Family Law for Legal Professionals

Laura Masella, B.A., LL.B., LL.M.
Marie Ferguson, B.A., LL.B.

THOMSON
CARSWELL

Library and Archives Canada Cataloguing in Publication

Masella, Laura
    Family law for legal professionals / Laura Masella, Marie Ferguson.

Includes index.
ISBN 0-459-24395-0

    1. Domestic relations—Ontario—Textbooks.   I. Ferguson, Marie E.
II. Title.

KEO213.M38 2006   346.71011'5   C2006-903402-8
KF505.ZB3M38 2006

Composition: Computer Composition of Canada Inc.

One Corporate Plaza
2075 Kennedy Road
Toronto, Ontario
MIT 3V4

Customer Relations:
Toronto 1-416-609-3800
Elsewhere in Canada/U.S. 1-800-387-5164
Fax 1-416-298-5094
www.carswell.com
Email: carswell.orders@thomson.com

DEDICATION

To my wonderful family,
especially my husband, Jim, and
my daughters, Christina and Julie

To my dear daughter, Sarah,
my wonderful mother, Jean Ferguson, and
in loving memory of my dear father, John Ferguson

PREFACE

We wrote this book with the intention that it should be a concise, thorough, and readable textbook for law clerks, paralegals, and other legal professionals. Rather than simply reiterating the language of the various statutes, we tried to explain and clarify the statutory provisions. The Application Questions that are scattered throughout the chapters are meant to reinforce the information presented, as well as illustrate how the statutory provisions would be applied in everyday situations. We have chosen and highlighted case excerpts that show how the various family law concepts and principles would be applied and determined. We also hope that our choice of cases will stimulate discussion and debate about family law policy in general.

We organized the text by statute, because we felt that this would be the most logical sequence for teaching the materials. We included practical procedural information in each chapter as well as completed forms that illustrate the types of applications discussed in several chapters. In addition, we have written a separate chapter that gives an overview of the most commonly used Family Law Rules.

We hope that students, instructors and other practicing legal professionals will find this text useful, informative, and interesting.

We would like to thank our colleague and friend, Kamini Steinberg, of Humber College, for sharing with us her detailed case scenario, which we used in the appendix to chapter 6 to illustrate the calculation of net family property.

We would also like to thank Julia Gulej of Carswell for her encouragement as we progressed with the manuscript and her unfailing belief that our book would fill a unique niche in the legal market. In addition, our thanks go to Ainsley Davison of Carswell for her competent, thorough, and timely editorial work on the book.

Laura Masella
Marie Ferguson
June 1, 2006

TABLE OF CONTENTS

PREFACE v
TABLE OF CASES xvii

CHAPTER 1 — FAMILY LAW: HISTORY AND COURTS 1
A BRIEF HISTORY OF FAMILY LAW IN ONTARIO 1
  The Beginning of Family Law 1
  Divorce 2
  Divorce and Family Law Reforms 3
FEDERAL AND PROVINCIAL LEGISLATION 6
  Federal 6
  Provincial (Ontario) 6
THE ONTARIO COURT SYSTEM AND THE FAMILY LAW COURTS 7
  The Ontario Court of Justice 7
  The Superior Court of Justice 7
    Divisional Court 8
    Small Claims Court 8
    Family Court 8
  The Court of Appeal for Ontario 9
SUPREME COURT OF CANADA 10
APPENDIX 1A 11

CHAPTER 2 — MARRIAGE AND ANNULMENT 13
MARRIAGE 13
  What is Marriage? 13
LEGAL CAPACITY TO MARRY 15
  Parties (Who Can Marry Whom) 15
  Marital Status 15
  Age 16
FORMALITIES OF MARRIAGE 16
  Who May Marry 16
  Marriage Licence or Publication of Banns Required 17
  Who Can Solemnize the Marriage 17
  Form of the Ceremony 18
  Failure to Comply With the Formalities of Marriage 19
ANNULMENT 21
  What is Annulment? 21
  Two Types of Annulment 21
  Marriage Void *Ab Initio* 22
    Age 22
    Prior Subsisting Marriage 22
    Consanguinity and Affinity 22
    Lack of Freedom to Consent to Marriage 23
      Mental Incapacity 23
      Duress 23
      Mistake 24
  Voidable Marriage 24
    Age 24

Inability to Consummate 24
     Marriages of Convenience (Ulterior Motive) 26
PROCEDURE TO OBTAIN ANNULMENT 28
Support and Property Division on Annulment 28
Custody of Children on Annulment 28
APPENDIX 2A — Form 8: Application (General) 29
APPENDIX 2B — Form 14A: Affidavit (general) dated 34

CHAPTER 3 — THE *DIVORCE ACT*: JURISDICTION AND OBTAINING A DIVORCE 37
JURISDICTION OVER DIVORCE 37
Where to Proceed 37
GROUND FOR DIVORCE 40
Separation 40
Adultery 41
Cruelty 43
DUTY OF LEGAL ADVISOR 44
DUTY OF THE COURT 44
Reconciliation 44
Bars 45
     Collusion 45
     Reasonable Arrangements for Child Support 45
     Condonation and Connivance 45
CERTIFICATE OF DIVORCE 47
Corollary Relief 47
Recognizing Foreign Divorces 47
DIVORCE PROCEDURE 48
Defended Divorce 48
Uncontested Divorces 49
APPENDIX 3A — Form 8A: Application (divorce) 51
APPENDIX 3B — Form 36: Affidavit for Divorce 56
APPENDIX 3C — Form 25A: Divorce Order 60

CHAPTER 4 — CHILD AND SPOUSAL SUPPORT UNDER THE *DIVORCE ACT* 63
CHILD SUPPORT UNDER THE *DIVORCE ACT* 63
The *Child Support Guidelines* 66
     The Presumptive Rule 67
     Special and Extraordinary Expenses 67
     Child Over the Age of Majority 68
     Incomes over $150,000 68
     Spouse in the Place of a Parent 69
     Split Custody 69
     Shared Custody 70
     Undue Hardship 71
SPOUSAL SUPPORT UNDER THE *DIVORCE ACT* 72
Who Can Apply 72
How Spousal Support is Determined 73
The Proposed Spousal Support Advisory Guidelines 77

CHAPTER 5 — CUSTODY AND VARIATION OF ORDERS UNDER THE *DIVORCE ACT* 79
CUSTODY AND ACCESS 79
WHAT IS CUSTODY? 79
CUSTODY UNDER THE *DIVORCE ACT*—WHO CAN APPLY 80
PRINCIPLES DETERMINING THE MERITS OF CUSTODY 81
    Best Interests of the Child 81
    Conduct as a Factor 82
    Maximum Contact Principle 82
    Joint Custody 84
        What is Joint Custody? 84
        Circumstances in which Joint Custody is Appropriate 85
        Parallel Parenting 87
ACCESS 88
    What is Access? 88
        Reasonable Access 88
        Specified Access 88
        Supervised Access 89
        Factors Affecting Access 89
VARIATIONS UNDER THE *DIVORCE ACT* 90
    Variation of Child Support 90
    Variation of Spousal Support 90
    Variation of Custody 92
APPENDIX 5A — Form 14: Notice of Motion 93
APPENDIX 5B — Form 15: Change Information Form (motion to change child support) 95

CHAPTER 6 — THE *FAMILY LAW ACT* — FAMILY PROPERTY 101
INTRODUCTION 101
EQUAL STATUS OF SPOUSES AND MARRIAGE AS PARTNERSHIP 101
WHO CAN APPLY FOR EQUALIZATION OF NET FAMILY PROPERTIES 102
    Married Spouses 102
    Surviving Spouse on Death of Other Spouse 102
    Common-Law Spouses Excluded 102
VALUATION DATE 104
    Permanent Separation 104
    Improvident Depletion 104
    Death of a Spouse 105
    Limitation Periods 105
DEFINING PROPERTY 105
    What is Property? 105
    What is *Not* Property? 106
WHAT IS "NET FAMILY PROPERTY" (NFP)? 108
    Deductions from "Net Family Property" 109
        Debts and Liabilities Outstanding on Valuation Date 109
        Net Value of Property Owned on Date of Marriage 109
        Matrimonial Home Excepted 110
    Exclusions from Net Family Property 110

Gift or Inheritance 111
Income from Gift or Inheritance 111
Damages for Personal Injuries 112
Life Insurance Proceeds 112
Tracing 112
Property Excluded by Domestic Contract 114
CALCULATING THE EQUALIZATION PAYMENT 115
Steps in Calculating "Net Family Property" 115
EQUALIZATION ON DEATH OF A SPOUSE 116
Election Where Spouse Dies Leaving a Will 116
Election Where Spouse Dies Intestate 117
Priority of Spouse's Entitlement 118
UNEQUAL DIVISION 118
Equalization "Unconscionable" 118
Factors Considered By the Courts 119
PROCEDURE IN AN EQUALIZATION APPLICATION 119
Commencement of Proceedings 119
Service of Documents 120
APPENDIX 6A — Fact Situation 121
APPENDIX 6B — Form 8: Application (General) 124
APPENDIX 6C — Form 13.1: Financial Statement (Property and Support
Claims) sworn/affirmed 129
APPENDIX 6D — Form 13B: Net Family Property Statement 138

**CHAPTER 7 — THE MATRIMONIAL HOME UNDER THE *FAMILY
LAW ACT*** 141
INTRODUCTION 141
WHO IS ENTITLED TO CLAIM SPECIAL RIGHTS TO THE
MATRIMONIAL HOME? 141
WHAT IS THE MATRIMONIAL HOME? 141
Property in Which a Spouse Has an Interest 142
More Than One Matrimonial Home 143
Ownership of Shares in Corporation Holding Title to Home 143
Part of Property Used For Other Purposes 143
DESIGNATION OF THE MATRIMONIAL HOME 144
POSSESSION OF THE MATRIMONIAL HOME 145
Right to Equal Possession 145
Spouse's Death 145
Exclusive Possession 145
Occupation Rent 146
Payments to the Spouse in Possession 146
Effect of Partition and Sale Application 147
DISPOSITION AND ENCUMBRANCE OF MATRIMONIAL HOME 148
Spousal Consent Required 149
Failure to Obtain Spousal Consent to Transaction 149
JOINT TENANCY IN THE MATRIMONIAL HOME 151

**CHAPTER 8 — SUPPORT OBLIGATIONS UNDER THE *FAMILY
LAW ACT*** 153

SPOUSAL SUPPORT 153
   Who Can Apply 153
   How Support is Determined 157
   Types of Orders 158
   Indexing 158
   Effect of Divorce Proceedings 159
   Variation of Spousal Support under the *Family Law Act* 159
CHILD SUPPORT UNDER THE *FAMILY LAW ACT* 160
   The *Child Support Guidelines* 161
   Effect of Divorce Proceeding 162
   Variation of Child Support 162
CHILD SUPPORT PROCEDURE 163
   Application and Financial Statements 163
   Motions for Temporary Orders 164
   Motions to Change a Final Order or Agreement 164
APPENDIX 8A — Form 8: Application (General) 166
APPENDIX 8B — Form 13: Financial Statement (Sworn Claims) sworn/
   affirmed 171

CHAPTER 9 — DOMESTIC CONTRACTS UNDER THE *FAMILY LAW ACT* 177
MARRIAGE CONTRACTS 177
COHABITATION AGREEMENT 178
SEPARATION AGREEMENTS 178
FORM AND CAPACITY 179
ENFORCEABILITY OF DOMESTIC CONTRACTS 180
   Custody, Access, and Child Support 180
   Spousal Support 181
   Circumstances Surrounding Negotiation and Execution 182
PATERNITY AGREEMENTS 184
REGISTERING A DOMESTIC CONTRACT WITH THE COURT 185
NEGOTIATING A DOMESTIC CONTRACT OR PATERNITY
   AGREEMENT 185
   Traditional Negotiations 185
   Mediation 186
   Arbitration 187
   Collaborative Family Law 188
APPENDIX 9A — Separation Agreement 189

CHAPTER 10 — THE *CHILDREN'S LAW REFORM ACT*: EQUAL STATUS OF CHILDREN AND PARENTAGE 199
SCOPE OF ACT 199
EQUAL STATUS OF CHILDREN 199
   Interpretation of Other Legislation and Documents 200
ESTABLISHING PARENTAGE OF CHILDREN 200
   Introduction 200
   Who Can Apply for a Declaration of Parentage? 201
   Limitations upon Application 202
   Nature of Declaratory Order 202

Presumptions of Paternity 203
Conflicting Presumptions 203
Proof of Parentage 204
    Written Acknowledgement of Paternity 204
    Blood Tests 204
    DNA Tests 205
    Inference from Refusal to Submit to Blood Tests 206
    Charter *Issues and Blood Tests* 206
JURISDICTION TO MAKE DECLARATION OF PARENTAGE 207

**CHAPTER 11 — CUSTODY UNDER THE *CHILDREN'S LAW
    REFORM ACT*** 209
INTRODUCTION 209
EQUAL ENTITLEMENT OF PARENTS 209
WHO CAN APPLY FOR CUSTODY UNDER THE CLRA 210
JURISDICTION TO APPLY FOR CUSTODY 210
Habitual Residence in Ontario 210
Child Physically Present in Ontario Coupled with Five Other
    Factors 211
Serious Harm to Child 212
Declining Jurisdiction 213
CLRA and the *Divorce Act* 213
PRINCIPLES DETERMINING THE MERITS OF CUSTODY 215
Best Interests of the Child 215
    Love, Affection and Emotional Ties 215
    Views and Preferences of the Child 217
    Length of Time in a Stable Home Environment 218
    *Ability and Willingness to Provide Guidance, Education, Necessaries
        and Special Needs* 218
    Plans for the Care and Upbringing of the Child 220
    Permanence and Stability of Proposed Family Unit 220
    Relationship to the Parties by Blood or Adoption 221
    Past Conduct as a Factor 221
TYPES OF CUSTODY ORDERS 223
VARIATION OF CUSTODY OR ACCESS ORDERS 223
Material Change in Circumstances 224
COURT ASSISTANCE IN CUSTODY MATTERS 224
Custody Assessments 224
Mediation 226
PROCEDURE 226
Application 226
Answer 227
Variation 227
INTERNATIONAL CHILD ABDUCTION – THE *HAGUE CONVENTION* ... 228
What is the *Hague Convention*? 228
Purpose 228
How it Works 228
APPENDIX 11A — Form 8: Application (General) 230

CHAPTER 12 — THE *FAMILY LAW RULES* 235
THE PRIMARY OBJECTIVE 235
DUTY TO MANAGE CASES 236
TIME 236
STARTING A CASE 238
    Application 238
    Financial Statement 238
    Continuing Record 239
    Service of Documents 239
ANSWERING A CASE 240
    Answer 240
    Financial Statement 241
    Continuing Record 241
    Service of Documents 242
REPLY 243
MANDATORY INFORMATION PROGRAM 243
MOTIONS FOR TEMPORARY ORDERS 244
    Motions without Notice 245
CONFERENCES 246
    Case Conferences 246
    Settlement Conferences 247
    Trial Management Conferences 248
CASE MANAGEMENT 248
    Family Court 249
    Ontario Court of Justice 250
    Superior Court of Justice 251
MOTIONS TO CHANGE A FINAL ORDER OR AGREEMENT 251
APPENDIX 12A — Formal Requirements of the Continuing Record under the
Family Law Rules 253

**CHAPTER 13 — ENFORCEMENT OF SUPPORT ORDERS AND
      AGREEMENTS** 261
THE DIRECTOR'S ROLE 261
SUPPORT ORDERS AND SUPPORT DEDUCTION ORDERS 262
    Income Source 263
    Dispute by Payor 264
SUSPENSION OF DRIVERS' LICENCES 264
    Motion to Refrain 265
    Final Notice 265
    Direction to Reinstate 265
DEFAULT HEARING 266
OTHER ENFORCEMENT MECHANISMS 266
    Registration against Land 266
    Registration under the *Personal Property Security Act* 266
    Garnishment of Joint Accounts 267
    Deduction from Lottery Prize 267
    Report to Consumer Reporting Agency 267
    Arrest of Absconding Debtor 267
    Director's Access to Information 267

APPENDIX 13A — Form 25: Order (general) 269
APPENDIX 13B — Support Deduction Order 271

CHAPTER 14 — THE *CHANGE OF NAME ACT* 273
ELECTION BY SPOUSE 273
    Married Spouses 273
    Common-Law Spouses 274
CHANGE OF CHILD'S NAME 274
PROCEDURE 277
DUTY OF THE REGISTRAR GENERAL 277
OFFENCES 278

CHAPTER 15 — *CHILD AND FAMILY SERVICES ACT* 279
INTRODUCTION 279
    Scope of Legislation 279
    Purpose of Legislation 279
CHILDREN'S AID SOCIETY 280
AGREEMENTS FOR CHILDREN'S CARE 280
    Temporary Care Agreements 280
    Special Needs Agreements 281
    Termination of Agreements 283
CHILD PROTECTION 284
    Overview of Child Protection Law 284
    Child Protection Distinguished from Custody 284
    Conflict between Community and Family Privacy Interests 284
    Who is a "Child in Need of Protection"? 286
        Physical Harm or Risk of Physical Harm 286
        Molestation or Risk of Molestation 286
        Denial of Medical Treatment 287
        Emotional Harm or Risk of Emotional Harm 287
        Mental, Emotional, or Developmental Condition 287
        Other Situations 288
    Parties to the Proceeding 289
        Children's Aid Society 289
        Parents 289
        Representative of Native Band 289
        Director 289
        Possessory Parents 289
        Child 290
    Jurisdiction of Courts 290
    Commencement of Child Protection Application 290
        Apprehension 290
            With a Warrant 291
            Without a Warrant 291
        Application 291
    Who May be Subject of a Child Protection Proceeding? 292
    Child Protection Hearing 293
        Adjournment 293
        Hearing in Private 294

Preliminary Findings 294
Finding of Child in Need of Protection 294
Orders the Court May Make 294
Supervision Order 295
Society Wardship 295
Crown Wardship 295
Consecutive Orders of Society Wardship and Supervision 296
Considerations in Making Order 296
Status Review 296
Application 296
Orders on Status Review 297
Appeals 298
APPENDIX 15A — Form 8B: Application (Child Protection and Status
Review) 299

INDEX 305

TABLE OF CASES

A. v. A. (1931), 40 O.W.N. 543 (Ont. H.C.) 25

A. (S.J.) v. A. (S.C.) (1994), 1994 CarswellOnt 4337 (Ont. Gen. Div.) 221

Alspector v. Alspector, 1957 CarswellOnt 39, [1957] O.R. 454, 9 D.L.R.
(2d) 679, 1 R.F.L. Rep. 140 (Ont. C.A.) 19

B. v. B. (1934), 1934 CarswellMan 110, [1935] S.C.R. 231, [1935] 1 D.L.R.
695 (S.C.C.) 25

B. (R.) v. Children's Aid Society of Metropolitan Toronto (1995), EYB 1995-
67419, 1995 CarswellOnt 105, 1995 CarswellOnt 515, [1994] S.C.J.
No. 24, 9 R.F.L. (4th) 157, 21 O.R. (3d) 479 (note), 122 D.L.R. (4th)
1, [1995] 1 S.C.R. 315, 26 C.R.R. (2d) 202, (sub nom. Sheena B., Re)
176 N.R. 161, (sub nom. Sheena B., Re) 78 O.A.C. 1 (S.C.C.) 285

B. (R.) v. G. (L.) (1992), 1992 CarswellOnt 3766 (Ont. Prov. Div.) 207

Bagaric v. Juric (1984), 1984 CarswellOnt 330, 44 O.R. (2d) 638, 40 C.P.C.
211, 5 D.L.R. (4th) 78, 2 O.A.C. 35 (Ont. C.A.) 201

Baker v. Baker (1979), 1979 CarswellOnt 367, 23 O.R. (2d) 391, 2 Fam.
L. Rev. 69, 8 R.F.L. (2d) 236, 95 D.L.R. (3d) 529 (Ont. C.A.) 85

Ballmick v. Ballmick, 2005 CarswellOnt 1205, [2005] O.J. No. 1209, 2005
ONCJ 101, 18 R.F.L. (6th) 10 (Ont. C.J.) 160

Bate v. Bate (1978), 1978 CarswellOnt 218, [1978] O.J. No. 113, 1 R.F.L.
(2d) 298 (Ont. H.C.) 48

Baxter v. Baxter, [1948] A.C. 274 (U.K. H.L.) 26

Belgiorgio v. Belgiorgio (2000), 2000 CarswellOnt 3060, [2000] O.J. No.
3246, 10 R.F.L. (5th) 239 (Ont. S.C.J.), affirmed (2001), 2001
CarswellOnt 4193, 23 R.F.L. (5th) 74 (Ont. C.A.) 113

Belisle v. Poole (1994), 1994 CarswellOnt 372, [1994] O.J. No. 364, 2
R.F.L. (4th) 165, 111 D.L.R. (4th) 717 (Ont. Gen. Div.) 275

Bender v. Bender (1993), 1993 CarswellOnt 1631 (Ont. Gen. Div.) 87

Berdette v. Berdette (1991), 1991 CarswellOnt 280, [1991] O.J. No. 788,
41 E.T.R. 126, 47 O.A.C. 345, 3 O.R. (3d) 513, 81 D.L.R. (4th) 194,
33 R.F.L. (3d) 113 (Ont. C.A.), leave to appeal refused [1991]
S.C.C.A. No. 306, 85 D.L.R. (4th) viii (note), 137 N.R. 388 (note),
55 O.A.C. 397 (note), [1991] 3 S.C.R. v, 5 O.R. (3d) xii (S.C.C.).. 115, 118

Binkley v. Binkley (1988), [1988] O.J. No. 414, 1988 CarswellOnt 250,
14 R.F.L. (3d) 336 (Ont. C.A.) 147

Blackwell v. Burden (1996), 1996 CarswellOnt 362, [1996] O.J. No. 472,
9 O.F.L.R. 185 (Ont. Gen. Div.) 218

Boots v. Sharrow, 2004 CarswellOnt 25, 49 R.F.L. (5th) 260, (sub nom.
J.S.B. v. D.L.S.) [2004] 3 C.N.L.R. 110 (Ont. S.C.J.) 82, 221

Bosch v. Bosch (1985), 1985 CarswellSask 118, 49 R.F.L. (2d) 157, 45
Sask. R. 189 (Sask. Q.B.) 218

Boukema v. Boukema (1997), 1997 CarswellOnt 3115, [1997] O.J. No.
2903, 31 R.F.L. (4th) 329, 33 O.T.C. 190 (Ont. Gen. Div.), additional
reasons at (1997), 1997 CarswellOnt 5151 (Ont. Gen. Div.) 217, 224

Bracklow v. Bracklow, 1999 CarswellBC 532, 1999 CarswellBC 533, [1999]
S.C.J. No. 14, 169 D.L.R. (4th) 577, 236 N.R. 79, 44 R.F.L. (4th) 1,

120 B.C.A.C. 211, 196 W.A.C. 211, [1999] 1 S.C.R. 420, 63 B.C.L.R. (3d) 77, [1999] 8 W.W.R. 740 (S.C.C.) 76

Brennen v. Brennen (1890), 19 O.R. 327 (Ont. H.C.)..............................24

Brooks v. Brooks (1998), 1998 CarswellOnt 3097, [1998] O.J. No. 3186, 111 O.A.C. 177, 163 D.L.R. (4th) 715, 39 R.F.L. (4th) 187, 22 C.P.C. (4th) 209, 41 O.R. (3d) 191 (Ont. C.A.)..211

Browne v. McLaughlin (1988), [1988] O.J. No. 1066, 1988 CarswellOnt 2563 (Ont. Dist. Ct.)..245

Brown, Re (1979), 1979 CarswellOnt 794, 26 O.R. (2d) 252 (Ont. Co. Ct.) 142

Bruce v. Bruce, 1947 CarswellOnt 73, [1947] O.R. 688 (Ont. C.A.)..............43

C. v. C., 1949 CarswellMan 21, [1949] 1 W.W.R. 911 (Man. K.B.) 25

C. (S.W.) v. C. (T.L.) (1996), 1996 CarswellOnt 5025, [1996] O.J. No. 4577, 20 O.T.C. 63 (Ont. Gen. Div.)..218

Capon v. McLay, 1965 CarswellOnt 192, [1965] 2 O.R. 83, 49 D.L.R. (2d) 675 (Ont. C.A.)..23

Caratun v. Caratun (1992), 1992 CarswellOnt 287, 42 R.F.L. (3d) 113, 47 E.T.R. 234, 96 D.L.R. (4th) 404, 10 O.R. (3d) 385, 58 O.A.C. 140 (Ont. C.A.), leave to appeal refused (1993), 46 R.F.L. (3d) 314 (note), 101 D.L.R. (4th) vii (note), 13 O.R. (3d) xvi (note), 157 N.R. 317 (note), 64 O.A.C. 273 (note) (S.C.C.) 106

Catholic Children's Aid Society of Metropolitan Toronto v. M. (C.), EYB 1994-67657, 1994 CarswellOnt 376, 1994 CarswellOnt 1157, [1994] S.C.J. No. 37, 2 R.F.L. (4th) 313, [1994] 2 S.C.R. 165, 165 N.R. 161, 71 O.A.C. 81, 113 D.L.R. (4th) 321, 18 O.R. (3d) 160 (note) (S.C.C.) 216, 297

Chartier v. Chartier, [1999] S.C.J. No. 79, 1999 CarswellMan 25, 1999 CarswellMan 26, 235 N.R. 1, 168 D.L.R. (4th) 540, 43 R.F.L. (4th) 1, [1999] 4 W.W.R. 633, 134 Man. R. (2d) 19, 193 W.A.C. 19, [1999] 1 S.C.R. 242 (S.C.C.)..64

Chertkow v. Feinstein (Chertkow), 1929 CarswellAlta 23, [1929] 2 W.W.R. 257, 24 Alta. L.R. 188, [1929] 3 D.L.R. 339, 1 R.F.L. Rep. 224 (Alta. C.A.), affirmed (1929), 1929 CarswellAlta 121, [1930] S.C.R. 335, [1930] 1 D.L.R. 137 (S.C.C.)..23

Contino v. Leonelli-Contino, 2005 CarswellOnt 6281, 2005 CarswellOnt 6282, [2005] S.C.J. No. 65, 2005 SCC 63, 19 R.F.L. (6th) 272, 259 D.L.R. (4th) 388, 341 N.R. 1 (S.C.C.)..70

Cooper v. Cooper (1972), 1972 CarswellOnt 98, [1972] O.J. No. 975, 10 R.F.L. 184 (Ont. H.C.)..40

Cox v. Stephen, 2002 CarswellOnt 2321, [2002] O.J. No. 2762, 30 R.F.L. (5th) 54, [2002] O.T.C. 499 (Ont. S.C.J.), affirmed (2003), 2003 CarswellOnt 4554, [2003] O.J. No. 4371, 47 R.F.L. (5th) 1, 179 O.A.C. 45 (Ont. C.A.) 215

Crousset v. Crousset (2003), 2003 CarswellOnt 1747 (Ont. S.C.J.) 87

D. (S.) v. B. (T.C.) (2000), 2000 CarswellOnt 3378, [2000] O.J. No. 3475 (Ont. S.C.J.)..221

Desramaux v. Desramaux (2002), 2002 CarswellOnt 2731, [2002] O.J. No. 3251, 28 R.F.L. (5th) 25, 216 D.L.R. (4th) 613, 162 O.A.C. 338 (Ont.

C.A.), leave to appeal refused (2003), 2003 CarswellOnt 1383, 2003 CarswellOnt 1384, [2002] S.C.C.A. No. 431, 189 O.A.C. 197 (note), 313 N.R. 400 (note) (S.C.C.) 156

Evans v. Evans, 2004 CarswellBC 762, 2004 BCSC 485 (B.C. S.C.), additional reasons at 2004 CarswellBC 1089, 2004 BCSC 658 (B.C. S.C.) 83

Evershed v. Evershed (1882), 46 L.T. 690 88

F. v. F., 1953 CarswellBC 70, 8 W.W.R. (N.S.) 84, [1953] 2 D.L.R. 318, 8 W.W.R. (N.S.) 84 (B.C. S.C.) 25

Fernandez (Alarcio) v. Fernandez, 1983 CarswellMan 113, [1983] 4 W.W.R. 755, 34 R.F.L. (2d) 249, 21 Man. R. (2d) 254 (Man. Q.B.) 26

Fisher v. Fisher (1985), 1985 CarswellNS 369, 70 N.S.R. (2d) 206, 166 A.P.R. 206 (N.S. T.D.) 80

Foucault v. Rouleau (2005), 2005 CarswellOnt 3583 (Ont. S.C.J.) 212

French v. Mackenzie (2003), 2003 CarswellOnt 1748, 38 R.F.L. (5th) 81 (Ont. S.C.J.) 213

Fulmer v. Kaleo-Fulmer (2002), 2002 CarswellOnt 2718, [2002] O.J. No. 3183 (Ont. S.C.J.), additional reasons at (2002), 2002 CarswellOnt 2944 (Ont. S.C.J.) 211

G. (F.) v. G. (F.) (1991), 1991 CarswellOnt 263, 32 R.F.L. (3d) 252 (Ont. Gen. Div.) 205

Gajamugan v. Gajamugan (1979), 1979 CarswellOnt 289, 10 R.F.L. (2d) 280 (Ont. H.C.) 24, 25

Gordon v. Goertz, 1996 CarswellSask 199, [1996] S.C.J. No. 52, 1996 CarswellSask 199F, [1996] 5 W.W.R. 457, 19 R.F.L. (4th) 177, 196 N.R. 321, 134 D.L.R. (4th) 321, 141 Sask. R. 241, 114 W.A.C. 241, [1996] 2 S.C.R. 27, [1996] R.D.F. 209 (S.C.C.) 79, 215, 216, 223

Grealy v. Lees, [2000] B.C.J. No. 249, 2000 CarswellBC 282, 2000 BCSC 217 (B.C. S.C.) 82

H. v. H. (1953), [1953] 2 All E.R. 1229, [1954] P. 258 (Eng. P.D.A.) 23

H. v. H. (1979), 1979 CarswellOnt 387, 25 O.R. (2d) 219, 100 D.L.R. (3d) 364, 1 F.L.R.A.C. 543, 9 R.F.L. (2d) 216 (Ont. Fam. Ct.) 205

H. (M.E.) v. F. (R.M.) (1994), 1994 CarswellSask 32, 10 R.F.L. (4th) 77, 128 Sask. R. 124, 85 W.A.C. 124 (Sask. C.A.) 221

Hagen v. Muir, 2000 CarswellBC 828, [2000] B.C.J. No. 786, 2000 BCSC 575 (B.C. S.C.) 89

Halpern v. Toronto (City) (2003), 2003 CarswellOnt 2159, [2003] O.J. No. 2268, 65 O.R. (3d) 161, 65 O.R. (3d) 201, 106 C.R.R. (2d) 329, 172 O.A.C. 276, 36 R.F.L. (5th) 127, 225 D.L.R. (4th) 529 (Ont. C.A.) 13

Hartling v. Hartling (July 11, 1979), Doc. Middlesex 05919 (Ont. S.C.) 143

Hartmann-Jorgensen v. Hartmann-Jorgensen (1986), 1986 CarswellOnt 340, [1986] O.J. No. 1821, 50 R.F.L. (2d) 430 (Ont. U.F.C.) 210

Heal v. Heal (1998), 1998 CarswellOnt 4468, 43 R.F.L. (4th) 88 (Ont. Gen. Div.) 118

Heil v. Heil, 1942 CarswellOnt 108, [1942] S.C.R. 160, [1942] 1 D.L.R. 657 (S.C.C.) 24

Hildinger v. Carroll (2004), 2004 CarswellOnt 444, [2004] O.J. No. 291, 2 R.F.L. (6th) 331 (Ont. C.A.), additional reasons at (2004), 2004

CarswellOnt 1334 (Ont. C.A.), leave to appeal refused (2004), 2004 CarswellOnt 4951, 2004 CarswellOnt 4952, 338 N.R. 193 (note) (S.C.C.) 85

Hodgson v. Hanson (2000), 2000 CarswellOnt 3769 (Ont. C.J.) 225

Hoffstrom v. Laderoute (1997), 1997 CarswellOnt 1062, [1997] O.J. No. 858 (Ont. Prov. Div.)..82

Ho v. Gallinger (2002), 2002 CarswellOnt 5308 (Ont. S.C.J.).....................219

Honsinger v. Kilmer (1984), 1984 CarswellOnt 1440, 12 C.R.R. 276 (Ont. Prov. Ct.)..206

Hyde v. Hyde (1866), L.R. 1 P.D. 130, 35 L.J. P. & M. 57 (Eng. P.D.A.) 13

Iantsis (Papatheodorou) v. Papatheodorou (1970), 1970 CarswellOnt 154, [1971] 1 O.R. 245, 15 D.L.R. (3d) 53, 3 R.F.L. 158 (Ont. C.A.)...............26

Jespersen v. Jespersen (1985), 1985 CarswellBC 564, [1985] B.C.J. No. 2440, 48 R.F.L. (2d) 193 (B.C. C.A.)..217

Jones v. Jones (1947), 1947 CarswellOnt 91, [1948] O.R. 22 (Ont. C.A.) 25

K. (K.) v. L. (G.), [1985] S.C.J. No. 7, 1985 CarswellNWT 54, 1985 CarswellNWT 58, [1985] 1 S.C.R. 87, [1985] 3 W.W.R. 1, [1985] N.W.T.R. 101, 16 D.L.R. (4th) 576, 57 N.R. 17, 58 A.R. 275, 44 R.F.L. (2d) 113 (S.C.C.) 81, 221

Katsigiannis v. Kottick-Katsigiannis (2001), 2001 CarswellOnt 2909, [2001] O.J. No. 1598, 144 O.A.C. 387, 203 D.L.R. (4th) 386, 18 R.F.L. (5th) 279, 55 O.R. (3d) 456, 12 C.P.C. (5th) 191 (Ont. C.A.).......................211

Kerr v. Kerr, 1952 CarswellMan 18, 5 W.W.R. (N.S.) 385, 60 Man. R. 118, [1952] 4 D.L.R. 578 (Man. C.A.)..23

Knoll v. Knoll, 1970 CarswellOnt 101, [1970] 2 O.R. 169, 10 D.L.R. (3d) 199, 1 R.F.L. 141 (Ont. C.A.)...43

Korutowska-Wooff v. Wooff (2004), 2004 CarswellOnt 3203, [2004] O.J. No. 3256, 242 D.L.R. (4th) 385, 5 R.F.L. (6th) 104, (sub nom. M.K.-W. v. M.S.W.) 188 O.A.C. 376 (Ont. C.A.), leave to appeal refused (2005), 2005 CarswellOnt 3135, 2005 CarswellOnt 3136 (S.C.C.)........211

Kosokowsky v. Kosokowsky (1992), 1992 CarswellOnt 816, 95 D.L.R. (4th) 309 (Ont. Gen. Div.) 218

Kruger v. Kruger (1979), 1979 CarswellOnt 299, 25 O.R. (2d) 673, 11 R.F.L. (2d) 52, 2 Fam. L. Rev. 197, 104 D.L.R. (3d) 481 (Ont. C.A.) 79, 85

LaChapelle v. LaChapelle (2000), 2000 CarswellOnt 4108, [2000] O.J. No. 4276 (Ont. C.A.) 82

Ladisa v. Ladisa (2005), 2005 CarswellOnt 268, [2005] O.J. No. 276, 193 O.A.C. 336, 11 R.F.L. (6th) 50 (Ont. C.A.) 85

Larcade v. Ontario (Minister of Community & Social Services) (2005), [2005] O.J. No. 1924, 2005 CarswellOnt 1912, 197 O.A.C. 287, 16 R.F.L. (6th) 156, 18 C.P.C. (6th) 21, (sub nom. A.L. v. Ontario (Ministry of Community and Social Services)) 77 O.R. (3d) 422 (Ont. Div. Ct.) 282

Lawreniuk v. Lawreniuk (October 26, 1995), Doc. Prince Albert Q.B. 04706/94, [1995] S.J. No. 593 (Sask. Q.B.) 82

Lehner v. Grundl (1995), [1995] O.J. No. 181, 1995 CarswellOnt 2077 (Ont. Gen. Div.), varied (1999), 1999 CarswellOnt 1318, [1999] O.J. No. 1573 (Ont. C.A.) 154

Linton v. Clarke (1994), 1994 CarswellOnt 361, [1994] O.J. No. 2999, 10 R.F.L. (4th) 92, 21 O.R. (3d) 568, 76 O.A.C. 363 (Ont. Div. Ct.) 225

Linton v. Linton (1990), 1990 CarswellOnt 316, [1990] O.J. No. 2267, 1 O.R. (3d) 1, 42 O.A.C. 328, 30 R.F.L. (3d) 1, 41 E.T.R. 85, 75 D.L.R. (4th) 637 (Ont. C.A.)...106

M. (B.P.) v. M. (B.L.D.E.) (1992), 1992 CarswellOnt 295, [1992] O.J. No. 2299, 42 R.F.L. (3d) 349, 59 O.A.C. 19, 97 D.L.R. (4th) 437 (Ont. C.A.), leave to appeal refused (1993), 48 R.F.L. (3d) 232 (note), 65 O.A.C. 290 (note), 157 N.R. 348 (note), 106 D.L.R. (4th) vii (note) (S.C.C.) 89

M. (E.C.D.), Re, 1980 CarswellSask 94, (sub nom. *E., Re*) 17 R.F.L. (2d) 274, (sub nom. *E., Re*) [1980] 4 W.W.R. 296 (Sask. Prov. Ct.)..............294

M. (M.) v. H. (J.) (2004), 2004 CarswellOnt 5548, [2004] O.J. No. 5314, 125 C.R.R. (2d) 161, 247 D.L.R. (4th) 361, 73 O.R. (3d) 337 (Ont. S.C.J.)..37

Major v. Major (1982), 1982 CarswellOnt 355, 31 R.F.L. (2d) 446 (Ont. U.F.C.)...142

Manella v. Manella, 1942 CarswellOnt 56, [1942] O.R. 630, [1942] 4 D.L.R. 712 (Ont. C.A.) 23

Mantesso v. Mantesso (1991), [1991] O.J. No. 643, 4 F.L.R.R. 128 (Ont. Gen. Div.) 225

Martin v. Martin (1936), 1936 CarswellMan 86, [1937] 1 W.W.R. 95, 44 Man. R. 436, [1937] 1 D.L.R. 411 (Man. K.B.) 25

McLeod v. Impey, [2003] S.J. No. 276, 2003 CarswellSask 289, 2003 SKQB 167 (Sask. Q.B.) 224

Medeiros v. Medeiros (2003), 2003 CarswellOnt 712, [2003] O.J. No. 817 (Ont. S.C.J.)..217

Miglin v. Miglin, REJB 2003-40012, 2003 CarswellOnt 1374, 2003 CarswellOnt 1375, [2003] S.C.J. No. 21, 2003 SCC 24, 66 O.R. (3d) 736 (note), [2003] 1 S.C.R. 303, 34 R.F.L. (5th) 255, 224 D.L.R. (4th) 193, 171 O.A.C. 201, 302 N.R. 201 (S.C.C.)..74

Mol v. Mol (1997), 1997 CarswellOnt 3693, [1997] O.J. No. 4060, 40 O.T.C. 1 (Ont. Gen. Div.) 87

Montreuil v. Montreuil (1999), 1999 CarswellOnt 3853, [1999] O.J. No. 4450 (Ont. S.C.J.), additional reasons at (2000), 2000 CarswellOnt 3566, [2000] O.J. No. 3617 (Ont. S.C.J.), affirmed (2001), 2001 CarswellOnt 3464, [2001] O.J. No. 3891 (Ont. C.A.) 183

Mooney v. Coutts (1996), 1996 CarswellOnt 3927 (Ont. Gen. Div.).............221

Mooswa v. Saskatchewan (Minister of Social Services) (1976), 1976 CarswellSask 20, 30 R.F.L. 101, 9 C.N.L.C. 241 (Sask. Q.B.)................294

Moss v. Moss, [2004] N.J. No. 164, 2004 CarswellNfld 125, 2 R.F.L. (6th) 121, 237 Nfld. & P.E.I.R. 223, 709 A.P.R. 223, 2004 NLSCTD 83 (N.L. T.D.)..64

Murdoch v. Murdoch (1973), 1973 CarswellAlta 156, 1973 CarswellAlta 119, [1974] 1 W.W.R. 361, 13 R.F.L. 185, 41 D.L.R. (3d) 367, [1975] 1 S.C.R. 423 (S.C.C.)...4, 101

Murphy v. Laurence (2002), 2002 CarswellOnt 1281, [2002] O.J. No. 1368 (Ont. S.C.J.)..221

N. v. D. (1985), 1985 CarswellOnt 1637, 49 O.R. (2d) 490, 13 C.R.R.
26 (Ont. Fam. Ct.) 206

N. (D.) v. K. (B.) (1999), 1999 CarswellOnt 1334, 48 R.F.L. (4th) 400
(Ont. S.C.J.)...89

N. (M.) v. B. (M.) (2000), 2000 CarswellOnt 2108, 9 R.F.L. (5th) 359
(Ont. S.C.J.), additional reasons at (2000), 2000 CarswellOnt 2433,
[2000] O.J. No. 2639 (Ont. S.C.J.) 216

N. (R.) v. D. (M.) (1986), 1986 CarswellOnt 1107, 54 O.R. (2d) 550, 16
O.A.C. 75 (Ont. Div. Ct.) 206

N. (W.P.) v. N. (B.J.), 2005 CarswellBC 10, [2005] B.C.J. No. 12, 2005
BCCA 7, 36 B.C.L.R. (4th) 330, 10 R.F.L. (6th) 440, 249 D.L.R. (4th)
352, 207 B.C.A.C. 76, 341 W.A.C. 76 (B.C. C.A.)......................64

Nairn v. Lukowski (2002), 2002 CarswellOnt 1119, [2002] O.J. No. 1082
(Ont. S.C.J.), additional reasons at (2002), 2002 CarswellOnt 2319,
[2002] O.J. No. 2680, 29 R.F.L. (5th) 117 (Ont. S.C.J.)...................221

Nane (Sykiotis) v. Sykiotis, 1966 CarswellOnt 54, [1966] 2 O.R. 428, 57
D.L.R. (2d) 118, 1 R.F.L. Rep. 246 (Ont. H.C.) 24

Neil v. Neil (2002), 2002 CarswellOnt 2513, [2002] O.J. No. 3003 (Ont.
S.C.J.)..64

O'Brien v. Thomson, 2004 CarswellNS 65, 1 R.F.L. (6th) 318, (sub nom.
C.J.M. v. A.T.) 221 N.S.R. (2d) 297, (sub nom. *C.J.M. v. A.T.*) 697
A.P.R. 297, 2004 NSCA 34 (N.S. C.A.) 81

O'Hara v. O'Hara (September 26, 2002), Doc. Brockville 01-0300 (Ont.
S.C.J.)...217

P. (K.) v. N. (P.) (1988), 1988 CarswellOnt 257, [1988] O.J. No. 1049,
15 R.F.L. (3d) 110, 37 C.R.R. 189 (Ont. H.C.) 206

P. (S.E.) v. P. (D.D.), 2005 CarswellBC 2137, [2005] B.C.J. No. 1971,
2005 BCSC 1290, 259 D.L.R. (4th) 358 (B.C. S.C.) 42

Papp v. Hunter (2004), 2004 CarswellOnt 1074, 3 R.F.L. (6th) 164 (Ont.
S.C.J.), additional reasons at (2004), 2004 CarswellOnt 1982 (Ont.
S.C.J.)...87

Parent v. Parent (2001), 2001 CarswellOnt 4962 (Ont. S.C.J.) 221

Pastway v. Pastway (1999), 1999 CarswellOnt 2055, 49 R.F.L. (4th) 375
(Ont. Gen. Div.) 89

Peterson v. Scalisi (2001), 2001 CarswellOnt 2404, [2001] O.J. No. 2774
(Ont. S.C.J.), additional reasons at (2001), 2001 CarswellOnt 3198
(Ont. S.C.J. [In Chambers])...218

Poole v. Poole, 1999 CarswellBC 649, (sub nom. *A.H.P. v. C.A.P.*) [1999]
B.C.J. No. 696, 45 R.F.L. (4th) 56, 173 D.L.R. (4th) 299, 123 B.C.A.C.
272, 201 W.A.C. 272, 64 B.C.L.R. (3d) 70, 1999 BCCA 203 (B.C.
C.A.) 215, 218

Powers v. Naston-Powers (1990), 1990 CarswellOnt 280, 28 R.F.L. (3d)
69 (Ont. H.C.) 106

R. v. R. (2002), 2002 CarswellOnt 902, [2002] O.J. No. 1095, 24 R.F.L.
(5th) 96, 211 D.L.R. (4th) 403, 58 O.R. (3d) 656, 159 O.A.C. 46
(Ont. C.A.)...68

R. (A.N.) v. W. (L.J.) (1983), 1983 CarswellMan 147, 1983 CarswellMan
186, [1984] 1 W.W.R. 1, [1983] 2 S.C.R. 173, 1 D.L.R. (4th) 193,

48 N.R. 362, 24 Man. R. (2d) 314, 36 R.F.L. (2d) I, [1984] I C.N.L.R.
    161 (S.C.C.) 216

R. (J.) v. H. (L.) (2002), 2002 CarswellOnt 3445, [2002] O.J. No. 3998
    (Ont. S.C.J.)..201

R. v. Millis (1844), 8 E.R. 844, 10 Cl. & F. 534 (U.K. H.L.) 24

Raft v. Shortt (1986), 1986 CarswellOnt 271, 2 R.F.L. (3d) 243, 54 O.R.
    (2d) 768 (Ont. H.C.) 202

Rapp v. Wagman (2001), 2001 CarswellOnt 3979, 22 R.F.L. (5th) 407
    (Ont. S.C.J.), additional reasons at (2002), 2002 CarswellOnt 4004
    (Ont. S.C.J.)..142

Riley v. Parsons (2002), 2002 CarswellOnt 1847, [2002] O.J. No. 2242
    (Ont. C.J.) 220

Romas v. Romas (1999), 1999 CarswellBC 512 (B.C. S.C.) 89

Rosien v. McCulloch (2000), [2000] O.J. No. 1744, 2000 CarswellOnt 1738
    (Ont. S.C.J.), additional reasons at (2000), 2000 CarswellOnt 2284,
    [2000] O.J. No. 2509 (Ont. S.C.J.), affirmed (2001), 2001
    CarswellOnt 1562 (Ont. C.A.) 220

Ruyter v. Samson (1992), 1992 CarswellOnt 311, 44 R.F.L. (3d) 35, 99
    D.L.R. (4th) 552 (Ont. Gen. Div.) 39

S. (A.) v. S. (A.) (1988), 1988 CarswellOnt 277, [1988] O.J. No. 1407,
    15 R.F.L. (3d) 443, 65 O.R. (2d) 720 (Ont. U.F.C.)............................23

Sayer v. Rollin (1980), 1980 CarswellOnt 252, [1980] O.J. No. 613, 16
    R.F.L. (2d) 289 (Ont. C.A.) 207

Scott v. Sebright (1886), 12 P.D. 21 (Eng. P.D.A.) 23

Silber v. Fenske (1995), 1995 CarswellOnt 81, [1995] O.J. No. 418, 11
    R.F.L. (4th) 145 (Ont. Gen. Div.) 206

Stafford v. Rebane (2004), 2004 CarswellOnt 4251 (Ont. S.C.J.)...................147

Starko v. Starko (1990), [1990] A.J. No. 432, 1990 CarswellAlta 83, (sub
    nom. *S. (D.G.) v. S. (S.L.)*) 74 Alta. L.R. (2d) 168, 106 A.R. 62 (Alta.
    Q.B.)..81

Starr v. Adam, 2003 CarswellSask 170, 2003 SKQB 101, 231 Sask. R. 31
    (Sask. Q.B.)..213

St. Pierre v. St. Pierre (2005), [2005] O.J. No. 1669, 2005 CarswellOnt
    1624, 17 R.F.L. (6th) 347 (Ont. S.C.J.) 85

Sukhu v. Hamid (2003), 2003 CarswellOnt 1102 (Ont. S.C.J.), additional
    reasons at (2004), 2004 CarswellOnt 181 (Ont. S.C.J.)........................87

Sullivan v. Sullivan (1986), 1986 CarswellOnt 343, 5 R.F.L. (3d) 28 (Ont.
    U.F.C.)..118

T. (K.A.) v. T. (J.) (1989), 1989 CarswellOnt 310, 23 R.F.L. (3d) 214 (Ont.
    U.F.C.)..220

T. (N.) v. C. (A.) (2000), 2000 CarswellOnt 39 (Ont. S.C.J.).........................206

Talbot v. Henry, 1990 CarswellSask 161, [1990] S.J. No. 159, 25 R.F.L.
    (3d) 415, 84 Sask. R. 170, [1990] 5 W.W.R. 251 (Sask. C.A.) 224

Talsky v. Talsky (1975), 1975 CarswellOnt 166, 1975 CarswellOnt 855,
    [1976] 2 S.C.R. 292, 21 R.F.L. 27, 7 N.R. 246, 62 D.L.R. (3d) 267
    (S.C.C.) 81

Tester v. Tester (1993), 1993 CarswellOnt 1632 (Ont. Prov. Div.)................87

Thomson v. Thomson, EYB 1994-67190, 1994 CarswellMan 91, 1994
    CarswellMan 382, [1994] S.C.J. No. 6, [1994] 10 W.W.R. 513, 173
    N.R. 83, [1994] 3 S.C.R. 551, 6 R.F.L. (4th) 290, 97 Man. R. (2d) 81,
    79 W.A.C. 81, 119 D.L.R. (4th) 253 (S.C.C.)..................................228
Tice v. Tice, 1937 CarswellOnt 165, [1937] O.W.N. 250, [1937] 2 D.L.R.
    591 (Ont. C.A.)...25
Tierney-Hynes v. Hynes (2005), 2005 CarswellOnt 2632, 200 O.A.C. 251,
    256 D.L.R. (4th) 193, 75 O.R. (3d) 737 (Ont. C.A.), leave to appeal
    refused (2005), 2005 CarswellOnt 7437, 2005 CarswellOnt 7438
    (S.C.C.)...91
Turner v. Viau (2002), 2002 CarswellOnt 991, [2002] O.J. No. 1229, 26
    R.F.L. (5th) 440 (Ont. C.A.)..211
Vamvakidis v. Kirkoff (1929), 64 O.L.R. 585, [1930] 2 D.L.R. 877 (Ont.
    C.A.)...24
Van Delft v. Colosimo (1996), 1996 CarswellOnt 3595, [1996] O.J. No.
    3387, (sub nom. *J.V-D. v. E.C.*) 14 O.T.C. 159 (Ont. Gen. Div.)...........225
Van de Perre v. Edwards, REJB 2001-25876, 2001 CarswellBC 1999, 2001
    CarswellBC 2000, [2001] S.C.J. No. 60, 2001 SCC 60, 204 D.L.R.
    (4th) 257, 94 B.C.L.R. (3d) 199, 19 R.F.L. (5th) 396, [2001] 11 W.W.R.
    1, (sub nom. *P. (K.V.) v. E. (T.)*) 275 N.R. 52, (sub nom. *K.V.P. v.
    T.E.*) 156 B.C.A.C. 161, (sub nom. *K.V.P. v. T.E.*) 255 W.A.C. 161,
    [2001] 2 S.C.R. 1014 (S.C.C.)...219
Walsh v. Bona, REJB 2002-36303, 2002 CarswellNS 511, 2002 CarswellNS
    512, [2002] S.C.J. No. 84, (sub nom. *Nova Scotia (Attorney General)
    v. Walsh*) [2002] 4 S.C.R. 325, 2002 SCC 83, 32 R.F.L. (5th) 81, (sub
    nom. *Nova Scotia (Attorney General) v. Walsh*) 221 D.L.R. (4th) 1, 297
    N.R. 203, 211 N.S.R. (2d) 273, 659 A.P.R. 273, 102 C.R.R. (2d) 1
    (S.C.C.)..103
Walduda v. Bell (2004), 2004 CarswellOnt 3029, 7 R.F.L. (6th) 205 (Ont.
    S.C.J.)..150
Wickham v. Wickham (1983), 1983 CarswellOnt 313, 35 R.F.L. (2d) 448
    (Ont. C.A.)...213
Willenbrecht v. Willenbrecht (1999), 1999 CarswellOnt 1483, 120 O.A.C.
    274, 47 R.F.L. (4th) 200 (Ont. C.A. [In Chambers])........................39
Winnipeg Child & Family Services (Northwest Area) v. G. (D.F.) (1997), 1997
    CarswellMan 475, 1997 CarswellMan 476, 152 D.L.R. (4th) 193, 31
    R.F.L. (4th) 165, (sub nom. *Child & Family Services of Winnipeg
    Northwest v. D.F.G.*) 219 N.R. 241, 121 Man. R. (2d) 241, 158 W.A.C.
    241, [1998] 1 W.W.R. 1, 39 C.C.L.T. (2d) 203 (Fr.), [1997] 3 S.C.R.
    925, 39 C.C.L.T. (2d) 155 (Eng.), 3 B.H.R.C. 611 (S.C.C.)...............292
Wright v. Zaver (2002), 2002 CarswellOnt 887, [2002] O.J. No. 1098,
    24 R.F.L. (5th) 207, 211 D.L.R. (4th) 260, 158 O.A.C. 146, 59 O.R.
    (3d) 26 (Ont. C.A.)..69, 181
Young v. Young, EYB 1993-67111, [1993] S.C.J. No. 112, 1993 CarswellBC
    264, 1993 CarswellBC 1269, [1993] 8 W.W.R. 513, 108 D.L.R. (4th)
    193, 18 C.R.R. (2d) 41, [1993] 4 S.C.R. 3, 84 B.C.L.R. (2d) 1, 160
    N.R. 1, 49 R.F.L. (3d) 117, 34 B.C.A.C. 161, 56 W.A.C. 161, [1993]
    R.D.F. 703 (S.C.C.)...81, 88

CHAPTER 1

FAMILY LAW: HISTORY AND COURTS

Family law is a dynamic, fast-paced and ever-changing area of law. It encompasses issues that are of primary importance to people, such as marriage, divorce, custody and support of children, spousal support, and division of property on marriage breakdown. Our concept of the family has undergone, and continues to undergo, massive transformations, with our increasing numbers of divorces, common-law marriages, children born outside of marriage, and same-sex marriages. Over the years, family law has evolved to keep up with changing values and attitudes of society. However, people are not always in agreement about what the values of society with respect to family law matters are or should be. Differing cultural and religious values make consensus on family law matters even more challenging. As the issues connected with family law matters are highly emotional, it is no surprise that family law continues to generate disagreement and controversy.

A BRIEF HISTORY OF FAMILY LAW IN ONTARIO

The Beginning of Family Law

The roots of family law in Ontario were planted in 1792, when the Governor and Legislature of Upper Canada established that the civil law of England would be the law of Upper Canada (as Ontario was then known). Rather than pass laws one at a time, Upper Canada simply imported and adopted all English law, including family law. This meant that that the doctrine of "unity of legal personality" became the law of Ontario. Upon marriage, the husband and the wife became one legal entity. Sir William Blackstone, famed English legal commentator, stated: "In law the husband and wife are one person, and the husband is that person."

Although the husband was expected to maintain the wife, he was not legally obliged to give her anything. On the other hand, the law required the wife to endow her husband with everything she had: her land, her furniture, the clothes on her back, and the ring on her finger. The wife's goods and chattels were vested absolutely in the husband. The wife had no legal capacity to hold or manage property, and no independent right to enter into contracts, or to sue or be sued. She could not dispose of property in her will without the consent of her husband. She could not vote. In other words, the legal status of the wife became identical to that of a minor child or an incompetent. However, it must be noted that single women were able to hold and sell property, enter into contracts, and sue and be sued.

The law with respect to property was revolutionized by the *Married Women's Property Act*[1] of 1884. Under this law, the doctrine of "separate property" was introduced. This meant that all real and personal property owned or acquired by a woman could be held, enjoyed, or disposed of, as though she were a single woman. A married woman now also had the right to retain her own earnings. Although this legislation gave new rights to women, for many women the situation did not change dramatically. Although women could retain their own earnings, few jobs were available to them. As men were the income earners in the family, most property would still have been registered in the name of the husband, and the wife would have no right to it.

Divorce

Until 1925, a husband could sue a wife for divorce on the grounds of the wife's adultery. However, a wife could only obtain a divorce against her husband if she could show not only that he had committed adultery, but also that he had committed another marital offence, such as cruelty, incest, or wilful desertion. Custody of the children was the right of the husband.

Prior to 1930, a divorce could only be obtained by a private act of Parliament, obtained by applying to the federal government in Ottawa. A Member of Parliament would have to introduce a private member's bill for the couple's divorce. That bill would then go though the process until it was finally passed into law, and the couple would be divorced. Needless to say, this was an expensive and cumbersome procedure that was only available to the very rich. In 1930, Ontario established its own divorce court.

The wife's right to financial support on marriage breakdown depended on fault. "Innocent" wives were entitled to lifelong financial support from their "guilty" husbands. If the wife had herself committed adultery, she was denied the right to spousal support, regardless of the conduct of her husband. A wife that had made no financial contribution to her husband's acquisition of assets had no legal right to share in the property he acquired during the marriage. However, a wife did have "dower rights", which

---

[1] S.O. 1884, c. 19.

entitled her to a life interest in one third of her husband's property after his death.

A major change came in 1968 when the federal government passed the first *Divorce Act*.[2] For the first time, everyone in Canada was subject to the same laws and procedures. This *Divorce Act* entitled either spouse to sue on the basis of a number of fault grounds, such as adultery, sodomy, bestiality, rape, homosexual act, or cruelty. The most radical change, though, was that for the first time spouses could also sue for a divorce on the basis of "marriage breakdown" — a "no-fault" ground for divorce. Marriage breakdown could be shown in a number of ways, such as imprisonment, gross addiction to alcohol or a narcotic, non-consummation, etc. Marriage breakdown could be also shown by a separation of three years where the parties agreed to separate or the petitioning spouse had been abandoned, or five years where the petitioner had deserted the other spouse.

Although it was no longer necessary to show fault in order to get a divorce, fault could still be taken in to consideration by the court when considering an award of alimony. Section 11(1) of that Act stated that the court could award maintenance "if it thinks it fit and just to do so having regard to the conduct of the parties and the condition, means and other circumstances of each of them."

In spite of the fact that fault was still relevant with regard to support, over time the emphasis in support orders shifted from misconduct to the economic consequences of marriage breakdown. The 1968 Act established formal legal equality between the spouses respecting support rights and obligations. The legal emphasis was on rehabilitative support orders that emphasized the obligation of each spouse to strive for economic self-sufficiency. Although the law was in keeping with the modern view of women as equal to men, it did not reflect the economic realities of women during that period. It was unduly optimistic and unrealistic to expect that women would be able to become self-supporting within a short period of time, especially where they had been in a long, traditional marriage.

Divorce and Family Law Reforms

By the 1960s, society's views on the role of women and marriage were undergoing substantial changes. The Women's Liberation Movement challenged the traditional role of women in families, in the workforce, and in

---

[2] R.S.C. 1970, c. D-8. When the Dominion of Canada was created by the *British North America Act, 1867*, legislative power was divided between the provincial and federal governments. Provinces were given power over The Solemnization of Marriage in the Province (s. 92(12)) and Property and Civil Rights in a Province (s. 92(13)) whereas the federal government was given power over Marriage and Divorce (s. 91(26)).

society, and the idea of marriage as a partnership was beginning to take hold. Major changes were also taking place at the provincial level regarding the economic consequences of marriage breakdown. The old fault system of awarding support was rejected in favour of a *needs* and *capacity to pay* approach.

With regard to property division, however, the law was not keeping up with society's changing attitudes regarding marriage as a partnership. The law required that in order to be awarded some part of the husband's property on marriage breakdown, the wife would need to show that she had made a financial contribution to acquiring the property.

Murdoch v. Murdoch (1973), [1975] I S.C.R. 423 (S.C.C.)

The appellant wife and respondent husband were married in 1943. They worked, as a couple, on several ranches, until 1947. The husband bought and sold several properties, until eventually, in 1958, the respondent purchased three quarter sections of land, known as the Brockway property. By the time they separated in 1968, Mr. Murdoch owned about 480 acres of ranch property. Mr. Murdoch, throughout most of the marriage, belonged to a stock association, which caused him to be away from home approximately five months of the year. During the periods of his absence, the wife did the husband's work. Both parties testified that the wife could do "just about anything" on the ranch. Her duties included "haying, raking, swathing, mowing, driving tractors and teams, taking cattle back and forth to the reserve, dehoming, vaccinating, branding, anything that was to be done," as well as taking care of the home and childcare.

Mrs. Murdoch argued that she was entitled to a share of the husband's property based on, among other things, her contribution of physical labour. The majority of the Supreme Court of Canada (Laskin J. dissenting) found that Mrs. Murdoch's contribution was "the work done by any ranch wife," and she was therefore not entitled to any part of her husband's property.

In the words of Beverley McLachlin, Chief Justice of the Supreme Court of Canada,

> The Supreme Court's decision may have marked the end of Mrs. Murdoch's saga. But it was only the beginning of the larger legal story. The decision galvanized Canadians, who reacted with a mix of astonishment and shock to the idea that married women had no property rights in the family home, farm or business. Public pressure was brought to bear. In short order, every province enacted laws recognizing the right of spouses to share family property, regardless of who holds legal title. The *Divorce Act* was amended to

the same effect. It was truly a revolution in the property rights of married couples.[3]

In Ontario, the *Family Law Reform Act* of 1978[4] provided that property would be classified as being either family assets or non-family assets. The family assets were to be divided equally between the parties on marriage breakdown, but the non-family assets would not be divided unless the non-owning spouse could show that he or she contributed to the acquisition of the non-family assets, in which case the court could award some portion of the non-family assets.

The next major change came with the *Divorce Act* of 1985,[5] which came into force on June 1, 1986. This Act continued the trend towards no-fault divorce by making marriage breakdown the sole grounds for divorce. Marriage breakdown can be based on adultery, cruelty, or separation for one year. Section 15(6) of the Act specifies that the misconduct of a spouse is to be ignored in determining spousal or child support. Further, the law also contains significant procedural changes. The application for divorce can be presented any time after separation, although the divorce cannot be granted until the parties have been separated for one year if the divorce is based on separation. The parties no longer have to appear before the courts, but instead uncontested divorces can be obtained on the basis of affidavit evidence. The divorce becomes final one month after the divorce judgment is granted.

Shortly after the changes to the *Divorce Act*, the Ontario government passed the *Family Law Act, 1986*.[6] This Act made sweeping changes to property law in Ontario. The distinction between family assets and non-family assets has been eliminated. Rather than being entitled to share particular assets, separated spouses were now entitled to an equalization of net family properties. This applied not only upon separation of spouses, but also upon the death of one of the spouses.

The current law as encompassed in the *Divorce Act* of 1985 and the *Family Law Act, 1986* will be discussed in detail throughout this book, as will other statutes and rules that pertain to family law matters in Ontario.

---

[3] Remarks of the Right Honourable Beverley McLachlin, P.C. Chief Justice of Canada, "Reaction and Pro-action: Bringing Family Law Advocacy Into the 21st Century" (Family Law Dinner, Ontario Bar Association, Toronto, Ontario, January 24, 2002).

[4] R.S.O. 1980, c. 152.

[5] R.S.C. 1985, c. 3 (2nd Supp.), as amended, s. 2(1).

[6] S.O. 1986, c. 4.

FEDERAL AND PROVINCIAL LEGISLATION

Both the federal government and the provincial government have the power to pass family law legislation. The division of legislative power is governed by the *Constitution Acts, 1867 to 1982*, which incorporates sections 91 and 92 of the *British North America Act, 1867*. Provinces were given power over The Solemnization of Marriage in the Province (s. 92(12)) and Property and Civil Rights in a Province (s. 92(13)) whereas the federal government was given power over Marriage and Divorce (s. 91(26)). Both levels of government have passed legislation that deal with family law matters. Below is a list of the most important pieces of family law legislation.

Federal

- *Civil Marriage Act;*[7]
- *Divorce Act;*[8] and
- *Marriage (Prohibited Degrees) Act.*[9]

Provincial (Ontario)

- *Change of Name Act;*[10]
- *Child and Family Services Act;*[11]
- *Children's Law Reform Act;*[12]
- *Family Law Act;*[13]
- *Family Responsibility and Support Arrears Enforcement Act, 1996;* and[14]
- *Marriage Act.*[15]

There is some overlap between the federal and provincial legislation. For example, both the *Divorce Act* and the *Family Law Act* make provision for child and spousal support, and child custody is dealt with in both the *Divorce Act* and the *Children's Law Reform Act*. Which legislation is applicable in a given situation and the similarities and differences between federal and provincial legislation in these areas will be dealt with in later chapters.

---

[7] S.C. 2005, c. 33.
[8] R.S.C. 1985, c. 3 (2nd Supp.), as amended.
[9] S.C. 1990, c. 46.
[10] R.S.O. 1990, c. C.7.
[11] R.S.O. 1990, c. C.11.
[12] R.S.O. 1990, c. C.12.
[13] R.S.O. 1990, c. F.3.
[14] S.O. 1996, c. 31.
[15] R.S.O. 1990, c. M.3.

THE ONTARIO COURT SYSTEM AND THE FAMILY LAW COURTS

Courts in Ontario are created and their jurisdiction is defined in the *Courts of Justice Act*.[16] The Act creates three levels of courts: the Court of Appeal for Ontario, the Superior Court of Justice, and the Ontario Court of Justice. In addition to its trial jurisdiction, the Superior Court of Justice has three other branches: the Divisional Court, the Small Claims Court, and the Family Court. The Ontario Court of Justice has both criminal jurisdiction and family jurisdiction. The chart in Appendix 1A shows the different levels of courts and gives an outline of the jurisdiction of each.

The Ontario Court of Justice

The Ontario Court of Justice is meant to handle smaller, less complex cases. It is less formal than the Superior Court of Justice, and a larger percentage of people who appear in this court do not have lawyers. With regard to criminal matters, it deals with Provincial Offences, summary conviction offences, most indictable offences until the end of the preliminary inquiry, and indictable trials where the accused elects to be tried by a magistrate.

The Ontario Court of Justice also handles certain family law cases. It cannot deal with any matter under the *Divorce Act*[17] or with equalization of net family properties, but can deal with matters such as child and spousal support under the *Family Law Act*,[18] custody under the *Children's Law Reform Act*,[19] enforcement of support orders, applications under the *Change of Name Act*,[20] and all matters under the *Child and Family Services Act*.[21] The Ontario Court of Justice is also a Youth Justice Court for the purposes of the *Youth Criminal Justice Act*.[22]

The Superior Court of Justice

The Superior Court of Justice is primarily a trial court. It handles criminal matters, mostly indictable offences after the accused has been committed for trial at a preliminary inquiry, and where the accused has elected to be

---

[16] R.S.O. 1990, c. C.43.

[17] R.S.C. 1985, c. 3 (2nd Supp.), as amended.

[18] R.S.O. 1990, c. F.3, as amended.

[19] R.S.O. 1990, c. C.12, as amended.

[20] R.S.O. 1990, c. C.7, as amended.

[21] R.S.O. 1990, c. C.11, as amended.

[22] S.C. 2002, c. 1.

tried either by a judge alone or by a judge and jury. It also deals with all types of civil cases, including bankruptcy, estates, personal injury, contract, and commercial cases.

In terms of family law, the Superior Court of Justice handles all matters under the *Divorce Act* and all applications where an equalization of net family properties is being sought. It will also deal with spousal and child support under the *Family Law Act* and custody under the *Children's Law Reform Act*. It will not deal with change of name applications, or hearings under the *Child and Family Services Act*.

Divisional Court

Divisional Court is a branch of the Superior Court of Justice. It deals with appeals from Small Claims Court and Administrative Tribunals and with appeals of civil matters (including family law matters) where the amount awarded was less than $25,000.

Small Claims Court

Small Claims Court is also a branch of the Superior Court of Justice. It deals with civil matters under $10,000.

Family Court

Because jurisdiction in family law matters is divided between the Superior Court of Justice and the Ontario Court of Justice and some of the jurisdiction is overlapping, the provincial government thought to create a new court that would handle all family law matters. As an experiment, in 1977 it created a court in Hamilton, which was called the Unified Family Court. The Unified Family Court had the entire jurisdiction of the Superior Court and of the Ontario Court of Justice and dealt only with family law matters. In 1995, the provincial government changed the name to Family Court and created Family Courts in four other judicial districts. Then, in 1998, the provincial government expanded the Family Court into 12 more locations. The Family Court is a branch of the Superior Court of Justice. Although the idea was that eventually, every judicial district in Ontario would have a Family Court, no new Family Courts have been created since 1998. Because these courts deal only with family law matters, they have Family Law Information Centres attached to them that offer integrated services such as mediation, information services, referral information for other community agencies, and legal services. Currently, Family Courts exist in the following locations:

- Hamilton-Wentworth (Hamilton);
- Middlesex County (London);
- Frontenac County (Kingston);
- Lennox & Addington County (Napanee);
- Simcoe County (Barrie);
- Ottawa;
- Newmarket;
- Oshawa;
- Peterborough;
- Lindsay;
- Cobourg;
- Bracebridge;
- St. Catharines;
- Cornwall;
- L'Orignal;
- Brockville; and
- Perth.

Where a location has a Family Court, all family law matters within that location are brought to the Family Court. If the location does not have a Family Court, then the applicant must decide whether to commence proceedings in the Superior Court of Justice or the Ontario Court of Justice, being careful to make sure that the court has jurisdiction in the matter.

Application Questions

In which court(s) would you commence the following applications?

1. A divorce application in Peterborough.

2. A divorce application in Toronto.

3. An application for spousal support under the *Family Law Act* in Napanee.

4. An application for spousal support under the *Family Law Act* in Brampton.

5. An application under the *Child and Family Services Act* in Toronto.

The Court of Appeal for Ontario

The Court of Appeal for Ontario hears appeals from the Divisional Court and from final orders of the Superior Court of Justice involving more than $25,000, including family law matters.

SUPREME COURT OF CANADA

The Supreme Court of Canada, located in Ottawa, Ontario, is a federal court that hears appeals from all of the provincial and territorial Courts of Appeal, and the Federal Court of Appeal. This is the final level of appeal available in Canada.

APPENDIX 1A

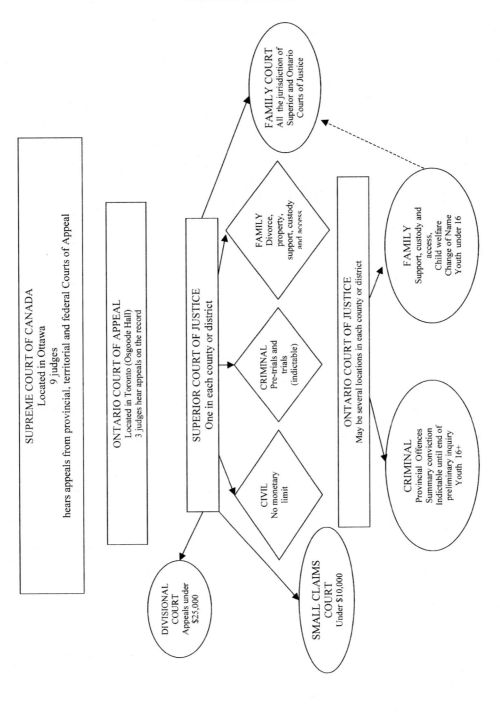

CHAPTER 2

MARRIAGE AND ANNULMENT

MARRIAGE

What is Marriage?

Marriage is a legal relationship that has many dimensions. It is a contract between two people and is therefore subject to the rules governing contracts. However, marriage is much more than simply a contract between two private individuals. It is also a status conferred by the state. Our laws attach conditions to the creation of a marriage, the ending of a marriage and the consequences of being married. Certain rights and obligations flow from the status of being a married person. Many of these rights and obligations govern the financial responsibilities between the spouses during the marriage and when the marriage breaks down, as well as the care of and responsibility for children of the marriage.

The Canadian definition of marriage was originally inherited from Britain where it was defined by the English common law as "the voluntary union of one man and one woman to the exclusion of all others."[1]

> ### *Halpern v. Toronto (City)* (2003), 36 R.F.L. (5th) 127, 172 O.A.C. 276, 65 O.R. (3d) 161, 225 D.L.R. (4th) 529, 65 O.R. (3d) 201 (Ont. C.A.)
>
> Seven gay and lesbian couples applied for civil marriage licences in Toronto. The clerk of the city refused to proceed with the licence applications until directions from the court were obtained. At about the same time, the Metropolitan Community Church of Toronto decided to conduct marriages for its homosexual members. After the marriage of two couples, the church submitted the required documentation to the Registrar who refused to accept the documents. The first group sought judicial review of the clerk's decision not to issue marriage licences and the church group sought judicial review of the refusal to register the marriages of the homosexual couples. The two applications were heard together by the Divisional Court. The Court held unanimously that the common-law definition of marriage infringed the couples' equality rights under section 15(1) of the *Charter of*

---

[1] *Hyde v. Hyde* (1866), L.R. 1 P.D. 130 (Eng. P.D.A.) at 133.

Rights and Freedoms and was not justified under section 1 of the *Charter*. The Attorney General of Canada appealed on the equality issue.

Held: The appeal by the Attorney General was dismissed.

> . . .The question at the heart of this appeal is whether excluding same-sex couples from one of the most basic elements of our civic life—marriage—infringes human dignity and violates the Canadian Constitution. [At 139 (R.F.L.).]

> Marriage is, without dispute, one of the most significant forms of personal relationships. For centuries, marriage has been a basic element of social organization in societies around the world. Through the institution of marriage, individuals can publicly express their love and commitment to each other. Through this institution, society publicly recognizes expressions of love and commitment between individuals, granting them respect and legitimacy as a couple. This public recognition and sanction of marital relationships reflect society's approbation of the personal hopes, desires and aspirations that underlie loving, committed conjugal relationships. This can only enhance an individual's sense of self-worth and dignity. [At 138 (R.F.L.).]

> The ability to marry, and therefore to participate in this fundamental societal institution, is something that most Canadians take for granted. Same-sex couples do not; they are denied access to this institution simply on the basis of their sexual orientation. [At 139 (R.F.L.).]

> The common law definition of marriage [the "voluntary union for life of one man and one woman to the exclusion of all others"] violated s. 15(1) [the equality rights section] of the Charter. The historical disadvantage suffered by same-sex couples favoured a finding of discrimination in the case-at-hand. A law prohibiting same-sex couples from marrying did not accord with the needs, capacities and circumstances of same-sex couples. Denying same-sex couples the right to marry perpetuated the view that same-sex couples were not capable of forming loving and lasting relationships. Equal treatment under the law with respect to benefits and obligations had not been afforded to same-sex couples. . . . The dignity of persons in same-sex relationships was violated by the exclusion of same-sex couples from the institution of marriage. [At 129 (R.F.L.).]

> [Furthermore,] [t]he violation of the seven couples' equality rights under s. 15(1) of the Charter was not justified under s. 1 of the Charter. The encouragement of procreation and childrearing could not be considered a pressing and substantial objective of maintaining marriage as an exclusively heterosexual institution. Encouraging companionship between only persons of the opposite sex perpetuated the view that persons in same-sex relationships were not equally capable of providing companionship and forming lasting and loving relationships. [At 129 (R.F.L.).]

An appropriate remedy to the infringement of the couples' constitutional rights was to declare the existing common law definition of marriage to be invalid to the extent that it referred to "one man and one woman", and to reformulate it as "the voluntary union for life of two persons to the exclusion of all others". [At 129 (R.F.L.).]

The federal *Civil Marriage Act*,[2] which came into effect in 2005, incorporated many of the principles outlined in the *Halpern* case. The Act now defines marriage in Canada as "the lawful union of two persons to the exclusion of all others."[3] In passing this legislation, the federal parliament noted that the right to equality without discrimination requires that couples of the same sex and couples of the opposite sex have equal access to the institution of marriage for civil purposes.[4]

LEGAL CAPACITY TO MARRY

Parties (Who Can Marry Whom)

The legal capacity to marry is governed by the law of the person's domicile (permanent residence) immediately before the marriage. In Canada, the legal capacity to marry is a matter of federal jurisdiction under the *Constitution Act*. The *Civil Marriage Act*[5] clearly states that a person has the legal capacity to marry another person of the opposite or the same sex. Prior to the Halpern decision, a person did not have the capacity to marry another person of the same sex.

The *Marriage (Prohibited Degrees) Act*[6] governs who a person is not permitted to marry. A person is prohibited from marrying anyone to whom he or she is too closely related by blood or adoption. In particular, a person cannot marry anyone to whom he or she is lineally related (i.e., parent, grandparent, child or grandchild); nor can he or she marry a sibling or half-sibling by blood or adoption. A marriage between two people who are related in any of these ways is void. On the other hand, a person is free to marry any other relatives not mentioned in the Act.

Marital Status

Neither party to a marriage can be married to anyone else (whether in Canada or in another jurisdiction) at the time of the marriage. Any person

---

[2] S.C. 2005, c. 33.
[3] *Civil Marriage Act*, s. 2.
[4] *Civil Marriage Act*, preamble.
[5] S.C. 2005, c. 33, s. 2.
[6] S.C. 1990, c. 46.

who has been previously married must demonstrate that his or her marriage has ended by divorce, annulment, or by the death of his or her spouse before remarriage can occur. For this purpose, a divorce that is recognized by the country granting it will be recognized in Canada. For example, a valid divorce granted in India would be recognized in Canada, even if the grounds for divorce in India were different from the grounds for divorce in Canada, as long as the parties met the residency requirements for recognition of foreign divorces in the *Divorce Act*.

Age

According to case law, a child under the age of 7 is not capable of entering a valid marriage. A marriage involving a boy between 7 and 14 and a girl between the ages of 7 and 12 can be annulled if the under-aged person applies to annul it.

FORMALITIES OF MARRIAGE

The formalities of marriage, which include such matters as the issuance of a marriage licence and the nature of the ceremony, are governed by the laws of the individual provinces and territories of Canada. This is because the "solemnization of marriage" is a matter within the jurisdiction of the provinces according to the *Constitution Act*. In Ontario, the formal aspects of the marriage are governed by the *Marriage Act*.[7]

Who May Marry

Any person who has the legal capacity to marry can marry if they are over the age of 18,[8] provided they are not mentally ill, mentally defective, or under the influence of drugs or alcohol.[9] Anyone between the ages of 16 and 18 can marry with the written consent of both parents.[10] Where one parent is dead or the parents are living apart, it is the parent having the actual or legal custody of the minor who can give consent.[11] If a minor has been made a ward of the Children's Aid Society or the Crown, the consent can be given by the person who is the child's lawful guardian.[12] In a situation where a person whose consent is necessary is not available

---

[7] R.S.O. 1990, c. M-3, as amended.
[8] *Marriage Act*, s. 5(1).
[9] *Marriage Act*, s. 7.
[10] *Marriage Act*, s. 5(2).
[11] *Marriage Act*, s. 5(4).
[12] *Marriage Act*, s. 5(6).

or arbitrarily refuses to give his or her consent, a minor can apply to a judge to obtain an order dispensing with the required consent.[13] Another alternative is to obtain the permission to marry from the Minister of Consumer and Business Services.[14]

Marriage Licence or Publication of Banns Required

In Ontario, before the marriage ceremony takes place, a couple who intends to marry must obtain a marriage licence or have their marriage banns "published" in the church or churches where the parties regularly attend. It is not necessary to do both. In order to obtain a marriage licence, a couple must go to city hall and prove their identity[15] and their marital status.[16] If a party has been married previously, he or she must have proof that the marriage was validly dissolved or annulled or possess a court declaration that the previous spouse has died.[17]

If a couple chooses to publish banns rather than obtain a marriage licence, their intention to marry must be announced openly, before the congregation, during divine service at their church. If the parties attend different churches, the announcement must be made at both places of religious worship. The church can be any denomination as long as the person is in the habit of attending regularly and the announcement complies with the normal customs of their religion.[18] However, a couple may not use the publication of banns if either of them has been previously married and the previous marriage was ended by divorce or annulment.[19] The parties must wait at least five days after the publication of their banns before they can marry. However, the couple must marry within three months of the issuance of a marriage licence or the publication of banns.[20]

Who Can Solemnize the Marriage

There are several different types of persons who are qualified to perform a marriage ceremony in Ontario. For religious ceremonies, a person is qualified if he or she is an Ontario resident who is ordained or appointed by a religious body that recognizes them as entitled to perform marriage ceremonies. The religious body can be any denomination as long as it is

---

[13] *Marriage Act*, s. 6.
[14] *Marriage Act*, s. 10.
[15] *Marriage Act*, s. 12.
[16] *Marriage Act*, s. 8.
[17] *Marriage Act*, s. 9.
[18] *Marriage Act*, s. 17.
[19] *Marriage Act*, s. 18.
[20] *Marriage Act*, ss. 27(2), (3).

a permanently established one.[21] The definition would include ministers, priests, rabbis, and officials ordained by other religions. A religious official must be registered with the Ministry in order to be qualified to perform a valid marriage.

It should also be noted that religious officials are free to refuse to perform marriages that violate their religious beliefs.[22] For example, a religious official is not obliged to perform a marriage ceremony between a same-sex couple if he or she cannot do so in good conscience. There are no legal sanctions for refusing to do so.

A civil marriage ceremony may be performed by a judge of the Ontario Court of Justice or the Superior Court of Justice, or a justice of the peace,[23] or a clerk of a local municipality.[24] Any marriage performed by a judge must take place in the judge's office between the hours of nine o'clock in the morning and five in the afternoon.[25]

Form of the Ceremony

A religious marriage, performed by a religious official registered under the Marriage Act, is valid if it is performed according to the usages and customs of the particular religion. With respect to a civil marriage, although no particular form of ceremony is required, there are three things that must occur during the ceremony in the presence of the witnesses and the person performing the ceremony:[26]

- each party must declare that they know of no "lawful impediment" why they should not be joined in matrimony;

- each party must ask the people present to witness that he or she takes the other to be their lawful wedded spouse or partner; and

- the person performing the ceremony must pronounce that the couple are married, pursuant to the powers vested in him/her by the *Marriage Act*.

Once the marriage ceremony has been performed, the person who performed the ceremony must immediately record the particulars in a register that must be signed by the parties, two witnesses and the person who

---

[21] *Marriage Act*, s. 20.
[22] *Civil Marriage Act*, s. 3.
[23] *Marriage Act*, s. 24(1).
[24] R.R.O. 1990, Reg. 738 as amended, s. 1.1.
[25] *Marriage Act*, s. 24(2).
[26] *Marriage Act*, s. 24(3).

solemnized the marriage.[27] If the parties ask for it, the person performing the ceremony must also give them a certificate of marriage.[28]

Failure to Comply With the Formalities of Marriage

If the parties fail to comply with the formal requirements to get married in Ontario, it does not necessarily follow that their marriage is invalid. As long as the parties have complied with three requirements, their marriage will be valid, even though the person who married them was not qualified by law, or they failed to obtain the proper marriage licence or publication of banns. The three necessary requirements are that:[29]

- the marriage was solemnized "in good faith" and intended to be in compliance with the *Marriage Act*;

- the parties cohabited as a married couple after the ceremony; and

- neither party lacked the legal capacity to enter the marriage.

Alspector v. Alspector, [1957] O.R. 454, 1957 CarswellOnt 39 (Ont. C.A.)

A couple who were adherents of the Jewish faith went through a marriage ceremony that complied with the requirements of the Jewish faith, but they did not obtain a marriage licence, as required by the *Marriage Act*. The parties were widow and widower at the time of the marriage and they lived together as husband and wife for seven years, until the husband died. The wife brought an application to determine the validity of the marriage. The marriage was found to be valid and the husband's children appealed the decision.

Held: The marriage was found to be valid.

> In considering [the equivalent to our present s. 31 of the Act, the Court had] to determine only the scope and meaning of the words "intended to be in compliance with this Act." It should be held that the legislature did not assume, believe or expect that every couple who should intermarry in the Province would be familiar with *this* Act. It would be the rare case, indeed, in which either of them would know of the existence of The Marriage Act. All that they would be expected to know is that there would be some law in effect in the Province respecting the solemnization of marriages. The phrase

---

[27] *Marriage Act*, s. 28(1).
[28] *Marriage Act*, s. 28(2).
[29] *Marriage Act*, s. 31.

should therefore be interpreted as meaning,—intended to be in compliance with that law. [At para. 34.]

Even if it should be held that [the wife] knew as a fact that a licence had not been issued, I think it fair to conclude on her evidence that she did not know that the absence of a licence in the circumstances of this case could affect the validity of her marriage; and that she intended that the marriage be in compliance with the law of the Province. As for [the husband], it is not unreasonable to conclude that although he knew that a licence had not been issued he proceeded in good faith believing that a licence was not necessary because of his intention shortly thereafter to go with the plaintiff to reside in Israel. [At para. 37.]

The appeal should be dismissed.

Application Questions

1. Joshua, aged 17, and Tara, aged 16 were madly in love and although they were still in high school, Tara became pregnant with Joshua's child. They wanted to marry immediately, but Joshua's parents were opposed to the marriage as they wanted their son to remain in school to become a doctor. Tara lived with her mother who was divorced from her dad. Her parents reluctantly supported the marriage.

   (a) Explain what steps Joshua and Tara must take before they can get married in Ontario.
   (b) If Joshua and Tara decide to get married in their church under the publication of banns, do they need a marriage licence? Can they get married the day after the banns are published? *Sec. 27(2)* *5days.*
   (c) If Joshua and Tara want to be married at sunrise on Wasaga Beach, can Tara's uncle, who is a judge, perform the ceremony? *yes*
   (d) If Joshua and Tara were first cousins, would they be permitted to get married in Ontario? *yes.*

2. Lisa came to Canada from Switzerland after her marriage to her first husband had been validly terminated by divorce. Shortly after arriving in Toronto, Lisa, who was of the Jewish faith, married Rabbi Morris at a ceremony at the Rabbi's home. The ceremony followed the proper customs of the Jewish religion. Although Lisa knew that they did not go down to City Hall, she was assured by the Rabbi prior to the marriage, that since they were older people, the local government recognized a solely Jewish marriage. The couple never obtained a marriage licence. Also, the person who married them was a cantor who was not registered to perform marriages under the *Marriage Act*. The couple lived together in the rabbi's home following the marriage and they were known as husband and wife in the community until his death three years later.

> (a) Was Lisa's marriage to the rabbi valid? Explain why or why not?
>
> (b) Assuming the same facts, would your answer be different if Lisa discovered that her divorce from her first husband in Switzerland was not valid? Explain.
>
> (c) What if the couple deliberately refrained from obtaining a marriage licence so that the husband could continue receiving his widower's pension? Would Lisa still be able to claim that the marriage was valid?

[Handwritten margin notes:]
yes. 2 technical defect.
Section 31

—no bc they didnt act in good faith under s.31

ANNULMENT

What is Annulment?

Annulment is a court judgment declaring that a marriage, which is apparently valid in form, is void in law. In other words, the marriage is of no force and effect. When a judgment of nullity is obtained, it is as if the marriage never existed. This kind of declaratory judgment from the court declares the legal status of the parties and it is binding on the whole world. This means that it is not merely a judgment that affects only the couple who are having their marriage annulled. The legal status of each party becomes that of a single person (or whatever it was immediately prior to the purported marriage). Each party is free to marry another person as if they were never married. Annulment is in contrast to divorce, which ends a valid marriage and results in the legal status of being "divorced". A declaration of annulment results from some defect or disability at the time of the marriage ceremony that renders the marriage either void or voidable. While the formalities of marriage are governed by statute, the law of annulment is primarily governed by the common law or case law.

Two Types of Annulment

With respect to annulment, there are marriages which are void *ab initio* and marriages that are voidable. A marriage that is void *ab initio* is void from the beginning because the parties never had the legal capacity to marry in the first place. Such a marriage never really existed at all and does not require a judgment of nullity to make the marriage void. However, most people still obtain a judgment in order to make their annulment official.

Some marriages are not necessarily void from the beginning, but are merely voidable. This means that the parties may, if they wish, stay married, but the marriage is voidable if one of the parties decides he or she wants to end the marriage. However, a voidable marriage, which is capable of being annulled, continues to be valid unless a declaration of nullity is granted. There are only a very few grounds annulling a voidable marriage. It is always necessary to obtain a judgment of nullity in this case. However, once the declaration is obtained, the marriage is retroactively erased and it is as if the parties were never married.

Marriage Void *Ab Initio*

Age

If either party to the marriage was younger than 7 years old at the time of the marriage, the marriage is void *ab initio*.

Prior Subsisting Marriage

A marriage is void from the beginning if one or both parties lack the legal capacity to marry. If one of the parties is already married to someone else at the time of the marriage, then the marriage was never valid because one party lacked the legal capacity to enter the marriage. Whether or not the parties married in good faith, if the previous divorce was not 'legal', then the marriage is void from the beginning.

Consanguinity and Affinity

Similarly, if a person marries someone to whom he or she is too closely related by blood or adoption, then the marriage is void from the beginning. It does not matter whether the parties knew at the time of the marriage that they were so related. The *Marriage (Prohibited Degrees) Act*[30] allows persons who are related by consanguinity, affinity or adoption to marry unless they are:

- linely related by consanguinity or adoption (grandparents, parents, children or grandchildren);

- brother and sister by consanguinity, whether by whole or half blood; or

- brother or sister by adoption.

---

[30] S.C. 1990, c. 46.

A marriage between two people who are related in any of these ways is void.

Lack of Freedom to Consent to Marriage

Just as with other contracts, the parties to a marriage must understand what they are doing and must voluntarily consent to the marriage. There are a number of factors that can negate a person's consent to a marriage; these include mental incapacity, duress and mistake.

Mental Incapacity

A person who marries must be able to understand the nature of the marriage contract and the duties and responsibilities that marriage creates.[31] This ability to understand must exist at the time of the marriage ceremony. Mental incapacity could result from a mental or emotional condition or from drug or alcohol intoxication.[32] However, if a person is relying upon intoxication as a ground of incapacity, he or she must prove that they were completely incapable of knowing what they were doing at the time of the marriage. In other words, the drugs or alcohol must completely deprive the person of their senses and ability to make choices at the time of the marriage ceremony.

Duress

A party's consent to the marriage can be negated by duress, which is the exertion of force upon the person, causing a person to marry out of fear that some dire circumstance will happen if he or she does not marry. Fear is a necessary ingredient to this ground[33] and it must be reasonably entertained fear arising from some external circumstance for which the person is not responsible.[34] In other words, a person's own paranoid fears arising from their mental illness would not qualify as duress. Threats or terrorizing acts—physical or mental—against a person or his or her loved ones to force that person to marry would definitely amount to duress. Threats against property may also suffice to negate consent. The threat of social alienation or exclusion from an important community to which a person belongs could amount to coercion, depending upon the circumstances.

---

[31] *Chertkow v. Feinstein (Chertkow)*, [1929] 2 W.W.R. 257 (Alta. C.A.), affirmed (1929), [1930] S.C.R. 335, [1930] 1 D.L.R. 137 (S.C.C.); *Manella v. Manella*, [1942] O.R. 630, [1942] 4 D.L.R. 712 (Ont. C.A.).

[32] *Capon, Re; Capon v. McLay*, [1965] 2 O.R. 83, 49 D.L.R. (2d) 675 (Ont. C.A.); *Kerr v. Kerr*, 5 W.W.R. (N.S.) 385, [1952] 4 D.L.R. 578 (Man. C.A.).

[33] *Scott v. Sebright* (1886), 12 P.D. 21 (Eng. P.D.A.); *H. v. H.* (1953), [1954] P. 258 (Eng. P.D.A.).

[34] *H. v. H., ibid.; S. (A.) v. S. (A.)* (1988), 65 O.R. (2d) 720, 15 R.F.L. (3d) 443 (Ont. U.F.C.).

Mistake

A mistake must be with respect to either the identity of the person one is marrying[35] or the nature of the ceremony[36] in order to render a marriage void *ab initio*. For example if you married the identical twin of your fiancé, honestly believing it was your intended partner, this kind of fundamental mistake would make the marriage void from the beginning. Similarly, marrying someone at a ceremony that you mistakenly believed was a baptismal service would render the marriage void. However, if you make a mistake about any other attributes of the person, such as their age or their wealth, this would not make the marriage void, even though the other person misrepresented himself or herself in that regard.[37] A mere change of heart would not amount to mistake.

Voidable Marriage

Age

A marriage involving a boy between 7 and 14 and a girl between the ages of 7 and 12 can be annulled if the under-aged person applies to annul it.

Inability to Consummate

The main ground for having a voidable marriage annulled is that of sexual impotence, which must be present at the time the marriage ceremony takes place. Many people hold the mistaken belief that sexual impotence means only that the parties have never consummated the marriage, or never had sexual intercourse. However, the mere refusal or failure to engage in a sexual relationship is not sufficient grounds to obtain an annulment of a marriage that is otherwise valid.[38]

The case law has clearly indicated that a person who wants to end the marriage on the basis of impotence must demonstrate that one of the parties to the marriage has an *incurable inability* to have normal sexual intercourse with him or her. It is only the inability that renders the marriage voidable. This inability can arise from either a physical abnormality or a psychological aversion to sexual intercourse.[39] The incapacity can be an aversion to sexual intercourse in general or merely an aversion to having

---

[35] *R. v. Millis* (1844), 10 Cl. & F. 534, 8 E.R. 844 (U.K. H.L.).

[36] *Nane (Sykiotis) v. Sykiotis*, [1966] 2 O.R. 428, 1 R.F.L. Rep. 246 (Ont. H.C.); *Vamvakidis v. Kirkoff* (1929), 64 O.L.R. 585 (Ont. C.A.).

[37] *Brennen v. Brennen* (1890), 19 O.R. 327 (Ont. H.C.).

[38] *Heil v. Heil*, [1942] S.C.R. 160, [1942] 1 D.L.R. 657 (S.C.C.).

[39] *Heil v. Heil, ibid.*; *Gajamugan v. Gajamugan* (1979), 10 R.F.L. (2d) 280 (Ont. H.C.).

sex with your particular partner.[40] Whatever the nature of the inability, it must be incurable and it must be present at the time of the marriage. If the incapacity occurs five years into the marriage, after the marriage has been consummated, the incapacity will not render the marriage voidable. If the problem can be alleviated by simple, safe surgery or therapy, and the person affected is willing to undergo a cure within a reasonable time, then it is not incurable.[41] However, if the person who is afflicted with the disability refuses to undergo a simple medical cure, that person cannot bring an action based on his or her own inability.[42] A court can also draw an inference of inability from a person's illness, disability, or refusal to consummate the marriage.

If one spouse marries with full knowledge that that other spouse is unable to consummate the marriage, the innocent spouse will not be in a position to seek an annulment. Similarly, where an older couple marries mainly for companionship, it is not open to either party to later apply for an annulment on the basis of impotence. However, it should be noted that age, in itself, is not a defence to an application for annulment based upon impotence.[43] An inability to consummate is not necessarily a disability associated with age.[44]

A long delay in bringing an application by an innocent spouse may preclude the spouse from seeking relief. After a period of time, there would be a presumption that the "innocent" spouse has approbated or approved of the voidable marriage.[45] Approbation occurs when the person claiming *acquienscence* annulment shows acquiescence or affirmative acceptance of the marriage, with full knowledge of his or her partner's impotency and is fully aware of the right to seek an annulment. However, if an innocent spouse has a credible explanation for the delay in bringing the application for annulment, such as a reasonably held belief that the other spouse could be cured, the presumption of approbation could be rebutted.

Tice v. Tice, [1937] O.W.N. 250, [1937] 2 D.L.R. 591 (Ont. C.A.)

After the parties married, they agreed not to have children for a year and on each occasion a contraceptive device was used. The wife testified that there had only been two or three attempts at intercourse, which resulted in failure on the husband's part. They continued to occupy the same bed, but except for those occasions, the husband made no further attempt. There was never any discussion about the problem as the wife claimed "she did not think it was her duty" to speak to her husband. After two

---

40 *Gajamugan v. Gajamugan, ibid.*

41 *C. v. C.,* [1949] 1 W.W.R. 911 (Man. K.B.).

42 *A. v. A.* (1931), 40 O.W.N. 543 (Ont. H.C.); *Jones v. Jones* (1947), [1948] O.R. 22 (Ont. C.A.).

43 *Martin v. Martin* (1936), [1937] 1 W.W.R. 95 (Man. K.B.).

44 *F. v. F.,* 8 W.W.R. (N.S.) 84, [1953] 2 D.L.R. 318 (B.C. S.C.).

45 *B. v. B.* (1934), [1935] S.C.R. 231, [1935] 1 D.L.R. 695 (S.C.C.).

months, the wife "put him out" of the flat they occupied with her mother and sister.

Medical evidence indicated that the wife was still a virgin as her hymen was unbroken. With respect to the husband, medical evidence indicated that he had rarely had an emission of sperm since he was 17 years old, which was not a normal condition. However, there was no sign that he was not capable of having intercourse.

The wife brought an action for annulment based upon the husband's impotence. At trial, her action was dismissed. The wife appealed.

Held: Her appeal was dismissed. The absence of sperm in the husband's discharge was insufficient ground to annul the marriage; otherwise, it would follow that every marriage without issue (biological children) could be dissolved. The mere incapability of conception was not a sufficient ground upon which to found a claim of impotence to annul a marriage.

Secondly, the evidence of the husband's impotence was far too flimsy. Even assuming that actual consummation had not taken place, it was too early to know whether the condition was permanent. Patience and mutual courtesy often overcome obstacles. The husband had not been shown to be incurably impotent. The wife had so conducted herself that that he was frigid toward her. Time alone could tell whether the condition was permanent and two months was too short a time span.

Marriages of Convenience (Ulterior Motive)

The parties' motive for getting married is not relevant as long as the parties knew what they were doing at the time of the marriage.[46] If they understood the nature and consequences of the marriage, then the marriage is not void or voidable. Marrying for immigration purposes so that one party can come to or stay in Canada is not a ground for annulment.[47] Contrary to popular belief, the ulterior motive, or limited purpose for the marriage does not, alone, affect its validity. In such a situation, the parties would be obliged to obtain a divorce in order to end their marriage and would have to comply with the grounds set out in the *Divorce Act*.

Application Questions

1. Zoe arrived in Canada from Greece and had no understanding of the English language. Shortly after her arrival, she went through a

---

[46] *Baxter v. Baxter*, [1948] A.C. 274 (U.K. H.L.); *Fernandez (Alarcio) v. Fernandez*, [1983] 4 W.W.R. 755, 34 R.F.L. (2d) 249 (Man. Q.B.).

[47] *Iantsis (Papatheodorou) v. Papatheodorou* (1970), [1971] 1 O.R. 245, 3 R.F.L. 158 (Ont. C.A.).

civil marriage ceremony in Ontario, believing it to be a "permission to marry" ceremony as was customary in her country. The marriage was never consummated. Zoe now seeks a declaration of nullity.

— void abinitio because of the language barrier

Does Zoe have any ground for annulment in Ontario? Explain.

— yes.

2. Samantha alleged that her mother had pressured her into marrying her husband when she was 17 in order to facilitate her husband's immigration status. Samantha's mother gave her consent to the marriage because she and her stepfather were paid $10,000 to arrange the marriage. Samantha never lived with her husband and never had sexual intercourse with him.

   (a) Does the fact that Samantha married solely for immigration purposes affect the validity of her marriage?

   — no.

   (b) Does the fact that parental consent may have been given for improper purposes affect the validity of the marriage?

   (c) Are there any other grounds upon which Samantha could apply for a declaration of nullity? Explain.

3. Kim married at age 18 and realized one hour after her marriage to Ryan that she had made a mistake and that she didn't love him, although she liked her husband as a friend. On her wedding night, Kim phoned her parents from the motel and her father convinced the couple to come back and stay with them. They lived with Kim's parents for several weeks but never slept together or had sexual intercourse. During this time, Kim slept with her mother. Finally Ryan left the home and has not seen Kim since. A gynaecologist who examined Kim said she was a virgin, but that she was capable of having intercourse. Kim said she would like to have intercourse some day with a man that she loved.

— shes 18

— no anullment scenarios exist here.

Ryan applied for a declaration of nullity on the basis of Kim's reluctance and refusal to consummate the marriage.

What are Ryan's chances of success? Explain. *— none.*

4. Shema alleged that she had agreed to get married, at age 23, under pressure from her family and other members of the Moslem community. No cohabitation ever took place and the marriage was never consummated. There was no evidence as to whether her husband was able to consummate the marriage.

What, if any, grounds, would Shema have for a declaration of nullity? Would the grounds, if any, make the marriage void *ab initio* or voidable?

✻ her age will work against her. Issue of consent is void ab initio.

5. When Brad and Rose married, mainly for companionship, Brad was 67 and Rose was 64 years of age. Both of them had been married before and had grown children. After the marriage, Brad was unable

*they have children no.
so at one point
they were able to
consumate.
must get a divorce.*

*marriages for inproper no.
purposes are not
voidable. must
get a divorce.*

to achieve an erection and the couple never engaged in sexual intercourse with each other. After a quarrel, Brad and Rose separated.

Rose now wants an annulment of the marriage? Will she be successful? Explain.

6. Boris and Sylvia were university students who met at their summer job. Boris suggested to Sylvia that they get married while in school because married students received much larger student loans than single students. Sylvia took Boris up on his offer and the two got married. Before the marriage, the two had a brief one-night fling, but they never lived together or had sexual intercourse after the marriage.

Sylvia now wants an annulment of her marriage to Boris. Will she be successful?

PROCEDURE TO OBTAIN ANNULMENT

An application for a judgment of annulment in Ontario must be brought in the Superior Court of Justice by application under the *Family Law Rules*.[48] The claim to be made is for a declaration of nullity. Such a claim is usually combined with a claim for support and property division under the *Family Law Act*[49] and, where necessary, a claim for custody under the *Children's Law Reform Act*.[50]

Support and Property Division on Annulment

Parties to a void or voidable marriage are covered by the property and support provisions of the *Family Law Act*, provided they have gone through a form of marriage and the person who is asserting the property or support rights entered the marriage in good faith.[51]

Custody of Children on Annulment

Parties to a void or voidable marriage can claim custody of, and access to, their children under the provisions of the Children's Law Reform Act. Under the Act, children of an invalid marriage have the same rights and their parents have the same responsibilities as children and parents from a valid marriage.[52]

[48] O. Reg. 114/99, as amended, Rules 1(2)(d), 8.
[49] R.S.O. 1990, c. F-3, as amended.
[50] R.S.O. 1990, c. C-12, as amended.
[51] *Family Law Act*, s. 1(1).
[52] *Children's Law Reform Act*, s. 1(1).

APPENDIX 2A

ONTARIO

(SEAL)

at

Superior Court of Justice Family Court Branch
(Name of court)
33 King Street West, First Floor, Oshawa, Ontario L1H 1A1
Court office address

Court File Number

Family Law Rules, O. Reg. 114/99
Form 8: Application (General)

Applicant(s)

Full legal name & address for service – street & number, municipality, postal code, telephone & fax numbers and e-mail address (if any).	*Lawyer's name & address – street & number, municipality, postal code, telephone & fax numbers and e-mail address (if any).*
Sheila Fenmore **70 Simcoe Street N., Apt. 710** **Oshawa, Ontario,** **L6P 1N0**	**Howard Feldstein** **Barrister & Solicitor** **4296 Yonge St. Suite 426** **North York, Ontario** **M6N 2E2** **Tel: 416 225-8679** **Fax: 416 225-8680**

Respondent(s)

Full legal name & address for service – street & number, municipality, postal code, telephone & fax numbers and e-mail address (if any).	*Lawyer's name & address – street & number, municipality, postal code, telephone & fax numbers and e-mail address (if any).*
Gerald Heinz **123 Limpey Lane,** **Markham, Ontario** **S7T 2E5**	

TO THE RESPONDENT(S):

A COURT CASE HAS BEEN STARTED AGAINST YOU IN THIS COURT. THE DETAILS ARE SET OUT ON THE ATTACHED PAGES.

☐ **THE FIRST COURT DATE IS** *(date)* _____ **AT** _____ ☐ a.m. ☐ p.m. or as soon as possible
after that time, at: *(address)*

NOTE: If this is a divorce case, no date will be set unless an Answer is filed. If you have also been served with a notice of motion, there may be an earlier court date and you or your lawyer should come to court for the motion.

☒ **THIS CASE IS ON THE FAST TRACK OF THE CASE MANAGEMENT SYSTEM.** A case management judge will be assigned by the time this case first comes before a judge.

☐ **THIS CASE IS ON THE STANDARD TRACK OF THE CASE MANAGEMENT SYSTEM. No court date has been set for this case** but, if you have been served with a notice of motion, it has a court date and you or your lawyer should come to court for the motion. A case management judge will not be assigned until one of the parties asks the clerk of the court to schedule a case conference or until a notice of motion under subrule 14(5) is served before a case conference has been held. If, after 200 days, the case has not been scheduled for trial, the clerk of the court will send out a warning that the case will be dismissed in 30 days unless the parties file proof that the case has been settled or one of the parties asks for a case conference or a settlement conference.

IF YOU WANT TO OPPOSE ANY CLAIM IN THIS CASE, you or your lawyer must prepare an Answer (Form 10 – a blank copy should be attached), serve a copy on the applicant(s) and file a copy in the court office with an Affidavit of Service (Form 6B). **YOU HAVE ONLY 30 DAYS AFTER THIS APPLICATION IS SERVED ON YOU (60 DAYS IF THIS APPLICATION IS SERVED ON YOU OUTSIDE CANADA OR THE UNITED STATES) TO SERVE AND FILE AN ANSWER. IF YOU DO NOT, THE CASE WILL GO AHEAD WITHOUT YOU AND THE COURT MAY MAKE AN ORDER AND ENFORCE IT AGAINST YOU.**

Form 8:   Application (General)   **(page 2)** | Court File Number |

Check the box of the paragraph that applies to your case

☐ This case includes a claim for support. It does not include a claim for property or exclusive possession of the matrimonial home and its contents. You **MUST** fill out a Financial Statement (Form 13 – a blank copy attached), serve a copy on the applicant(s) and file a copy in the court office with an Affidavit of Service even if you do not answer this case.

☐ This case includes a claim for property or exclusive possession of the matrimonial home and its contents. You **MUST** fill out a Financial Statement (Form 13.1 – a blank copy attached), serve a copy on the applicant(s) and file a copy in the court office with an Affidavit of Service even if you do not answer this case.

IF YOU WANT TO MAKE A CLAIM OF YOUR OWN, you or your lawyer must fill out the claim portion in the Answer, serve a copy on the applicant(s) and file a copy in the court office with an Affidavit of Service.

- If you want to make a claim for support but do not want to make a claim for property or exclusive possession of the matrimonial home and its contents, you **MUST** fill out a Financial Statement (Form 13), serve a copy on the applicant(s) and file a copy in the court office.

- However, if your only claim for support is for child support in the table amount specified under the Child Support Guidelines, you do not need to fill out, serve or file a Financial Statement.

- If you want to make a claim for property or exclusive possession of the matrimonial home and its contents, whether or not it includes a claim for support, you **MUST** fill out a Financial Statement (Form 13.1, not Form 13), serve a copy on the applicant(s), and file a copy in the court office.

YOU SHOULD GET LEGAL ADVICE ABOUT THIS CASE RIGHT AWAY. If you cannot afford a lawyer, you may be able to get help from your local Legal Aid Ontario office. *(See your telephone directory under LEGAL AID.)*

_____   _____
            Date of issue   *Clerk of the court*

Form 8:   Application (General)   **(page 3)**   Court file number

FAMILY HISTORY

APPLICANT: Age: **26**   Birthdate: *(d,m,y)* **February 20, 1980**

Resident in *(municipality & province)*   **Oshawa, Ontario**

since *(date)* **February 14, 2006**

Surname at birth: **Fenmore**   Surname just before marriage: **Fenmore**

Divorced before?   ☒ No   ☐ Yes *(Place and date of previous divorce)*

RESPONDENT: Age: **45**   Birthdate: *(d,m,y)* **April 23, 1960**

Resident in *(municipality & province)*   **Markham, Ontario**

since *(date)* **December 28, 2004**

Surname at birth: **Heinz**   Surname just before marriage: **Heinz**

Divorced before?   ☐ No   ☒ Yes *(Place and date of previous divorce)*

RELATIONSHIP DATES:

☒   Married on *(date)*   July 22, 2005   ☐   Started living together on *(date)*

☒   Separated on *(date)* February 14, 2006   ☐   Never lived together   ☐   Still living together

THE CHILD(REN)
List all children involved in this case, even if no claim is made for these children.

Full legal name	Age	Birthdate *(d,m,y)*	Resident in *(municipality & province)*	Now Living With *(name of person and relationship to child)*

PREVIOUS CASES OR AGREEMENTS

Have the parties or the children been in a court case before?

☒ No   ☐ Yes *(Attach a Summary of Court Cases – Form 8E.)*

Have the parties made a written agreement dealing with any matter involved in this case?

☒ No   ☐ Yes *(Give date of agreement. Indicate which of its terms are in dispute. Attach an additional page if you need more space.)*

Form 8:   Application (General)   **(page 4)**   Court file number

CLAIM BY APPLICANT

I ASK THE COURT FOR THE FOLLOWING:
(Claims below include claims for temporary orders.)

Claims under the *Divorce Act* *(Check boxes in this column only if you are asking for a divorce and your case is in the Family Court of the Superior Court of Justice.)*	**Claims under the *Family Law Act* or *Children's Law Reform Act***	**Claims relating to property** *(Check boxes in this column only if your case is in the Family Court of the Superior Court of Justice.)*
00 ☐ a divorce 01 ☐ support for me 02 ☐ support for child(ren) – table amount 03 ☐ support for child(ren) - other than table amount 04 ☐ custody of child(ren) 05 ☐ access to child(ren)	10 ☐ support for me 11 ☐ support for child(ren) – table amount 12 ☐ support for child(ren) - other than table amount 13 ☐ custody of child(ren) 14 ☐ access to child(ren) 15 ☐ restraining/non-harassment order 16 ☐ indexing spousal support 17 ☐ indexing same-sex partner support 18 ☐ declaration of parentage 19 ☐ guardianship over child's property	20 ☐ equalization of net family properties 21 ☐ exclusive possession of matrimonial home 22 ☐ exclusive possession of contents of matrimonial home 23 ☐ freezing assets 24 ☐ sale of family property
Other claims 30 ☒ costs 31 ☒ annulment of marriage 32 ☐ prejudgment interest	50 ☐ Other *(Specify.)*	

Give details of the order that you want the court to make. *(Include any amounts of support (if known) and the names of the children for whom support, custody or access is claimed.)*

1, a judgment annulling my marriage to the respondent, Gerald Heinz,

2. costs of this application

Form 8:	Application (General)	(page 5)	Court File Number

IMPORTANT FACTS SUPPORTING MY CLAIM FOR DIVORCE

☐ **Separation:** The spouses have lived separate and apart since *(date)* _____ and

   ☐ have not lived together again since that date in an unsuccessful attempt to reconcile.

   ☐ have lived together again during the following period(s) in an unsuccessful attempt to reconcile: *(Give dates.)*

☐ **Adultery:** The respondent has committed adultery. *(Give details. It is not necessary to name any other person involved but, if you do name the other person, then you must serve this application on the other person.)*

☐ **Cruelty:** The respondent has treated the applicant with physical or mental cruelty of such a kind as to make continued cohabitation intolerable. *(Give details.)*

IMPORTANT FACTS SUPPORTING MY OTHER CLAIM(S)
(Set out below the facts that form the legal basis for your other claim(s). Attach an additional page if you need more space.)

1. Since the date of our marriage on July 22, 2005, the parties have been unable to consummate the marriage or have normal sexual intercourse because the respondent is unable to have an erection.

2. From August through December 2005, the respondent tried several drugs, under the supervision of a urologist, in an attempt to alleviate the problem, but this was unsuccessful.

3. The respondent refuses to go back to a doctor or attempt to find other ways to deal with the problem.

4. As a result of this situaion, I am being treated for depression, am under a doctor's care and am living with my parents.

Put a line through any space left on this page. If additional space is needed, extra pages may be attached.

_____   _____
Date of signature   Signature of applicant

LAWYER'S CERTIFICATE

For divorce cases only

My name is: _____
and I am the applicant's lawyer in this divorce case. I certify that I have complied with the requirements of section 9 of the *Divorce Act.*

_____   _____
Date   Signature of Lawyer

APPENDIX 2B

ONTARIO

Superior Court of Justice Family Court Branch	Court File Number
(Name of court)	

at 33 King Street West, First Floor, Oshawa, Ontario, L1H 1A1

Court office address

Family Law Rules, O. Reg. 114/99

Form 14A: Affidavit (general) dated

Applicant(s)

Full legal name & address for service — street & number, municipality, postal code, telephone & fax numbers and e-mail address (if any).	Lawyer's name & address — street & number, municipality, postal code, telephone & fax numbers and e-mail address (if any).
Sheila Fenmore 70 Simcoe Street N., Apt. 710 Oshawa, Ontario, L6P 1N0	Howard Feldstein Barrister & Solicitor 4296 Yonge St., Suite 426 North York, Ontario M6N 2E2 Tel: 416 225-8679 Fax: 416 225-8680

Respondent(s)

Full legal name & address for service — street & number, municipality, postal code, telephone & fax numbers and e-mail address (if any).	Lawyer's name & address — street & number, municipality, postal code, telephone & fax numbers and e-mail address (if any).
Gerald Heinz 123 Limpey Lane Markham, Ontario S7T 2E5	

My name is *(full legal name)* Sheila Fenmore

I live in *(municipality & province)* Oshawa, Ontario

and I swear that the following is true:

Set out the statements of fact in consecutively numbered paragraphs. Where possible, each numbered paragraph should consist of one complete sentence and be limited to a particular statement of fact. If you learned a fact from someone else, you must give that person's name and state that you believe that fact to be true.

1. The respondent, Gerald Heinz, and I were married on July 22, 2005 at Wellington United Church in Oshawa, Ontario.

2. Since the date of our marriage, the respondent and I have been unable to consummate our marriage or have normal sexual relations because the respondent is unable to have an erection.

3. From August through December 2005, the respondent has tried several prescription drugs, under the supervision of a urologist, Dr. Sydney Weiser, in an attempt to remedy his problem. The drugs were not helpful in alleviating the problem of the respondent.

4. The respondent now refuses to see a doctor to attempt to find other ways to deal with his problem.

5. As a result of this situation, I am presestly being treated for severe depression, am under the care of my physician, Dr. Maria Medicini, and am living with my parents, who are caring for me.

6. I no longer wish to live with or be married to the respondent.

7. I want to obtain annulment of my marriage to the respondent.

Form 14A: **Affidavit (general) dated**   **(page 2)** | Court File Number |

Put a line through any blank space left on this page.

Sworn before me at   **CITY of OSHAWA**
                                          municipality

in   **the PROVINCE of ONTARIO**
                              province, state, or country

on **March 3, 2006**
          date   *Commissioner for taking affidavits*
                              (Type or print name below if signature is illegible.)

                                          _____
                                                  Signature
                              *(This form is to be signed in front of a
                              lawyer, justice of the peace, notary public
                              or commissioner for taking affidavits.)*

CHAPTER 3

THE *DIVORCE ACT*: JURISDICTION AND OBTAINING A DIVORCE

JURISDICTION OVER DIVORCE

Divorce in Ontario is governed by the *Divorce Act*.[1] The *Divorce Act* is federal legislation, which means that the substantive law of divorce is the same across Canada, even though the forms used and the procedure for obtaining a divorce will vary from province to province.

The *Divorce Act* defines "court" in respect of Ontario as the Superior Court of Justice.[2] In jurisdictions where a Family Court has been created, then the Family Court, being a branch of the Superior Court of Justice,[3] would have the ability to grant divorces and corollary relief under the *Divorce Act*. In jurisdictions where no Family Court has been created, then it is only the Superior Court of Justice, and not the Ontario Court of Justice, that can deal with matters under the *Divorce Act*.

"Spouse" was defined as either of a man or woman who are married to each other. On November 19, 2004, the Ontario Superior Court of Justice struck down the definition of "spouse" in the *Divorce Act* as being discriminatory, and redefined "spouse" to mean "either of two persons who are married to each other."[4] As a result of this case, same-sex couples could also be divorced under the *Divorce Act*. The definition in the Act has now been amended by the *Civil Marriage Act* to "either of two persons who are married to each other."[5]

Where to Proceed

In our highly mobile society, it is not unusual for a couple to be married in one place, to live for all or part of their marriage in another place, and

---

[1] R.S.C. 1985, c. 3 (2nd Supp.), as amended.

[2] *Ibid.*, s. 2(1).

[3] *Courts of Justice Act*, R.S.O. 1990, c. C.43, s. 21.1.

[4] *M. (M.) v. H. (J.)* (2004), [2004] O.J. No. 5314, 73 O.R. (3d) 337, 247 D.L.R. (4th) 361, 2004 CarswellOnt 5548 (Ont. S.C.J.).

[5] *Civil Marriage Act*, S.C. 2005, c. 33, s.8(1).

for one or both of them to move to different places after separation. The question then becomes, in which province can the parties get a divorce? Many mistakenly believe that the parties can always be divorced in the province in which they where married, but this is not necessarily so. By section 3 of the *Divorce Act*, a proceeding for a divorce can be commenced in any province where either spouse has been ordinarily residing for at least one year. If a province has jurisdiction, either spouse can commence proceedings in that province. The ability to commence proceedings is not restricted to the spouse who resides there. If both the spouses have changed provinces in the last 12 months, neither of them will be able to commence divorce proceedings. On the other hand, it may be possible that two provinces have jurisdiction. If this is the case, it is conceivable that the spouses may commence proceedings in different provinces. If this happens, then the divorce will proceed in the province where the divorce was commenced first.[6] If, however, proceedings are commenced in different provinces on the same day, then the Federal Court – Trial Division has jurisdiction.

The rules are slightly different if instead of a divorce proceeding, the parties wish to commence corollary relief proceedings (for support or custody under the *Divorce Act*) or variation proceedings (to change the support or custody provisions in an existing divorce judgment). In these cases, it is not necessary that a spouse reside in a jurisdiction for any particular length of time, because a province will have jurisdiction as long as one of the spouses is residing there at the time proceedings are commenced.[7] In fact, it is not even necessary that either of the spouses reside in the province, if the spouses accept that the matter proceeds in that province. Again, if the spouses commence proceedings in different provinces, then the matter will proceed in the province where proceedings were commenced first, and, if they were commenced on the same day, then the Federal Court – Trial Division would hear and determine the proceedings.

However, if custody is in issue in any of these proceedings, the court may transfer the proceedings to the province that has the most substantial connection with the child or children.[8] In determining whether a child is most substantially connected to another province, the court will consider a number of factors, including the child's present physical location, the length of the child's residence in each province, the bonds the child has with people in each province, and the extent of the child's involvement in education and other activities in the province of current residence. The application to transfer the proceeding must be brought before the court that has initial jurisdiction and not before the court in the province to

---

[6] *Divorce Act*, s. 3(2).
[7] *Divorce Act*, s. 4(1), 5(1).
[8] *Divorce Act*, s. 6.

which the proceeding might be transferred. The general practice has been to transfer the entire proceeding to the other province, whether it is a divorce proceeding, a corollary relief proceeding, or a variation proceeding.[9]

Application Questions

1. Joe and Mary were married in Quebec ten years ago. They moved to Ontario five years ago, and separated year years ago. Joe has been living in British Columbia for the last 18 months, and Mary moved to Nova Scotia, where she now resides, one month ago.

   (a) Where can Joe commence divorce proceedings?
   (b) Where can Mary commence divorce proceedings?
   (c) Where can Joe commence corollary relief proceedings?
   (d) Where can Mary commence variation proceedings?

2. John and Amy obtained a divorce in British Columbia, but did not obtain an order for custody at that time because they had a shared custody arrangement that was working well for everybody concerned. Amy subsequently moved to Ontario with the children to accept a teaching position at York University. She wished to apply for custody of the children immediately after she arrived in Toronto.

   (a) Can Amy still apply for a custody order under the *Divorce Act*? If so, what kind of proceeding must she begin?
   (b) In which province should Amy begin her proceeding? (Which province has jurisdiction to hear the case?)

3. Ryan and Kerry obtained a divorce in Newfoundland at which time custody of two young children was awarded to Kerry. Ryan then moved to Oshawa, Ontario to accept a position with General Motors. After Ryan had lived in Ontario for three years, his teenaged son decided he wanted to move to Ontario to live with his dad. Ryan therefore wanted to vary the original custody order so that his son could live with him in Oshawa. The son had visited Ryan on several occasions in Ontario and had made some friends there over the past three years.

   (a) In which province can Ryan bring his application to vary the original custody order? Why?
   (b) If the variation proceeding were commenced in Ontario, would the Ontario court have the power to transfer the proceeding to Newfoundland? Why or why not?

---

[9] *Ruyter v. Samson* (1992), 44 R.F.L. (3d) 35 (Ont. Gen. Div.); see also *Willenbrecht v. Willenbrecht* (1999), 47 R.F.L. (4th) 200 (Ont. C.A. [In Chambers]).

GROUND FOR DIVORCE

The *Divorce Act* recognizes only one ground for divorce, which is that there has been a breakdown of the marriage.[10] There are, however, three ways of establishing a breakdown of the marriage, which are:

(a) separation for at least one year;

(b) adultery; and

(c) cruelty.

Separation

In order to proceed on the basis of separation, the parties must actually be living separate and apart at the time the proceedings are commenced. They can begin proceedings any time after separation, but the divorce cannot be granted until they have been separated for at least one year.[11] Parties often mistakenly believe that there is some process for getting a "legal separation", whereas in fact the parties are considered separated when they are living separate and apart and at least one of them has the intention to be separated. Although parties may be living in separate accommodations for a variety of reasons, they are not separated within the meaning of the *Divorce Act* unless at least one of them intends to end the marriage. Once one party leaves with the intention of ending the marriage, if that party becomes incapable of forming or having the intention to live separate and apart, the court can still find that the period of separation has not been interrupted, if it appears to the court that the separation probably would have continued.[12]

Although the *Divorce Act* requires that the parties be living separate and apart, the cases have made it clear that it is possible to be separated even if the parties are living under the same roof.

Cooper v. Cooper (1972), [1972] O.J. No. 975, 10 R.F.L. 184, 1972 CarswellOnt 98 (Ont. H.C.), Holland J.

. . .For the last year or two there has been practically no communication between the parties whatsoever. They have not cohabited as man and wife since 1967 and have not shared the same bedroom since that year. Over the last few months the wife alleges that the husband has only spent three or four nights at home in a month. The wife testified that she moved out of the bedroom that she originally shared with her husband because he was

---

[10] *Divorce Act*, s. 8(1).

[11] *Divorce Act*, s. 8(2)(a).

[12] *Divorce Act*, s. 8(3)(b)(i).

not coming home at night and she found it degrading. The wife admitted quite frankly that she had not done any "chores" for her husband for the last two years.. . . [At para. 3.]

Can it be said that the parties in this case are living separate and apart? Certainly spouses living under the same roof may well in fact be living separate and apart from each other. The problem has often been considered in actions brought under s. 4(1)(e)(i) of the Divorce Act and, generally speaking, a finding that the parties were living separate and apart from each other has been made where the following circumstances were present:

(i) Spouses occupying separate bedrooms.
(ii) Absence of sexual relations.
(iii) Little, if any, communication between spouses.
(iv) Wife performing no domestic services for husband.
(v) Eating meals separately.
(vi) No social activities together. [At paras. 9, 10.]

In the present case all of the above six circumstances exist and it could well be said that the parties are living separate and apart from each other and have been living separate and apart from each other for the last two years. [At para. 17.]

During the period of separation, it is possible for the parties to make attempts at reconciliation, without losing their grounds for divorce. Section 8(3)(b)(ii) of the *Divorce Act* stipulates that the parties can resume cohabitation for one or more periods to try to reconcile without having to start "counting" all over again, as long as the total of all the periods for which the parties have resumed cohabitation in the year does not add up to more than 90 days. In other words, during the one-year period of separation, the parties can actually live together on and off for up to 90 days, in attempting to reconcile, and the time they live together still counts as part of the period of separation. The purpose of this section is to encourage reconciliation by removing the risk of losing the grounds for divorce.

Adultery

If one of the spouses can prove adultery, there is no need to wait for one year; the divorce can be granted immediately. In order to be able to rely on adultery, a spouse must show that the other spouse has committed adultery since the celebration of the marriage.[13] The case law has defined adultery as consensual sexual intercourse between a married person and a person of the opposite sex who is not his or her spouse. Now that marriage between same-sex couples has been legalized, at least one court has rejected the common-law definition of spouse and has redefined it as

---

[13] *Divorce Act*, s. 8(2)(b)(i).

"intimate sexual activity outside of marriage." It is highly likely that other courts will also change their definition of adultery as well.

P. (S.E.) v. P. (D.D.), [2005] B.C.J. No. 1971, 2005 BCSC 1290, 2005 CarswellBC 2137 (B.C. S.C.)

The petitioner (Ms. P) applied for a divorce from her husband (Mr. P) on the grounds of his admitted "adultery" with another man.

Held:

Judges can and should adapt the common law to reflect the changing social, moral and economic fabric of the country. Judges should not be quick to perpetuate rules whose social foundation has long since disappeared. Nonetheless, there are significant constraints on the power of the judiciary to change the law. [At para. 39.]

The traditional definition of adultery included the requirement that the sexual activity be intercourse. Because sexual relations might involve no penetration at all, this requirement could serve to deny a divorce to a man or a woman whose partner is having a sexual affair with a person of the same sex. However, the uncertainty about precisely what would constitute adultery in a same-sex relationship is not a reasonable basis for denying spouses the ability to divorce on the basis of same-sex sexual activity.

In the modern understanding of marriage, the wrong for which the petitioner seeks redress is something akin to violation of the marital bond. Viewed from this perspective, the heterosexual nature of the sexual acts is not determinative. Intimate sexual activity outside of marriage may represent a violation of the marital bond and be devastating to the spouse and the marital bond regardless of the specific nature of the sexual act performed.

In this case, the evidence of an intimate sexual relationship outside of Mr. and Ms. P's marriage is sufficient to grant the divorce on the grounds of adultery, notwithstanding that the act alleged was a same-sex sexual act. Adultery may include same-sex sexual acts where as here the evidence supports a finding that such has occurred.

In this case I do not consider it is necessary or desirable for me to define what type of intimate sexual activity constitutes adultery. Questions about the meaning of adultery in same-sex marriages should be clarified over time on a case-by-case basis, just as those questions have been resolved on a case-by-case basis in the context of heterosexual marriages. [At paras. 47-50.]

The spouse who commences the divorce proceedings cannot rely on his or her own adultery, but only on the other spouse's. Also, the adultery has to have taken place since the celebration of the marriage. In other words, a spouse who finds out after marriage that his or her spouse had cheated before marriage would not be able to obtain a divorce on that basis.

In order to be able to prove adultery, circumstantial evidence is often relied on. To succeed, the applicant would have to show that the respondent had both the opportunity and the inclination to commit adultery.[14] Under Ontario's *Evidence Act*,[15] no witness in a proceeding instituted in consequence of adultery can be asked any question tending to show that he or she is guilty of adultery, and is not required to answer such questions. However, even though a person cannot be forced to testify that he or she has committed adultery, a person may give this evidence voluntarily, if he or she chooses.

Cruelty

A spouse can also obtain a divorce based on cruelty. Again, if cruelty can be proven, it would not be necessary to be separated for a year and the divorce could be granted immediately. In order to establish a breakdown of the marriage based on cruelty, a spouse would have to show that the other spouse treated him or her with such cruelty as to render continued cohabitation impossible.[16] The cruelty can be either physical or mental.

Knoll v. Knoll, [1970] 2 O.R. 169 (Ont. C.A.)

Over the years the courts have steadfastly refrained from attempting to formulate a general definition of cruelty. As used in ordinary parlance "cruelty" signifies a disposition to inflict suffering; to delight in or exhibit indifference to the pain or misery of others; mercilessness or hard-heartedness as exhibited in action. If in the marriage relationship one spouse by his conduct causes wanton, malicious or unnecessary infliction of pain or suffering upon the body, the feelings or emotions of the other, his conduct may well constitute cruelty which will entitle a petitioner to dissolution of the marriage if, in the court's opinion, it amounts to physical or mental cruelty "of such a kind as to render intolerable the continued cohabitation of the spouses". [At para. 29]

Care must be exercised in applying the standard set forth in s. 3(*d*) that conduct relied upon to establish cruelty is not a trivial act, but one of a "grave and weighty" nature, and not merely conduct which can be characterized as little more than a manifestation of incompatability of temperament between the spouses. The whole matrimonial relations must be considered, especially if the cruelty consists of reproaches, complaints, accusations, or constant carping criticisms. A question most relevant for consideration is the effect of the conduct complained of upon the mind of the affected spouse. The determination of what constitutes cruelty in a given case must, in the final analysis, depend upon the circumstances of the particular case, having

---

[14] *Bruce v. Bruce*, [1947] O.R. 688 (Ont. C.A.).
[15] R.S.O. 1990, c. E.23, as amended, s. 10.
[16] *Divorce Act*, s. 8(2)(b)(ii).

due regard to the physical and mental condition of the parties, their character and their attitudes towards the marriage relationship. [At para. 30.]

DUTY OF LEGAL ADVISOR

The *Divorce Act* requires that every legal advisor who acts for a spouse in a divorce proceeding to discuss certain matters with his or her client. Firstly, the legal advisor must point out the provisions in the *Divorce Act* that allow the parties to attempt reconciliation. Secondly, the legal advisor must discuss the possibility of reconciliation and let the spouse know what is available in the community in terms of marriage counselling or guidance. However, the *Divorce Act* makes an exception where the circumstances of the case make discussions about reconciliation or marriage counselling inappropriate.[17]

If support or custody is in issue, the legal advisor must also talk to the client about the advisability of negotiating these issues and the mediation facilities that are available to assist the parties to reach an agreement.[18]

If the legal advisor is acting for the applicant, then he or she must certify that he or she has complied with these sections in the application.[19]

DUTY OF THE COURT

Reconciliation

Under section 10 of the *Divorce Act*, before beginning a hearing, the judge in a divorce case must satisfy himself or herself that there is no possibility of reconciliation, unless the circumstances of the case make inquiries into reconciliation inappropriate. If either spouse indicated that there is a possibility of reconciliation at any stage, the judge must adjourn the hearing and refer the spouses to marriage counselling.[20] Either party can apply to resume the hearing after 14 days. Any person who acts as a marriage counsellor in these circumstances cannot be called as a witness for either party and nothing that is said in the course of the marriage counselling can be used as evidence by either party.[21]

---

[17] *Divorce Act*, s. 9(1).
[18] *Divorce Act*, s. 9(2).
[19] *Divorce Act*, s. 9(3).
[20] *Divorce Act*, s. 10 (1), (2).
[21] *Divorce Act*, s. 10 (3), (4).

Bars

The court cannot grant a divorce unless that judge first satisfies himself or herself about several matters.

Collusion

Firstly, the court must assure itself that there has been no collusion with respect to the divorce.[22] "Collusion" is defined as "an agreement, or conspiracy. . .[for] subverting the administration of justice, and includes any agreement, understanding or arrangement to fabricate or suppress evidence or to deceive the court. . .."[23] In other words, the court must be assured that the evidence regarding the grounds for divorce is genuine, and the court is not being mislead.

Reasonable Arrangements for Child Support

Secondly, the court must satisfy itself that reasonable arrangements have been made regarding child support.[24] Support must be reasonable having regard to the *Guidelines*, and if the court is not satisfied, it cannot grant the divorce. Custody arrangements are not mentioned.

Condonation and Connivance

Thirdly, the court must also be sure that if the divorce is being sought on the basis of adultery or cruelty, the spouse bringing the proceeding has not condoned the behaviour complained about, nor has connived at such behaviour.[25] A spouse condones an offence by forgiving the offending spouse. Once behaviour has been condoned or forgiven, it cannot be used any more to prove a breakdown of the marriage.[26] However, because of subsection 11(3), parties may resume cohabitation to attempt reconciliation for a period or periods not totalling more than 90 days without losing their grounds. Connivance means plotting or cooperating with a spouse to come up with a basis for divorce. Nevertheless, if the court is of the opinion that it is in the public interest to grant a divorce, the court may still do so despite finding condonation or connivance.

---

[22] *Divorce Act*, s. 11(1)(a).
[23] *Divorce Act*, s. 11(4).
[24] *Divorce Act*, s. 11(1)(b).
[25] *Divorce Act*, s. 11(1)(c).
[26] *Divorce Act*, s. 11(2).

Application Questions

1. Jamal wishes to divorce his wife, Talesia, based on adultery. When asked for the details, he states, "Oh, I have cheated on my wife many times since we were married." Will Jamal be successful?

2. Ron finds out that his wife, Jill, had sexual intercourse with his best friend the night of the rehearsal party for the wedding. Can Ron obtain a divorce on the basis of adultery?

3. Alicia and Peter separated on January 31. They cohabited for the purpose of reconciliation from March 1 to April 30 (61 days), then again from July 1 to July 31 (31 days), then again from September 1 to September 15 (15 days). What is the earliest date that Alicia and Peter can be divorced based on separation? April 30th 2015.

4. Robert has accepted a six-month contract in China. He phones his wife frequently, telling her that he misses her and cannot wait to come home again. Robert's wife says she is waiting impatiently for him to return. Are Robert and his wife separated within the meaning of the *Divorce Act*?

5. Yolanda moves out of the matrimonial home, telling her husband, Charles, that she cannot stand to be married to him any longer. One week later, Yolanda comes back to get some of her clothes and things. Yolanda and Charles have a terrible fight, during which Charles begs Yolanda to come back home. Yolanda runs out of the house and into the street, where she is hit by a car. Yolanda is now in a deep coma. Charles is constantly by her bedside. Are Yolanda and Charles separated within the meaning of the *Divorce Act*?

6. At the start of the divorce trial, the judge asks Victoria and Joe if there is any chance of reconciliation. Joe answers quickly, "None whatsoever," but Victoria starts to cry, claiming she still loves Joe. What should the judge do?

7. Brenda moves out and commences divorce proceedings against her husband, Rick, based on cruelty. Two weeks later Rick persuades Brenda to "give him another chance" and move back in with him. She stays with him for one month, and then decides to move out again and proceed with the divorce. No new instances of cruelty have occurred. Can Brenda obtain a divorce based on Rick's behaviour before she moved back in with him?

Handwritten margin notes:

no. S8(2)bi

no. happened before

can start counting by April 30th. cant count the 61 day period.

no. physically seperated s. 8(3)

yes. bc she had the intention.

Judge must pursue possibility of reconciliation but only under consent of the spouses. sec. 10 no adjournmunt no reconciliation.

can still pursue seperation bc it hasnt been 90 days. Sect. 11

domestic violence expert should be called in to prove that abused ppl go back even after abuse.

CERTIFICATE OF DIVORCE

At trial or on a motion (in the case of an uncontested divorce), the court will grant a Divorce Order. However, usually the divorce is not effective immediately. Section 12 states that a divorce generally takes effect on the 31st day after it is granted. This gives the other party 30 days in which to appeal the granting of the divorce.[27] If, in fact, an appeal is launched within 30 days, then the divorce does not take effect until the appeals have been completed or abandoned.[28]

It is possible for the court to order that the divorce be effective sooner than the 31st day.[29] For the court to make such an order, special circumstances must exist and both spouses must state in writing that they will not appeal the judgment or that they will abandon any appeal that has been commenced.

When the divorce is effective, either party can apply to the court for a Certificate of Divorce.[30] The Certificate of Divorce is conclusive proof that the marriage has been dissolved and has legal effect throughout Canada.[31]

Corollary Relief

The *Divorce Act* also has provisions for child support orders, spousal support orders, custody orders, and variation orders. These will be discussed in other chapters.

Recognizing Foreign Divorces

If parties are divorced in another country, that divorce may be legal and valid in Canada, and it will not be necessary for the parties to obtain a Canadian divorce. However, not all foreign divorces are recognized in Canada. A divorce will be valid in Canada if one of the spouses was ordinarily resident in the place that granted the divorce for at least one year before having commenced the divorce proceeding.[32] The *Divorce Act* also preserves the common-law rules for recognizing foreign divorces,[33] which is that a foreign divorce will be recognized where there exists some real and substantial connection between the petitioner or the respondent

---

[27] *Divorce Act*, s. 21(2).
[28] *Divorce Act*, s. 12(3)-(6).
[29] *Divorce Act*, s. 12(2).
[30] *Divorce Act*, s. 12(7).
[31] *Divorce Act*, s. 12(8), 13, 14.
[32] *Divorce Act*, s. 22(1).
[33] *Divorce Act*, s. 22(3).

and the granting jurisdiction.[34] Therefore, if a party goes to a jurisdiction for the purpose of obtaining a "quickie" divorce, most likely that divorce will not be recognized in Canada.

DIVORCE PROCEDURE

Divorce procedure in Ontario is governed by the *Family Law Rules*.[35] Rules 5 requires that proceedings be commenced where either party resides, or where the child resides if custody and/or access are in issue. The parties may also agree to a different municipality, but require the court's permission.

A spouse begins a divorce proceeding by filing an application.[36] If the spouse seeks only a divorce, Form 8A is used. If the applicant is seeking other relief as well, then Form 8 is used. The parties are the applicant and the respondent.[37] The parties can also file a joint application, in which neither is named as a respondent. If the divorce is based on adultery, it is not necessary to name the person with whom the spouse is alleged to have committed the adultery, but if that person is named, then he or she must be served with the application and can participate as a respondent.[38] At the time of filing the application, a Central Divorce Registry Form must also be filed. The applicant must serve the respondent(s) immediately by special service.[39]

Defended Divorce

As well as asking for a divorce, the applicant can also include other claims in the application, such as claims for custody, support, or equalization of net family properties.[40] If the application includes a claim for support, property, or exclusive possession, then the applicant must serve and file a financial statement with the application.[41]

The respondent then has 30 days to serve and file an answer, unless the respondent has been served outside of Canada or the U.S.A., in which case he or she has 60 days.[42] The respondent must also serve and file a

---

[34] See *Bate v. Bate* (1978), [1978] O.J. No. 113, 1 R.F.L. (2d) 298, 1978 CarswellOnt 218 (Ont. H.C.).

[35] O. Reg. 114/99, as amended.

[36] Rule 36(1).

[37] Rule 7(3).

[38] Rule 36(3).

[39] Rule 8(5).

[40] Rule 8(3)(b).

[41] Rule 13(1).

[42] Rule 10(1), (2).

financial statement if support, custody, or exclusive possession are in issue.[43] Defended divorce cases are described in more detail in Chapter 12.

Uncontested Divorces

If the respondent does not file an answer, or withdraws it, the applicant can proceed to obtain an uncontested divorce. The steps to obtain an uncontested divorce are as follows:

1. The applicant must file a copy of the marriage certificate or the marriage registration certificate. If the applicant does not have the original marriage certificate, a marriage registration certificate can be obtained from the Office of the Registrar General, if the parties were married in Ontario. Application forms are available online. If the parties were not married in Ontario, then a marriage certificate must be obtained from the government of the place where the parties were married. If it is impractical to obtain a marriage certificate, then the application must state why it is impractical. It is wise to obtain a copy of the marriage certificate prior to filing the application to ensure that the names of the parties on the application are the same as they appear in the marriage certificate.[44]

2. The applicant must file an affidavit (Form 36).[45] If the applicant wishes the divorce to take effect sooner than 31 days after the divorce order is granted, the applicant must set out what the special circumstances are, and must attach undertakings from both parties not to appeal the divorce order. If the divorce is being sought on the basis of adultery, unless there is sufficient evidence of the adultery, the respondent should also file an affidavit. The respondent should state that he or she is aware that he or she is not obliged to give evidence of the adultery.

3. Upon filing the affidavit(s), applicant must also file three copies of the draft divorce order (Form 25A) and a stamped envelope addressed to each party. If the divorce order contains a support order, then the applicant must also file an extra copy of the draft divorce order (for the Director of the Family Responsibility Office) and two copies of a draft support deduction order.[46]

4. When the documents are filed, the court clerk reviews the documents, fills out a form, and then presents them to a judge.[47] If the judge is satisfied with the materials, he or she will grant the divorce and the

---

[43] Rule 13(1)(b).
[44] Rule 36(4).
[45] Rule 36(5).
[46] Rule 36(6).
[47] Rule 36(7).

Divorce Order will be sent to the parties in the envelopes provided. The Divorce Order will show when the divorce takes effect.

5. After the divorce has taken effect, either party may request a Divorce Certificate (Form 36B).

APPENDIX 3A

ONTARIO

(SEAL)	

SUPERIOR COURT OF JUSTICE
_____
(Name of court)

at __393 University Ave., Toronto, Ontario, M5G 2M2__
Court office address

Court File Number

Family Law Rules, O. Reg. 114/99
Form 8A: Application
(divorce)

☒ **Simple**
☐ **Joint**

Applicant(s)

Full legal name & address for service – street & number, municipality, postal code, telephone & fax numbers and e-mail address (if any).	Lawyer's name & address – street & number, municipality, postal code, telephone & fax numbers and e-mail address (if any).
Mallory Jane Lutzen **261 Catalina Dr.** **Toronto, Ontario,** **M2N 1H7**	**Cloe Christopholous** **Barrister & Solicitor** **269 Neilson Rd.** **Toronto, Ontario** **M2N 2N4** **Tel: 416 284-9876** **Fax: 416 284-9877**

Respondent(s)

Full legal name & address for service – street & number, municipality, postal code, telephone & fax numbers and e-mail address (if any).	Lawyer's name & address – street & number, municipality, postal code, telephone & fax numbers and e-mail address (if any).
Gordon Bjorn Lutzen **789 Grassy Knoll Place,** **Newmarket, Ontario** **L0G 0B0**	

☒ **IN THIS CASE, THE APPLICANT IS CLAIMING DIVORCE ONLY.**

TO THE RESPONDENT(S): A COURT CASE FOR DIVORCE HAS BEEN STARTED AGAINST YOU IN THIS COURT. THE DETAILS ARE SET OUT ON THE ATTACHED PAGES.

THIS CASE IS ON THE STANDARD TRACK OF THE CASE MANAGEMENT SYSTEM. No court date has been set for this case but, if you have been served with a notice of motion, it has a court date and you or your lawyer should come to court for the motion. A case management judge will not be assigned until one of the parties asks the clerk of the court to schedule a case conference or until a notice of motion under subrule 14(5) is served before a case conference has been held. If, after 200 days, the case has not been scheduled for trial, the clerk of the court will send out a warning that the case will be dismissed in 30 days unless the parties file proof that the case has been settled or one of the parties asks for a case conference or settlement conference.

IF YOU WANT TO OPPOSE ANY CLAIM IN THIS CASE, you or your lawyer must prepare an Answer (Form 10 – a blank copy should be attached), serve a copy on the applicant and file a copy in the court office with an Affidavit of Service (Form 6B). **YOU HAVE ONLY 30 DAYS AFTER THIS APPLICATION IS SERVED ON YOU (60 DAYS IF THIS APPLICATION IS SERVED ON YOU OUTSIDE CANADA OR THE UNITED STATES) TO SERVE AND FILE AN ANSWER. IF YOU DO NOT, THE CASE WILL GO AHEAD WITHOUT YOU AND THE COURT MAY MAKE AN ORDER AND ENFORCE IT AGAINST YOU.**

IF YOU WANT TO MAKE A CLAIM OF YOUR OWN, you or your lawyer must fill out the claim portion in the Answer, serve a copy on the applicant(s) and file a copy in the court office with an Affidavit of Service.

- If you want to make a claim for support but do not want to make a claim for property or exclusive possession of the matrimonial home and its contents, you MUST fill out a Financial Statement (Form 13), serve a copy on the applicant(s) and file a copy in the court office.
- However, if your only claim for support is for child support in the table amount specified under the Child Support Guidelines, you do not need to fill out, serve or file a Financial Statement.
- If you want to make a claim for property or exclusive possession of the matrimonial home and its contents, whether or not it includes a claim for support, you MUST fill out a Financial Statement (Form 13.1, not Form 13), serve a copy on the applicant(s), and file a copy in the court office.

YOU SHOULD GET LEGAL ADVICE ABOUT THIS CASE RIGHT AWAY. If you cannot afford a lawyer, you may be able to get help from your local Legal Aid Ontario office. *(See your telephone directory under LEGAL AID.)*

Form 8A: **Application (divorce)**   **(page 2)** | Court File Number |

☐ **THIS CASE IS A JOINT APPLICATION FOR DIVORCE. THE DETAILS ARE SET OUT ON THE ATTACHED PAGES.** The application and affidavits in support of the application will be presented to a judge when the materials have been checked for completeness

If you are requesting anything other than a simple divorce, such as support or property or exclusive possession of the matrimonial home and its contents, then refer to page 1 for instructions regarding the Financial Statement you should file.

_____   _____
Date of issue   *Clerk of the court*

Form 8A:	Application (Divorce)	(page 3)	Court file number

FAMILY HISTORY

HUSBAND: Age: **42** Birthdate: *(d,m,y)* **July 29, 1963**

Resident in *(municipality & province)* **Newmarket, Ontario**

since *(date)* **April 29, 2004**

Surname at birth: **Lutzen** Surname just before marriage: **Lutzen**

Divorced before? ☒ No ☐ Yes *(Place and date of previous divorce)*

WIFE: Age: **39** Birthdate: *(d,m,y)* **November 21, 1966**

Resident in *(municipality & province)* **Toronto, Ontario**

since *(date)* **November 21, 1966**

Surname at birth: **Johnson** Surname just before marriage: **Johnson**

Divorced before? ☒ No ☐ Yes *(Place and date of previous divorce)*

RELATIONSHIP DATES:

☒ Married on *(date)* **June 24, 1985** ☐ Started living together on *(date)*

☒ Separated on *(date)* **April 29, 2004** ☐ Never lived together

THE CHILD(REN)

List all children involved in this case, even if no claim is made for these children.

Full legal name	Age	Birthdate *(d,m,y)*	Resident in *(municipality & province)*	Now Living With *(name of person and relationship to child)*
Kimberley Ann Lutzen	20	1 July, 1985	Toronto, Ontario	Mallory Lutzen, mother

PREVIOUS CASES OR AGREEMENTS

Have the parties or the children been in a court case before?

☒ No ☐ Yes *(Attach a Summary of Court Cases – Form 8E.)*

Have the parties made a written agreement dealing with any matter involved in this case?

☐ No ☒ Yes *(Give date of agreement. Indicate which of its terms are in dispute. Attach an additional page if you need more space.)*

September 6, 2004. No terms of the agreement are in dispute.

Form 8A: **Application (divorce)**   **(page 4)**

Court file number

CLAIMS

USE THIS FRAME ONLY IF THIS CASE IS A JOINT APPLICATION FOR DIVORCE

WE JOINTLY ASK THE COURT FOR THE FOLLOWING:

Claims under the *Divorce Act*

- 00 ☐ a divorce
- 01 ☐ spousal support
- 02 ☐ support for child(ren) – table amount
- 03 ☐ support for child(ren) – other than table amount
- 04 ☐ custody of child(ren)
- 05 ☐ access to child(ren)

Claims under the *Family Law Act* or *Children's Law Reform Act*

- 10 ☐ spousal support
- 11 ☐ support for child(ren) – table amount
- 12 ☐ support for child(ren) – other than table amount
- 13 ☐ custody of child(ren)
- 14 ☐ access to child(ren)
- 15 ☐ restraining/non-harassment order
- 16 ☐ indexing spousal support
- 17 ☐ declaration of parentage
- 18 ☐ guardianship over child's property

Claims relating to property

- 20 ☐ equalization of net family properties
- 21 ☐ exclusive possession of matrimonial home
- 22 ☐ exclusive possession of contents of matrimonial home
- 23 ☐ freezing assets
- 24 ☐ sale of family property

Other claims

- 30 ☐ costs
- 31 ☐ annulment of marriage
- 32 ☐ prejudgment interest
- 50 ☐ Other *(Specify)*

USE THIS FRAME ONLY IF THE APPLICANT'S ONLY CLAIM IN THIS CASE IS FOR DIVORCE.

I ASK THE COURT FOR:
(Check if applicable.)

00 ☒ a divorce   30 ☐ costs

IMPORTANT FACTS SUPPORTING THE CLAIM FOR DIVORCE

☒ **Separation:** The spouses have lived separate and apart since *(date)* **April 29, 2004**   and

    ☐ have not lived together again since that date in an unsuccessful attempt to reconcile.

    ☒ have lived together again during the following periods(s) in an unsuccessful attempt to reconcile: *(Give dates.)*

      June 7, 2004 to June 30, 2004
      September 1, 2004 to September 15, 2004

☒ **Adultery:** *(Name of spouse)*   **Gordon Bjorn Lutzen**   has committed adultery.
    (Give details. It is not necessary to name any other person involved but if you do name the other person, then you must serve this application on the other person.)

  The respondent has resided with another woman as husband and wife at 789 Grassy Knoll Place in Newmarket, Ontario since on or about October 2004 to the date of this application, and during that time has engaged in acts of sexual intercourse with her on numerous occasions.

☐ **Cruelty:** *(Name of spouse)*   has treated *(name of spouse)*   with physical or mental cruelty of such a kind as to make continued cohabitation intolerable. *(Give details.)*

Form 8A: **Application (General)** **(page 5)** Court File Number

---

USE THIS FRAME ONLY IF THIS CASE IS A JOINT APPLICATION FOR DIVORCE.

The details of the other order(s) that we jointly ask the court to make are as follows: *(Include any amounts of support and the names of the children for whom support, custody or access is to be ordered.)*

IMPORTANT FACTS SUPPORTING OUR CLAIM(S)

(Set out the facts that form the legal basis for your claim(s). Attach an additional page if you need more space.)

Put a line through any space left on this page.

In a joint application for divorce, there will be two signatures - one for each spouse. But in an application where the applicant's only claim is for divorce, you and your lawyer are the only ones who will sign and you should strike out the inappropriate zone for your spouse's signature and corresponding date.

_____	_____
Date of signature	*Signature of applicant husband*
_____	_____
Date of signature	*Signature of applicant wife*

LAWYER'S CERTIFICATE

My name is: **Cloe Christopholous**

and I am the lawyer for *(name)* **Mallory Jane Lutzen**   in this divorce case. I certify that I have complied with the requirements of section 9 of the *Divorce Act*.

_____	_____
Date	*Signature of Lawyer*

APPENDIX 3B

ONTARIO

Superior Court of Justice
(Name of court)

at **393 University Ave., Toronto, Ontario, M5G 2N2**
Court office address

Court File Number

Family Law Rules, O. Reg. 114/99

Form 36:
Affidavit for Divorce

Applicant(s)

Full legal name & address for service — street & number, municipality, postal code, telephone & fax numbers and e-mail address (if any).	Lawyer's name & address — street & number, municipality, postal code, telephone & fax numbers and e-mail address (if any).
Mallory Jane Lutzen **261 Cataline Cr.** **Toronto, Ontario** **M2N 1H7**	**Cloe Christopholous** **Barrister & Solicitor** **269 Neilson Rd.** **Toronto, Ontario** **M2N 2N4** **Tel: 416 284-9876** **Fax: 416 284-9877**

Respondent(s)

Full legal name & address for service — street & number, municipality, postal code, telephone & fax numbers and e-mail address (if any).	Lawyer's name & address — street & number, municipality, postal code, telephone & fax numbers and e-mail address (if any).
Gordon Bjorn Lutzen **789 Grassy Knoll Place** **Newmarket, Ontario** **L0G 0B0**	

My name is *(full legal name)* **Mallory Jane Lutzen**

I live in *(municipality & province)* **Toronto, Ontario**

and I swear/affirm that the following is true:

1. I am the applicant in this divorce case.

2. There is no chance of a reconciliation between the respondent and me.

3. All the information in the application in this case is correct, except:
   (State any corrections or changes to the information in the application. Write "NONE" if there are no corrections or changes.)
   NONE

4. ☒ The certificate or registration of my marriage to the respondent has been signed and sealed by the Registrar General of Ontario and:

   ☒ has been filed with the application.

   ☐ is attached to this affidavit.

   ☐ The certificate of my marriage to the respondent was issued outside Ontario. It is called *(title of certificate)*

   It was issued at *(place of issue)* _____

   on *(date)* _____

   by *(name and title of person who issued certificate)* _____

   and the information in it about my marriage is correct.

   ☐ I have not been able to get a certificate or registration of my marriage. I was married to the respondent on *(date)* _____ at *(place of marriage)* _____

   The marriage was performed by *(name and title)* _____

   who had the authority to perform marriages in that place.

Form 36:   **Affidavit for Divorce**   **(page 2)**

Court File Number

5.   The legal basis for the divorce is:

☒   that the respondent and I have been separated for at least one year.

We separated on *(date)* **April 29, 2004**

☒   *(Other; specify.)*

That the respondent has committed adultery. Although I have no personal knowledgge of the adultery, the respondent has told me on numerous occasions that he is living as husband and wife with another woman with whom he is having sexual relations on a regular basis.

5a. I have not condoned or connived at the respondent's adultery.

6.   I do not know about and I am not involved in any arrangement to make up or to hide evidence or to deceive the court in this divorce case.

Strike out the following paragraphs if they do not apply.

7.   I do not want to make a claim for a division of property in this divorce case, even though I know that it may be legally impossible to make such a claim after the divorce.

8.   I want the divorce order to include the following paragraph numbers of the attached consent, settlement, separation agreement or previous court order: *(List the numbers of the paragraphs that you want included in the divorce order.)*

9.   There are *(number)* **1**   children of the marriage. They are:

Full legal name of child	Birth date *(d, m, y)*
Kimberley Ann Lutzen	**1 July, 1985**

10. The custody and access arrangements for the child(ren) are as follows: *(Give summary.)*
The child of our marriage has completed community college and is self-supporting. She presently lives with me.

11. These are the arrangements that have been made for the support of the child(ren) of the marriage:

(a) The income of the party paying child support is $ _____ per year.

(b) The number of children for whom support is supposed to be paid is *(number)* _____

(c) The amount of support that should be paid according to the applicable table in the child support guidelines is

$ _____ per month.

(d) The amount of child support actually being paid is $ _____ per month.
*(**NOTE:** - Where the dollar amounts in clauses [c] and [d] are different, you must fill out the frame on the next page. If the amounts in clauses [c] and [d] are the same, skip the frame and go directly to paragraph 12.)*

Form 36:   **Affidavit for Divorce**   **(page 3)** | Court File Number |

(Paragraph 11 continued.)

Fill out the information in this frame only if the amounts in paragraphs 11(c) and 11(d) are different. If they are the same, go to paragraph 12.

a) Child support is already covered by:

(i) ☐ a court order dated *(date)* _____ that was made before the child support guidelines came into effect (before 1 May 1997). I attach a copy of the order.

(ii) ☐ a domestic contract order dated *(date)* _____ that was made before the child support guidelines came into effect (before 1 May 1997). I attach a copy of the contract.

(iii) ☐ a court order or written agreement dated *(date)* _____ made after the guidelines came into effect that has some direct or indirect benefits for the child(ren). I attach a copy.

(iv) ☐ a written consent between the parties dated *(date)* _____ agreeing to the payment of an amount different from that set out in the guidelines.

b) The child support clauses of this order or agreement require payment of $ _____ per _____ in child support.

c) These child support clauses

☐ are not indexed for any automatic cost-of-living increases.

☐ are indexed according to *(Give indexing formula.)*

d) These child support clauses

☐ have not been changed since the day the order or agreement was made.

☐ have been changed on *(Give dates and details of changes.)*

e) *(If you ticked off box [i] above, you can go to paragraph 12. If you ticked off boxes [ii], [iii] or [iv] above, then fill out the information after box of the corresponding number below. For example, if you ticked off box [iii] above, you would fill out the information alongside box [iii] below.)*

(ii) ☐ The amount being paid under this agreement is a fair and reasonable arrangement for the support of the child(ren) because: *(Give reasons.)*

(iii) ☐ The order or agreement directly or indirectly benefits the child(ren) because: *(Give details or benefits.)*

(iv) ☐ The amount to which the parties have consented is reasonable for the support of the child(ren) because: *(Give reasons.)*

Form 36:   **Affidavit for Divorce**   **(page 4)** | Court File Number |

12. I am claiming costs in this case. The details of this claim are as follows: *(Give details.)*
    N/A

13. The respondent's address last known to me is: *(Give address.)*

    789 Grassy Knoll Place
    Newmarket, Ontario
    L0G 0B0

Put a line through any blank space left on this page.

Sworn/Affirmed before me at **the CITY of TORONTO**
                                        municipality

in **the PROVINCE of ONTARIO**
                                province, state or country

on _____   _____
        date   *Commissioner for taking affidavits*
                                (Type or print name below if signature is illegible.)

_____
                Signature
*(This form is to be signed in front of a
lawyer, justice of the peace, notary public
or commissioner for taking affidavits.)*

APPENDIX 3C

ONTARIO

Superior Court of Justice	Court File Number **123456**
(Name of court)	

at _____

Court office address

Family Law Rules, O. Reg. 544/99
Form 25A: Divorce Order

(SEAL)

Applicant(s)

Full legal name & address for service — street & number, municipality, postal code, telephone & fax numbers and e-mail address (if any).	Lawyer's name & address — street & number, municipality, postal code, telephone & fax numbers and e-mail address (if any).
Mallory Jane Lutzen **261 Catalina Dr.** **Toronto, Ontario** **M2N 1H7**	**Cloe Christopholous** **Barrister & Solicitor** **269 Neilson Rd.** **Toronto, Ontario** **M2N 2N4** **Tel: 416 284-9876** **Fax: 416 284-9877**

Judge (print or type name)

_____

Date of order

_____

Respondent(s)

Full legal name & address for service — street & number, municipality, postal code, telephone & fax numbers and e-mail address (if any).	Lawyer's name & address — street & number, municipality, postal code, telephone & fax numbers and e-mail address (if any).
Gordon Bjorn Lutzen **789 Grassy Knoll Place** **Newmarket, Ontario** **L0G 0B0**	

The court considered an application of *(name)* **Mallory Jane Lutzen**

on *(date)* _____

The following persons were in court *(Give names of parties and lawyers in court. This paragraph may be struck out if the divorce is uncontested.)*

The court received evidence and considered submissions on behalf of *(name or names)*
Mallory Jane Lutzen

THIS COURT ORDERS THAT:

If the court decides that the divorce should take effect earlier, replace "31" with the smaller number.

1. *(full legal names of spouses)* **Mallory Jane Lutzen and Gordon Bjorn Lutzen**

   who were married at *(place)* **Newmarket, Ontario**

   on *(date)* **June 24, 1985**

   be divorced and that the divorce take effect 31 days after the date of this order.

   (Add further paragraphs where the court orders other relief.)

Form 25A: **Divorce Order** (page 2)

Court File Number

123456

Put a line through any blank space left on this page. If additional space is needed, extra pages may be attached.

_____
Date of signature

_____
Signature of judge or clerk of the court

NOTE: _Neither spouse is free to remarry until this order takes effect, at which time you can get a_ **Certificate of Divorce** _from the court office._

FLR 25A (01/00)

CHAPTER 4

CHILD AND SPOUSAL SUPPORT UNDER THE *DIVORCE ACT*

Both child support and spousal support are available as corollary relief under the *Divorce Act.*[1] It is also possible to obtain spousal and child support under the *Family Law Act.*[2] The *Divorce Act* is only applicable where the spouses have been married and are seeking a divorce. All other support applications must be brought pursuant to the *Family Law Act.* The support provisions under these Acts are very similar. Support under the *Family Law Act* will be dealt with in Chapter 8.

CHILD SUPPORT UNDER THE *DIVORCE ACT*

The way that the amount of child support is determined changed dramatically in May of 1997, when the federal government passed the *Federal Child Support Guidelines*[3] and amended the *Income Tax Act.*[4] Provincial *Child Support Guidelines*[5] soon followed. Prior to this, child support was decided by determining the child's financial needs, having regard to the lifestyle of the child prior to separation, and the obligation of both parents to contribute to the child's support, proportionately to their respective incomes. The parent who made the child support payment could deduct the amount paid from income, therefore reducing the amount of income tax that the parent needed to pay. On the other hand, the parent receiving child support had to include it in income and was obliged to pay tax on it. The *Child Support Guidelines* completely changed the way the amount of support is determined, and the *Income Tax Act* was amended so that any child support paid pursuant to the *Guidelines* is not deductible by the payor spouse and does not have to be included in the income of the recipient spouse.

The *Divorce Act* defines a "child of the marriage" as a child of two spouses who is under the age of majority (18 years in Ontario) and has not withdrawn from their charge, or the age of majority or over and unable to

---

[1] R.S.C. 1985, c. 3 (2nd Supp.), as amended.

[2] R.S.O. 1990, c. F.3, as amended.

[3] Regulations made under the *Divorce Act*, Can. Reg. 97-175, as amended [hereinafter the "*Guidelines*"].

[4] R.S.C. 1985, c. 1(5th Supp.), as amended.

[5] Regulations made under the *Family Law Act*, O. Reg. 391/97, as amended.

withdraw from their charge because of illness, disability, or other cause.[6] It is clear that "other cause" includes full-time attendance at an educational institution. Although the rule of thumb is one degree or diploma, the courts will extend the definition to children pursuing advanced degrees in certain circumstances.[7] A "child of the marriage" also includes a child that is not the natural child of the spouse, but for whom the spouse "stands in the place of a parent."[8] A person who treats a child as his or her own child will be obligated to support that child, whether or not the child is related to the person by blood or adoption.[9]

Chartier v. Chartier, [1999] 1 S.C.R. 242, [1999] S.C.J. No. 79, 1999 CarswellMan 25 (S.C.C.)

The parties began a common law relationship in November 1989 and married on June 1, 1991. Their child, Jeena, was born on August 29, 1990. The parties separated in May 1992, later reconciled for a month or two, then permanently separated in September 1992. [At para. 2.]

Jessica is the child of the wife from a previous relationship. While the parties lived together, the husband played an active role in caring for both children and was a father-figure for Jessica. The parties discussed, but did not proceed with, the husband's adoption of Jessica. The parties did amend Jessica's birth registration to indicate, falsely, that the husband was Jessica's natural father and to change her name to his. [At para. 3.]

In divorce proceedings, a request was made for a declaration that the husband stood in the place of a parent to the Jessica. The husband contested the claim, and wished to sever his relationship with the Jessica

Held:

> . . .[A] person cannot unilaterally withdraw from a relationship in which he or she stands in the place of a parent and that the court must look to the nature of the relationship to determine if a person in fact does stand in the place of a parent to a child. [At para. 17.]

> The relevant factors in defining the parental relationship include, but are not limited to, whether the child participates in the extended family in the same way as would a biological child; whether the person provides financially for the child (depending on ability to pay); whether the person disciplines the child as a parent; whether the person represents to the child, the family, the world, either explicitly or implicitly, that he or she is responsible as a parent

---

[6] *Divorce Act*, s. 2(1).

[7] See *Moss v. Moss*, [2004] N.J. No. 164, 2004 NLSCTD 83, 2004 CarswellNfld 125 (N.L. T.D.), where child support was payable for children while they pursued Master's Degrees and *N. (W.P.) v. N. (B.J.)*, [2005] B.C.J. No. 12, 2005 BCCA 7, 2005 CarswellBC 10 (B.C. C.A.), where support was payable for a child attending medical school.

[8] *Divorce Act*, s. 2(2).

[9] See *Neil v. Neil* (2002), [2002] O.J. No. 3003, 2002 CarswellOnt 2513 (Ont. S.C.J.).

> to the child; the nature or existence of the child's relationship with the absent biological parent. [At para. 39.]

The concern that a child might collect support from both the biological parent and the step-parent was not a valid one.

> The respondent's unilateral withdrawal from the relationship with Jessica does not change the fact that he acted, in all ways, as a father during the time the family lived together. Therefore, Jessica was a "child of the marriage" when the parties separated and later divorced, with all of the rights and responsibilities which that status entails under the *Divorce Act*. With respect to support from the respondent, Jessica is to be treated in the same way as Jeena. [At para. 47.]

Either or both spouses can make an application for child support, but the child cannot apply.[10] Where an application is made for child support, the court can order interim child support.[11] Both interim and final orders must be in accordance with the applicable guidelines,[12] unless there are "special provisions" made for the child, such as a trust account or a property transfer that directly or indirectly benefits a child.[13] The court must find that awarding the guideline amount in light of the special provisions would result in an amount that was inequitable. The court must give reasons in this case.[14] If the parties agree on an amount of support that is different than the guideline amount, the court can only make an order in that amount if the amount is reasonable, with regard to the applicable guidelines.[15] Orders can be for a limited amount of time or no limit may be specified. The court can order that child support ends on the happening of certain events and can impose terms and conditions on child support.[16]

---

[10] *Divorce Act*, s. 15.1(1).
[11] *Divorce Act*, s. 15.1(2).
[12] *Divorce Act*, s. 15.1(3).
[13] *Divorce Act*, s. 15.1(5).
[14] *Divorce Act*, s. 15.1(6).
[15] *Divorce Act*, s. 15.1(7), (8).
[16] *Divorce Act*, s. 15.1(4).

Application Questions

For each of the following situations, state whether the child is a "child of the marriage" within the meaning of the *Divorce Act*:

1. Tom, who is 23 years old, has quit school and refuses to get a job, even though his former employer has offered to take him back.

2. Charlene, 20, is in full time attendance in college, taking a law clerk course. She is living in residence during the school year, but comes back home on holidays and on some weekends, and intends to move back home in the summer, when she will be working at her summer job.

3. Steve, 16, is not Greg's biological child. Greg married Steve's mother when Steve was 7 years old. Greg has coached Steve's soccer team and usually takes Steve to his hockey practices and games. Greg has gone to most of Steve's parent-teacher interviews and other school events. Steve calls Greg "Dad," and they have always had a good relationship. Greg's relationship with Steve's mother has now ended, and Greg has moved out. Greg has not seen Steve since he left.

4. Katherine is 24 years of age. She suffers from physical and developmental problems that prevent her from ever being able to support herself.

5. Amanda, 15, has moved in with her boyfriend, against her parent's strong objections. She continues to attend high school.

The *Child Support Guidelines*

Section 1 of the *Federal Child Support Guidelines* set out the objectives of the *Guidelines*, which are:

- to ensure a fair standard of support;
- to reduce conflict and tension;
- to improve efficiency; and
- to ensure consistent treatment of parents and children.

The *Guidelines* attempt to meet these objectives by providing tables that set out the amount of child support that will be payable in most cases, indicating the specific circumstances where child support is to be calculated in a different way, and providing either a method of calculation or enumerating factors to be considered in determining the appropriate amount of child support in the exceptional circumstances.

The Presumptive Rule

The general rule is that the amount of child support is determined by going to the proper table and looking up the amount of child support, based on the income of the payor spouse. There is a set of tables for each province, and for each set of tables there are separate sections based on the number of children for which support is payable. The sections cover from one child to six or more children. For example, to determine the amount of support that would be payable for two children in Ontario, you would first go to the Ontario tables and then go to the section for two children. You would then use the income of the payor spouse to look up the amount of child support. The tables show income ranges (for example, between $45,000 and $45,999). They then show a base amount of child support ($680) and how to calculate the additional amount (1.49 per cent of the amount over $45,000).

Special and Extraordinary Expenses

In addition to the table amount, the court can order an extra amount to cover special and extraordinary expenses. The court can order that all, or a portion, of the special or extraordinary expense be covered. In deciding whether or not to order that all or part of the expense be paid, the court must consider:

- the necessity of the expense in the child's best interest;
- the reasonableness of the expense in relation to the means of the parties and the child; and
- the spending pattern of the parties regarding the child, while they were together.[17]

The spouses must share the special and extraordinary expenses in proportion to their incomes, after deducting from the expense any contribution from the child.[18] The court can decide how much of the expense should be covered by each party or whether the expense should be covered at all.

The categories that fall into special and extraordinary expenses are:

- childcare expenses;
- medical and dental insurance;
- health-related expenses (orthodontist, counselling, etc.);
- educational programs (e.g., private schools, tutoring);
- post-secondary education; and
- extra-curricular activities.

---

[17] *Guidelines*, s. 7(1).
[18] *Guidelines*, s. 7(2).

Child over the Age of Majority

Where the child is the age of majority (18 years) or over, the court has the discretion not to award the table amount. The court should begin by looking at the table amount and award that amount unless the court considers it inappropriate, having regard to the circumstances of the child, and the financial ability of each parent to contribute to the support of the child. This is one of the cases where the income of both parents will be considered, instead of just the income of the payor spouse. The court can award more or less than the table amount.

Incomes over $150,000

The tables cover incomes up to $150,000 and then provide a base amount and a percentage to calculate child support on the amount over $150,000. The court begins by calculating what support would be according to the formula, but then has discretion regarding the amount over the base amount. The court should award the amount it considers appropriate, based on the circumstances of the children, and the ability of each parent to contribute to the support of the children. Again, the income of both parents is taken into account.

R. v. R. (2002), 58 O.R. (3d) 656, [2002] O.J. No. 1095, 2002 CarswellOnt 902 (Ont. C.A.)

The parties separated after eight years of marriage. In the last five years of the marriage, the husband's annual income averaged $1.4 million. After separation, his income doubled to $4.1 million annually. Under the *Federal Child Support Guidelines*, the table amount of child support for four children at that income was over $65,000 per month. The trial judge declined to award child support for four children in the *Guidelines* table amount. He found that the family lifestyle before separation was "conservative and modest". This "comfortable but not extravagant lifestyle" constituted for the trial judge "clear and compelling evidence" that the table amount was inappropriate. He ordered the husband to pay $16,000 per month for the four children. He also ordered the husband to pay spousal support in the amount of $5,000 per month. The wife appealed.

Held: The appeal should be allowed in part.

> . . .It is one thing for the family to live modestly and save money while together; it is quite another, and seemingly unfair, for the paying parent to hold his children to the family's pre-separation lifestyle while saving the increase in his post-separation income, but now for his benefit alone. [At para. 58.]

> Given the increase in [the husband's] income, [there was] nothing wrong with [the wife] having included in her proposed budget items not previously

acquired or even contemplated by the parties. Instead of dismissing [the] budget out of hand, the trial judge should have considered whether [the wife's] options were reasonable having regard to the substantial increase in [the husband's] income. [At para. 61.]

An appropriate amount of child support under s. 4 of the *Guidelines* in the circumstances of this case was $32,000 for four children. The trial judge did not err in the exercise of his discretion by ordering spousal support of $5,000 per month.

Spouse in the Place of a Parent

As discussed earlier, a person may be obliged to support a child who is not the biological or adoptive child of that person, if that person has treated the child as his or her own child. However, the court does not necessarily have to award the table amount against that person. The court can award the amount it considers appropriate and in determining the appropriate amount, the court must consider the duty of any other person to support the child.[19] It is therefore quite possible for the court to order child support for the same child against more than one person, but the person or persons that stood in the place of a parent of that child would not necessarily be ordered to pay the table amount.[20]

Split Custody

If each of the parents has custody of one or more of the children, then determining the amount of child support payable is fairly simple. The Guidelines require that the table amount for each parent be ascertained and the smaller amount be subtracted from the larger amount. The amount left over is the child support payable.[21] For example, if the mother had custody of two children and the father had custody of one, then to determine the mother's table amount, we would go to the table for one child and use the mother's income to determine her amount. We would then go to the table for two children and use the father's income to determine his amount. If the father's amount was larger than the mother's amount, then the mother's amount would be subtracted from the father's amount, and the father would pay the mother the difference.

---

[19] *Guidelines*, s. 5.

[20] For an interesting twist on this situation, see *Wright v. Zaver* (2002), 59 O.R. (3d) 26 (Ont. C.A.), where the biological father argued that his child support should be reduced, because the person who stood in the place of a parent to the child was paying the full table amount.

[21] *Guidelines*, s. 8.

Shared Custody

Shared custody, on the other hand, has caused quite a bit more difficulty. Section 9 of the *Guidelines* stipulates that the court must determine the appropriate amount of support where the parent paying support has the child for 40 per cent of the time or more. The 40 per cent is calculated over the course of a year. There has been a fair amount of litigation surrounding the issue of how the 40 per cent is to be calculated, such as whether time spent asleep or at school is counted, etc. Once it has been established that the payor spouse has the child at least 40 per cent of the time, the court must then determine the amount of child support payable. The *Guidelines* require the court to take into account:

(a) the table amount for each parent;

(b) the increased cost of shared custody arrangements; and

(c) the circumstances of each parent and the child.

The *Guidelines* do not set out how these factors should be weighed.

Contino v. Leonelli-Contino, [2005] S.C.J. No. 65, 2005 SCC 63, 2005 CarswellOnt 6281 (S.C.C.)

Appeal of a reduction in child support. Upon separation in 1992, Contino (the father) and Leonelli-Contino (the mother) maintained joint custody of their son, whose daily residence was with the mother. Nine years later, the father applied for a reduction in child support payments pursuant to section 9 of the *Child Support Guidelines*, on the basis that he and the mother were now sharing custody. The motions judge agreed and reduced child support to $100 a month. That decision was set aside by the Divisional Court and the father was ordered to pay the full table amount of $688 per month. The Ontario Court of Appeal reduced that amount to $399 after consideration of section 9.

Held: Appeal allowed. Child support was increased to $500 per month. Section 9 of the *Guidelines* provided a particular regime for determining support in the context of shared custody, with an emphasis on flexibility and fairness to all parties. There were three factors that the court must consider: 1) section 9(a) required the court to take the financial situations of both parents into account, including the effective contributions each parent made and their continuing ability to meet the needs of the child; 2) section 9(b) required the court to determine whether shared custody had resulted in increased costs overall; if so, those costs would be apportioned based on the party's incomes; and 3) section 9(c) required the court to make a broad analysis of the resources and needs of all parties, including the child. The court must keep in mind the objectives of *Guide-*

lines, including a fair standard support for the child and fair contributions from the parents.

Undue Hardship

If the court finds that ordering the *Guideline* amount would cause a parent or spouse or child to suffer undue hardship, the court can award an amount of child support different from the *Guideline* amount.[22] The circumstances that may cause undue hardship include:

- the parent or spouse has reasonably incurred an unusually high level of debt;
- the parent or spouse has unusually high access expenses;
- the parent or spouse is obliged by a court order, judgment, or separation agreement to support any person;
- the spouse has a legal duty to support another child; or
- the parent or spouse has a legal duty to support someone who is ill or disabled.[23]

The court cannot order an amount different from the *Guideline* amount if the household of the person claiming undue hardship would have a higher standard of living than the household of the other parent or spouse.[24] If the court does order a different amount of child support, it can specify for what period the different amount is payable, and what the amount of support will be when the period is over.[25] If the court does order a different amount, it must give reasons for doing so.[26]

Application Questions

1. Naseem and Masi have two children, aged 12 and 10. Naseem has custody of both children and Masi has access. Naseem earns $40,000 per year, and Masi earns $45,000. Both children attend a before-and-after-school program and play hockey. How will child support be determined?

2. Michael and Melissa have one daughter, aged 19. She is in her first year of university. She has a scholarship that pays her $10,000 per year as long as she maintains an "A" average and she works in the summer. What factors will be considered in determining child support?

---

[22] *Guidelines*, s.10(1).
[23] *Guidelines*, s.10(2).
[24] *Guidelines*, s.10(3), (4).
[25] *Guidelines*, s.10(5).
[26] *Guidelines*, s.10(6).

3. Lydia and Jasik have two children. Lydia has custody of their daughter, aged 5, and Jasik has custody of their son, aged 9. Lydia earns $20,000 per year and Jasik earns $100,000. How will child support be determined?

4. Derek has three children by three different women. How is child support determined for these children? Would the amount Derek is required to pay be different if all three children had the same mother?

SPOUSAL SUPPORT UNDER THE *DIVORCE ACT*

Spousal support remains one of the most difficult and contentious areas of family law. Over the years, the courts have maintained that spousal support is to be determined on a case-by-case basis. Because spousal support orders are so fact-specific, and because there are so many variables, this area of law has been fraught with unpredictability and controversy. An attempt is being made to bring some consistency and predictability to this area by promulgating new Spousal Support Guidelines.

Unlike child support, spousal support payments are tax deductible to the payor and must be included in the income of the recipient spouse. This means that the payor pays less income tax as a result of being able to deduct spousal support payments. These tax savings can be quite significant and the payor may be able to get a very substantial portion of the spousal support payments back as a tax refund. On the other hand, the support recipient must pay income tax on spousal support payments received, therefore having less disposable income after taxes. The effect of income taxes is taken into account by the courts when deciding on the amount of spousal support.

There are major differences between the *Divorce Act*[27] and the *Family Law Act*[28] in terms of who qualifies as a spouse and minor differences regarding the principles upon which spousal support is awarded. Spousal Support under the *Family Law Act* will be examined in Chapter 8.

Who Can Apply

Only spouses who have been legally married to each other and have commenced divorce proceedings can seek spousal support pursuant to the *Divorce Act*. As mentioned in Chapter 3, as a result of the court striking down the definition of "spouse" as discriminatory and unconstitutional, the

---

[27] R.S.C. 1985, c. 3 (2nd Supp.), as amended, s. 2(1).
[28] R.S.O. 1990, c. F.3, as amended.

definition has now been amended by the *Civil Marriage Act* to read "either of two persons who are married to each other."[29] The Act therefore applies equally to opposite-sex and same-sex couples, as long as they were legally married. The term "spouse" also includes former spouses for the purpose of support orders.[30]

Either or both spouses can apply for spousal support. The court can order either a lump sum or periodic payments (usually monthly) or a combination of both. The court can also order the payor spouse to secure payment of support against real or personal property.[31] Once an application for support has been commenced, the court can also order interim support.[32] Support orders can be indefinite, which means they continue until changed, or for a definite period. The court can specify a particular date or period after which support ends, or an event (such as the spouse completing a course, or a child graduating from high school), which will cause support to terminate.[33]

Application Questions

Would the following be spouses within the meaning of the *Divorce Act*?

(a) Krista and Kyle where married in 1990 and separated in 2005.

(b) George and Steven were married in 2004 and have just recently separated.

(c) Anna and Cameron have been living together in a conjugal relationship for five years, and have two children. Although they were never legally married, they have gone thorough a "promising" ceremony in front of their friends.

(d) Veronica and Shawn were married in 2000. Veronica has just found out that Shawn was married before, but never divorced. His first wife is still alive.

How Spousal Support is Determined

In deciding what amount of support is reasonable, the court must take into consideration each spouse's condition, means, need, and other circumstances, and specifically must consider:

---

[29] *Civil Marriage Act*, S.C. 2005, c. 33, s. 8(1).
[30] *Divorce Act*, s. 15.
[31] *Divorce Act*, s. 15.2(1).
[32] *Divorce Act*, s. 15.2(2).
[33] *Divorce Act*, s. 15.2(3).

- the length of time the parties cohabited (which would include living together before marriage);
- the functions performed by each spouse during cohabitation; and
- any order, agreement or arrangement relating to support.[34]

Although the court must consider previous orders and agreements or arrangements made by the parties, the court is not bound by such orders, agreements, or arrangements and can order any amount it considers reasonable.

Miglin v. Miglin, [2003] 1 S.C.R. 303, [2003] S.C.J. No. 21, 2003 SCC 24, 2003 CarswellOnt 1374 (S.C.C.).

The parties were married in 1979. They were co-owners of a hotel, which was managed by the husband. The wife was responsible for administrative and housekeeping tasks and received a salary of $80,500 each year. She was also the primary caregiver of the parties' four children. The parties separated in 1993 and entered into a separation agreement in 1994 in which the wife released the husband from the obligation to pay spousal support. The parties also entered into a five-year consulting agreement that could be renewed from time to time by mutual consent, whereby the husband agreed to pay the wife $15,000 in annual consulting fees through the business. The parties were to share responsibility for raising the children, but the children's primary residence was to be with the wife. The husband's initially amicable relationship with the wife changed when the wife sold the matrimonial home and converted to Judaism. The husband caused the hotel not to extend the consulting agreement. Before the agreement was terminated, the wife brought proceedings pursuant to section 15 of the *Divorce Act*, R.S.C. 1985, c. 3 (2nd Supp.), for sole custody of the children, spousal support, and child support in accordance with the *Child Support Guidelines*. The trial judge awarded the wife monthly spousal support in the amount of $4,400 for five years and monthly child support of $3,000. The husband appealed. The wife cross-appealed the five-year time limit in the support order.

> An initial application for spousal support inconsistent with a pre-existing agreement requires an investigation into all the circumstances surrounding that agreement, first, at the time of its formation, and second, at the time of the application. [At para. 64.]

At the first stage, the court should look at the circumstances in which the agreement was negotiated and executed to determine whether there is any reason to discount it, including any circumstances of oppression, pressure or other vulnerabilities. Circumstances less than "unconscionability" in the commercial law context may be relevant, but a court should not

---

[34] *Divorce Act*, s. 15.2(4).

presume an imbalance of power. Further, the degree of professional assistance received by the parties may be sufficient to overcome any systemic imbalances between the parties. Next, the court must consider the substance of the agreement to determine whether it is in substantial compliance with the Act.

At the second stage, the court must assess whether the agreement still reflects the original intentions of the parties and the extent to which it is still in substantial compliance with the objectives of the Act. Accordingly, the party seeking to set aside the agreement will need to show that these new circumstances were not reasonably anticipated by the parties and have led to a situation that cannot be condoned. Some degree of change in the circumstances of the parties is always foreseeable. Parties are presumed to be aware that health, job markets, parental responsibilities, housing markets, and values of assets are all subject to change. It is only where the current circumstances represent a significant departure from the range of reasonable outcomes anticipated by the parties, in a manner that puts them at odds with the objectives of the Act, that the court may be persuaded to give the agreement little weight.

The consulting contract reflects the parties' intention to provide the wife with a source of employment income for a limited time. The non-renewal of the contract did not render continued reliance on the original separation agreement inappropriate.

Section 15.2(5) of the Act specifies that in determining the amount of spousal support, the court must not take into consideration any misconduct that either spouse may have committed in relation to the marriage. In other words, it should make no difference whatsoever who ended the marriage and why. The court will not enquire into whose fault the marriage breakdown was, as this is irrelevant to support.

The *Divorce Act* requires the court to fulfill certain objectives with a support order, which are to:

- recognize any economic advantages or disadvantages to the spouses arising from the marriage or its breakdown;
- apportion between the spouses any financial consequences arising from the care of any child of the marriage over and above any obligation for the support of any child of the marriage;
- relieve any economic hardship of the spouses arising from the breakdown of the marriage; and,
- in so far as practicable, promote the economic self-sufficiency of each spouse within a reasonable period of time.[35]

---

[35] *Divorce Act*, s. 15.2(6).

Bracklow v. Bracklow, [1999] I S.C.R. 420, [1999] S.C.J. No. 14, 1999 CarswellBC 532 (S.C.C.)

Appeal by the wife from the dismissal of her appeal from a trial judge's decision not to award her spousal support. The husband and wife cohabited for four years before they married in 1989. During the first two years of their relationship, the wife paid for most of the household expenses as she earned more than the husband and her two children from a previous marriage were living with them. They then shared expenses and chores equally. When the wife was unemployed, the husband supported the family. In 1991, the wife was hospitalized for psychiatric problems and did not work again. The parties separated in 1992 and divorced in 1995. The husband earned $3,764 per month and had expenses of $2,284 per month. The wife was ill with no means of support other than $787 in monthly disability benefits. The wife obtained interim monthly spousal support of $275, which increased to $400 in May 1994. The wife was awarded no spousal support as the judge found that she experienced no economic hardship from the marriage or its breakdown and that her health problems were not due to the marriage. He also found that there was no express or implied agreement between the parties that they would support each other. At the husband's suggestion, the trial judge ordered that spousal support continue to September 1, 1996. The Court of Appeal upheld the trial decision.

Held: Appeal allowed. The matter was ordered remitted to the trial judge for assessment of the amount and duration of support. The wife was legally eligible for spousal support. The early years of the parties' relationship suggested a fairly independent partnership; however, by the end, the parties had established an interdependent relationship. They had adjusted their expenses equally and the husband had covered the wife's needs in the early stages of her illness. Thus, it followed that the divorce rendered the wife in a state of economic hardship within the meaning of section 15.2(6)(c) of the *Divorce Act*.

> . . .While the law has evolved to accept compensation as an important basis of support and to encourage the self-sufficiency of each spouse when the marriage ends, where compensation is not indicated and self-sufficiency is not possible, a support obligation may nonetheless arise from the marriage relationship itself. Turning to the specific provisions, the factors judges must consider in resolving support issues reveal the three different conceptual bases for spousal support obligations—contractual, compensatory, and non-compensatory. The judge must consider them all, and any or all of them may figure in the ultimate order, as may be appropriate in the circumstances of the case. [At para. 37.]

Given the statutory objectives of support and the relevant factors, the wife was eligible for support given the length of the cohabitation, the hardship marriage breakdown imposed on her, her palpable need, and the husband's financial ability to pay. The wife was unlikely to work again. While the combined cohabitation and marriage of seven years was not long, neither was it very short. As the wife did contribute financially to the family at times, it would be unjust to find that she was ineligible for support.

Application Questions

Which of the following factors would the court take into consideration in awarding spousal support?

(a) Violetta and Yuri lived together for three years before they were married.

(b) In the early years of their marriage, John supported the family while Caroline went to medical school.

(c) All through the marriage, Andrea had numerous affairs.

The Proposed Spousal Support Advisory Guidelines[36]

The Draft Spousal Support Advisory Guidelines are intended to bring more certainty and predictability to determining spousal support under the *Divorce Act*. These advisory guidelines are very different from the *Federal Child Support Guidelines*. They are not being legislated by the federal government. They are informal guidelines that will operate on an advisory basis only. The proposed advisory guidelines do not deal with entitlement, just amount and duration once entitlement has been found. The advisory guidelines do not deal with the effect of a prior agreement on spousal support.

There are two basic formulas in the proposal: the *without child support* formula and the *with child support* formula. Both formulas use income sharing as the method for determining the amount of spousal support, not budgets. The formulas produce ranges for the amount and duration of support, not just a single number. The precise number chosen within that range will be a matter for negotiation or adjudication, depending upon the facts of a particular case.

The *without child support* formula is built around two crucial factors: the gross income difference between the spouses and the length of the marriage. Cases with dependent children and concurrent child support obligations require a different formula, the *with child support* formula.

Because the guidelines are only advisory, departures are always possible on a case-by-case basis where the formula outcomes are inappropriate. Under both formulas, the proposed guidelines do offer a short list of exceptions, intended to identify common categories of departures: a compensatory ex-

---

[36] Prepared by Professor Carol Rogerson, Faculty of Law, University of Toronto, and Professor Rollie Thompson, Dalhousie Law School [excerpts].

ception in short relationships, illness and disability, debt payment, prior support obligations, and compelling financial circumstances in the interim period.

As with the *Federal Child Support Guidelines*, there is a ceiling and a floor that sets the range of incomes to which the formulas apply. The ceiling is the income level for the payor spouse above which any formula gives way to discretion, set here at a gross annual income for the payor of $350,000. The floor is the income level for the payor below which no support is to be paid, here set at $20,000.

As the calculations are very complex, practitioners are most likely to use computer software to determine the spousal support ranges. In Ontario, two software programs are currently available: DIVORCEmate, and ChildView.

The authors of the Draft Spousal Support Advisory Guidelines continue to seek comments, suggestions and feedback from those who are working with the Guidelines. The Guidelines continue to be reviewed and revised.

CHAPTER 5

CUSTODY AND VARIATION OF ORDERS UNDER THE *DIVORCE ACT*

CUSTODY AND ACCESS

An application for custody or access to a child can be made under both the *Divorce Act*[1] and the *Children's Law Reform Act*[2] in Ontario. The *Divorce Act* is only applicable where the parents of the child who is the subject of the dispute have been married and are seeking a divorce. All other custody applications must be brought pursuant to the *Children's Law Reform Act*, which will be dealt with in Chapter 11.

WHAT IS CUSTODY?

Custody has been defined as full parental control over, and ultimate parental responsibility for, the care, upbringing and education of the child. The other parent has no right to interfere in the decisions that are made by the parent who has been granted sole custody.[3] A person who is granted custody is responsible for the child on a day-to-day basis and makes the day-to-day and major decisions on behalf of the child.[4] It is clear from the cases that a person who has custody of a child has both the responsibility and the authority to make decisions about the child's residence, health care, education, religion, social activities, and parenting time. "Parenting time" refers to the period that a child spends under the care of a person, whether or not the child is physically with that person during all of the period. For example, a child could spend time in day care, yet the child would still be in the parent's care.

---

[1] R.S.C. 1985, c. 3 (2nd Supp.), as amended.
[2] R.S.O. 1990, c. C.12, as amended.
[3] *Kruger v. Kruger* (1979), 25 O.R. (2d) 673, 104 D.L.R. (3d) 481 (Ont. C.A.) at 677 [O.R.], per Thorson J.A.
[4] *Gordon v. Goertz* (1996), 19 R.F.L. (4th) 177 (S.C.C.).

CUSTODY UNDER THE DIVORCE ACT—WHO CAN APPLY

Under the *Divorce Act*, either or both spouses or former spouses have the status to apply for custody of a child or children of the marriage if they are seeking a divorce.[5] A "child of the marriage" includes not only biological and adopted children of the couple; the definition also includes any children for whom the parties both stand in the place of parents and also any children of whom one is a parent and the other stands in place of a parent.[6] The section clearly contemplates that spouses may apply for custody of stepchildren when they divorce.

In addition, non-spouses can apply for custody under the *Divorce Act*, but must first obtain the court's permission to become a party to the divorce proceeding, a corollary relief proceeding, or a variation proceeding.[7] However, non-spouses, such as grandparents, will not generally be included as parties in a custody dispute if they are not themselves seeking custody and their participation is not necessary to make an effective custody decision.[8]

Application Questions

Sarah and Mohammed brought an application for divorce in Ontario and each applied for custody of their baby, Sahara. Mohammed's parents, who had looked after Sahara most of her life, wanted to have custody of the child or, at least generous access to the child.

(a) Can the grandparents apply for custody under the *Divorce Act*? If so, how should they go about doing this?

(b) If Sarah and Mohammed decide they do not want to get divorced after they have started the divorce proceeding, can a custody order still be granted?

(c) If the parties had been married for five years and Sahara was Mohammed's child from a previous relationship, could Sarah still apply for custody? Why or why not?

---

[5] *Divorce Act*, s. 16(1).
[6] *Divorce Act*, s. 2(2).
[7] *Divorce Act*, s. 16(3).
[8] *Fisher v. Fisher* (1985), 166 A.P.R. 206, 70 N.S.R. (2d) 206 (N.S. T.D.).

PRINCIPLES DETERMINING THE MERITS OF CUSTODY

Best Interests of the Child

In making a custody order under the *Divorce Act*, the *only* consideration is the best interests of the child, which is to be determined by reference to the condition, means, needs and other circumstances of the child.[9] The focus on the "best interests of the child" principle is one of relatively recent origin. Early in the nineteenth century, a father had a near-absolute right to custody of a child unless he was disqualified by some serious circumstance having to do with the child's welfare.[10] The rule of paternal preference was later displaced by a rule establishing that the mother had a primary right to custody of a child of tender years.[11] By the 1970s, a number of western countries began passing legislation that incorporated the "best interests" or "welfare of the child" test. Under the former 1968 *Divorce Act* in Canada, the court was obliged to determine custody based upon what was "fit and just. . .having regard to the conduct of the parties and the condition, means and other circumstances [of the spouses]."[12] The emphasis was still upon the circumstances of the spouses rather than those relevant to the child. In the *Divorce Act* of 1985, the best interests of the child was clearly established as the *paramount* consideration, and soon thereafter, the legislation was amended to make it the only criterion for determining child custody.[13]

Now that the best interests of the child are the only consideration, parental preferences and "rights" no longer play a role in determining custody. However, by setting out general factors to be considered, Parliament has established a legal test that is a flexible one. The test should be applied according to the evidence in each particular case.[14] The Supreme Court of Canada has elaborated upon the factors that should be considered, which include the general psychological, spiritual and emotional welfare of the child. The court should choose the course that will best provide for the healthy growth, development and education of the child.[15]

---

[9] *Divorce Act*, s. 16(8).
[10] See *K. (K.) v. L. (G.)*, [1985] 1 S.C.R. 87, 44 R.F.L. (2d) 113 (S.C.C.).
[11] *Talsky v. Talsky* (1975), 21 R.F.L. 27, 62 D.L.R. (3d) 267 (S.C.C.).
[12] R.S.C. 1970, c. D-8, s. 11(1).
[13] R.S.C. 1985, c. 3 (2nd Supp.), as amended.
[14] *Young v. Young* (1993), 49 R.F.L. (3d) 117 (S.C.C.).
[15] *K. (K.) v. L. (G.)*, *supra* note 10; see also *O'Brien v. Thomson* (2004), 2004 CarswellNS 65 (N.S. C.A.); for an interesting and detailed discussion of factors considered in determining best interests, see *Starko v. Starko* (1990), 1990 CarswellAlta 83 (Alta. Q.B.).

Conduct as a Factor

The court is directed, in determining best interests, not to consider the past conduct of any person unless the conduct is relevant to the ability of a person to act as a parent.[16] In order to be relevant, the conduct must affect a person's ability to recognize and meet a child's needs. A parent would not be disentitled to custody merely because he or she commits adultery or cohabits with another person, unless that parent's new partner poses a risk to the child. Even a parent's fault for the marriage breakdown has been found to be irrelevant to the issue of custody.[17] A parent should not be disentitled to custody merely because he or she is involved in a same-sex relationship, especially where the parent is capable of handling any problems that the children might encounter in the community.[18]

The type of conduct that would, in fact, be relevant to determining custody would include situations where the parent has committed a serious criminal offence[19] or the conduct raises questions about the parent's stability or the parent's ability to act as a suitable role model. For example, a parent who drives intoxicated with the child in the car[20] or lies about having terminal cancer and threatens suicide to get the child's attention,[21] would fall into this category.

Maximum Contact Principle

The court must apply the principle that a child should have as much contact with each spouse as is consistent with the child's best interests. The court is specifically directed to take into consideration the willingness of the parent seeking custody to facilitate contact with the other parent.[22] Consequently, a parent who has custody has a positive obligation to promote contact with the other parent. A parent who deliberately attempts to undermine a child's relationship with the other parent could place himself or herself at a disadvantage in a custody dispute.

---

[16] *Divorce Act*, s. 16(9).

[17] *LaChapelle v. LaChapelle* (2000), [2000] O.J. No. 4276, 2000 CarswellOnt 4108 (Ont. C.A.).

[18] See *Boots v. Sharrow* (2004), 2004 CarswellOnt 25, 49 R.F.L. (5th) 260 (Ont. S.C.J.).

[19] See *Grealy v. Lees*, 2000 CarswellBC 282, 2000 BCSC 217 (B.C. S.C.), where the father was convicted of killing the mother.

[20] See *Hoffstrom v. Laderoute* (1997), [1997] O.J. No. 858, 1997 CarswellOnt 1062 (Ont. Prov. Div.).

[21] See *Lawreniuk v. Lawreniuk* (October 26, 1995), Doc. Prince Albert Q.B. 04706/94, [1995] S.J. No. 593 (Sask. Q.B.).

[22] *Divorce Act*, s. 16(10), 17(9) (variation proceedings).

Evans v. Evans (2004), 2004 CarswellBC 762 (B.C. S.C.), additional reasons at (2004), 2004 CarswellBC 1089 (B.C. S.C.)

The parents of three girls, aged 8, 10 and 12, separated following 15 years of marriage. During the marriage, Mrs. Evans stayed home to raise the children and each of the parents played a significant role in parenting the children. Up until the separation, Mr. Evans had a close, loving relationship with his daughters and was very involved with their lives.

The relationship between the parents had been troubled for some time. When Mr. Evans told his wife that he was going to get his own apartment, a number of incidents occurred that threatened to undermine the father's relationship with the children. Soon after she found out her husband was leaving, Mrs. Evans called the children into the living room and demanded that Mr. Evans tell the children why he wanted to leave and why he did not love them. The father was portrayed as the "bad guy" and the children became upset. For the next six months, Mr. Evans had difficulty exercising access to the children. Mrs. Evans told him he could not see the children until she received an agreement giving her the family home. If she did not get the house, she threatened to leave with the children and he would never see them again. The children would telephone their father and say that their mother had told them to call and ask why he wanted to sell the house and not give them any money. Mr. Evans received more than 60 calls of a similar nature and each time he heard Mrs. Evans prompting the children in the background and also insisting that they not let their father ruin their plans for the weekend. At least 100 times, when he called Mrs. Evans about seeing the children, Mr. Evans was rebuffed. Even after a consent order was made specifying the times each parent would have the children, the access problems continued. The mother then attempted to encourage the youngest daughter not to visit her father and conveniently had her engaged in other activities during access times. She insisted that the child hated her father, did not want to visit her father, and refused to facilitate the access in any way.

In a divorce proceeding, the father applied for sole custody or in the alternative, joint custody. The mother denied in her testimony that she had ever interfered with the father's access to the children.

Held: The parties were granted joint custody with primary residence with the father.

Based on the evidence, the court found that Mr. Evans' concerns were justified; i.e., that if the children were residing primarily with Mrs. Evans, there would be continuous undermining and excluding of him as the father. On the other hand, Mrs. Evans did not express similar concerns in the event that Mr. Evans was granted sole custody. It was in the best interests of the children that maximum contact with both parents be fostered. Having in mind the requirements of section 16(10) of the *Divorce Act*, the court concluded on the evidence that Mr. Evans was more likely than Mrs. Evans to facilitate maximum contact by the children with each parent.

Application Questions

Luke and Jasmin were married for 11 years and had three children. They separated when Luke became involved with another woman and eventually went to live with her. Both parents loved the three children very much and during the marriage they had shared the care and raising of the children. The children were close to both parents. After the separation, Jasmin, who was very bitter about the way the marriage ended, refused to allow the children to see their father. Whenever he tried to have them over, she would make excuses that they were busy and said they hated him. She told the children their father was a "good-for-nothing cheater" and that he did not love them any more. In all other respects she had always been a good mother. In the divorce application, Jasmin applied for sole custody with no access to Luke. The father also applied for sole custody with generous access to Jasmin.

(a) Is the fact that Luke committed adultery an important factor in deciding the issue of custody? Why or why not?

(b) In considering the custody application, what conduct of the parents, if any, is relevant in determining the children's best interests? Explain how the conduct would be viewed in the context of the factors in the *Divorce Act*.

Joint Custody

The *Divorce Act* permits the court to award custody or access to "one or more persons", which provides the authority to grant joint custody orders.[23]

What is Joint Custody?

Joint custody can take several different forms. However, the most important feature of a joint custody arrangement is that each parent who shares custody is entitled to participate in the major decisions affecting the child's life; i.e., health, religion, social activities, and general welfare. In addition each parent is entitled to exercise the incidents of custody when the child is with him or her. The parents' legal rights do not necessarily co-exist at the same time and therefore the court will usually define when

---

[23] *Divorce Act*, s. 16(4).

a child is under the care and control of each parent. Even though the parents have joint decision-making powers, they may not share physical custody to the same extent. In reality, one parent is usually designated as the parent having primary residence of the child while the other parent spends generous periods of time with the child. Although joint custody orders are usually made between parents, it is also possible to award joint custody between a parent and another person, such as a grandparent.

Circumstances in which Joint Custody is Appropriate

At one time, joint custody was viewed as an exceptional order that could only be imposed if both parents agreed to it.[24] Joint custody could only be granted where each parent accepted the other as a fit parent and each believed they could cooperate with the other. Above all, it required a willingness on the part of both parents to work together to make the arrangement successful.[25] Unless both parents were willing to cooperate and communicate, joint custody was not awarded.[26]

The courts presently take a more expansive and less restrictive view of joint custody and when it should be awarded. A court will sometimes award joint custody if it is in the best interests of the children, even if one or both parents do not want joint custody. It appears that there must be some history of cooperation and appropriate communication between the parents in order for the courts to award what is sometimes referred to as "coercive joint custody".[27] Increasingly, the courts are awarding joint custody if both parents are capable of meeting the children's needs and neither parent has disentitled himself or herself to custody. The court will examine whether the parent seeking joint custody is the cause of the parental conflict that undermines the parents' ability to communicate. If so, joint custody might be denied.

Ladisa v. Ladisa (2005), 193 O.A.C. 336, 11 R.F.L. (6th) 50 (Ont. C.A.)

Mr. and Mrs. Ladisa were married for 16 years and had three children, aged 16, 13 and 9. The mother had worked outside the home during most

---

[24] *Baker v. Baker* (1979), 8 R.F.L. (2d) 236 (Ont. C.A.); *Kruger v. Kruger* (1979), 11 R.F.L. (2d) 52, 25 O.R. (2d) 673, 104 D.L.R. (3d) 481 (Ont. C.A.). For a more current case following this principle, see *Hildinger v. Carroll* (2004), 2004 CarswellOnt 444, [2004] O.J. No. 291, 2 R.F.L. (6th) 331 (Ont. C.A.), additional reasons at (2004), 2004 CarswellOnt 1334 (Ont. C.A.), leave to appeal refused (2004), 2004 CarswellOnt 4951 (S.C.C.).

[25] *Kruger v. Kruger, ibid.*

[26] *Baker v. Baker, supra* note 24.

[27] See *St. Pierre v. St. Pierre* (2005), 2005 CarswellOnt 1624 (Ont. S.C.J.) (although parents had extreme friction, there was absence of evidence of conflict involving children or causing children difficulty; parties had three-year history of joint custody).

of the marriage. The father worked in construction until his health deteriorated and he required surgery in 1991. Thereafter, the father worked only part-time and devoted his free time to caring for the home and the children until the parents separated. The mother also participated in the children's activities during the marriage, to the extent that she was able. After the parents separated, the two youngest remained with their mother while the oldest child was permitted to move between her parents' homes as she wished. The mother arranged for counselling for the children and the father had agreed to cooperate with her efforts.

At trial, there was evidence that there was intense conflict between the parents. However, there was also evidence of the parents' ability to cooperate. For example, when the daughter had emergency treatment for her fall, the parents were able to work out their differences. Teachers, neighbours, a sports coach and other hockey parents all testified that the parents had always acted appropriately towards each other and the children when together. When a child forgot something at the other parent's house, the parents always worked out an arrangement to fetch the item or sports equipment. Both parents made efforts to meet the financial needs of the children when those needs arose, without considering whether the other parent should be paying, or anticipating whether they would be reimbursed by the other.

The trial judge found that the children needed the parenting that both parents could give them and awarded the parties joint custody. The two youngest children were to reside with both parents on an alternating weekly basis. The eldest child was to reside primarily with the father. The parents were to communicate through a "communication book" or by e-mail. The mother appealed, arguing that joint custody was not appropriate in the circumstances because the parents were repeatedly in conflict.

Held: The appeal was dismissed, except that no order for custody was made with respect to the oldest child. Joint custody of the two youngest children was affirmed.

The trial judge properly took into consideration the history of co-parenting by the parents while they were married and following separation as well as the ties that the children had with both of their parents. Despite their personal strife and animosity, the parents had demonstrated that they could communicate effectively and place the interests of their children ahead of their own.

It is even more difficult to convince a court to change a joint custody agreement or order that is already in place. The onus is on the parent who seeks to change the order to sole custody to show why it would be in the best interests of the children to do so.[28] However, where both parents agree that joint custody is unworkable, this is a sufficient reason to change to sole custody.[29]

Parallel Parenting

Sometimes a court will award joint custody under a highly structured regime that allows each parent to make independent decisions with respect to the best interests of the children while the children are with him or her. In a parallel parenting arrangement, each parent is given equal status and he or she is entitled to exercise the rights and responsibilities of custody over independent spheres of a child's life, independently of one another. Parallel parenting arrangements are sometimes awarded where the court is concerned that the parent who has primary care of the children will try to force the other parent out of the children's lives, but the parental relationship is too full of conflict to make joint custody work.[30] Instead of co-parenting, the court awards parallel parenting. Such parenting orders often contain detailed arrangements about where the children will live, when the children will have contact with each parent, and methods for resolving disputes between the parents. The parents usually communicate through a "communication book" or through e-mail about all issues related to the children because they find it difficult to deal directly with each other in a civil manner. Parallel parenting arrangements are only ordered where the court is of the view that the children will benefit from a heightened involvement of both parents.

---

[28] See *Bender v. Bender* (1993), 1993 CarswellOnt 1631 (Ont. Gen. Div.) (agreement upheld); *Tester v. Tester* (1993), 1993 CarswellOnt 1632 (Ont. Prov. Div.) (agreement upheld); *Papp v. Hunter* (2004), 2004 CarswellOnt 1074 (Ont. S.C.J.), additional reasons at (2004), 2004 CarswellOnt 1982 (Ont. S.C.J.) (communication problems insufficient to change interim joint custody to sole custody).

[29] See *Crousset v. Crousset* (2003), 2003 CarswellOnt 1747 (Ont. S.C.J.).

[30] See *Sukhu v. Hamid* (2003), 2003 CarswellOnt 1102 (Ont. S.C.J.), additional reasons at (2004), 2004 CarswellOnt 181 (Ont. S.C.J.) (since whoever got sole custody would consider it a victory, which was not in the child's best interests, shared parenting continued under a highly structured regime); see also *Mol v. Mol* (1997), [1997] O.J. No. 4060, 1997 CarswellOnt 3693 (Ont. Gen. Div.) (parallel parenting imposed as form of joint custody even though mother adamantly opposed).

ACCESS

What is Access?

Access means permission to see a child or children who are in the legal custody of someone else.[31] Our current legislation generally gives an access parent the right to visit and be visited by the child, together with a right to make inquiries and be given information about the health, education and welfare of the child.[32] The Supreme Court of Canada has held that an access parent has the right to share his or her day-to-day life with the child unless this poses some risk to the child. On the other hand, a custodial parent does not have the right to dictate how the access parent should spend his or her time with the child. A court should only step in to control access in a situation where access poses a risk (physical or emotional) to the child or the child is unable to handle the stress resulting from the very different lifestyles of the parents.[33] Access is intended to facilitate the child building and continuing a meaningful relationship with the parent who does not have custody. As a general rule, access is unsupervised and should maximize contact between the access parent and the child.[34]

Reasonable Access

It is common for judges to order "reasonable access" and leave it up to the parents to work out the day-to-day terms of access. This arrangement works well when the parents are child focused and able to place the children's interests ahead of their own. Reasonable access is best for the children because of its flexibility to meet their needs. Children's needs change as they become older, their friends and peers become more important in their lives and they become involved in more extra-curricular activities. The adaptability of reasonable access allows the parents to vary their plans and time with the children in keeping with the children's changing needs and interests.

Specified Access

Where the parties are unable or unwilling to agree upon what amounts to "reasonable access", the court will order specified access, or partially specified access. Specified access sets minimum parameters of parenting

---

[31] *Evershed v. Evershed* (1882), 46 L.T. 690 at 691.
[32] *Divorce Act*, s. 16(5); *Children's Law Reform Act*, s. 20(5).
[33] *Young v. Young* (1993), 49 R.F.L. (3d) 117 (S.C.C.).
[34] *Young v. Young, ibid.*

responsibilities and usually deals with high-conflict dates, such as holidays, vacations, birthdays, setting out with whom they should be spent. In situations of high conflict, specified access can provide a very structured access schedule, setting out specific days and times of the week or month, also delineating places and activities for access.

Supervised Access

Supervised access means that access can only be exercised under the supervision of a third party, such as a trusted relative or friend or an agency that hires professionals to supervise access. It would only be ordered as a temporary measure where unsupervised access poses a physical or emotional risk to the child. For example, if the access parent were an alcoholic who could not be trusted not to become intoxicated while the child was in his or her care, supervision might be ordered. Sometimes, supervised access is ordered where a child is being re-introduced to a parent with whom he or she has not had a relationship for a long period of time.[35] The onus is on the person who seeks to limit access to demonstrate that supervised access is in the child's best interests.[36]

Supervised access is not seen as a long-term solution to access or parenting difficulties.[37] Usually, supervised access orders are made for a fixed period of time. If the problem requiring supervision cannot be addressed by a period of supervised access, the court might suspend access until the child is old enough to deal with the problem or, in extreme cases, terminate access altogether.

Factors Affecting Access

Just as with custody, a parent's conduct is only relevant insofar as it affects that parent's ability to meet the child's needs while they are together. The maximum contact principle continues to be an important factor in determining access to the parent who does not have custody. Most of the same factors that are relevant in determining best interests are similarly relevant to both entitlement to, and nature of, access.

---

[35] See *Romas v. Romas* (1999), 1999 CarswellBC 512 (B.C. S.C.) (access structured to address past difficulty in mother-daughter relationship); *N. (D.) v. K. (B.)* (1999), 48 R.F.L. (4th) 400 (Ont. S.C.J.) (restrictions imposed on resuming access after six-year lack of access).

[36] *Pastway v. Pastway* (1999), 49 R.F.L. (4th) 375 (Ont. Gen. Div.) (supervised access unnecessary); *Hagen v. Muir*, 2000 BCSC 575 (B.C. S.C.) (onus on person seeking supervision).

[37] *M. (B.P.) v. M. (B.L.D.E.)* (1992), 42 R.F.L. (3d) 349 (Ont. C.A.), leave to appeal refused (1993), 48 R.F.L. (3d) 232 (note) (S.C.C.).

VARIATIONS UNDER THE *DIVORCE ACT*

Variation of Child Support

Section 17(1)(a) of the *Divorce Act* allows the court to vary, rescind or suspend a support order, prospectively or retroactively, and section 17(4) requires the court to satisfy itself that there has been a change of circumstances as provided in the *Guidelines*. Section 17 of the *Guidelines* lists the changes of circumstances that would allow the court to make a variation order. These are:

- if the original order was a table amount, any change that would affect the amount. The change may be that there is a different number of children, or that the income of the payor has changed;

- if the original order was a non-table amount, any change in the circumstances of either parent, or child; and

- the coming into force of the *Guidelines*. In other words, anyone who had a support order before the *Guidelines* can have it recalculated as a *Guideline* amount.

Variation of Spousal Support

Section 15.3(1) of the *Divorce Act* requires the court to give priority to child support orders over spousal support orders. Therefore, where the payor spouse cannot pay the full amount of child support and spousal support the court would order, the court is obligated to make the full child support order and to reduce or eliminate spousal support, but must give reasons for doing so.[38] When child support is reduced or eliminated, the court can reconsider the question of spousal support.[39]

Section 17(1)(a) also allows a court to vary a spousal support order. The court can include in the variation order any terms and conditions it could have included in the original order.[40] Before making a variation order, the court must be satisfied that there has been a change in the circumstances of either spouse.[41] Again, the court cannot take into consideration any misconduct related to the marriage.[42] The variation order should fulfill the same objectives as an original order.[43]

---

[38] *Divorce Act*, s. 15.3(2).
[39] *Divorce Act*, s. 15.3(3).
[40] *Divorce Act*, s. 17(3).
[41] *Divorce Act*, s. 17(4.1).
[42] *Divorce Act*, s. 17(6).
[43] *Divorce Act*, s. 17(7).

Where the original order for support is time-limited or expires on the happening of an event, and support has expired, in order to have support re-instituted, the spouse would have to show that:

- a change is necessary to relieve economic hardship;

- the economic hardship results from a change of circumstances that is related to the marriage; and,

- if the changed circumstances had existed at the time of the order, they would have resulted in a different order.[44]

Tierney-Hynes v. Hynes (2005), [2005] O.J. No. 2661, 2005 CarswellOnt 2632 (Ont. C.A.), leave to appeal refused (2005), 2005 CarswellOnt 7437 (S.C.C.)

Appeal by the wife, Tierney-Hynes, from the order granting the husband, Hynes, summary judgment dismissing the wife's motion to reinstate spousal support. The parties had been married for ten years. They had three children. The wife had helped the husband during his medical education and training. During the marriage, the wife maintained the home and assumed responsibility for the children. The original divorce judgment required the husband to pay $300 per month in spousal support to the wife. Following separation, the husband's income fell from $72,000 to $62,000 per year and he left family practice to begin a residency in psychiatry. During his residency, his income fell to $30,000 per year. The husband applied to terminate spousal support and reduce the child support payable by him during his residency. The husband completed his training and subsequently earned an income of $250,000 per year. The wife argued that the termination of spousal support and decrease in child support were temporary until the completion of the husband's residency. The wife claimed that she was suffering from health problems that prevented her from becoming self-sufficient. The husband argued that the court did not have jurisdiction to vary the order, as it was not a positive order for support.

Held: Appeal allowed. The court had jurisdiction to vary the order terminating spousal support. There had been a statutory and jurisprudential shift away from the ideas of finality, certainty and self-sufficiency in spousal support. A spouse could move in and out of spousal support. The current *Divorce Act* did not restrict the court's jurisdiction to vary orders to those "providing for the support" of a spouse and contemplated applications for support subsequent to divorce proceedings.

---

[44] *Divorce Act*, s. 17(10).

Variation of Custody

A child custody or access order made under the *Divorce Act* can also be varied by the court, on the application of either spouse, or any other person.[45] If someone other than a spouse is applying for the variation, that person must obtain permission from the court.[46] The court can make any order on a variation application that it could have made in the original proceeding.[47] The court will only make a variation order if it finds that there has been a change in the conditions, means, needs, or other circumstances of the child since the order was made.[48] Again, the variation order must be in the best interest of the child.[49] The conduct of the adults is only relevant if it goes to the ability of that person to parent the child.[50] The maximum contact principle applies equally to variation proceedings as it does to the original order.[51]

---

[45] *Divorce Act*, s. 17(1)(b).
[46] *Divorce Act*, s. 17(2).
[47] *Divorce Act*, s. 17(3).
[48] *Divorce Act*, s. 17(5).
[49] *Divorce Act*, s. 17(5).
[50] *Divorce Act*, s. 17(6).
[51] *Divorce Act*, s. 17(9).

APPENDIX 5A

ONTARIO

Superior Court of Justice	Court File Number
(Name of court)	
at 114 Worsley Street, Barrie, Ontario, L4M 1M1	*Family Law Rules, O. Reg. 114/99*
Court office address	**Form 14: Notice of Motion**

Applicant(s)

Full legal name & address for service — street & number, municipality, postal code, telephone & fax numbers and e-mail address (if any).	*Lawyer's name & address — street & number, municipality, postal code, telephone & fax numbers and e-mail address (if any).*
Andrea Jane Carson **231 Lake Street** **Barrie, Ontario** **L4M 2J7**	**Allistair Ryan** **Barrister & Solicitor** **729 Simcoe Street, Suite 107** **Barrie, Ontario** **L4M 1M1** **Tel: (705) 739-7777** **Fax: (705) 739-7778**

Respondent(s)

Full legal name & address for service — street & number, municipality, postal code, telephone & fax numbers and e-mail address (if any).	*Lawyer's name & address — street & number, municipality, postal code, telephone & fax numbers and e-mail address (if any).*
Robert Bruce Carson **177 Downing Street, Unit 216** **Barrie, Ontario** **L4M 2J8**	

The person making this motion or the person's lawyer must contact the clerk of the court by telephone or otherwise to choose a time and date when the court could hear this motion.

TO THE PARTIES:

THE COURT WILL HEAR A MOTION on *(date)* **April 6, 2006**

at   **9:30 a.m.**   **, or as soon as possible after that time, at** *(place of hearing)*

114 Worsley Street, Barrie, Ontario, L4M 1M1

This motion will be made by *(name of person making the motion)* **Andrea Jane Carson**

who will be asking the court for an order for the item(s) listed on page 2 of this notice.

☒   A copy of the affidavit(s) in support of this motion is/are served with this notice.

☐   A notice of a case conference is served with this notice to change an order.

If this material is missing, you should talk to the court office immediately.

The person making this motion is also relying on the following documents in the continuing record: *(List documents.)*

1. Change Information Form (motion to change child support) Form 15 sworn on (date)

If you want to oppose this motion or to give your own views, you should talk to your own lawyer and prepare your own affidavit, serve it on all other parties not later than 4 days before the date above and file it at the court office not later 2 days before that date. Only written and affidavit evidence will be allowed at a motion unless the court gives permission for oral testimony. You may bring your lawyer to the motion.

IF YOU DO NOT COME TO THE MOTION, THE COURT MAY MAKE AN ORDER WITHOUT YOU AND ENFORCE IT AGAINST YOU.

_____ *Date of signature*	**Allistair Ryan** **Barrister & Solicitor** **729 Simcoe Street, Suite 107** **Barrie, Ontario** **L4M 1M1**
_____ *Signature of person making this motion or of person's lawyer*	**Tel: (705) 739-7777** **Fax: (705) 739-7778**
	Typed or printed name of person or of person's lawyer, address for service, telephone & fax number and e-mail address (if any)

NOTE TO PERSON MAKING THIS MOTION: *You MUST file a confirmation (Form 14C) not later than 2:00 p.m. 2 days before the date set out above.*

If this is a motion to change past and future support payments under an order that has been assigned to a government agency, you must also serve this notice on that agency. If you do not, the agency can ask the court to set aside any order that you may get in this motion and can ask for costs against you.

Form 14:	Notice of Motion	(page 2)	Court File Number

State the order or orders requested on this motion.

1. An order changing child support in accordance with the Child Support Guidelines from $1,148 per month to $1,225 per month.

2. An order requiring the respondent to pay $6,000 annually toward the university costs of the child Justin Bruce Carson, as extraordinary expenses in accordance with the Child Support Guidelines.

NOTE: You must attach a *summary of court cases* (Form 8E) to this notice of motion.

APPENDIX 5B

ONTARIO

Superior Court of Justice

_____
(Name of court)

at **114 Worsley Street, Barrie, Ontario, L4M 1M1**
_____
Court office address

Court File Number

Family Law Rules, O. Reg. 202/01

**Form 15: Change
Information Form
(motion to change
child support)**

Recipients(s)

Full legal name & address for service — street & number, municipality, postal code, telephone & fax numbers and e-mail address (if any).	*Lawyer's name & address — street & number, municipality, postal code, telephone & fax numbers and e-mail address (if any).*
Andrea Jane Carson **231 Lake Street** **Barrie, Ontario** **L4M 2J7**	**Allistair Ryan** **Barrister & Solicitor** **729 Simcoe Street, Suite 107** **Barrie, Ontario** **L4M 1M1** **Tel: (705) 739-7777** **Fax: (705) 739-7778**

Payor

Full legal name & address for service — street & number, municipality, postal code, telephone & fax numbers and e-mail address (if any).	*Lawyer's name & address — street & number, municipality, postal code, telephone & fax numbers and e-mail address (if any).*
Robert Bruce Carson **177 Downing Street, Unit 216** **Barrie, Ontario** **L4M 2J8**	

PART 1 – GENERAL INFORMATION

(This part should be filled out to the best ability of the party asking for a change in a child support order.)

My name is *(full legal name)* **Andrea Jane Carson**

I live in *(municipality & province)* **Barrie, Ontario**

and I swear that the following is true:

1.   I am the   ☒ support recipient.   ☐ support payor.

2.   The payor, *(payor's full legal name)* **Robert Bruce Carson**

     was born on *(date of birth) (d, m, y)* **15 September, 1961**

     lives in *(municipality & province)* **Barrie, Ontario**

     and, at the present time, is   ☐ married   ☐ living in a spousal relationship   ☒ *(Other. Specify.)*
                             ☐ separated   ☐ living in a same-sex partner relationship   **divorced**

3.   The recipient, *(recipient's full legal name)* **Andrea Jane Carson**

     was born on *(date of birth) (d,m,y)* **28 February, 1963**

     lives in *(municipality & province)* **Barrie, Ontario**

     and, at the present time, is   ☐ married   ☐ living in a spousal relationship   ☒ *(Other. Specify.)*
                             ☐ separated   ☐ living in a same-sex partner relationship   **divorced**

4.   The payor and the recipient:

     ☒ were married on *(date)* **July 23, 1986**

     ☒ separated on *(date)* **August 20, 2002**

     ☐ started living together on *(date)* _____

     ☐ never lived together.

Form 15:   **Change Information Form**   **(page 2)**
           (motion to change child support)

Court File Number

5.   The following chart gives basic information about the child(ren) in this case:
List all children involved in this case, even those for whom no support is being claimed.

Child's full legal name	Age	Birthdate *(d, m, y)*	Lives in *(municipality & province)*	Now living with *(name of person and relationship to child)*	Support claimed for child? *(YES or NO)*
Justin Bruce Carson	18	19 April, 1988	Barrie, Ontario	Andrea Jane Carson, mother	Yes
Tara Lynn Carson	15	31 January, 1991	Barrie, Ontario	Andrea Jane Carson, mother	Yes
Kimberley Anne Carson	12	2 August, 1994	Barrie, Ontario	Andrea Jane Carson, mother	Yes

6.   The access arrangements for the child(ren) are as follows:

Child's name	Access arrangement
Justin Bruce Carson	reasonable access
Tara Lynn Carson	alternate weekends with father
Kimberley Anne Carson	alternate weekends with father

7.   I attached a copy of the existing   ☒ court order   ☐ agreement
that deals with the child support to be varied. The details of this **order/agreement** are as follows:

Date of order or Agreement	Present child support payment	Other terms of child support *(such as cost-of-living increases)*	Present support payment (if any) for spouse or same-sex partner
September 25, 2003	$ 1,148.00 *per* **month**		$ _____ , *per* _____

8.   The payment status of this order/agreement as of today is as follows:

Child support owed to recipient	Child support owed to other(s) *(such as Ministry of Community & Social Services)*	Spousal or same-sex partner support owed to recipient	Spousal or same-sex partner support owed to other(s) *(such as Ministry of Community & Social Services)*
$ 0.00	$	$	$

(If money is owing, attach a statement of money owed (Form 26)).

Form 15:	**Change Information Form** (motion to change child support)	**(page 3)**	Court File Number

9. This order/agreement ☒ has never been ☐ has been

assigned to ☒ the Ontario Ministry of Community and Social Services

☐ the municipality of *(name)* _____

☐ *(Other. Specify.)* _____

The details of this assignment are *(Give date of assignment, indicate whether it is still in effect and add any other information known to you.)*

10. I am asking to change the child support in the order/agreement because:

☐ the order/agreement was made before the applicable Child Support Guidelines came into effect.

☒ a change in circumstances has taken place. *(Give details of change in circumstances.)*

1. The oldest child, Justin Bruce Carson is now 18 years of age, has completed high school and has been accepted into a science program at the University of Guelph. The cost of the program, including tuition, books and residence fees will be $12,000 annually for four years. The recipient is unable to pay these expenses and proposes that the parties share the expenses in proportion to their incomes.

2. The payor's income has increased from $65,000 to $71,000 annually since the making of the previous order.

11. I ask that the child support be calculated as follows:

☒ the basic table amount listed in the Child Support Guidelines of *(give a dollar amount where possible)*

$ _____ 1,225.00 _____ per month for the *(number of children)* **3** child(ren) on the basis of the payor's total

annual income of *(give a dollar amount where possible)* $ _____ **71,000.00** _____, with payments to begin on

(date) **June 1, 2006** _____

☒ the following special or extraordinary expenses (add-ons):

Child's name	Type of expense	Amount	Payor's share	Child's contribution	Termination date (if known)
Justin Bruce Carson	**University tuition, residence, books**	12,000.00	**6,000.00**	3,000.00	

☐ an amount of $ _____ per month, which is different from the table amount listed in the Child Support

Guidelines, with payments to start on *(date)* _____

The reason(s) for my request for a different amount is/are that:

☐ the parties consent to a different amount.
   ☐ I have attached a separate sheet to this form that explains why this is a reasonable arrangement for the child(ren).
   ☐ The recipient is getting social assistance payments from a public agency whose consent to this arrangement is needed. I am attaching the agency's consent to this form.

☐ as can be seen from paragraphs 5 and 6 above, the parties have shared custody to the child(ren) *(the payor has a child at least 40% of the time).*
   ☐ I have attached a separate sheet to this form that compares the table amounts from the Child Support Guidelines for each of the parties and that shows the increased cost of the shared custody arrangement and shows the financial circumstances of each party and of each child for whom support is claimed.
   ☐ The parties are consenting to this arrangement and I have attached a separate sheet to this form that explains why this is a reasonable arrangement for the child(ren).

☐ as can be seen from paragraph 5 above, custody of the children is split between the parties. I have attached a separate sheet to this form that calculates the difference between the amount that each party would otherwise pay to the other under the guidelines.

FLR 15 (07/01)

Form 15:   **Change Information Form**   **(page 4)**   Court File Number
              (motion to change child support)

☐ a child is 18 or more years old and I attach to this form a separate sheet that calculates the amount of support for this child.

☒ a child contributes to **his** own support and I attach to this form a separate sheet showing the amount of the child's own income.

☐ the payor's annual income is over $150,000 and I have attached to this form a separate sheet that calculates the amount of support that I want to be put in an order.

☐ under the order/agreement, *(name of child)* _____ is the subject of special provisions that I have detailed on a separate sheet that I have attached to this form.

☐ the payor stands in the place of a natural parent to *(name of child)* _____ and I attach to this form a separate sheet that gives the details of another parent's duty to pay support for this child as well as the details of the calculation of the amount of support requested.

☐ the amount listed in the Child Support Guidelines would cause undue hardship to me or to the child(ren) for whom support is claimed. I attach to this form a separate sheet that compares the living standards of the parties.

12. I ask that the child support owed be paid off as follows:

☐ the child support owed to *(name of recipient)* _____

should be fixed at $ _____ as of *(date)* _____

and to be paid off at the rate of $ _____ per month, with _____

payments to begin on *(date)* _____

☐ the child support owed to *(name of agency or other person)* _____

should be fixed at $ _____ as of *(date)* _____

and to be paid off at the rate of $ _____ per month, with _____

payments to begin on *(date)* _____

Sworn before me at   **CITY of BARRIE** _____
                                          municipality

In **PROVINCE of ONTARIO** _____
                          province, state or country

On _____   _____
       date   _____   *Signature*
                               Commissioner for taking affidavits   *(This form is to be signed in front*
                               (Type or print name below if signature is illegible.)   *of a lawyer, justice of the peace,*
                                                          notary public or commissioner
                                                          for taking affidavits.)

| Form 15: | **Change Information Form** (motion to change child support) | **(page 5)** | Court File Number |

PART 2 – INFORMATION FROM SUPPORT PAYOR

My name is *(full legal name)* Robert Bruce Carson

I live in *(municipality & province)* Barrie, Ontario

and I swear that the following is true:

13. I am the support payor in this case.

14. My total income will be $ _____ **58,000.00** _for this year.

15. On the basis of my annual income, the table amount from the Child Support Guidelines for *(number of children)*

     3 _____ child(ren) is $ _____ **1,045.00** per month.

16. My financial statement ☒ is attached   ☐ is not attached.

     (NOTE: *You do not need to attach a financial statement if you and the other party have filled out the appropriate portion of the consent (Form 15A) and have agreed not to file a financial statement. Nevertheless, because the Child Support Guidelines have a new way of computing the amount of child support, YOU MUST PROVIDE THE COURT WITH NEW ADDITIONAL INFORMATION. That amount is set out in a table that is geared to the payor's annual income and to the number of children who are entitled to support. Under certain conditions, the annual income of the recipient may also be taken into account, in which case, the recipient will have to provide the court with the same additional information in paragraphs 19 and 20 below.)*

17. I attach the following financial information about me:

     (a) a copy of every personal income tax return that I filed with Revenue Canada for the 3 most recent taxation years;

     (b) a copy of every notice of assessment or re-assessment from Revenue Canada of those returns; and

     (c) ☒ *(applies only if you are an employee)* proof of this year's earnings from my employer as required by clause 21(1)(c) of the Child Support Guidelines.

     ☐ *(applies only if you are self-employed, or you are a partner in a partnership or you control a corporation or are a beneficiary under a trust)* the documents listed in clauses 21(1)(d), (e), (f) or (g) of the Child Support Guidelines.

Sworn before me at   **CITY of BARRIE** _____
                                                          municipality

In **PROVINCE of ONTARIO** _____
                                       province, state or country

On _____
        date   _____
                        Commissioner for taking affidavits
                        (Type or print name below if signature is illegible.)

_____
Signature
(This form is to be signed in front of a lawyer, justice of the peace, notary public or commissioner for taking affidavits.)

Form 15:	**Change Information Form** (motion to change child support)	**(page 6)**	Court File Number

PART 3 – INFORMATION FROM SUPPORT RECIPIENT

Because the Child Support Guidelines have a new way of computing the amount of child support, YOU MUST PROVIDE THE COURT WITH NEW ADDITIONAL INFORMATION. That amount is set out in a table that is geared to the payor's annual income and to the number of children who are entitled to support. Under certain conditions, the annual income of the recipient may also be taken into account, in which case, the recipient will have to provide the court with the same additional information in paragraph 19 and 20 below.

My name is *(full legal name)* **Andrea Jane Carson**

I live in *(municipality & province)* **Barrie, Ontario**

and I swear that the following is true:

18. I am the support recipient in this case.

Fill in paragraphs 19 and 20 only if:

- *the change for which you are asking is for an amount that is different from that calculated under the appropriate table in the Child Support Guidelines;*
- *the change for which you are asking relates to a child over the age of 18 years, a child for whom the payor stands in the place of a parent or a child with respect to whom the payor has access or physical custody not less than 40% of the time over the course of the year,*
- *each party has custody of one or more children;*
- *the payor's annual income as determined under the guidelines is more than $150,000*
- *either party claims that an order according to the guidelines amount would result in undue hardship.*

19. My total income

☒ will be $ **35,500.00** for this year;

☒ was $ **34,729.00** for last year; and

☒ was $ **34,100.00** for the year before that.

20. I attach the following financial information about me:
    (a) a copy of every personal income tax return that I filed with Revenue Canada for the three most recent taxation years;
    (b) a copy of every notice of assessment or re-assessment from Revenue Canada of those returns; and
    (c) ☒ *[applies only if you are an employee]* proof of this year's earnings from my employer as required by clause 21(1)*(c)* of the Child Support Guidelines.
    ☐ *[applies only if you are self-employed, or you are a partner in a partnership or you control a corporation or are a beneficiary under a trust]* the documents listed in clauses 21(1)*(d)*, *(e)*, *(f)*, or *(g)* of the Child Support Guidelines.

21. My financial statement   ☒ is attached   ☐ is not attached.

(NOTE: *You do not need to attach a financial statement if you and the other party have signed a consent in Form 15A.)*

Sworn before me at   **CITY of BARRIE**

                            municipality

In **PROVINCE of ONTARIO**

                     province, state or country

On

              date   *Commissioner for taking affidavits*
 (Type or print name below if signature is illegible.)

Signature
(This form is to be signed in front of a lawyer, justice of the peace, notary public or commissioner for taking affidavits.)

CHAPTER 6

THE *FAMILY LAW ACT*—FAMILY PROPERTY

INTRODUCTION

In response to the Supreme Court of Canada *Murdoch*[1] decision, discussed in Chapter 1, all provinces, including Ontario, have passed laws that give effect to an equitable distribution of property on marriage breakdown. In Ontario, the division of property is governed by Part 1 of the *Family Law Act*.[2] Upon marriage breakdown or on the death of a spouse, the spouses or the surviving spouse are entitled to an "equalization of net family properties". Rather than actually dividing the property itself, each spouse calculates the value of his or her net family property and the spouse with the higher net family property is required to pay half the difference in values to the other spouse.

EQUAL STATUS OF SPOUSES AND MARRIAGE AS PARTNERSHIP

The shift in society's perspective on the marital relationship is reflected in the preamble to the FLA itself. The most notable elements of the preamble are the concept of the equal status of the spouses in the marriage and the view of marriage as a partnership. The preamble represents the philosophical underpinning of the FLA and is intended to assist in explaining its purpose and object. It is particularly evident in the Part 1 dealing with property division. The FLA must be interpreted in light of the preamble in a way that brings the concepts of equal status of the spouses and marriage as a partnership to life.

The section of the FLA authorizing the actual division of property further elaborates upon the philosophy behind the division of property. The purpose of the section is to "recognize that child care, household management and financial provision are the joint responsibilities of the spouses and that inherent in the marital relationship there is equal contribution, whether financial or otherwise, by the spouses to the assumption of these respon-

---

[1] *Murdoch v. Murdoch* (1973), [1975] 1 S.C.R. 423 (S.C.C.).
[2] R.S.O. 1990, c. F.3, as amended [hereinafter "FLA"].

sibilities, entitling each spouse to the equalization of the net family properties. . . ."[3] This section appears to address directly the inequitable result in the *Murdoch* case. There is now a presumption that the spouses make an equal contribution to the marriage, whether financially or in less tangible ways.

WHO CAN APPLY FOR EQUALIZATION OF NET FAMILY PROPERTIES

Married Spouses

Pursuant to the FLA, only a married spouse or a formerly married spouse is entitled to make a claim for equalization of property. The spousal rights to equalization apply equally to opposite-sex and same-sex marriages. However, "spouse" also includes anyone who went through a form a marriage in good faith. The definition includes parties to a void or voidable marriage, as long as the person who seeks the equalization entered the marriage in good faith.[4] The result of this could mean that in an invalid marriage, one party may have equalization rights while the other (who did not act in good faith) does not.

The definition of "spouse" also extends to polygamous marriages, provided that the marriage took place in a jurisdiction that recognizes such marriages as valid.[5]

Surviving Spouse on Death of Other Spouse

In addition, on the death of a spouse, the surviving spouse may choose his or her equalization rights instead of other inheritance rights to which he or she is entitled. This election is only available where the net family property of the deceased spouse is greater than that of the surviving spouse.[6]

Common-Law Spouses Excluded

In Ontario, the equalization of property is not available to cohabiting couples who have never married. In other words, contrary to popular belief, common-law couples do not qualify in Ontario for a division of property

---

[3] FLA, s. 5(7).
[4] FLA, s. 5(1), s. 1(1).
[5] FLA, s. 5(2).
[6] FLA, s. 6(1)-(3).

pursuant to the FLA regime, no matter how long they have lived together in a marriage-like relationship. Other provinces, such as Saskatchewan, have changed their matrimonial property legislation to specifically include common-law spouses. Some Canadian lawyers and scholars have argued that by excluding common-law spouses from the provincial property regimes, the legislation violates the equality rights section of the *Charter of Rights and Freedoms*. They claimed that it is discrimination based on marital status, based on section 15 of the *Charter*, to permit greater benefits to married spouses than to common-law spouses.

**Walsh v. Bona, 32 R.F.L. (5th) 81,
(sub nom. *Nova Scotia (Attorney General) v. Walsh*)
221 D.L.R. (4th) 1, (sub nom. *Nova Scotia
(Attorney General) v. Walsh*) [2002] 4 S.C.R. 325 (S.C.C.)**

A man and a woman in Nova Scotia cohabited together for ten years, but never married. During that time, they had two children together and owned a home. When the couple separated, the woman applied for a division of assets acquired during their "marriage". The term "spouse" in the Nova Scotia *Matrimonial Property Act* did not include common-law spouses. The woman asked the court to determine whether the exclusion of common-law spouses from the Act violated section 15(1) of the *Charter of Rights and Freedoms*. The trial judge dismissed the application and held that marital status was not an analogous ground to those listed in section 15(1) of the *Charter*. The trial judge also held that even if it was discrimination, it was saved by section 1 of the *Charter*. The woman's appeal was allowed by the Nova Scotia Court of Appeal, which held that, as a person, in a common-law relationship, the woman was denied the benefits granted to similar persons in a marriage relationship simply on the ground that she and the man were not married. The Crown appealed this decision.

Held: The appeal was allowed. Excluding common-law spouses from the matrimonial property regime did not violate the *Charter*. The decision to marry or not was an intensely personal one that involved a complex set of considerations by an individual. Many people in relationships of some permanence have chosen to avoid the institution of marriage and the legal consequences that flow from it. The application of the Act to married persons only respects the fundamental autonomy and dignity of the individual to make choices about their relationships. There was no implication that unmarried spouses were less valued members of Canadian society than married spouses. By refusing to impose limitations that restrict freedom of choice among persons in conjugal relationships, the court was actually ensuring that the object of section 15(1) of the *Charter* was respected.

VALUATION DATE

The valuation date is the date on which property is valued for purposes of equalization between the spouses. The FLA establishes an inflexible valuation date, which is the close of business on the earliest of the following dates:

- the date the spouse separate with no reasonable prospect of reconciliation;
- the date the divorce is granted;
- the date the marriage is declared a nullity;
- the date one of the spouses commences an application based on subsection 5(3) (improvident depletion) that is subsequently granted; and
- the date before the date on which one spouse dies leaving the other spouse surviving.

Permanent Separation

In the vast majority of cases, the parties will use the date of permanent separation as their valuation date, as a permanent separation will almost always occur before the parties are divorced or the marriage is declared a nullity. The parties must therefore establish when they commenced living separate and apart. For this purpose, the courts use similar principles to those used for establishing "separate and apart" under the *Divorce Act*. The parties must also show that there was no reasonable prospect that cohabitation would resume. For example, if the spouses were attending marriage counselling after they separated, then a reasonable prospect of resuming cohabitation would exist. Just as under the *Divorce Act*, it is also possible for the parties to live separate and apart under the same roof, as long as they can prove they are living completely separate lives.

Improvident Depletion

Another situation that is invoked much less frequently is where there is a serious danger that the other spouse might deplete his or her net family property.[7] If a spouse begins to reduce his or her property by either giving it away, selling it, or spending it, this conduct could seriously prejudice the property rights of the other spouse. If a spouse commences an application for improvident depletion that is subsequently granted, then valuation day is the day the application is commenced. Once an equalization of net family

---

[7] FLA, s. 5(3).

properties has been granted under section 5(3), neither spouse can make a further application for an equalization of net family properties.

Death of a Spouse

If the surviving spouse chooses an equalization of net family properties (which will be discussed in more detail later in this chapter), then the valuation date is the day before the date of death. The day before is used to avoid transfers that take place by operation of law on death (such as property held in joint tenancy transferring to the joint owner).

Limitation Periods

Where an application is brought on the basis of divorce, nullity, or permanent separation of the spouses, the application must be commenced within six years of separation or two years after the divorce, whichever comes first.[8] An application based on the death of a spouse must be brought within six months of the death of the spouse.[9]

The FLA provides for extending a limitation period if there are obvious grounds for relief, the delay was incurred in good faith, and no one would be prejudiced by the delay.[10] A delay would be considered to be in good faith if one of the spouses did not know of his or her rights or if the delay was caused by ongoing settlement negotiations. However, if a spouse has the opportunity to make inquiries about his or her rights, but instead chooses to be ignorant or wilfully blind of those rights, this would not be acting in good faith. Similarly, if one spouse arranges his or her financial affairs in reliance upon the two-year limitation period, that spouse would be prejudiced, if an extension were permitted.

DEFINING PROPERTY

What is Property?

When spouses separate, each spouse must include in his or her net family property the value of all property that he or she owned on valuation day, subject to certain deductions and exclusions, which will be discussed later in this chapter. The FLA has defined property to include any present or

---

[8] FLA, s. 7(3)(a), (b).
[9] FLA, s. 7(3)(c).
[10] FLA, s. 2(8).

future interest in real or personal property, whether it is vested or contingent.[11] A property right that is contingent means that it only comes into effect on the happening of a specified future event, such as the right to receive an inheritance when your brother reaches age 30.

All property, unless expressly excluded by the Act, is included in a spouse's net family property. This includes such assets as the family residence, the cottage, family vehicles, bank accounts, stocks, bonds, shares, pensions, annuities, RRSPs, farms, and businesses. There is no distinction between business assets and family assets. If the asset is owned on valuation day, it must be included unless it comes within the list of specified deductions or exclusions in the FLA. There is no discretion in the court to withdraw an asset from the accounting, as all property must be included and valued.[12]

Some specific assets that the courts have found to constitute property include the following:

- the right to receive income from a trust even if the recipient has no right to the body of the trust;
- a doctor's accounts receivable from OHIP;
- an interest in a professional practice or partnership;
- banked sick leave benefits and vacation pay accumulated during marriage; and
- air miles credits.

What is *Not* Property?

On the other hand, there are certain things that should not be classed as "property" under the FLA. For example, the courts have refused to include "debts" in defining property under the FLA. There is no provision for an equalization of the parties' debts.[13] Neither is a spouse's job classed as property under the FLA.[14] A job cannot be sold and has no exchange value and is uncertain, as it may be lost for business or personal reasons.

Caratun v. Caratun (1992), 42 R.F.L. (3d) 113, 10 O.R. (3d) 385, 96 D.L.R. (4th) 404, 58 O.A.C. 140 (Ont. C.A.), leave to appeal refused (1993), 13 O.R. (3d) xvi (note) (S.C.C.)

...[T]he parties met in Romania in 1972 [when] the husband was completing his internship in medicine. The wife moved to Israel in 1973, and following

---

[11] FLA, s. 4(1).

[12] *Caratun v. Caratun* (1992), 42 R.F.L. (3d) 113, 96 D.L.R. (4th) 404, 10 O.R. (3d) 385, 58 O.A.C. 140 (Ont. C.A.), leave to appeal refused (1993), 46 R.F.L. (3d) 314 (note), 101 D.L.R. (4th) vii (note), 13 O.R. (3d) xvi (note) (S.C.C.).

[13] *Powers v. Naston-Powers* (1990), 28 R.F.L. (3d) 69 (Ont. H.C.).

[14] *Linton v. Linton* (1990), 1 O.R. (3d) 1, 30 R.F.L. (3d) 1, 75 D.L.R. (4th) 637, 42 O.A.C. 328, 41 E.T.R. 85 (Ont. C.A.).

their marriage she arranged for the husband to join her in 1977. Three months later the husband unilaterally decided to leave that country. He wanted to immigrate to North America to practise dentistry. The wife gave up a tenured position that she held at a university and joined the husband in a refugee camp. The parties arrived in Canada in 1978 and both parties worked while the husband continued his efforts to obtain his dental licence. In May 1981, after a number of attempts, the husband finally obtained his licence to practise dentistry in Ontario; two days later he told his wife that he wanted a divorce. In divorce proceedings the wife claimed support and an interest in the husband's dental licence and right to practise. The trial judge held that the licence and right to practise were property. . .[and the] wife was awarded a lump sum of $30,000 for her contribution to the acquisition of the husband's dentistry licence. . . .. [She was also awarded lump sum spousal support.]

The husband appealed. [At 113-114 (R.F.L.).]

Held: The appeal was dismissed, but the dental licence was *not* property.

A professional licence or right to practise did not constitute property within the meaning of section 4 of the *Family Law Act*. The broad definition of property in the FLA clearly encompasses many forms of intangibles, which are "bundles of rights" such as share certificates. However, the only right attached to a professional licence is a present and future right to work in a particular profession. The nature of this right causes insurmountable difficulties in treating it as property for matrimonial purposes. First, the right, by its very nature is personal to the holder and is incapable of transfer. Although a practice itself is capable of transfer, where the spouses separate before a practice is built up, there is nothing of value to transfer. Second, a licence requires the personal efforts of the holder in order to be of any value in the future. Third, the only difference between a professional licence and any other right to work is its exclusivity. Without the personal efforts of the licensee, the licence will produce nothing. The only provisions of the FLA that allow one spouse to share in the fruits of the other spouse's future labours are the support provisions that do not form part of the equalization payment. When a marriage ends, the partnership envisioned by the FLA ends. Placing a value on future labours of either spouse for purposes of equalization would frustrate the policy objectives of the Act.

However, the wife had made a significant contribution to the marriage and to the husband's ability to obtain his dental licence. She had sacrificed, or at least, delayed her own career advancement to assist her husband in furthering his. Therefore, a compensatory support order pursuant to the *Divorce Act* was appropriate. The $30,000 calculated by the trial judge would fairly compensate the wife for her efforts and the court had no reason to interfere with that assessment. The lump sum award should be maintained, but as compensatory support rather than as an interest in property.

Application Questions

1. Which of the following couples would be eligible for equalization of net family property under the *Family Law Act*?

   (a) Olga and Peter had been married for six years prior to separation.

   yes

   (b) Pat and Nick had cohabited for four years, but never married, and had two children prior to separation.

   (Kids dont mean anything) *no, not legally married*

   (c) Kendra and Obama had married in good faith, but later discovered that Obama's previous divorce was not recognized in Canada. They are now separated.

   yes bc they married in good faith

   (d) Anna and Sandra were married for six months prior to their separation. *yes doesnt matter how long.*

   (e) Ken and Shirley were married for twenty years before Ken dropped dead suddenly of a heart attack. Ken had accumulated significantly more property than Shirley during the marriage. Three months after Ken's death, Shirley wants to apply for equalization, even though Ken has included her in his will.

   yes.

2. Which of the following items would be defined as "property" under the FLA? *(are these defined as property)*

   (a) shares in a company *yes.*

   (b) money in a savings account *yes.*

   (c) a wife's licence to practise medicine where the husband had put her through medical school *no.*

   (d) a husband's accumulated sick leave *yes. (accumulated means property)*

   (e) a wife's debts to pay for a family vacation *no.*

   (f) a husband's real estate business *yes.* *(partnership = only half)*

WHAT IS "NET FAMILY PROPERTY" (NFP)?

"Net family property" is essentially all property that is owned by a spouse on the valuation date, after subtracting the deductions and exclusions set out in the FLA.[15] These deductions and exclusions are set out below.

Each spouse must calculate his or her net family property separately. The spouse must add up the value of all the property owned by him or her on the valuation date. If assets are owned jointly, then each spouse would

---

[15] FLA, s. 4(1).

include one-half the value of that asset in his or her NFP. No spouse is allowed to have a net family property that is less than zero.[16]

Deductions from "Net Family Property"

There are two classes of property that are considered deductions from NFP. These are 1) a spouse's debts and liabilities on valuation date; and 2) the net value of property (other than the matrimonial home) owned on the date of marriage.

Debts and Liabilities Outstanding on Valuation Date

The debts and liabilities owed by a spouse on valuation date must be deducted from the value of the property owned on that date. These debts can include unpaid income or property taxes, mortgages, loans, and credit card debts. If the spouses jointly own the matrimonial home, then each will deduct one-half of the value of the mortgage from his or her NFP. If the parents of one spouse have provided money to purchase an asset, such as a home, unless there is satisfactory evidence that it was a loan, the court will find that the money was a gift to the spouses. Evidence that it was a loan would be either a written agreement or evidence that part of the amount had been repaid. A contingent liability, such as co-signing of a loan for another person, is also included as a liability on valuation date, but it is usually reduced in value to reflect the fact that the spouse may not be called upon to pay it.

Net Value of Property Owned on Date of Marriage

A spouse is entitled to subtract from the value of property owned on valuation date the net value of property owned at the date of marriage. Property owned at the date of marriage could be property that was purchased or received as a gift or inheritance by the spouse prior to the marriage. A person may bring both assets and debts into the marriage. If a spouse brings a vehicle and stocks and bonds into the marriage, but also has an outstanding student loan, then the loan must be subtracted from his or her assets to arrive at his or her net worth at the date of marriage. If a spouse's debts at the date of marriage are greater than their assets, then they will bring a negative value into the marriage. This negative deduction will actually form an "addition" to the spouse's NFP on valuation date.

---

[16] FLA, s. 4(5).

Where a spouse deducts an asset brought into the marriage, if that same asset, such as stocks, is still owned on valuation date, the value on valuation date must be included in NFP. The result of this will be that any increase in value, since the date of marriage, would be shared with the spouse. However, the deduction is available regardless of what happens to the pre-marital property during the marriage. It is not necessary that a spouse still own the asset on valuation day in order to be able to deduct it as a pre-marriage asset.

Matrimonial Home Excepted

There is one exception to a spouse's ability to deduct the value of property brought into the marriage and that is the matrimonial home. If a spouse brings a home into the marriage, and that home is ordinarily occupied by the couple as their family residence at the time of separation, then the spouse cannot deduct the value of the home on the date of marriage. However, if the home, at the time of separation, has been sold, or is rented while the parties live elsewhere, then the spouse who brought the home into the marriage is entitled to deduct its value on the date of marriage from his or her NFP. In the latter case, the home would not be a matrimonial home under the Act.

Application Questions

When Darla and Jim got married, Darla had a Visa debt of $765, a student loan of $6,000, and a car loan in the amount of $2,000. Before the marriage, she had received an inheritance from her grandfather, which included a coin collection worth $10,000 and some shares in the family company valued at $16,000. Jim brought bonds valued at $20,000 and a Corvette worth $80,000 into the marriage, and had $8,000 in a savings account. He also owned a home that the couple lived in until the date of their separation, four years later. The home was worth $250,000 when the parties married. Jim owed $30,000 on a line of credit and had a mortgage of $100,000 on the home at the time of marriage.

(a) What, if anything, can Darla claim as a pre-marital deduction?

(b) What, if anything, can Jim claim as a pre-marital deduction?

Exclusions from Net Family Property

All property must be included in a spouse's NFP on valuation date unless it can be deducted under section 4(1) or excluded under section 4(2) of the FLA. It is up to the person who is alleging a deduction or exclusion to prove its existence.[17] In order to be counted as an exclusion, the property must still be owned by the spouse on valuation date. If the money has been spent or used up, then a spouse is not entitled to subtract it from his or her NFP.

Gift or Inheritance

A spouse is entitled to exclude from NFP a gift or inheritance received during the marriage from a third party.[18] The value to be excluded is the value of the asset on valuation date, rather than its value on the date it was received. The gift or inheritance must have been one that was received after the marriage. Gifts received prior to marriage will be deducted as pre-marital property. If the gift is spent on something other than property, such as a family vacation, then it cannot be excluded on separation. On the other hand, if a gift, such as shares in company, is still owned on valuation date and has increased in value by that date, the increased value of the gift can be excluded from the spouse's NFP. If a spouse places a gift of money in a joint account with his or her spouse, there is a presumption of a gift of one-half of the inheritance or gift. Finally, the gift must be from a third party rather than from the other spouse. Gifts between spouses are not excluded from the NFP of the spouse who received the gift.

However, if the spouse inherited or received the matrimonial home as a gift during the marriage, the spouse cannot exclude the value of the home on valuation date. Similarly, if a gift is used to purchase a matrimonial home, then the value of the home on valuation date can no longer be excluded.

Income from Gift or Inheritance

If a spouse inherits or receives an income-producing asset as a gift, such as a rental building, the spouse will exclude the value of the building itself from his or her NFP.[19] However, the spouse may also accumulate rental income from the building to the date of separation. This accumulated rental income can only be excluded if the person who gave the gift expressly states that the income is to be excluded. Therefore, if it was received by will, for example, the will must expressly provide for the exclusion of the

---

[17] FLA, s. 4(3).
[18] FLA, s. 4(2)1.
[19] FLA, s. 4(2)2.

rental income. Otherwise the accumulated rental income would be included in the spouse's NFP.

Damages for Personal Injuries

A spouse is entitled to exclude the value on valuation date of a judgment or settlement for damages for personal injuries, nervous shock, mental distress, or loss of guidance, care and companionship.[20] The damages excluded are generally those received for personal injury, pain, and suffering. Damages for loss of income or wages are generally not excluded under this subsection. For example, that part of a medical malpractice or motor vehicle accident settlement that was attributable to personal injury could be excluded from NFP.

Life Insurance Proceeds

A spouse is entitled to exclude from NFP the value of proceeds or a right to proceeds of a life insurance policy that are payable on the death of the life insured.[21] The insurance must be on the life of a third party, such as a spouse's parent. Only proceeds that are available on death are excluded, but not annuities payable to the insured person.

Tracing

If a spouse owns any property on valuation day that can be traced back to a gift or inheritance, a personal injury damages award, or life insurance proceeds, the spouse is entitled to exclude the value of that property from his or her NFP. It is the value on valuation date of the traceable property that is excluded. If the money or asset was given away, disposed of, or spent on a vacation before the couple separated, then the asset or money cannot be traced to anything on valuation date. On the other hand, if a gifted asset, such as money, was used to purchase an Oriental rug, which increased in value by valuation date, the spouse is entitled to exclude the increased value of the Oriental rug on valuation date. The onus of tracing an asset is on the spouse who seeks to claim the exclusion and it is difficult to prove without documentation such as bank records, receipts, and dates of purchase of an asset.

Of course, there is one exception to the value of property that can be excluded through tracing. If a spouse takes funds that would be otherwise

---

[20] FLA, s. 4(2)3.
[21] FLA, s. 4(2)4.

excluded and uses those funds to purchase a matrimonial home, then the value of the matrimonial home cannot be excluded on valuation date.

Belgiorgio v. Belgiorgio (2000), 10 R.F.L. (5th) 239 (Ont. S.C.J.), affirmed (2001), 23 R.F.L. (5th) 74 (Ont. C.A.)

Martina and John Belgiorgio were married for ten years. John Belgiorgio was involved in a motor vehicle accident the year prior to marriage and he received an insurance settlement during the first year of the parties' marriage. However, at trial, the husband was unable to produce any documentation to prove the existence or amount of the settlement he received.

During the marriage, John Belgiorgio also received an inheritance from his father's estate. The evidence indicated that he received the inheritance in the form of GICs, which he collapsed and placed in a joint account in the name of himself and his wife, Martina. Much of the money was spent to support the family's high standard of living and to support the family during Mr. Belgiorgio's periods of unemployment. Other portions of the inheritance monies were spent on expenditures such as family vacations, a hot tub, refrigerator, television, and dining room suite. The husband admitted that these items were used and enjoyed by the whole family. The husband sought to deduct the accident settlement and exclude the goods purchased from his inheritance received during the marriage from his net family property.

Held: The husband was not permitted to deduct the insurance settlement or exclude the inheritance.

Although the cause of action arising before the marriage constituted property under section 4(1) of the FLA, the husband failed to meet the onus of proof under section 4(3) of the Act. The FLA clearly places the burden of proving such a deduction, as well as its value, on the claiming party. With respect to the inheritance monies, again, the husband failed to produce any documentary evidence indicating the deposit of the inheritance funds into the joint bank account, and the subsequent application of those funds to the goods he now sought to exclude. The court was unable to accept oral testimony in order to trace the inheritance funds. Secondly, most of the property he claimed to have purchased with the inheritance was used for the common purposes of the family. Such property can, therefore, not be excluded from net family property. Finally, since the husband placed his inheritance funds in a joint bank account with his wife, section 14 of the FLA created a presumption that the monies were intended to be jointly owned. Although the husband later regretted having placed the monies in a joint account, it was his intention at the time he deposited the funds that was relevant. The inheritance lost its exclusionary nature when placed in the joint account.

Application Questions

1. During her marriage to Jacob, Anna inherited $75,000 from her father's estate. She spent $10,000 on an extended trip to Europe with Jacob and their four children. Anna purchased some expensive paintings in Europe worth $45,000 and had them shipped back to her home in Ontario. She placed the remaining $20,000 in an RRSP in her name alone. When the couple separated five years later, the paintings were worth $95,000 and the RRSP had decreased in value to $10,000 as Anna had to spend some of it on orthodontic work for her children.

   How much can Anna exclude from her NFP on valuation date? Explain your answer. *(part c)*

2. Clayton inherited $300,000 during his marriage to Dina and he used the money to purchase a home on the Scarborough bluffs. When the parties separated seven years later, the family was living in the home as their residence. At the date of separation, the home was worth $750,000.

   How much is Clayton entitled to exclude from his NFP? Explain your answer. *0 bc it went towards a home and joint bank account.*

3. Larry, a real estate agent, received $350,000 from a medical malpractice settlement during his marriage to Linda. He put the money towards the purchase of a rental building which cost $500,000. The couple both contributed the rest of the funds from their savings during cohabitation. When the couple separated, the building was worth $1,000,000.

   How much can Larry exclude from his NFP on valuation date?

Property Excluded by Domestic Contract

The spouses are free under the FLA to rearrange their property regime by entering into a valid domestic contract. This can be either a marriage contract or a separation agreement, both of which are discussed in Chapter 9, "Domestic Contracts under the *Family Law Act*". The spouses can agree to withdraw specific assets of a spouse's net family property or they can override the entire FLA property regime by a domestic contract. The parties can even agree to exclude the matrimonial home from their NFP. An example of a partial exclusion would be the spouses agreeing to release any interest in each other's pre-marital property. As previously noted, although the spouses can deduct the value of pre-marital property at the date of marriage, any increase in value of the property during the marriage is still open to sharing on separation. Any agreement must be in proper form in order to be enforceable.

CALCULATING THE EQUALIZATION PAYMENT

Each spouse must calculate his or her net family property separately. Once you have calculated the NFP of each spouse on valuation date (after deducting and excluding all of the appropriate items), you are in a position to calculate the equalization payment that one spouse must pay to the other. The first step is to determine the difference between the spouses' NFPs by subtracting the lesser NFP from the greater NFP. The difference is then divided in half to arrive at the equalization payment. It is always the spouse with the greater NFP who makes the equalization payment to the spouse with the lesser NFP. If there is no difference between the NFPs, the court has no jurisdiction to order an equalization payment. Each spouse will simply be left with his or her own "pile" of assets.[22]

Example:
Husband's NFP = $300,000 on V-Day
Wife's NFP = $160,000 on V-day
Difference between the two = $140,000
Wife receives $70,000 (one-half the difference)

Application Questions

On valuation date, the husband had a NFP of $695,000 while the wife had a NFP of minus $32,000.

(a) Who should pay the equalization payment to whom?

(b) How much will the equalization payment be? Explain how you calculated it.

Steps in Calculating "Net Family Property"

The following is a list of suggested steps to simplify the process of calculating the NFP and the resulting equalization payment:

1. **Determine the valuation date.** This is almost always the date when the parties separated with no reasonable prospect of resuming cohabitation [FLA s. 4(1)].

2. **Add up the value of all property held by each spouse on valuation**

---

[22] *Berdette v. Berdette* (1991), 33 R.F.L. (3d) 113 (Ont. C.A.), leave to appeal refused (1991), 85 D.L.R. (4th) viii (note), 55 O.A.C. 397 (note) (S.C.C.).

date. List separately for each spouse the property and its value held at valuation date. If assets are owned jointly, each spouse would include one-half the value of the asset in his or her NFP. Determine the total gross worth of each spouse, before the deductions and exclusions, on valuation date.

3. **Subtract each spouse's debts and liabilities at valuation date.**

4. **Subtract the net value of property owned by each spouse at the date of marriage, not including the matrimonial home.** The matrimonial home refers only to property that is actually used as a residence at the valuation date. You must calculate the net worth of each spouse at the date of marriage (subtract debts from assets).

5. **Take away any excluded property to which each spouse is entitled** [FLA s. 4(2)]. The most common exclusions will be gifts and inheritances received during the marriage by one spouse. Exclusions will also include any property that can be traced back to a gift or inheritance received during the marriage. Remember, if the excluded property was consumed or used during the marriage and there is nothing to show for it on V-day, then there can be no exclusion for it.

6. **The value remaining is the NFP of each spouse.**

7. **Determine the difference between the NFPs by subtracting the lesser NFP from the greater NFP.**

8. **Divide the difference by 2 to arrive at the equalization payment.** This is the amount that the spouse with the greater NFP must pay to the spouse with the lesser NFP.

EQUALIZATION ON DEATH OF A SPOUSE

A surviving married spouse has a choice to make under the FLA when his or her spouse dies. However, in many cases, a spouse is not aware that he or she has an election to make when the other spouse dies leaving property in his or her estate. The election only applies where the deceased spouse has a greater net family property than the surviving spouse.

Election Where Spouse Dies Leaving a Will

If a spouse dies, leaving a will, then the surviving spouse can choose between taking what he or she would receive under the will, or bringing an application under section 5 of the FLA for equalization of net family property.[23] If a spouse chooses the equalization route, he or she effectively gives up any rights under the will. In other words, his or her rights under the will are revoked.[24] However, if the deceased spouse has specifically stated in the will that the surviving spouse is to receive both his or her entitlement under the will and the equalization entitlement, then the surviving spouse can receive both.[25] The surviving spouse can make the election by filing the prescribed forms in the Office of the Estate Registrar for Ontario within six months of the other spouse's death.[26] If the surviving spouse fails to file an election within the required time, then he or she is deemed to have elected to take under the will.[27]

Election Where Spouse Dies Intestate

If a spouse dies intestate (without a will), then the surviving spouse can choose between whatever entitlement he or she may have under Part II of the *Succession Law Reform Act* and what he or she would be entitled to pursuant to equalization under section 5 of the FLA.[28] If the surviving spouse elects to take his or her equalization entitlement under the FLA, then he or she effectively waives or gives up any entitlement under the *Succession Law Reform Act*.[29] Before making such a decision, the surviving spouse must be in a position to assess, usually in consultation with a lawyer or accountant, the advantages and disadvantages of each potential choice. If a surviving spouse fails to file the prescribed election forms within six months of the date of death, then he or she will be deemed to have chosen to take whatever he or she is entitled to under the *Succession Law Reform Act*.[30]

Where a spouse dies partially intestate, i.e., has a will with respect to some of his or her property, but not in relation to other property, the surviving spouse must choose between the will plus any entitlement under the SLRA, or the equalization entitlement under the FLA.[31]

---

[23] FLA, s. 6(1).
[24] FLA, s. 6(8).
[25] FLA, s. 6(5).
[26] FLA, s. 6(10).
[27] FLA, s. 6(11).
[28] FLA, s. 6(2).
[29] FLA, s. 6(9).
[30] FLA, s. 6(11).
[31] FLA, s. 6(3).

Priority of Spouse's Entitlement

In the case of a surviving spouse who makes an election to take under the FLA that spouse's entitlement to equalization takes priority over any gifts made in the deceased spouse's will and any person's right to share in the estate pursuant to the SLRA provisions.[32] However, there is an exception where a spouse has made a will in accordance with a contract that was entered in good faith for valuable consideration with a third party. The surviving spouse's entitlement under the FLA does not take priority over such a gift that was made pursuant to a contract. For example, a deceased spouse might have entered into a separation agreement in which he or she agreed, for valuable consideration, to give his or her former spouse an interest in a company owned at his or her death. Such a gift would take priority over any rights that the current surviving spouse has under the FLA.

UNEQUAL DIVISION

Equalization "Unconscionable"

The FLA provides limited discretion to a court to award an amount that is less than or greater than half the difference between the spousal NFPs.[33] In order to do so, the court must be satisfied that equalization would be "unconscionable". The courts have interpreted this to mean that equalization must be "shockingly unfair" and not merely inconvenient or inequitable to one spouse.[34] Merely because an equalization payment would create hardship for the paying spouse would not render the payment unconscionable. When interpreting the word "unconscionable", the courts are directed to consider the purpose set out in section 5(7) of the FLA.[35] The spouses' contributions during the marriage are deemed to be equal, whether financial or otherwise. The fact that one spouse makes a larger contribution does *not*, in itself, lead to the conclusion that the spouse is entitled to a larger share upon separation.

---

[32] FLA, s. 6(12).

[33] FLA, s. 5(6).

[34] See *Sullivan v. Sullivan* (1986), 5 R.F.L. (3d) 28 (Ont. U.F.C.); *Heal v. Heal* (1998), 43 R.F.L. (4th) 88 (Ont. Gen. Div.) (unconscionable a very high threshold).

[35] *Berdette v. Berdette, supra* note 22.

Factors Considered By the Courts

The court is obliged to consider the following factors in determining whether equalization would be unconscionable:[36]

- a spouse's failure to disclose debts and liabilities at the date of marriage;
- a spouse claiming debts that were incurred recklessly or in bad faith;
- part of a spouse's NFP consisting of gifts made by the other spouse;
- a spouse intentionally or recklessly reducing his or her assets;
- a period of cohabitation less than five years *and* the amount is disproportionately large, considering the short period of cohabitation;
- the fact that one spouse has incurred a disproportionately larger amount of debts for the support of the family;
- a written agreement between the spouses other than a domestic contract; and
- any other circumstance relating to the acquisition, disposition, preservation, maintenance or improvement of property.

Some situations where a spouse might be awarded an unequal division include the following:

- a spouse recklessly depleting his or her NFP through a drug or alcohol addiction;
- a marriage lasting for only a year and one spouse bringing a matrimonial home into the marriage; or
- a husband spending $175,000 on lavish living with his mistress without the wife's knowledge or consent.

PROCEDURE IN AN EQUALIZATION APPLICATION

Commencement of Proceedings

An equalization proceeding is commenced by application, using Form 8 under the *Family Law Rules*.[37] The party making the claim must also file a financial statement (Form 13.1)[38] and a net family property statement (Form 13B).[39] In addition, the party responding to a property claim must file and serve these two statements.[40] The financial statement must be verified by oath and sets out the details of the parties' property, debts, and liabilities as of the date of marriage, the valuation date, and the date

---

[36] FLA, s. 5(6)(a)-(h).
[37] Rule 8(1).
[38] Rule 13(1)(a), (1.2).
[39] FLA, s. 8; Rule 13(14).
[40] Rule (13(1)(b), FLA, s. 8.

the statement is sworn. It must also set out all deductions and exclusions claimed by each party. Finally, the financial statement must set out all property disposed of during the previous two years by the parties, or during the marriage, whichever is shorter. The net family property statement summarizes the sworn property information of both parties in one document and shows the net family property for each spouse in a comparative fashion.

Service of Documents

The financial statement must be served along with the application, answer, or notice of motion.[41] The court will not accept the documents without the financial statement[42] and the financial statement must be updated if it is more than 30 days old at the time of a case conference, motion settlement conference, or trial.[43] The net family property statement must be served and filed at least 7 days prior to a settlement conference, and not more than 30 days but not less than 7 days before trial.[44]

---

[41] Rule 13(1.2).
[42] Rule 13(10).
[43] Rule 13(12).
[44] Rule 13(14).

APPENDIX 6A

Fact Situation—Jack Nesbitt and Jill Fairbanks

Jack Nesbitt was a fairly successful accountant back in the late 1990s. He was a single man, and as a result, was able to live quite well. In 2000, he bought some original art for $20,000. He needed somewhere to display the art, so he bought a penthouse condominium in downtown Toronto for $300,000. Because he lived downtown, he did not need to have a car at the time. However, he did invest $5,000 in an RRSP and had an additional $30,000 in the bank. To make his apartment comfortable, he bought modern stereo and television equipment worth about $10,000. Despite doing well in his career, Jack chose to take out loans on some of his possessions when he purchased them. He had a mortgage on the condo in the amount of $280,000, a bank loan for $2000, and a student loan in the amount of $13,500.

In late 2001, Jack met Jill Fairbanks. It was a whirlwind romance and they got married in June 2002. Everything was wonderful for the first few months. They bought a house in Toronto's west end and moved in two months after they were married. The house was put in Jill's name, as was the mortgage. The house cost $590,000 and the mortgage was $400,000. Jack kept his condo, figuring that it might come in handy for those late nights they would be spending in the city on weekends.

Jill was a doctor with a practice at the Toronto Hospital. She earned a good living so before she met Jack, she had bought a beautiful Jaguar for $87,500. She took a loan out at the bank for $43,000 to purchase the Jag. Right after that, she received as a gift from her favourite aunt, a beautiful diamond ring worth about $4,000, and $30,000 to help her get started in life. She put $15,000 against her bank loan for the car, and $1,000 in Canada Savings Bonds and put the rest in her savings account in the bank.

When Jill and Jack got married, they opened a joint bank account. Jill closed her own savings account, and they used the joint bank account for everyday bills and expenses. As a wedding gift, Jill bought Jack a used BMW for $20,000. During the first two months of their marriage, Jack spent his $30,000 savings on a variety of different things such as bills, vacations and possessions purchased during their marriage. He also paid off his $2,000 bank loan and all of his remaining student loans. Jack bought Jill emerald earrings and matching necklace worth $2,000. They also bought furniture worth about $30,000, and a cottage, where they planned to spend their summers for the rest of their lives. The cottage cost $258,000 with a mortgage of $150,000. The cottage was placed in Jack's name. In addition, Jack received a gift of $15,000 from his parents during the marriage to furnish the cottage and buy water toys.

Jack never got to furnish the cottage because he and Jill split up in January 2006. He moved back to his condo on January 17, 2006. He couldn't believe he'd married her, and couldn't wait to get a divorce. He filed his application for divorce on January 31, 2006.

At the time that they separated, Jack and Jill had $16,347.68 in their joint bank account. The $15,000 gift from his parents was in a separate savings account that Jack had.

By the time the couple separated, Jack's VISA bills amounted to $1,600, and Jill had a MasterCard bill for $900 and gas card with $80 outstanding. They also had a joint personal bank loan in the amount of $7,000. Jill had paid off the Jaguar completely. The mortgage on the matrimonial home was now $350,000 and the mortgage on the cottage was now $123,000.

Also, at the time of separation, Jack's art was worth $67,000, and his condo was now only worth $285,000, with the mortgage still outstanding of $250,000.

Jack wants to apply for an equalization of net family property.

The following illustration demonstrates how net family property is to be calculated for each spouse, Jack and Jill, following the procedure in the *Family Law Act*. Also included are the following completed forms:

1. An application for equalization of net family property (Form 8);

2. A Financial Statement for support and property claims (Form 13.1); and

3. A Net Family Property Statement (Form 13B).

Calculation of Net Family Property

Property Type	Jack Nesbitt		Jill Fairbanks	
Pre-marriage Assets	condo	300,000.00	Jaguar	87,500.00
	furniture	1,000.00	ring	4,000.00
	stereo, TV	10,000.00	CSB	1,000.00
	RRSP	5,000.00	bank account	14,000.00
	bank account	30,000.00		
	art	20,000.00		
	Total	**$366,000.00**	**Total**	**$106,500.00**
Pre-marriage Liabilities	mortgage on condo		car loan	28,000.00
		280,000.00		
	loan	2,000.00		
	student loan	13,500.00		
	Total	**$295,500.00**	**Total**	**$28,000.00**

Property Type	Jack Nesbitt		Jill Fairbanks	
Net Pre-marriage Assets	**$70,500.00** (assets minus liabilities)		**$78,500.00** (assets minus liabilities)	
Valuation Day Assets	condo	285,000.00	home	590,000.00
	cottage	258,000.00	furniture (joint)	15,000.00
	furniture (joint)	15,000.00	Jaguar	87,500.00
	furniture (pre-mar.)		jewellery	2,000.00
		1,000.00	ring (pre-mar.)	4,000.00
	stereo, TV	10,000.00	bank (joint)	8,173.84
	BMW	20,000.00	CSB	1,000.00
	bank (sole)	15,000.00		
	bank (joint)	8,173.84		
	RRSP	5,000.00		
	art	67,000.00		
	Total	**$684,173.84**	**Total**	**$707,673.84**
Valuation Day Debts and Liabilities	mortgage (condo)		mortgage (home)	
		250,000.00		350,000.00
	mortgage (cottage)		loan (joint)	3,500.00
		123,000.00	MasterCard	900.00
	loan (joint)	3,500.00	Gas card	80.00
	VISA	1,600.00		
	Total	**$378,100.00**	**Total**	**$354,480.00**
Subtract V-day debts from V-day assets		684,173.84 - 378,100.00		707,673.84 - 354,480.00
		$306,073.84		**$353,193.84**
Excluded Property	bank account 15,000.00 (gift from parents during marriage)		none	
	Total	**$15,000.00**		
Complete Calculations V-day Assets/Liabilities		306,073.84		353,193.84
1. Subtract net pre-marriage assets		- 70,500.00		- 78,500.00
2. Subtract excluded property		- 15,000.00		
Net Family Property		**$220,573.84**		**$274,693.84**

Difference between net family properties

$274,693.84
- $220,573.84
$ 54,120.00

Equalization payment

$54,120.00 divided by 2 = **$27,060.00**

APPENDIX 6B

ONTARIO

SEAL		

ONTARIO SUPERIOR COURT OF JUSTICE
(Name of court)

at   393 University Ave., Toronto, Ontario, M5G 2M2
Court office address

Court File Number

Family Law Rules, O. Reg. 114/99

Form 8: Application (General)

Applicant(s)

Full legal name & address for service – street & number, municipality, postal code, telephone & fax numbers and e-mail address (if any).	Lawyer's name & address – street & number, municipality, postal code, telephone & fax numbers and e-mail address (if any).
Jack Ritchie Nesbitt **75 Swingers Tower, PH 2** **Toronto, Ontario** **M2N 1P6**	**Marla Fairmeadow** **Barrister & Solicitor** **330 Bay Street, Stuie 1703** **Toronto, Ontario** **M2N 6P7** **Tel: 416 657-9999** **Fax: 416 657-9910**

Respondent(s)

Full legal name & address for service – street & number, municipality, postal code, telephone & fax numbers and e-mail address (if any).	Lawyer's name & address – street & number, municipality, postal code, telephone & fax numbers and e-mail address (if any).
Jill Roberta Fairbanks **729 Whirlwind Court** **Etobicoke, Ontario** **M6P 2L9**	

TO THE RESPONDENT(S):

A COURT CASE HAS BEEN STARTED AGAINST YOU IN THIS COURT. THE DETAILS ARE SET OUT ON THE ATTACHED PAGES.

☐ **THE FIRST COURT DATE IS** *(date)* _____ **AT** _____ ☐ a.m. ☐ p.m. or as soon as possible
after that time, at: *(address)*

NOTE: If this is a divorce case, no date will be set unless an Answer is filed. If you have also been served with a notice of motion, there may be an earlier court date and you or your lawyer should come to court for the motion.

☐ **THIS CASE IS ON THE FAST TRACK OF THE CASE MANAGEMENT SYSTEM.** A case management judge will be assigned by the time this case first comes before a judge.

☒ **THIS CASE IS ON THE STANDARD TRACK OF THE CASE MANAGEMENT SYSTEM. No court date has been set for this case** but, if you have been served with a notice of motion, it has a court date and you or your lawyer should come to court for the motion. A case management judge will not be assigned until one of the parties asks the clerk of the court to schedule a case conference or until a notice of motion under subrule 14(5) is served before a case conference has been held. If, after 200 days, the case has not been scheduled for trial, the clerk of the court will send out a warning that the case will be dismissed in 30 days unless the parties file proof that the case has been settled or one of the parties asks for a case conference or a settlement conference.

IF YOU WANT TO OPPOSE ANY CLAIM IN THIS CASE, you or your lawyer must prepare an Answer (Form 10 – a blank copy should be attached), serve a copy on the applicant(s) and file a copy in the court office with an Affidavit of Service (Form 6B). **YOU HAVE ONLY 30 DAYS AFTER THIS APPLICATION IS SERVED ON YOU (60 DAYS IF THIS APPLICATION IS SERVED ON YOU OUTSIDE CANADA OR THE UNITED STATES) TO SERVE AND FILE AN ANSWER. IF YOU DO NOT, THE CASE WILL GO AHEAD WITHOUT YOU AND THE COURT MAY MAKE AN ORDER AND ENFORCE IT AGAINST YOU.**

Form 8:   Application (General)   **(page 2)** | Court File Number

Check the box of the paragraph that applies to your case

☐ This case includes a claim for support. It does not include a claim for property or exclusive possession of the matrimonial home and its contents. You **MUST** fill out a Financial Statement (Form 13 – a blank copy attached), serve a copy on the applicant(s) and file a copy in the court office with an Affidavit of Service even if you do not answer this case.

☒ This case includes a claim for property or exclusive possession of the matrimonial home and its contents. You **MUST** fill out a Financial Statement (Form 13.1 – a blank copy attached), serve a copy on the applicant(s) and file a copy in the court office with an Affidavit of Service even if you do not answer this case.

IF YOU WANT TO MAKE A CLAIM OF YOUR OWN, you or your lawyer must fill out the claim portion in the Answer, serve a copy on the applicant(s) and file a copy in the court office with an Affidavit of Service.

   ▪ If you want to make a claim for support but do not want to make a claim for property or exclusive possession of the matrimonial home and its contents, you **MUST** fill out a Financial Statement (Form 13), serve a copy on the applicant(s) and file a copy in the court office.

   ▪ However, if your only claim for support is for child support in the table amount specified under the Child Support Guidelines, you do not need to fill out, serve or file a Financial Statement.

   ▪ If you want to make a claim for property or exclusive possession of the matrimonial home and its contents, whether or not it includes a claim for support, you **MUST** fill out a Financial Statement (Form 13.1, not Form 13), serve a copy on the applicant(s), and file a copy in the court office.

YOU SHOULD GET LEGAL ADVICE ABOUT THIS CASE RIGHT AWAY. If you cannot afford a lawyer, you may be able to get help from your local Legal Aid Ontario office. *(See your telephone directory under LEGAL AID.)*

_____   _____
          Date of issue   *Clerk of the court*

Form 8: Application (General)	(page 3)	Court file number

FAMILY HISTORY

APPLICANT: Age: **34**   Birthdate: *(d,m,y)* **January 31, 1972**

Resident in *(municipality & province)* **Toronto, Ontario**

since *(date)* **1972**

Surname at birth: **Nesbitt**   Surname just before marriage: **Nesbitt**

Divorced before?   ☒ No   ☐ Yes *(Place and date of previous divorce)*

RESPONDENT: Age: **31**   Birthdate: *(d,m,y)* **May 27, 1974**

Resident in *(municipality & province)* **Toronto, Ontario**

since *(date)* **1974**

Surname at birth: **Fairbanks**   Surname just before marriage: **Fairbanks**

Divorced before?   ☒ No   ☐ Yes *(Place and date of previous divorce)*

RELATIONSHIP DATES:

☒ Married on *(date)* June 24, 2002   ☐ Started living together on *(date)*

☒ Separated on *(date)* January 17, 2006   ☐ Never lived together   ☐ Still living together

THE CHILD(REN)
List all children involved in this case, even if no claim is made for these children.

Full legal name	Age	Birthdate *(d,m,y)*	Resident in *(municipality & province)*	Now Living With *(name of person and relationship to child)*

PREVIOUS CASES OR AGREEMENTS

Have the parties or the children been in a court case before?

        ☒ No   ☐ Yes *(Attach a Summary of Court Cases – Form 8E.)*

Have the parties made a written agreement dealing with any matter involved in this case?

        ☒ No   ☐ Yes *(Give date of agreement. Indicate which of its terms are in dispute. Attach an additional page if you need more space.)*

Form 8: **Application (General)** **(page 4)**

Court file number

CLAIM BY APPLICANT

I ASK THE COURT FOR THE FOLLOWING:
(Claims below include claims for temporary orders.)

Claims under the *Divorce Act* *(Check boxes in this column only if you are asking for a divorce and your case is in the Family Court of the Superior Court of Justice.)*	**Claims under the *Family Law Act* or *Children's Law Reform Act***	**Claims relating to property** *(Check boxes in this column only if your case is in the Family Court of the Superior Court of Justice.)*
00 ☐ a divorce 01 ☐ support for me 02 ☐ support for child(ren) – table amount 03 ☐ support for child(ren) - other than table amount 04 ☐ custody of child(ren) 05 ☐ access to child(ren)	10 ☐ support for me 11 ☐ support for child(ren) – table amount 12 ☐ support for child(ren) - other than table amount 13 ☐ custody of child(ren) 14 ☐ access to child(ren) 15 ☐ restraining/non-harassment order 16 ☐ indexing spousal support 17 ☐ indexing same-sex partner support 18 ☐ declaration of parentage 19 ☐ guardianship over child's property	20 ☒ equalization of net family properties 21 ☐ exclusive possession of matrimonial home 22 ☐ exclusive possession of contents of matrimonial home 23 ☐ freezing assets 24 ☐ sale of family property
Other claims 30 ☒ costs 31 ☐ annulment of marriage 32 ☐ prejudgment interest	50 ☐ Other *(Specify.)*	

Give details of the order that you want the court to make. *(Include any amounts of support (if known) and the names of the children for whom support, custody or access is claimed.)*

1. An equalization of net family property of the parties pursuant to s. 5 of the *Family Law Act*, R.S.O. 1990, c. F.3.

2. Costs of this application.

Form 8:	Application (General)	(page 5)	Court File Number

IMPORTANT FACTS SUPPORTING MY CLAIM FOR DIVORCE

☐ **Separation:** The spouses have lived separate and apart since *(date)* _____ and

    ☐ have not lived together again since that date in an unsuccessful attempt to reconcile.

    ☐ have lived together again during the following period(s) in an unsuccessful attempt to reconcile: *(Give dates.)*

☐ **Adultery:** The respondent has committed adultery. *(Give details. It is not necessary to name any other person involved but, if you do name the other person, then you must serve this application on the other person.)*

☐ **Cruelty:** The respondent has treated the applicant with physical or mental cruelty of such a kind as to make continued cohabitation intolerable. *(Give details.)*

IMPORTANT FACTS SUPPORTING MY OTHER CLAIM(S)

(Set out below the facts that form the legal basis for your other claim(s). Attach an additional page if you need more space.)

1. The parties were married on June 24, 2002 and separated on January 17, 2006 There is no prospect that the parties will resume cohabitation. The applicant therefore seeks an equalization of net family property of the parties.

Put a line through any space left on this page. If additional space is needed, extra pages may be attached.

_____   _____
Date of signature   *Signature of applicant*

LAWYER'S CERTIFICATE

For divorce cases only

My name is: _____

and I am the applicant's lawyer in this divorce case. I certify that I have complied with the requirements of section 9 of the *Divorce Act.*

_____   _____
Date   *Signature of Lawyer*

APPENDIX 6C

ONTARIO

ONTARIO SUPERIOR COURT OF JUSTICE
_____
(Name of court)

at 393 University Avenue, Toronto, Ontario, M5G 2M2
_____
Court office address

Court File Number

Family Law Rules, O. Reg. 114/99

Form 13.1: Financial Statement (Property and Support Claims) sworn/affirmed

_____

Applicant(s)

Full legal name & address for service — street & number, municipality, postal code, telephone & fax numbers and e-mail address (if any).	Lawyer's name & address — street & number, municipality, postal code, telephone & fax numbers and e-mail address (if any).
Jack Ritchie Nesbitt **75 Swingers Tower, PH 2** **Etobicoke, Ontario** **M2N 1P6**	**Marla Fairmeadow** **Barrister & Solicitor** **330 Bay Street, Suite 1703** **Toronto, Ontario** **M2N 6P7** **Tel: (416) 657-9999** **Fax: (416) 657-9910**

Respondent(s)

Full legal name & address for service — street & number, municipality, postal code, telephone & fax numbers and e-mail address (if any).	Lawyer's name & address — street & number, municipality, postal code, telephone & fax numbers and e-mail address (if any).
Jill Roberta Fairbanks **729 Whirlwind Court** **Etobicoke, Ontario** **M6P 2L9**	

INSTRUCTIONS

1. USE THIS FORM IF:
   - you are making or responding to a claim for property or exclusive possession of the matrimonial home and its contents; or
   - you are making or responding to a claim for property or exclusive possession of the matrimonial home and its contents together with other claims for relief.

2. DO NOT USE THIS FORM AND INSTEAD USE FORM 13 IF:
   - you are making or responding to a claim for support but NOT making or responding to a claim for property or exclusive possession of the matrimonial home and its contents.

1. **My name** is *(full legal name)* **Jack Ritchie Nesbitt**

   I live in *(municipality & province)* **Toronto, Ontario**

   and I swear/affirm that the following is true:

   My financial statement set out on the following *(specify number)* _____ pages is accurate

   to the best of my knowledge and belief and sets out the financial situation as of *(give date for which information is*

   accurate) _____ **for**

Check one or more boxes, as circumstances require.	☒	me
	☐	the following person(s): *(Give name(s) and relationship to you.)*

Form 13.1: **Financial Statement (Property and** **(page 2)**
Support Claims)

Court File Number

NOTE: *When you show monthly income and expenses, give the current actual amount if you know it or can find out. To get a monthly figure you must multiply any weekly income by 4.33 or divide any yearly income by 12.*

PART 1: INCOME

for the 12 months from *(date)* **January 1, 2005** to *(date)* **December 31, 2005**

Include all income and other money that you get from all sources, whether taxable or not. Show the gross amount here and show your deductions in Part 3.

	CATEGORY	Monthly
1.	Pay, wages, salary, including overtime (before deductions)	12,886.14
2.	Bonuses, fees, commissions	
3.	Social assistance	
4.	Employment insurance	
5.	Workers' compensation	
6.	Pensions	
7.	Dividends	
8.	Interest	

	CATEGORY	Monthly
9.	Rent, board received	
10.	Canada Child Tax Benefit	
11.	Support payments actually received	
12.	Income received by children	
13.	G.S.T. refund	
14.	Payments from trust funds	
15.	Gifts received	
16.	Other *(Specify. If necessary, attach an extra sheet.)*	
17.	**INCOME FROM ALL SOURCES**	12,886.14

PART 2: OTHER BENEFITS

Show your non-cash benefits — such as the use of a company car, a club membership or room and board that your employer or someone else provides for you or benefits that are charged through or written off by your business.

ITEM	DETAILS	Monthly Market Value
	18. TOTAL	

19. GROSS MONTHLY INCOME AND BENEFITS *(Add* [17] *plus* [18].) **$** 12,886.14

PART 3: AUTOMATIC DEDUCTIONS FROM INCOME

for the 12 months from *(date)* **January 1, 2005** to *(date)* **December 31, 2005**

	TYPE OF EXPENSE	Monthly
20.	Income tax deducted from pay	4,179.40
21.	*Canada Pension Plan*	155.10
22.	Other pension plans	846.59
23.	Employment insurance	63.38
24.	Union or association dues	

	TYPE OF EXPENSE	Monthly
25.	Group insurance	
26.	Other *(Specify. If necessary, attach an extra sheet.)*	
27.	**TOTAL AUTOMATIC DEDUCTIONS**	5,244.47

28. NET MONTHLY INCOME *(Do the subtraction:* [19] *minus* [27].) **$** 7,641.67

Form 13.1:   **Financial Statement (Property and Support (page 3) Claims)**

<table>
<tr><td>Court File Number</td></tr>
</table>

PART 4: TOTAL EXPENSES

for the 12 months from *(date)* _____ to *(date)* _____

NOTE: This part must be completed in all cases. You must set out your TOTAL living expenses, including those expenses involving any children now living in your home. This part may also be used for a proposed budget. To prepare a proposed budget, photocopy Part 4, complete as necessary, change the title to "Proposed Budget" and attach it to this form.

TYPE OF EXPENSE		Monthly
Housing		
29.	Rent/mortgage	$2,126.98
30.	Property taxes & municipal levies	$560.00
31.	Condominium fees & common expenses	$320.00
32.	Water	$62.71
33.	Electricity & heating fuel	$337.97
34.	Telephone	$105.72
35.	Cable television & pay television	$132.87
36.	Home insurance	$78.96
37.	Home repairs, maintenance, gardening	$200.00
	Sub-total of items [29] to [37]	3,925.21
Food, Clothing and Transportation etc.		
38.	Groceries	$1,000.00
39.	Meals outside home	$350.00
40.	General household supplies	$100.00
41.	Hairdresser, barber & toiletries	$75.00
42.	Laundry & dry cleaning	$35.00
43.	Clothing	$150.00
44.	Public transit	
45.	Taxis	
46.	Car insurance	$252.00
47.	Licence	$12.00
48.	Car loan payments	
49.	Car maintenance and repairs	$100.00
50.	Gasoline & oil	$350.00
51.	Parking	
	Sub-total of items [38] to [51]	2,424.00
Health and Medical *(do not include child(ren)'s expenses)*		
52.	Regular dental care	$35.00
53.	Orthodontics or special dental care	
54.	Medicine & drugs	
55.	Eye glasses or contact lenses	
56.	Life or term insurance premiums	$65.00
	Sub-total of items [52] to [56]	100.00

TYPE OF EXPENSE		Monthly
Child(ren)		
57.	School activities (field trips, etc.)	
58.	School lunches	
59.	School fees, books, tuition, *etc.* (for children)	
60.	Summer camp	
61.	Activities (music lessons, clubs, sports)	
62.	Allowances	
63.	Baby sitting	
64.	Day care	
65.	Regular dental care	
66.	Orthodontics or special dental care	
67.	Medicine & drugs	
68.	Eye glasses or contact lenses	
	Sub-total of items [57] to [68]	
Miscellaneous and Other		
69.	Books for home use, newspapers, magazines, videos, compact discs	$125.00
70.	Gifts	$100.00
71.	Charities	
72.	Alcohol & tobacco	$150.00
73.	Pet expenses	$100.00
74.	School fees, books, tuition, *etc.*	
75.	Entertainment & recreation	$200.00
76.	Vacation	$300.00
77.	Credit cards (*but not for expenses mentioned elsewhere in the statement*)	$200.00
78.	R.R.S.P. or other savings plans	
79.	Support actually being paid in any other Case	
80.	Income tax and *Canada Pension Plan* (*not deducted from pay*)	
81.	Other (*Specify. If necessary attach an extra sheet.*)	
	Sub-total of items [69] to [81]	1,175.00
82.	**Total of items [29] to [81]**	7,624.21

SUMMARY OF INCOME AND EXPENSES

Net monthly income *(item [28] above)* =$ 7,641.67

Subtract actual monthly expenses *(item [82] above)* =$ 7,624.21

ACTUAL MONTHLY SURPLUS/DEFICIT =$ 17.46

Form 13.1:	Financial Statement (Property and Support (page 4) Claims)	Court file number

PART 5: OTHER INCOME INFORMATION

1.   I am   ☒   employed by *(name and address of employer)*

    Accurate & Efficient Accounting Services
    1762 Dividend Court, Suite 307
    Toronto, Ontario
    M2N 7Y8

    ☐   self-employed, carrying on business under the name of *(name and address of business)*

    ☐   unemployed since *(date when last employed)*

2.   I attach the following required information *(if you are filing this statement to update or correct an earlier statement, then you do not need to attach income tax returns that have already been filed with the court):*

    ☒   a copy of my income tax returns that were filed with the Canada Customs and Revenue Agency for the past 3 taxation years, together with a copy of all material filed with the returns and a copy of any notices of assessment or re-assessment that I have received from the Canada Customs and Revenue Agency for those years; or

    ☐   a statement from the Canada Customs and Revenue Agency that I have not filed any income tax returns from the past 3 years; or

    ☐   a direction in Form 13A signed by me to the Taxation Branch of the Canada Customs and Revenue Agency for the disclosure of my tax returns and notices of assessment to the other part for the past 3 years.

    I attach proof of my current income, including my most recent

    ☒ pay cheque stub.   ☐ employment insurance stub.   ☐ worker's compensation stub.
    ☐ pension stub.   ☐ Other. *(Specify.)*

3.   ☐   *(check if applicable)* I am an Indian within the meaning of the *Indian Act* (Canada) and all my income is tax exempt and I am not required to file an income tax return. I have therefore not attached an income tax return for the past three years.

PART 6: OTHER INCOME EARNERS IN THE HOME

Complete this part only if you are making a claim for undue hardship or spousal support. Indicate at paragraph 1 or 2, whether you are living with another person (for example, spouse, same sex partner, roommate or tenant). If you complete paragraph 2, also complete paragraphs 3 to 6.

1.   ☒ I live alone.

2.   I am living with *(full legal name of person)* _____

3.   This person has *(give number)* _____ child(ren) living in the home.

4.   This person   ☐ works at *(place of work or business)* _____
                 ☐ does not work outside the home.

5.   This person   ☐ earns (give amount) $ _____ per _____
                 ☐ does not earn anything.

6.   This person   ☐ contributes about $ _____ per _____ towards the household expenses.
                 ☐ contributes no money to the household expenses.

Form 13.1:	Financial Statement (Property and (page 5) Support Claims)	Court file number

PART 7: ASSETS IN AND OUT OF ONTARIO

If any sections of Parts 7 to 12 do not apply, do not leave blank, print "NONE" in the section.

The date of marriage is: *(give date)* **June 24, 2002**

The valuation date is: *(give date)* **January 17, 2006**

The date of commencement of cohabitation is (if different from date of marriage): *(give date)* **May 20, 2002**

PART 7(a): LAND

*Include any interest in land **owned** on the dates in each of the columns below, including leasehold interests and mortgages. Show estimated market value of your interest, but do not deduct encumbrances or costs of disposition; these encumbrances and costs should be shown under Part 8, "Debts and Other Liabilities".*

Nature & Type of Ownership *(Give your percentage interest where relevant.)*	Address of Property	Estimated Market Value of YOUR Interest		
		on date of marriage	on valuation date	today
100%	75 Swingers Tower, PH 2 Toronto, Ontario	300,000.00	285,000.00	285,000.00
100%	R. R. # 2, Buckhorn, Ontario		258,000.00	258,000.00
83. TOTAL VALUE OF LAND		$ 543,000.00		543,000.00

PART 7(b): GENERAL HOUSEHOLD ITEMS AND VEHICLES

Show estimated market value, not the cost of replacement for these items owned on the dates in each of the columns below. Do not deduct encumbrances or costs of disposition; these encumbrances and costs should be shown under Part 8, "Debts and Other Liabilities".

Item	Description	Indicate if NOT in your possession	Estimated Market Value of YOUR Interest		
			on date of marriage	on valuation date	today
Household goods & furniture	furniture (pre-marriage)		1,000.00	1,000.00	1,000.00
	furniture (jointly owned with wife)	in wife's possession		15,000.00	15,000.00
Cars, boats, vehicles	BMW Car			20,000.00	20,000.00
Jewellery, art, electronics, tools, sports & hobby equipment	art		20,000.00	67,000.00	67,000.00
	stereo, TV equipment		10,000.00	10,000.00	10,000.00
Other special items					
84. TOTAL VALUE OF GENERAL HOUSEHOLD ITEMS AND VEHICLES			$ 113,000.00		113,000.00

Form 13.1:	Financial Statement (Property and (page 6) Support Claims)	Court file number

PART 7(c): BANK ACCOUNTS, SAVINGS, SECURITIES AND PENSIONS

Show the items owned on the dates in each of the columns below by category, for example, cash, accounts in financial institutions, pensions, registered retirement or other savings plans, deposit receipts, any other savings, bonds, warrants, options, notes and other securities. Give your best estimate of the market value of the securities if the items were to be sold on the open market.

Category	INSTITUTION (including location)/ DESCRIPTION (including issuer and date)	Account number	Amount/Estimated Market Value		
			on date of marriage	on valuation date	today
joint savings	TD Canada Trust, Toronto	777334		8,173.84	8,000.00
RRSP	TD Canada Trust, Toronto	987000	5,000.00	5,000.00	5,000.00
savings	Royal Bank, Toronto	956444	30,000.00		
savings	CIBC, Toronto	778009		15,000.00	15,000.00
85. TOTAL VALUE OF ACCOUNTS, SAVINGS, SECURITIES AND PENSIONS			$ 28,173.84		28,000.00

PART 7(d): LIFE AND DISABILITY INSURANCE

List all policies in existence on the dates in each of the columns below.

Company, Type & Policy No.	Owner	Beneficiary	Face Amount	Cash Surrender Value		
				on date of marriage	on valuation date	today
86. TOTAL CASH SURRENDER VALUE OF INSURANCE POLICIES				$		

PART 7(e): BUSINESS INTERESTS

Show any interest in an unincorporated business owned on the dates in each of the columns below. An interest in an incorporated business may be shown here or under "BANK ACCOUNTS, SAVINGS, SECURITIES, AND PENSIONS" in Part 7(c). Give your best estimate of the market value of your interest.

Name of Firm or Company	Interest	Estimated Market Value of YOUR Interest		
		on date of marriage	on valuation date	today
87. TOTAL VALUE OF BUSINESS INTERESTS		$		

Form 13.1:	Financial Statement (Property and (page 7) Support Claims)	Court file number

PART 7(f): MONEY OWED TO YOU

Give details of all money that other persons owe to you on the dates in each of the columns below, whether because of business or from personal dealings. Include any court judgments in your favour, any estate money and any income tax refunds owed to you.

Details	Amount Owed to You		
	on date of marriage	on valuation date	today
88. TOTAL OF MONEY OWED TO YOU	$		

PART 7(g): OTHER PROPERTY

Show other property or assets owned on the dates in each of the columns below. Include property of any kind not listed above. Give your best estimate of market value.

Category	Details	Estimated Market Value of YOUR interest		
		on date of marriage	on valuation date	today
89. TOTAL VALUE OF OTHER PROPERTY		$		
90. VALUE OF ALL PROPERTY OWNED ON THE VALUATION DATE (Add items [83] to [89].)		$ 684,173.84		

PART 8: DEBTS AND OTHER LIABILITIES

Show your debts and other liabilities on the dates in each of the columns below. List them by category such as mortgages, charges, liens, notes, credit cards, and accounts payable. Don't forget to include:

- *any money owed to the Canada Customs and Revenue Agency;*
- *contingent liabilities such as guarantees or warranties given by you (but indicate that they are contingent); and*
- *any unpaid legal or professional bills as a result of this case.*

Category	Details	Amount Owing		
		on date of marriage	on valuation date	today
mortgage	75 Swingers Tower, PH2, Toronto	280,000.00	250.000.00	247,596.00
mortgage	R. R. # 2, Buckhorn, Ontario		123.000.00	122,586.00
loan (joint with wife)	TD Canada Trust, Toronto		3,500.00	3,250.00
credit card	CIBC VISA		1,600.00	1,350.00
91. TOTAL OF DEBTS AND OTHER LIABILITIES		$ 378,100.00		374,782.00

Form 13.1:	Financial Statement (Property and (page 8) Support Claims)	Court file number

PART 9: PROPERTY, DEBTS AND OTHER LIABILITIES ON DATE OF MARRIAGE

*Show by category the value of your property and your debts and other liabilities **as of the date of your marriage**. DO NOT INCLUDE THE VALUE OF A MATRIMONIAL HOME THAT YOU OWNED ON THE DATE OF MARRIAGE IF THIS PROPERTY IS STILL A MATRIMONIAL HOME ON VALUATION DATE.*

Category and details	Value on date of marriage	
	Assets	Liabilities
Land		
Condominium at 75 Swingers Tower, PH 2, Toronto	300,000.00	280,000.00
General household items & vehicles		
furniture	1,000.00	
Stereo, TV	10,000.00	
Bank accounts, savings, securities & pensions		
RRSP	5,000.00	
Savings Account (CIBC)	30,000.00	
Life & disability insurance		
Business interests		
Money owed to you		
Other property *(Specify.)*		
art	20,000.00	
Debts and other liabilities *(Specify.)*		
student loan	0	13,500.00
bank loan at TD Canada Trust		2,000.00
TOTALS	$ 366,000.00	$ 295,500.00
92. NET VALUE OF PROPERTY OWNED ON DATE OF MARRIAGE *(From the total of the "Assets" column, subtract the total of the "Liabilities" column.)*	$ 70,500.00	
93. VALUE OF ALL DEDUCTIONS *(Add items [91] and [92].)*	$ 448,600.00	

PART 10: EXCLUDED PROPERTY

Show by category the value of property owned on the valuation date that is excluded from the definition of "net family property" (such as gifts or inheritances received after marriage).

Category	Details	Value on valuation date
Gift	**CIBC Savings Account**	15,000.00
	94. TOTAL VALUE OF EXCLUDED PROPERTY	$ 15,000.00

Form 13.1: **Financial Statement (Property and Support Claims)** **(page 9)**

Court file number

PART 11: DISPOSED-OF PROPERTY

Show by category the value of all property that you disposed of during the two years immediately preceding the making of this statement, or during the marriage, whichever period is shorter.

Category	Details	Value
	95. TOTAL VALUE OF DISPOSED-OF PROPERTY	$

PART 12: CALCULATION OF NET FAMILY PROPERTY

	Deductions	BALANCE
Value of all property owned on valuation date *(from item [90] above)* $	684,173.84	$ 684,173.84
Subtract value of all deductions *(from item [93] above)* $	448,600.00	$ 235,573.84
Subtract total value of excluded property *(from item [94] above)* $	15,000.00	$ 220,573.84
96. NET FAMILY PROPERTY		$ 220,573.84

☒ I do not expect changes in my financial situation.

☐ I do expect changes in my financial situation as follows:

☐ I attach a proposed budget in the format of Part 4 of this form.

NOTE: As soon as you find out that the information in this financial statement is incorrect or incomplete, or there is a material change in your circumstances that affects or will affect the information in this financial statement, you MUST serve on every other party to this case and file with the court:

- *a new financial statement with updated information, or*
- *if changes are minor, an affidavit in Form 14A setting out the details of these changes.*

Sworn/Affirmed before me at   **CITY of TORONTO**

_____
municipality

in   **the PROVINCE of ONTARIO**

_____
province, state or country

on

_____
date   Commissioner for taking affidavits
(Type or print name below if signature is illegible.)

_____
Signature
(This form is to be signed in front of a lawyer, justice of the peace, notary public or commissioner for taking affidavits.)

APPENDIX 6D

ONTARIO

Superior Court of Justice

(Name of court)

at **393 University Avenue, Toronto, Ontario, M5G 2M2**

Court office address

Court File Number

Family Law Rules, O. Reg. 114/99

Form 13B: Net Family Property Statement

Applicant(s)

Full legal name & address for service — street & number, municipality, postal code, telephone & fax numbers and e-mail address (if any).	Lawyer's name & address — street & number, municipality, postal code, telephone & fax numbers and e-mail address (if any).
Jack Ritchie Nesbitt **75 Swingers Tower, PH 2** **Toronto, Ontario** **M2N 1P6**	**Marla Fairmeadow** **Barrister & Solicitor** **330 Bay Street, Suite 1703** **Toronto, Ontario** **Tel: (416) 657-9999** **Fax: (416) 657-9910**

Respondent(s)

Full legal name & address for service — street & number, municipality, postal code, telephone & fax numbers and e-mail address (if any).	Lawyer's name & address — street & number, municipality, postal code, telephone & fax numbers and e-mail address (if any).
Jill Roberta Fairbanks **729 Whirlwind Court** **Etobicoke, Ontario** **M6P 2L9**	

My name is *(full legal name)* **Jack Ritchie Nesbitt**

The valuation date for the following material is *(date)* **January 17, 2006**

(Complete the tables by filling in the columns for both husband and wife, showing your assets, debts, etc., and those of your spouse.)

Table 1: Value of assets owned on valuation date
(List in the order of the categories in the financial statement.)

ITEM	HUSBAND	WIFE
1. condominium at 75 Swingers Tower, PH 2, Toronto (sole owner)	$285,000.00	
2. matrimonial home at 729 Whirlwind Court, Etobicoke (sole owner)		$590,000.00
3. cottage at R.R. 2, Buckhorn, Ontario (sole owner)	$258,000.00	
4. household furniture (jointly owned)	$15,000.00	$15,000.00
5. pre-marriage furniture, stereo, TV	$11,000.00	
6. BMW car	$20,000.00	
7. Jaguar		$87,500.00
8. bank account at TD Canada Trust (joint)	$8,173.84	$8,173.84
9. bank account at CIBC	$15,000.00	
10. Canada Savings Bonds		$1,000.00
11. RRSP at TD Canada Trust	$5,000.00	
12. art	$67,000.00	
13. earings, necklace		$2,000.00
14. ring (pre-marriage)		$4,000.00
TOTAL 1	$684,173.84	$707,673.84

Form 13B: **Net Family Property Statement**   **(page 2)**

Court File Number

Table 2: Value of debts and liabilities on valuation date
(List in the order of the categories in the financial statement.)

ITEM	HUSBAND	WIFE
1. mortgagae on condominium	$250,000.00	
2. mortgage on matrimonial home		$350,000.00
3. mortgage on cottage	$123,000.00	
4. bank loan (joint) at TD Canada Trust	$3,500.00	$3,500.00
5. Visa	$1,600.00	
6. Mastercard		$900.00
7. Esso card		$80.00
TOTAL 2	$378,100.00	$354,480.00

Table 3: Net value of property (other than a matrimonial home) and debts on date of marriage
(List in the order of the categories in the financial statement.)

3(a) PROPERTY ITEM	HUSBAND	WIFE
1. Condominium	$300,000.00	
2. Furniture, stereo, TV	$11,000.00	
3. Jaguar		$87,500.00
4. Savings account	$30,000.00	$14,000.00
5. RRSP Canada Savings Bond	$5,000.00	$1,000.00
6. art, jewellery	$20,000.00	$4,000.00
TOTAL OF PROPERTY ITEMS	$366,000.00	$106,500.00
3(b) DEBIT ITEM		
1. mortgage on condominium	$280,000.00	
2. bank loan (TD Canada Trust)	$2,000.00	
3. student loan	$13,500.00	
4. car loan		$28,000.00
TOTAL OF DEBIT ITEMS		
NET TOTAL 3 *[3(a) minus 3(b)]*	$70,500.00	$78,500.00

Form 13B: **Net Family Property Statement**   **(page 3)**   Court File Number

Table 4: Value or property excluded under subsection 4(2) of the *Family Law Act* *(List in the order of the categories in the financial statement.)*		
ITEM	HUSBAND	WIFE
1. CIBC bank account (gift from parents)	$15,000.00	
TOTAL 4	$15,000.00	

	HUSBAND	WIFE
TOTAL 2 *(from page 2)*	$378,100.00	$354,480.00
TOTAL 3 *(from page 2)*	$70,500.00	$78,500.00
TOTAL 4 *(from above)*	$15,000.00	
TOTAL 5 *([Total 2] + [Total 3] +[Total 4])*	$463,600.00	$432,980.00

	HUSBAND	WIFE
TOTAL 1 *(from page 1)*	$684,173.84	$707,673.84
TOTAL 5 *(from above)*	$463,600.00	$432,980.00
TOTAL 6: NET FAMILY PROPERTY *([Total 1] minus [Total 5])*	$220,573.84	$274,693.84

_____   _____
Signature   Date of signature

CHAPTER 7

THE MATRIMONIAL HOME UNDER THE *FAMILY LAW ACT*

INTRODUCTION

The matrimonial home occupies a unique place in family law. In most families, it is the asset having the greatest cash value and is the focal point for family life. Under the *Family Law Act*, the matrimonial home is treated differently from other family property. As we have seen in the previous chapter, there is no deduction for the value of the matrimonial home brought into the marriage. Neither is there an exclusion for a gift or inheritance of the matrimonial home after the marriage or in respect of any excluded property that can be traced to the matrimonial home. Part II of the FLA provides the spouses with special rights with respect to the matrimonial home, which include rights to possession and limitations upon encumbrance of the home.

WHO IS ENTITLED TO CLAIM SPECIAL RIGHTS TO THE MATRIMONIAL HOME?

As with equalization rights, the special rights with respect to the matrimonial home can only be claimed by married spouses and those who went through a form of marriage in good faith and are now seeking an annulment. Common-law spouses, whether opposite sex or same sex, have no status to claim the special rights to the matrimonial home under the FLA.

WHAT IS THE MATRIMONIAL HOME?

The FLA defines the matrimonial home in very specific terms in order to qualify for the protections set out in the Act. The matrimonial home is every property in which one spouse has an interest that was ordinarily occupied by the spouses as their family residence at the time of separation.[1]

---

[1] *Family Law Act*, R.S.O. 1990, c. F-3, s. 18(1) [hereinafter "FLA"].

Property in Which a Spouse Has an Interest

Property includes real or personal property;[2] therefore, a matrimonial home can be any kind of property such as a mobile home, trailer, cottage or even a boat, provided the spouses ordinarily use it as their family home at the relevant time. It is not essential that both spouses have an interest in the property as long as one of the spouses has an interest in it. The nature of a spouse's interest can be an ownership interest or some lesser interest such as a leasehold interest, a life interest, or a vested future interest. For example, if the spouses are renting the premises where they live, whether the lease is in one or both names, the premises would be their matrimonial home. Similarly, if a husband's father transfers the home to the spouses, subject to a life interest to himself, even if the parties separate before the father dies, the home is a matrimonial home at the time of separation, provided the parties lived there as their family residence. In that case, the spouse had a vested future interest at the time they received the deed.[3] In another case, the rights of a veteran spouse under the *Veteran's Land Act* contract were sufficient to amount to an interest in property.[4] There must be some enforceable right held by a spouse in the property in order for it to qualify as a matrimonial home.

Rapp v. Wagman (2001), 22 R.F.L. (5th) 407 (Ont. S.C.J.), additional reasons at (2002), 2002 CarswellOnt 4004 (Ont. S.C.J.)

The parties married in 1998 and lived in a home that was inherited by the husband's parent until they separated in 2001. The parent and the husband signed a licence agreement that permitted the husband to live in the house as a licensee only and not as a tenant. The agreement was signed by the husband and his parent and was witnessed by the wife. The wife claimed that the home was now owned by the husband and his siblings. The husband's parent applied for a declaration that the wife had no interest in the home.

Held: The application was dismissed.

Although a licence did not create an interest in land, the licence agreement may have been a lease agreement disguised as a licence agreement for the purpose of defeating any claims by the wife. The existence of the licence was irrelevant if, in fact, the husband had a beneficial interest in the property since that would be sufficient to bring the home within the definition of matrimonial home in the *Family Law Act*. The court could not declare that the wife had no interest in the property until the issues of ownership and the effect of the licence agreement were determined at trial.

---

[2] FLA, s. 17.
[3] See *Major v. Major* (1982), 31 R.F.L. (2d) 446 (Ont. U.F.C.).
[4] See *Brown, Re* (1979), 26 O.R. (2d) 252 (Ont. Co. Ct.).

More Than One Matrimonial Home

The matrimonial home is the place where the parties carry on their ordinary pattern of family life. The FLA states that "every" such property is a matrimonial home, provided one spouse has an interest in it.[5] Therefore, it is possible for a family to have more than one matrimonial home. For example, a couple could spend six months of each year in their Toronto home, three months each winter in their condominium in Florida. and three months at their cottage in Muskoka during the summer. If the spouses' normal lives revolve around each home for a significant part of each year, then each home is a matrimonial home. In many cases, a cottage that has been used by the family for vacations and weekends over several years has been considered to be a matrimonial home. On the other hand, a cottage that is only used on odd weekends would not be considered a matrimonial home.

Since the use of the home is a key ingredient in the definition, the character of a home can change throughout a marriage. For example, if the family discontinues the practice of using a cottage for family vacations, the cottage may lose its character as a matrimonial home.

Ownership of Shares in Corporation Holding Title to Home

The FLA also provides for the situation where one of the spouses owns shares in a corporation that entitles the owner of the shares to occupy a housing unit owned by the corporation.[6] Such ownership of shares is deemed to be an interest in the housing unit for purposes of defining the matrimonial home. However, the right to occupy the home must arise out of the ownership of the shares. It is insufficient if the person who owns shares occupies the home as a manager or as an employment "perk".[7]

Part of Property Used For Other Purposes

Sometimes a portion of the property that includes the family residence is used for other non-residential purposes. The FLA provides that where this is the case, only the portion of the property that may reasonably be regarded as necessary for the use and enjoyment of the residence will be the matrimonial home.[8] The most common cases involving other uses of

---

[5] FLA, s. 18(1).
[6] FLA, s. 18(2).
[7] See *Hartling v. Hartling* (July 11, 1979), Doc. Middlesex 05919 (Ont. S.C.) (occupancy arising from lease and not from shareholding in corporation that owned building).
[8] FLA, s. 18(3).

the property involve farmland. The portion of the land used for the farming operation would not be considered part of the matrimonial home. Similarly, if part of a property is rented out to third parties or used for commercial purposes such as a family business, that portion would not be considered part of the matrimonial home. Only the small surrounding area necessary for using and enjoying the residence would be the matrimonial home.

Application Questions

Which of the following would be a matrimonial home?

(a) a trailer, owned by a husband, situated in a trailer park where the family spent the entire summer each year;

(b) an apartment rented by a couple for two years prior to separation;

(c) a home owned by the wife's parents where the couple lived free of charge;

(d) a home owned jointly by a couple that was used as a rental property;

(e) a chalet in Collingwood, Ontario, owned by a couple, where they went skiing occasionally with friends;

(f) a home owned by a corporation in which a wife owned shares that entitled her to live there, assuming the couple lived in the home;

(g) a home that a couple lived in when they first married, in which their grown daughter and son-in-law now lived.

DESIGNATION OF THE MATRIMONIAL HOME

Where more than one property qualifies as a matrimonial home, the spouses may wish to designate one property as the matrimonial home and release other properties from the provisions of the Act. The FLA provides for one or both spouses to designate a property as their matrimonial home and this can include property contiguous to the home.[9] The registration of a designation by both spouses results in all other non-designated homes losing their status as a matrimonial home.[10] However, if only one spouse registers a designation, the other homes remain matrimonial homes.[11]

A designation of the matrimonial home can be cancelled by a cancellation executed by the person who made the original designation, by a certificate of divorce or judgment of nullity, by a court order, or proof of a spouse's

---

[9] FLA, s. 20(1), (2).
[10] FLA, s. 20(4).
[11] FLA, s. 20(5).

death.[12] Once a designation by both spouses is cancelled, all other properties that lost their status as a matrimonial home as a result of the designation will again become subject to the Act.

POSSESSION OF THE MATRIMONIAL HOME

Right to Equal Possession

During the marriage, both spouses have an equal right to possession of the matrimonial home.[13] The right to possession is distinct from any ownership rights or other interest a spouse may have in the property. A spouse has a right to equal possession even though only the other spouse has an interest in the matrimonial home. In such a case, the non-owning spouse's right to possession is a personal right against the other spouse and the right ends when they are no longer spouses.[14] Therefore, when a marriage ends by divorce, annulment, or by one spouse's death, the right of the non-owning spouse ceases to exist. However, it is possible to extend the right of the non-owning spouse after the marriage ends, either by court order or separation agreement. The right to equal possession cannot be limited or waived by a spouse in any provisions of a marriage contract. In such a case, the provision would be unenforceable.[15]

Spouse's Death

Where a spouse who has no interest in the matrimonial home is occupying the home at the time of the other spouse's death, the surviving spouse is entitled to remain in possession, rent-free, for 60 days after the spouse's death.[16]

Exclusive Possession

Regardless of who owns the matrimonial home, and regardless of the right to equal possession, the court has the discretionary power to order that one spouse be given exclusive possession of the home or part of it.[17] This kind of application is made where the spouses are unable to continue living together and one spouse applies for an order that the other spouse leave.

---

[12] FLA, s. 20(6).
[13] FLA, s. 19(1)
[14] FLA, s. 19(2).
[15] FLA, s. 52(2).
[16] FLA, s. 26(2).
[17] FLA, s. 24(1).

An order for exclusive possession is discretionary. The court must consider the following factors in making a decision about exclusive possession:[18]

- the best interests of the children involved;
- any existing family property or support orders;
- the financial position of the parties;
- any written agreement between the parties;
- the availability of other suitable affordable accommodation; and
- any violence against a spouse or children.

In determining the best interests of the child, the court is obliged to consider the disruptive effects upon a child of a move and the child's views and preferences.[19]

In addition to the factors listed above, the court may also consider other factors. These factors include:

- the likelihood that violence will occur if the parties remain together;
- the extent to which the property was acquired by gift or by special efforts;
- the number of children who would continue to reside in the home;
- the need of one spouse for immediate funds;
- in whose name the property is registered; and
- whether the person seeking to stay in the house is paying appropriate child support for children residing elsewhere with the other parent.

Occupation Rent

Where one spouse is awarded exclusive possession of the matrimonial home, the court is permitted to order the spouse who has exclusive possession to make periodic payments to the other spouse for the loss of use of the property.[20] Sometimes, the cost of maintaining the house that is paid by the person remaining in possession will cancel out any obligation to pay occupation rent to the other spouse.

Payments to the Spouse in Possession

After the court has ordered one party to vacate the matrimonial home, the court can nevertheless order that party to pay for all or part of the repairs and maintenance of the matrimonial home or liabilities arising in

---

[18] FLA, s. 24(3).
[19] FLA, s. 24(4).
[20] FLA, s. 24(1)(c).

respect of it, or to make periodic payments to the spouse who has exclusive possession for those purposes.[21] In other words, the court can order the spouse who has been forced to leave the matrimonial home to continue to make payments on the mortgage, for taxes and other expenses related to the matrimonial home, or can order that spouse to make payments to the other spouse so that the spouse in possession can make mortgage payments, etc.

If a party has been ordered to vacate the matrimonial home, it is an offence for that person to violate the exclusive possession order.[22] If convicted, that person is liable to a fine of up to $5,000 and/or imprisonment for up to three months; for a second or subsequent offence, to a fine of up to $10,000 and/or imprisonment for up to two years. A police officer can arrest anyone he or she has reasonable and probable grounds to believe has contravened an exclusive possession order, without a warrant.[23]

Effect of Partition and Sale Application

Where the spouses co-own the matrimonial home, the *Partition Act*[24] permits an application by one of the owners for partition and sale of the property if such a sale is considered by the court to be advantageous to the parties.[25]

> ### *Stafford v. Rebane* (2004), 2004 CarswellOnt 4251 (Ont. S.C.J.)
>
> When the parties separated, the wife left the matrimonial home and the husband remained living there with the children of the marriage. Before the family law issues had been resolved i.e. exclusive possession and equalization, the wife applied for partition and sale of the home pursuant to the provisions of the *Partition Act*. The husband applied for interim exclusive possession of the matrimonial home under the *Family Law Act*.
>
> Held: The wife's application for partition and sale was denied. Husband was granted interim exclusive possession of the matrimonial home.
>
> . . .[A]n order directing the sale of a matrimonial home before trial should only be made in cases where, in all of the circumstances, such an order is appropriate. Orders for the sale of a matrimonial home made before the resolution of *Family Law Act* issues (particularly the determination of the equalization payment), should not be made as a matter of course. See Binkley v. Binkley (1988), 14 R.F.L. (3d) 336 (Ont. C.A.). In addition, spousal rights

---

[21] FLA, s. 24(1)(e).
[22] FLA, s. 24(5).
[23] FLA, s. 24(6).
[24] R.S.O. 1990, c. P.4.
[25] *Partition Act*, s. 3(1).

of possession (s. 19) and any order for interim exclusive possession should be taken into account. [At para. 30.]

Also, the order for partition and sale would prejudice the husband's claim for exclusive possession until the youngest son has finished high school in four-and-a-half years. The court accepted the husband's testimony that it would be harmful to the children if they were forced to leave the home at this time. The children had lived in the home since 1989. The son's school was a five-minute walk away and the home provided stability and continuity for the children. As well, the home was only five minutes away from the husband's job.

Application Questions

Heather and Terry separated after a 24-year marriage, although they both continued to live in the matrimonial home. Their two daughters, aged 20 and 21, and their son, aged 15, lived in the home with them. Terry admitted that he was an alcoholic and that he was in a state of depression and was no longer working. He had hit rock bottom and was under medical care for his depression.

The couple had originally afforded the matrimonial home through a generous long-term loan of about $35,000 from Terry's mother. The mother had lived in the self-contained "granny suite" that Terry had constructed in the basement. Terry had now repaid the loan to his mother through a severance package he had received. His mother was now living in a nursing home.

Heather and the two adult daughters wanted to have Terry removed from the home. The accusations of verbal abuse went both ways. The physical abuse alleged by Heather was never substantiated. There was no evidence that the son wanted his father out of the home.

(a) List the factors in this case that are relevant to the application for exclusive possession.

(b) Which factors *must* the court consider and which ones are discretionary?

(c) Would Heather likely be successful in obtaining an order for exclusive possession? Why or why not?

DISPOSITION AND ENCUMBRANCE OF MATRIMONIAL HOME

Part II of the FLA places certain restrictions upon a married spouse's ability to dispose of or encumber his or her interest in the matrimonial home.

Spousal Consent Required

In general, a spouse cannot transfer the matrimonial home (i.e., sell it or give it away) or create any kind of encumbrance such as mortgage on the home unless the other spouse consents to the transaction.[26] The other spouse's consent is required even though the consenting spouse has no interest in the property. The other spouse can consent by signing the transaction document or executing a consent, or they can release all of his or her rights to the home in a separation agreement.[27] Otherwise, the spouse wishing to deal with the matrimonial home must obtain a court order releasing the property from the application of the FLA provisions or make sure that another property has been designated and registered as a matrimonial home by the parties.[28] This provision does not apply to liens on the matrimonial home arising by operation of law.[29] Thus, if an automatic lien arose as a result of failing to pay property taxes on the matrimonial home, this would not require the consent of the non-owning spouse.

For example, if a wife owned both a city home and a cottage that qualified as a matrimonial home, as long as the city home was designated and registered by herself and her husband as the matrimonial home, she would be free to sell the cottage without the husband's consent. Otherwise, the wife could not sell the cottage without the husband's consent unless she obtained a court order or the husband had released his rights to the cottage under a separation agreement.

Failure to Obtain Spousal Consent to Transaction

If a spouse fails to obtain the proper consent of the other spouse to a sale or mortgage transaction involving the matrimonial home, the entire transaction can be set aside. However, the transaction will not be set aside if the person received the interest in the home for value, in good faith and without notice that it was a matrimonial home, at the time they entered the transaction.[30] The spouse who makes the disposition or encumbrance of the home usually makes a statement pursuant to the Act verifying either that they are not a spouse, that the property is not a matrimonial home, or that the other spouse has released their interest, if it is a matrimonial home.[31] If such a statement is made, then the person receiving the interest

---

[26] FLA, s. 21(1).
[27] FLA, s. 21(1)(a), (b).
[28] FLA, s. 21(1)(c), (d).
[29] FLA, s. 21(5).
[30] FLA, s. 21(2).
[31] FLA, s. 21(3).

in the matrimonial home is entitled to presume that it is not a matrimonial home, unless the person had other evidence to the contrary.[32]

Where a person makes a false statement in order to sell or encumber the matrimonial home, the court can set aside the transaction.[33] In such a situation, the court can also order the person who made the false statement, and anyone who bought the property knowing the statement was false and then resold it, to substitute other real property in the place of the matrimonial home, or to set aside money or security to stand in place of the matrimonial home.[34]

Walduda v. Bell (2004), 7 R.F.L. (6th) 205 (Ont. S.C.J.)

The parties were joint owners of the matrimonial home. After the wife left the matrimonial home with the parties' three children, the wife's sister obtained judgments against the wife in the total amount of $249,995.51 with respect to promissory notes issued by the wife to her sister within the six-month period after separation. All of the promissory notes indebted the wife to her sister. The funds received were used to fund the wife's litigation against the husband. The sister then filed writs of execution against the matrimonial home to realize upon the judgments against the wife. When the parties divorced, the husband was awarded custody of the three children and exclusive possession of the matrimonial home.

The husband brought an application for an order under section 23(d) of the FLA to set aside the writs of execution because they were encumbrances against the matrimonial home that were obtained without his consent, contrary to section 21(1) of the Act. He also sought an order revesting his interest in the matrimonial home pursuant to section 23(d) of the FLA.

Held: The husband's applications were granted.

The wife's actions in obtaining funds from her sister through a series of unsecured transactions did not directly result in an encumbrance against the wife's interest in the matrimonial home. The plain meaning of the terms "disposition" and "encumbrance" could not be extended to include executions taken by creditors of one of the parties to the marriage. The circumstances indicated that the loan arrangements between the wife and her sister were not "normal commercial transactions". The sister was not an arms-length creditor and it was the shared intent of the wife and her sister to encumber the wife's interest in the matrimonial home, in order to "tie up" the matrimonial home against the husband's occupancy. At no time during the matrimonial litigation did the wife indicate that she had

---

[32] FLA, s. 21(3).
[33] FLA, s. 23(d).
[34] FLA, s. 24(1)(g).

obtained loans from her sister. At no time did the sister attempt to enforce the writs. The timing and conditions surrounding the loans undermined the evidence of the wife and her sister that the transactions were *bona fide*.

Application Questions

1. A father, who was suffering from Alzheimer's disease, granted a valid power of attorney to his daughter, Sandra. Sandra's parents owned the matrimonial home jointly. Sandra used the power of attorney to co-sign the transfer of the matrimonial home to herself. She convinced her mother to sign her share of the home over to her by telling her mother it was necessary to prevent the government from taking the house when she went into a nursing home. Sandra now had full title to her parents' matrimonial home.

   Would either of Sandra's parents have grounds to have the transfer of the home to Sandra set aside under the FLA? Explain.

2. While her husband Gerhard was in Europe on business, Candice forged her husband's signature on documents in order to obtain a mortgage on the matrimonial home from the CIBC. The bank had no reason to doubt the husband's signature.

   Would Gerhard be able to have the transaction set aside upon his return to Canada? Why or why not?

JOINT TENANCY IN THE MATRIMONIAL HOME

When the spouses own the matrimonial home in joint tenancy, the right of survivorship arises, by operation of law, upon the death of one of the spouses. This means that the property vests completely in the surviving spouse who becomes the sole owner of the property. However, if one spouse owns the matrimonial home jointly with someone other than his or her spouse, the FLA provides a solution to the potential problem that could arise if the spouse dies before the other joint tenant. The law deems the joint tenancy to be severed immediately before the time of death.[35] The joint tenancy becomes a tenancy-in-common at that time, thus preventing the right of survivorship from vesting the matrimonial home solely in the third party.

As an example, a husband might own the matrimonial home jointly with his brother, although the husband and wife reside in the home as their matrimonial home. If the husband dies before his brother, the joint tenancy

---

[35] FLA, s. 26(1).

would be deemed severed right before the husband's death and the husband would then own the home as a tenant-in-common with his brother. The husband's portion of the matrimonial home would fall into his estate and would most likely devolve to the wife.

CHAPTER 8

SUPPORT OBLIGATIONS UNDER THE *FAMILY LAW ACT*

Part III of the *Family Law Act* creates an obligation on every person to support his or her dependants. A "dependant" is defined as "a person to whom another has an obligation to provide support under this Part."[1] This Part creates three support obligations; to your spouse, to your child, and to your parent. Every child over the age of majority is obligated to support his or her parent who has cared for or provided support to him or her.[2] However, there have been few cases claiming parental support. This chapter will focus on spousal support and child support.

SPOUSAL SUPPORT

Who Can Apply

The definition of "spouse" under the *Family Law Act* is much broader and more inclusive than under the *Divorce Act*. For the purposes of support, "spouse" means not only either of two persons who are married to each other,[3] but also includes:

- persons who have entered into a marriage that is void or voidable in good faith on the part of the person claiming support;[4]

- spouses to a polygamous marriage, if it was celebrated in a place where such marriages are valid;[5] and

- either of two persons who are not married to each other and have cohabited,

    (a) continuously for a period of not less than three years, or

---

[1] *Family Law Act*, R.S.O. 1990, c. F.3, s. 29, "dependant" [hereinafter "FLA"].

[2] FLA, s. 32.

[3] FLA, s.1(1), "spouse" (a).

[4] FLA, s.1(1), "spouse" (b).

[5] FLA, s. 1(2).

(b) in a relationship of some permanence, if they are the natural or adoptive parents of a child.[6]

"Cohabit" is defined as "to live together in a conjugal relationship, whether within or outside marriage."[7]

This definition of spouse encompasses married couples, people whose marriage is invalid, and couples who were never married. It embraces both opposite-sex and same-sex partners.

Lehner v. Grundl (1995), [1995] O.J. No. 181, 1995 CarswellOnt 2077 (Ont. Gen. Div.), affirmed on this point by the Ontario Court of Appeal at (1999), [1999] O.J. No. 1573, 1999 CarswellOnt 1318 (Ont. C.A.)

In the spring of 1986, when the parties began their relationship, both parties were working. . . . In the latter part of 1986 the parties discussed and actively pursued purchasing a home together. Sixty-five Bow Valley Drive was a two-bedroom bungalow and was not large enough to accommodate the furnishings of both Mr. Lehner and Mrs. Grundl. Mr. Lehner planned to sell 65 Bow Valley Drive, and Mrs. Grundl planned to liquidate some of her investments then held in mortgages. The plan was for each of the parties to equally contribute to the purchase of a new home. . . . It was clear that Mrs. Grundl and Mr. Lehner shared day-to-day tasks of laundry, cooking, cleaning and gardening. I conclude from the evidence that 65 Bow Valley was Mrs. Grundl's main base and primary home where she spent time each day. I find that she stayed overnight frequently. However, it was important for Mrs. Grundl to maintain a separate residence for her own sense of security and to maintain her independence from Mr. Lehner. Occasionally she spent time with family and on her own at her separate apartment. . . . Throughout the relationship each of the parties kept their finances separate. They maintained separate bank accounts. They shared the cost of food. Mr. Lehner paid the operating expenses of 65 Bow Valley and the Cottage, perhaps with assistance from Mrs. Grundl on one hydro bill for the Cottage. Mrs. Grundl paid for her apartment. [At paras. 9, 11, 14 and 17.]

In December, 1992, the parties separated.

Held: Mrs. Grundl's claim for support was dismissed. The court concluded that she was not a spouse within the meaning of the *Family Law Act*. The parties had distinct financial arrangements and the woman received no direct financial support from the man. Although Mrs. Grundl had contributed to the relationship by cooking, cleaning, decorating, gardening and organizing social events, she had her own residence. Consenting adults

---

[6] FLA, s. 29.
[7] FLA, s. 1(1).

with separate residences who visited one another could not be said to cohabit.

Section 30 of the Act creates an obligation on every spouse to support him- or herself and the other spouse, in accordance with need, to the extent he or she is capable of doing so. An application for support can be made by a spouse,[8] and also by agencies (such as the Ministry of Community and Social Services), which provide benefits to the spouse.[9]

The *Limitations Act, 2002*,[10] applies to applications for support. Therefore, an application for support must be made within two years of separation. This is so whether the application is being made by the spouse or by an agency.[11]

Application Questions

Would the following be spouses within the meaning of the *Family Law Act*?

(a) Krista and Kyle where married in 1990 and separated in 2005. *yes*

(b) George and Steven were married in 2004 and have just recently separated. *yes*

(c) Anna and Cameron have been living together in a conjugal relationship for five years and have two children. Although they were never legally married, they have gone thorough a "promising" ceremony in front of their friends. *no*

(d) Veronica and Shawn were married in 2000. Veronica has just found out that Shawn was married before, but never divorced. His first wife is still alive. *yes*

(e) Dim is one of Hake's five wives. In the place where they were married, polygamous marriages are legal. *yes*

(f) Diana and Cory were only together for a "one-night stand." Henry was born as a result. *no*

(g) Lisa and Nadine have been living together continuously in a conjugal relationship for seven years. They have no children. *no*

---

[8] FLA, s. 30.
[9] FLA, s. 33(3).
[10] S.O. 2002, c. 24. Sched. B.
[11] FLA, s. 33(2.1).

Even where support has been agreed to by the parties in a contract, it may still be possible to apply to the court for a different amount of support. If the parties have entered into a domestic contract wherein the parties have either agreed to support, or have agreed that no support is payable, the court can set aside the contract, and decide spousal support, where any one of the following can be shown:

- the agreement for support or not to pay support results in circumstances that are unconscionable;

- the agreement results in a spouse qualifying to be supported out of public money; or

- the payor spouse has defaulted on the support payment.

The court can intervene in these circumstances, even if the contract says otherwise.[12]

Desramaux v. Desramaux (2002), [2002] O.J. No. 3251, 2002 CarswellOnt 2731 (Ont. C.A.), leave to appeal refused (2003), 2003 CarswellOnt 1383 (S.C.C.)

Appeal by the wife from a judgment dismissing her claim for spousal support and ordering her to repay child support of $5,142. The parties were married in 1971 and separated in 1991. The wife had a grade 10 education. She worked as a nurse's aid until their first child was born in 1974. She then remained at home raising the children. She returned to part-time sales work in 1989 and never obtained further training. The husband was continuously employed with a bank throughout the marriage. The family had moved six times during the marriage to enable the husband to further his career. The husband gave the wife no financial support after the separation, although his annual income was $70,000. The parties' separation agreement provided the wife with time-limited spousal support and contained a release and waiver of further claims to spousal support. At the time of the trial, the husband's annual income was $102,400. The wife worked as a babysitter in her home and suffered from numerous health problems. Her weekly income was $150. The trial judge dismissed her claim for spousal support on the basis of the agreement and release. He refused to apply section 33(4) of the *Family Law Act* and set aside the support provisions in the agreement. The trial judge also ordered the wife to repay child support paid by the husband for the time when one child reached the age of majority and was no longer in school.

Held: Appeal allowed in part. The trial judge erred in refusing to consider the applicability of section 33(4).

---

[12] FLA, s. 33(4).

The wife had sacrificed her career potential in order to advance that of her husband's. She had a limited income and there was no realistic expectation that her employment situation would change, given her limited education and sparse, outdated work experience. The husband, conversely, was enjoying a $100,000 per year income. The waiver of spousal support provision was set aside on the basis that it resulted in unconscionable circumstances. The husband was ordered to pay spousal support of $3,000 per month. Although it seemed unfair to require the wife to repay the overpayment of child support, the trial judge did not err in making this decision.

How Support is Determined

The purposes of an order for spousal support under the *Family Law Act* are very similar to the objectives of a spousal support order under the *Divorce Act*. They are to:

- recognize the spouse's contribution to the relationship and the economic consequences of the relationship for the spouse;

- share the economic burden of child support equitably;

- make fair provisions to assist the spouse to become able to contribute to his or her own support; and

- relieve financial hardship, if this has not been done by orders under Parts I (Family Property) and II (Matrimonial Home).[13]

The *Family Law Act* also requires the court to consider a long list of factors before deciding on the amount and duration of support.[14] Despite the *Family Law Act* being more specific in terms of what the court needs to consider, the amount and duration of spousal support would be the same under both the *Divorce Act* and the *Family Law Act*.

With regard to a spouse's conduct that leads to the relationship's breakdown, the court cannot consider conduct unless it is "so unconscionable as to constitute an obvious and gross repudiation of the relationship."[15] Despite being able to take extreme conduct into consideration in deciding the amount or duration of spousal support, the courts very rarely do so. In effect, conduct leading to the relationship's breakdown is virtually never a factor in spousal support.

---

[13] FLA, s. 33(8).
[14] FLA, s. 33(9).
[15] FLA, s. 33(10).

Types of Orders

As with the *Divorce Act*, the court has very wide powers to make different kinds of orders for support under the *Family Law Act*.[16] The court can make both interim and final orders. Support can be in the form of a lump sum or periodic payments or both, it can be for a definite or unlimited amount of time, and it can be secured against property. However, under the *Family Law Act*, the court can also make other orders such as ordering property to be transferred or held in trust for the dependant, ordering money be paid into court, making orders for exclusive possession of the matrimonial home, and ordering one spouse to designate another as irrevocable beneficiary under a life insurance policy.

Both child and spousal support orders bind the estate of the person obligated to make the support payments, unless the court orders otherwise.[17] This means that if the support payor should die while the obligation to pay support exists, then the persons entitled to support can make a claim against the property that the support payor left behind.

Indexing

Section 34(5) of the *Family Law Act* allows spousal support (but not child support) to be indexed. This means that when ordering spousal support, the court can include a clause stating that the amount of spousal support will increase every year with the cost of living. The increase takes effect each year on the day the order was made. The change is based on the percentage increase in the All Items Consumer Price Index (CPI) for Canada[18] each November. This percentage increase is usually available by the third or fourth week of December of each year. You can find out what the increase is by telephoning Statistics Canada at 1-800-263-1136 or consulting the website at www.statcan.ca.

For example, if the court ordered spousal support of $1,000 per month on May 12, 2004, and ordered that spousal support be indexed, then the support recipient would be entitled to an increase on the anniversary date, which is May 12, 2005. Regardless of what month the order is made, the increase is always based on the change in the CPI for November. The increase for November 2004 was 2.4 per cent. This means that the support recipient is entitled to a 2.4 per cent increase in support ($1,000 x 2.4 per cent = $24). Therefore, as of May 12, 2005, the support recipient would be entitled to support of $1,024.

---

[16] FLA, s. 34(1).
[17] FLA, s. 34(4).
[18] FLA, s. 34(6).

If support is being paid pursuant to a domestic contract that does not contain an indexing clause, that contract can be filed with the Ontario Court of Justice or with the Family Court, and then the court can order that spousal support be indexed.[19] This is so even if the contract contains a clause to the contrary.[20]

If the original support order does not contain an indexing clause, then the spouse, or an agency that could have applied for support on behalf of the spouse, can apply to the court to have the order indexed.[21]

Effect of Divorce Proceedings

An application for spousal support under the *Divorce Act* has precedence over an application under the *Family Law Act*. If an application under the *Family Law Act* has already begun when an application under the *Divorce Act* is commenced, then:

- the application under the *Family Law Act* is stayed, which means it cannot proceed any further. Proceedings continue under the *Divorce Act*;

- any arrears that have accumulated under the *Family Law Act* order can be included in the order under the *Divorce Act*;

- an interim order under the *Family Law Act* continues in force until it is changed pursuant to the *Divorce Act*; and

- if the Divorce Order does not contain any support provisions, any previous final orders under the *Family Law Act* continue in force.[22]

Variation of Spousal Support under the *Family Law Act*

Variations of spousal support can be made under section 37 of the *Family Law Act*. Applications can be made by the spouse or by an agency that provides benefits to the spouse.[23] In order to make a variation order, the court must be satisfied that there has been a material change in either spouse's circumstances or evidence that was not available at the previous hearing becomes available.[24] Orders can be retroactive. A variation appli-

---

[19] FLA, s. 35(1), (2).
[20] FLA, s. 35(4).
[21] FLA, s. 38(2).
[22] FLA, s. 36.
[23] FLA, s. 37(1).
[24] FLA, s. 37(2).

cation cannot be made for at least six months after the order was first made or varied, unless the court gives permission.[25]

As mentioned previously, if the court has awarded a lower amount or no spousal support because of a child support order, when the child support is reduced or ends, the spouse would be entitled to have spousal support re-determined.[26]

CHILD SUPPORT UNDER THE *FAMILY LAW ACT*

Although for the most part, child support obligations are the same under the *Divorce Act* and *the Family Law Act*, the differences between the two acts are worth examining.

Section 31 of the *Family Law Act* creates an obligation on every parent to provide support to his or her child that is:

- unmarried, and

- a minor, or enrolled in a full time program of education.

There is no obligation to support a child that is 16 years of age or older and has withdrawn from parental control, whereas it would appear under the *Divorce Act*, parents have no obligation to support a child who has withdrawn from their charge, regardless of age. The *Family Law Act* also makes no provision for support of disabled children over the age of majority.

Under the *Family Law Act*, the definition of "child" includes someone that a person has demonstrated a "settled intention" to treat as a child of his or her family. Although the wording is different from the *Divorce Act*'s definition, the effect is the same. If a person treats the child as his or her own child, then the person will be obligated to support that child.

> ### *Ballmick v. Ballmick*, 2005 ONCJ 101, 2005 CarswellOnt 1205, (sub nom. *B.B. v. C.P.B.*), [2005] O.J. No. 1209 (Ont. C.J.)
>
> This matter arises in the context of an application by [Mrs. B.] for support for her three children, [R.B.] (born on 26 December 1990) and [N.B.] (born on 12 August 1994) (hereinafter referred to as "the boys") and [C.B.] (born on 5 December 1997). The threshold issue is whether [Mr. B.] has demonstrated a settled intention to treat the boys as children of his family under the *Family Law Act*, R.S.O. 1990, c. F-3, as amended. . . . The parties married on 1 June 19[8]8 in Guyana. The three children named above were born

---

[25] FLA, s. 37(3).
[26] FLA, s. 38.1.

> during the course of the marriage. Until the parents' separation in July 2001, the children resided with them, with the exception of one year when [C.B.] lived with relatives in Guyana. The parents separated after 13 years of marriage and the children had their primary residence with their mother. The parents were divorced in January 2003. . . . At some point after separation, [Mr. B.] received information that suggested that the older two children were not his biological offspring. . . . [O]nce [Mr. B.] was certain in his own mind that the older two children were not his, he voluntarily ceased to exercise any access to them and cut all ties with them. Paternity testing was eventually completed in April 2004 that established that [Mr. B.] was indeed not the father of [R.B.] or [N.B.]. [Mr. B.] has remained steadfast in his position that, since the older two children are not biologically his, he wants nothing to do with them. He has put a claim forward for sole custody of [C.B.]. [At paras. 1-3.]
>
> It is clear and undisputed that [Mr. B.] acted as a father to all three of the children, without discrimination, prior to the separation. . . . Indeed, he is the only father whom the children have known for their entire lives. . . . The emotional bonding, shared memories and trust that was built up over time cannot be wiped out with the stroke of a pen. For better or for worse, with intention or without it, [Mr. B.] is the boys' father. In all the ways that fatherhood matters—love, guidance, pride, nurturing, role modeling, connection—[Mr. B.] is a father to these boys. It is their concept of him as father that was—and continues to be—important. This was not a relationship entered into by either child or parent in a tentative or temporary fashion. It has been, since the children's birth, the only paternal relationship that either the boys or [Mr. B.] has known. [At paras. 4, 20.]

In addition to creating an obligation on parents to support their children, the *Family Law Act* also creates an obligation on children to support their parents. Every child over the age of majority is obligated to support his or her parent who has cared for, or provided support to him or her.[27] The *Divorce Act* does not have any similar provision. Another difference is that the *Family Law Act* allows a child to bring a support application,[28] whereas the *Divorce Act* does not. The *Family Law Act* also allows agencies, such as the Ministry of Community and Social Service, to bring an application on behalf of a person, if they have provided benefits to that person, or if the person has applied for benefits.[29]

The *Child Support Guidelines*

A court making an order for child support under the *Family Law Act* must do so in accordance with the *Child Support Guidelines*. Therefore, the

---

[27] FLA, s. 32.
[28] FLA, s. 33(2).
[29] FLA, s. 33(3).

amount of child support will be identical, whether the application is made under the *Divorce Act* or the *Family Law Act*. Like the *Divorce Act*, the *Family Law Act* allows the court to order a non-*Guideline* amount, where special provision is made for the child, such as a trust account or transfer of property, if it would be inequitable to order the *Guideline* amount under the circumstances, but must give reasons for doing so.[30] The court can also order an amount that the parties have agreed to that is different from the *Guideline* amount, if it is reasonable to do so having regard to the *Guidelines*.[31]

Effect of Divorce Proceedings

An application for child support under the *Divorce Act* has precedence over an application under the *Family Law Act*. If an application under the *Family Law Act* has already begun when an application under the *Divorce Act* is commenced, then:

- the application under the *Family Law Act* is stayed, which means it cannot proceed any further. Proceedings continue under the *Divorce Act*;

- any arrears that have accumulated under the *Family Law Act* order can be included in the order under the *Divorce Act*;

- an interim order under the *Family Law Act* continues in force until it is changed pursuant to the *Divorce Act*; and

- if the Divorce Order does not contain any support provisions, any previous final orders under the *Family Law Act* continue in force.[32]

Variation of Child Support

Variations of child support can be made under section 37 of the *Family Law Act*. A variation application can be made by anyone who could have applied for child support in the first place, namely the child, the parents of the child, an agency, and also the personal representative of a dependant or a respondent.[33] In order to make a variation order, the court must be satisfied that there has been a change of circumstances within the meaning of the *Child Support Guidelines*, or that evidence has become available that

---

[30] FLA, s. 33(12), (13).
[31] FLA, s. 33(14).
[32] FLA, s. 36.
[33] FLA, s. 37(1).

was not available at the hearing. The new child support order must be in accordance with the *Guidelines*,[34] unless special provision has been made for the child, or the parties have agreed to an amount that is reasonable, having regard to the *Guidelines*.[35] A variation application cannot be made for at least six months after the order was first made or varied, unless the court gives permission.[36]

Application Questions

1. Carly, 17, lives with her father. She has had little contact with her mother, who has never paid any child support. Carly's father never bothered to pursue a child support claim against Carly's mother because he was just as happy that she left them alone. Carly now wishes to apply herself for a child support order against her mother. Can she?

2. Russell is paying $755 per month in child support, which is the table amount, to his ex-wife Elena for their two minor children, who are in Elena's custody. At the time the order was made, Elena was not working, but now she has a good job and is earning $50,000 per year. Can Russell have his child support varied, based on this change?

CHILD SUPPORT PROCEDURE

Application and Financial Statements

To begin an application for child support, the applicant would file and serve a Form 8 Application.[37] The applicant can ask for other relief as well, such as a divorce, custody, or equalization of net family properties.[38] If the claim is only for child support, and a table amount only is being requested, it is not necessary to file a financial statement.[39] If support is otherwise being claimed, but no claims to property or exclusive possession are being made, then the applicant must serve and file a Form 13 Financial Statement with the Application.[40] If property and/or exclusive possession are also being claimed, then a Form 13.1 Financial Statement must be served and filed with the claim.[41] The court cannot accept documents filed without a fi-

---

[34] FLA, s. 37(2.2).

[35] FLA, s. 37(2.3)-(2.6).

[36] FLA, s. 37(3).

[37] FLA, O. Reg. 114/99, as am., s. 8(1).

[38] Rule 8(3)(b).

[39] Rule 13(1.3).

[40] Rule 13(1.1).

[41] Rule 13(1.2).

nancial statement, if the Rules require them.[42] A Continuing Record must also be served and filed.[43] The respondent then has 30 days to serve and file a Form 10 Answer,[44] unless he or she was served outside of Canada and the U.S., in which case the respondent has 60 days.[45] The applicant can serve and file a Form 10A Reply within ten days.[46]

Motions for Temporary Orders

A party in the case can make a motion for a temporary order.[47] The party making a motion on notice must serve and file a Form 14 Motion, a Form 14A Affidavit, and any other evidence he or she will be relying on in the motion, on all the other parties, at least four days before the motion.[48] These materials should be filed as soon as possible, but must be filed by 2:00 p.m. at least two days before the motion date.[49] A Form 14C Confirmation must also be filed by 2:00 p.m. two days before the motion date.[50]

However, no motion material may be served, and no motion may be heard, until a Case Conference has taken place,[51] unless it is a situation of urgency or hardship.[52]

Motions to Change a Final Order or Agreement

If a person wishes to change a final order for child support, whether the order was made under the *Divorce Act* or the *Family Law Act*, the procedure under Rule 15 must be followed. The person wishing to change the order must serve the Notice of Motion by special service, at least 30 days before the motion is to be heard (or 60 days, if the Notice is served outside of the U.S. or Canada).[53] However, the motion cannot be heard until a Case Conference has been held.[54] Rule 15(7) sets out the information that must be included in the affidavit in support of the motion. A copy of the existing order or agreement must be attached as an exhibit to the affidavit.[55] Al-

---

[42] Rule 13(10).
[43] Rule 9(1).
[44] Rule 10(1).
[45] Rule 10(2).
[46] Rule 10(6).
[47] Rule 14(1).
[48] Rule 14(11)(a).
[49] Rule 14(11)(b), (11.1).
[50] Rule 14(11)(c).
[51] Rule 14(4).
[52] Rule 14(4.2).
[53] Rule 15(1).
[54] Rule 15(2.1).
[55] Rule 15(8).

ternatively, the party asking for the change can serve and file a Form 15 Change Information Form, with all the required attachments, instead of an affidavit.[56] The responding party may serve and file an affidavit if he or she disagrees with any of the evidence.[57] If either party is claiming that the amount of child support should not be the table amount, then the parties must serve and file affidavits containing information on why the order should be an exception to the presumptive rule (e.g., split custody, income over $150,000), and financial statements.[58]

If the parties are in agreement as to what the child support order should be, then, instead of proceeding by way of a motion, they can simply file the following materials:

- a Change Information Form (Form 15);

- a Consent (Form 15A);

- five copies of a draft Order;

- a stamped envelope addressed to each of the parties;

- a Support Deduction Order Information Form; and

- a draft Support Deduction Order.[59]

The Clerk then presents this material to a judge. If everything is in order, the judge will sign the order and copies will be sent to the parties in the envelopes provided.[60] This avoids the necessity of anyone having to appear in court.

---

[56] Rule 15(12)(a).
[57] Rule 15 (12)(b).
[58] Rule 15 (12)(c).
[59] Rule 15 (10).
[60] Rule 15(11).

APPENDIX 8A

ONTARIO

SUPERIOR COURT OF JUSTICE FAMILY COURT BRANCH

SEAL

(Name of court)

at **80 Dundas Street, London, Ontario, N6A 2P3**

Court office address

Court File Number

Family Law Rules, O. Reg. 114/99

Form 8: Application (General)

Applicant(s)

Full legal name & address for service – street & number, municipality, postal code, telephone & fax numbers and e-mail address (if any).	*Lawyer's name & address – street & number, municipality, postal code, telephone & fax numbers and e-mail address (if any).*
Patricia Ann Seymour **325 Traditional Lane** **London, Ontario** **N6P 5L7**	**Cassandra Burton** **Barrister & Solicitor** **68 Dundas Street, Suite 1108** **London, Ontario** **N6A 2P2** **Tel: (519) 777-8822** **Fax: (519) 777-8823**

Respondent(s)

Full legal name & address for service – street & number, municipality, postal code, telephone & fax numbers and e-mail address (if any).	*Lawyer's name & address – street & number, municipality, postal code, telephone & fax numbers and e-mail address (if any).*
Richard John Seymour **78 Cherry Hill Park** **London, Ontario** **N6P 5L9**	

TO THE RESPONDENT(S):

A COURT CASE HAS BEEN STARTED AGAINST YOU IN THIS COURT. THE DETAILS ARE SET OUT ON THE ATTACHED PAGES.

☒ **THE FIRST COURT DATE IS** *(date)* **Tues. April 4, 2006** **AT** **9:30** ☒ a.m. ☐ p.m. or as soon as possible after that time, at: *(address)*

80 Dundas Street, London, Ontario, N6A 2P3.

NOTE: If this is a divorce case, no date will be set unless an Answer is filed. If you have also been served with a notice of motion, there may be an earlier court date and you or your lawyer should come to court for the motion.

☒ **THIS CASE IS ON THE FAST TRACK OF THE CASE MANAGEMENT SYSTEM.** A case management judge will be assigned by the time this case first comes before a judge.

☐ **THIS CASE IS ON THE STANDARD TRACK OF THE CASE MANAGEMENT SYSTEM. No court date has been set for this case** but, if you have been served with a notice of motion, it has a court date and you or your lawyer should come to court for the motion. A case management judge will not be assigned until one of the parties asks the clerk of the court to schedule a case conference or until a notice of motion under subrule 14(5) is served before a case conference has been held. If, after 200 days, the case has not been scheduled for trial, the clerk of the court will send out a warning that the case will be dismissed in 30 days unless the parties file proof that the case has been settled or one of the parties asks for a case conference or a settlement conference.

IF YOU WANT TO OPPOSE ANY CLAIM IN THIS CASE, you or your lawyer must prepare an Answer (Form 10 – a blank copy should be attached), serve a copy on the applicant(s) and file a copy in the court office with an Affidavit of Service (Form 6B). **YOU HAVE ONLY 30 DAYS AFTER THIS APPLICATION IS SERVED ON YOU (60 DAYS IF THIS APPLICATION IS SERVED ON YOU OUTSIDE CANADA OR THE UNITED STATES) TO SERVE AND FILE AN ANSWER. IF YOU DO NOT, THE CASE WILL GO AHEAD WITHOUT YOU AND THE COURT MAY MAKE AN ORDER AND ENFORCE IT AGAINST YOU.**

FLR 8 (Rev. 04/03)

Form 8: Application (General)	(page 2)	Court File Number

Check the box of the paragraph that applies to your case

☒ This case includes a claim for support. It does not include a claim for property or exclusive possession of the matrimonial home and its contents. You **MUST** fill out a Financial Statement (Form 13 – a blank copy attached), serve a copy on the applicant(s) and file a copy in the court office with an Affidavit of Service even if you do not answer this case.

☐ This case includes a claim for property or exclusive possession of the matrimonial home and its contents. You **MUST** fill out a Financial Statement (Form 13.1 – a blank copy attached), serve a copy on the applicant(s) and file a copy in the court office with an Affidavit of Service even if you do not answer this case.

IF YOU WANT TO MAKE A CLAIM OF YOUR OWN, you or your lawyer must fill out the claim portion in the Answer, serve a copy on the applicant(s) and file a copy in the court office with an Affidavit of Service.

- If you want to make a claim for support but do not want to make a claim for property or exclusive possession of the matrimonial home and its contents, you **MUST** fill out a Financial Statement (Form 13), serve a copy on the applicant(s) and file a copy in the court office.

- However, if your only claim for support is for child support in the table amount specified under the Child Support Guidelines, you do not need to fill out, serve or file a Financial Statement.

- If you want to make a claim for property or exclusive possession of the matrimonial home and its contents, whether or not it includes a claim for support, you **MUST** fill out a Financial Statement (Form 13.1, not Form 13), serve a copy on the applicant(s), and file a copy in the court office.

YOU SHOULD GET LEGAL ADVICE ABOUT THIS CASE RIGHT AWAY. If you cannot afford a lawyer, you may be able to get help from your local Legal Aid Ontario office. *(See your telephone directory under LEGAL AID.)*

_____
Date of issue

_____
Clerk of the court

Form 8:   Application (General)   **(page 3)**   Court file number

FAMILY HISTORY

APPLICANT: Age: **54**   Birthdate: *(d,m,y)* **30 April, 1952**

Resident in *(municipality & province)* **London, Ontario**

since *(date)* **30 April, 1952**

Surname at birth: **Walsh**   Surname just before marriage: **Walsh**

Divorced before?   ☒ No   ☐ Yes *(Place and date of previous divorce)*

RESPONDENT: Age: **55**   Birthdate: *(d,m,y)* **7 August, 1951**

Resident in *(municipality & province)* **London, Ontario**

since *(date)* **31 January, 1970**

Surname at birth: **Seymour**   Surname just before marriage: **Seymour**

Divorced before?   ☒ No   ☐ Yes *(Place and date of previous divorce)*

RELATIONSHIP DATES:

☒   Married on *(date)* **June 5, 1973**   ☐   Started living together on *(date)*

☒   Separated on *(date)* **February 27, 2006**   ☐   Never lived together   ☐   Still living together

THE CHILD(REN)

List all children involved in this case, even if no claim is made for these children.

Full legal name	Age	Birthdate *(d,m,y)*	Resident in *(municipality & province)*	Now Living With *(name of person and relationship to child)*

PREVIOUS CASES OR AGREEMENTS

Have the parties or the children been in a court case before?

          ☒ No   ☐ Yes *(Attach a Summary of Court Cases – Form 8E.)*

Have the parties made a written agreement dealing with any matter involved in this case?

          ☒ No   ☐ Yes *(Give date of agreement. Indicate which of its terms are in dispute. Attach an additional page if you need more space.)*

Form 8: **Application (General)** **(page 4)** | Court file number |

CLAIM BY APPLICANT

I ASK THE COURT FOR THE FOLLOWING:
(Claims below include claims for temporary orders.)

Claims under the *Divorce Act* *(Check boxes in this column only if you are asking for a divorce and your case is in the Family Court of the Superior Court of Justice.)*	**Claims under the *Family Law Act* or *Children's Law Reform Act***	**Claims relating to property** *(Check boxes in this column only if your case is in the Family Court of the Superior Court of Justice.)*
00 ☐ a divorce 01 ☐ support for me 02 ☐ support for child(ren) – table amount 03 ☐ support for child(ren) - other than table amount 04 ☐ custody of child(ren) 05 ☐ access to child(ren)	10 ☒ support for me 11 ☐ support for child(ren) – table amount 12 ☐ support for child(ren) - other than table amount 13 ☐ custody of child(ren) 14 ☐ access to child(ren) 15 ☐ restraining/non-harassment order 16 ☒ indexing spousal support 17 ☐ indexing same-sex partner support 18 ☐ declaration of parentage 19 ☐ guardianship over child's property	20 ☐ equalization of net family properties 21 ☐ exclusive possession of matrimonial home 22 ☐ exclusive possession of contents of matrimonial home 23 ☐ freezing assets 24 ☐ sale of family property
Other claims 30 ☒ costs 31 ☐ annulment of marriage 32 ☐ prejudgment interest	50 ☐ Other *(Specify.)*	

Give details of the order that you want the court to make. *(Include any amounts of support (if known) and the names of the children for whom support, custody or access is claimed.)*

1. Interim and permanent support for the applicant pursuant to s. 34(1) of the *Family Law Act*, including:

(a) periodic support in the amount of $2,000 per month pursuant to s. 34(1)(a) of the *Family Law Act*;

(b) compensatory support by way of lump sum in the amount of $100,000 pursuant to s. 34(1)(b) of the *Family Law Act*;

(c) an order requiring the respondent to maintain OHIP, dental, medical and extended health plan coverage for the applicant so long as she is entitled to be supported by the respondent.

2. Indexing of the periodic spousal support order in accordance with s. 34(5) of the *Family Law Act*; and

3. Costs.

Form 8:	**Application (General)**	**(page 5)**	Court File Number

IMPORTANT FACTS SUPPORTING MY CLAIM FOR DIVORCE

☐ **Separation:** The spouses have lived separate and apart since *(date)* _____ and

    ☐ have not lived together again since that date in an unsuccessful attempt to reconcile.

    ☐ have lived together again during the following period(s) in an unsuccessful attempt to reconcile: *(Give dates.)*

☐ **Adultery:** The respondent has committed adultery. *(Give details. It is not necessary to name any other person involved but, if you do name the other person, then you must serve this application on the other person.)*

☐ **Cruelty:** The respondent has treated the applicant with physical or mental cruelty of such a kind as to make continued cohabitation intolerable. *(Give details.)*

IMPORTANT FACTS SUPPORTING MY OTHER CLAIM(S)

(Set out below the facts that form the legal basis for your other claim(s). Attach an additional page if you need more space.)

1. The applicant is in need of spousal support because of the financial hardship suffered as a result of the parties' separation and the respondent has the ability to pay such support.

2. The applicant has a part-time contract teaching position that fails to meet her monthly expenses and provides her with no medical or other benefits. The applicant was accustomed to relying upon the respondent for the shortfall in her income.

3. The resondent is a physician and a qualified anesthetist, who practises and teaches at the University of Western Ontario Hospital, and earns in excess of $250,000 per year.

4. The applicant recently contributed to the career potential of the respondent by supporting the family from 2000 through 2003 while the husband returned to school to become an anesthetist. It would now be fair and equitable for the respondent to compensate the applicant with a lump sum award, which would assist her in her retirement.

Put a line through any space left on this page. If additional space is needed, extra pages may be attached.

_____   _____
Date of signature   *Signature of applicant*

LAWYER'S CERTIFICATE

For divorce cases only

My name is: _____
and I am the applicant's lawyer in this divorce case. I certify that I have complied with the requirements of section 9 of the *Divorce Act.*

_____   _____
Date   *Signature of Lawyer*

APPENDIX 8B

ONTARIO

Superior Court of Justice Family Court Branch
(Name of Court)

at   **80 Dundas Street, London, Ontario, N6A 2P3**
Court office address

Court File Number

Family Law Rules, O. Reg. 114/99

**Form 13: Financial
Statement (Support Claims)
sworn/affirmed**

Applicant(s)

Full legal name & address for service — street & number, municipality, postal code, telephone & fax numbers and e-mail address (if any).	Lawyer's name & address — street & number, municipality, postal code, telephone & fax numbers and e-mail address (if any).
Patricia Ann Seymour **325 Traditional Lane** **London, Ontario** **N6P 5L7**	**Cassandra Burton** **Barrister & Solicitor** **68 Dundas Street, Suite 1108** **London, Ontario** **N6A 2P2** **Tel: (519) 777-8822** **Fax: (519) 777-8823**

Respondent(s)

Full legal name & address for service — street & number, municipality, postal code, telephone & fax numbers and e-mail address (if any).	Lawyer's name & address — street & number, municipality, postal code, telephone & fax numbers and e-mail address (if any).
Richard John Seymour **78 Cherry Hill Park** **London, Ontario** **N6P 5L9**	

INSTRUCTIONS

1. YOU DO NOT NEED TO COMPLETE THIS FORM IF:
   - your only claim for support is for child support in the table amount specified under the Child Support Guidelines and you are not making or responding to a claim described in paragraph 3 below.

2. USE THIS FORM IF:
   - you are making or responding to a claim for spousal support; or
   - you are responding to a claim for child support; or
   - you are making a claim for child support in an amount different from the table amount specified under the Child Support Guidelines.

   You must complete all parts of the form **UNLESS** you are **ONLY** responding to a claim for child support in the table amount specified under the Child Support Guidelines **AND** you agree with the claim. In that case only complete Parts 1, 2 and 3.

3. DO NOT USE THIS FORM AND INSTEAD USE FORM 13.1 IF:
   - you are making or responding to a claim for property or exclusive possession of the matrimonial home and its contents; or
   - you are making or responding to a claim for property or exclusive possession of the matrimonial home and its contents together with other claims for relief.

---

1. **My name is** *(full legal name)*   **Patricia Ann Seymour**

   I live in *(municipality & province)*   **London, Ontario**

   and I swear/affirm that the following is true:

   My financial statement set out on the following *(specify number)* _____ pages is accurate to the best of my knowledge and belief and sets out the financial situation as of *(give date for which information is accurate)*

   March 10, 2006   for

Check one or more boxes, as circumstances require.	☒	me
	☐	the following person(s): *(Give name(s) and relationship to you.)*

FLR 13 (Rev. 04/03)

Form 13:   **Financial Statement (Support Claims)**   **(page 2)**

Court File Number

NOTE: When you show monthly income and expenses, give the current actual amount if you know it or can find out. To get a monthly figure you must multiply any weekly income by 4.33 or divide any yearly income by 12.

PART 1: INCOME

for the 12 months from *(date)*   **January 1, 2005**   to *(date)*   **December 31, 2005**

Include all income and other money that you get from all sources, whether taxable or not. Show the gross amount here and show your deductions in Part 3.

	CATEGORY	Monthly			CATEGORY	Monthly
1.	Pay, wages, salary, including overtime (before deductions)	3,208.33		9.	Rent, board received	
2.	Bonuses, fees, commissions			10.	Canada Child Tax Benefit	
3.	Social assistance			11.	Support payments actually received	
4.	Employment insurance			12.	Income received by children	
5.	Workers' compensation			13.	G.S.T. refund	
6.	Pensions			14.	Payments from trust funds	
7.	Dividends			15.	Gifts received	
8.	Interest			16.	Other *(Specify. If necessary, attach an extra sheet.)*	
				17.	**INCOME FROM ALL SOURCES**	$3.208.33

PART 2: OTHER BENEFITS

Show your non-cash benefits — such as the use of a company car, a club membership or room and board that your employer or someone else provides for you or benefits that are charged through or written off by your business.

ITEM	DETAILS	Monthly Market Value
	18. TOTAL	

19. GROSS MONTHLY INCOME AND BENEFITS *(Add [17] plus [18].)* $ $3,208.33

PART 3: AUTOMATIC DEDUCTIONS FROM INCOME

for the 12 months from *(date)*   **January 1, 2005**   to *(date)*   **December 31, 2005**

	TYPE OF EXPENSE	Monthly			TYPE OF EXPENSE	Monthly
20.	Income tax deducted from pay	640.00		25.	Group insurance	
21.	*Canada Pension Plan*	146.60		26.	Other *(Specify. If necessary, attach an extra sheet.)*	
22.	Other pension plans					
23.	Employment insurance	62.56				
24.	Union or association dues	57.70		27.	**TOTAL AUTOMATIC DEDUCTIONS**	$906.86

28. NET MONTHLY INCOME *(Do the subtraction: [19] minus [27].)* $ $2,301.47

Form 13: **Financial Statement (Support Claims)** (page 3)

Court File Number

PART 4: TOTAL EXPENSES

for the 12 months from *(date)* _____ to *(date)* _____

NOTE: If you need to complete this Part (see instructions on page 1), you must set out your TOTAL living expenses, including those expenses involving any children now living in your home. This part may also be used for a proposed budget. To prepare a proposed budget, photocopy Part 4, complete as necessary, change the title to "Proposed Budget" and attach it to this form.

TYPE OF EXPENSE		Monthly	TYPE OF EXPENSE		Monthly
Housing			**Child(ren)**		
29.	Rent/mortgage	1,146.72	57.	School activities (field trips, etc.)	
30.	Property taxes & municipal levies	212.00	58.	School lunches	
31.	Condominium fees & common expenses		59.	School fees, books, tuition, *etc.* (for children)	
32.	Water	30.00	60.	Summer camp	
33.	Electricity & heating fuel	275.00	61.	Activities (music lessons, clubs, sports)	
34.	Telephone	76.00	62.	Allowances	
35.	Cable television & pay television	42.00	63.	Baby sitting	
36.	Home insurance	48.06	64.	Day care	
37.	Home repairs, maintenance, gardening	56.00	65.	Regular dental care	
			66.	Orthodontics or special dental care	
	Sub-total of items [29] to [37]	1,885.78	67.	Medicine & drugs	
Food, Clothing and Transportation etc.			68.	Eye glasses or contact lenses	
38.	Groceries	650.00		**Sub-total of items [57] to [68]**	
39.	Meals outside home		**Miscellaneous and Other**		
40.	General household supplies	50.00	69.	Books for home use, newspapers, magazines, videos, compact discs	
41.	Hairdresser, barber & toiletries				
42.	Laundry & dry cleaning		70.	Gifts	20.00
43.	Clothing	35.00	71.	Charities	
44.	Public transit		72.	Alcohol & tobacco	
45.	Taxis		73.	Pet expenses	75.00
46.	Car insurance	121.00	74.	School fees, books, tuition, *etc.*	
47.	Licence	12.00	75.	Entertainment & recreation	30.00
48.	Car loan payments	367.00	76.	Vacation	100.00
49.	Car maintenance and repairs	35.00	77.	Credit cards *(but not for expenses mentioned elsewhere in the statement)*	
50.	Gasoline & oil	225.00			
51.	Parking	17.50	78.	R.R.S.P. or other savings plans	
	Sub-total of items [38] to [51]	1,512.50	79.	Support actually being paid in any other case	
Health and Medical *(do not include child(ren)'s expenses)*			80.	Income tax and *Canada Pension Plan (not deducted from pay)*	
52.	Regular dental care				
53.	Orthodontics or special dental care		81.	Other *(Specify. If necessary attach an extra sheet.)*	
54.	Medicine & drugs				
55.	Eye glasses or contact lenses			**Sub-total of items [69] to [81]**	225.00
56.	Life or term insurance premiums		82.	**Total of items [29] to [81]**	3,623.28
	Sub-total of items [52] to [56]				

SUMMARY OF INCOME AND EXPENSES

Net monthly income *(item [28] above)* =$ 2301.47

Subtract actual monthly expenses *(item [82] above* =$ 3,623.28

ACTUAL MONTHLY SURPLUS/DEFICIT =$ $1,321.81 (deficit)

Form 13: **Financial Statement (Support Claims)** **(page 4)** | Court File Number

PART 5: OTHER INCOME INFORMATION

1. I am ☒ employed by *(name and address of employer)*

    Churchill Community College
    856 Churchill Way
    London, Ontario
    N6A 2P8

    ☐ self-employed, carrying on business under the name of *(name and address of business)*

    ☐ unemployed since *(date when last employed)*

2. I attach the following required information *(if you are filing this statement to update or correct an earlier statement, then you do not need to attach income tax returns that have already been filed with the court.):*

    ☒ a copy of my income tax returns that were filed with the Canada Customs and Revenue Agency for the past 3 taxation years, together with a copy of all material filed with the returns and a copy of any notices of assessment or re-assessment that I have received from the Canada Customs and Revenue Agency for those years; or

    ☐ a statement from the Canada Customs and Revenue Agency that I have not filed any income tax returns from the past 3 years; or

    ☐ a direction in Form 13A signed by me to the Taxation Branch of the Canada Customs and Revenue Agency for the disclosure of my tax returns and notices of assessment to the other party for the past 3 years.

    I attach proof of my current income, including my most recent

    ☒ pay cheque stub. ☐ employment insurance stub. ☐ worker's compensation stub.
    ☐ pension stub. ☐ Other. *(Specify.)*

3. ☐ *(check if applicable)* I am an Indian within the meaning of the *Indian Act* (Canada) and all my income is tax exempt and I am not required to file an income tax return. I have therefore not attached an income tax return for the past three years.

PART 6: OTHER INCOME EARNERS IN THE HOME

Complete this part only if you are making a claim for undue hardship or spousal support. Indicate at paragraph 1 or 2, whether you are living with another person (for example, spouse, same sex partner, roommate or tenant). If you complete paragraph 2, also complete paragraphs 3 to 6.

1. ☒ I live alone.

2. I am living with *(full legal name of person)* _____

3. This person has *(give number)* _____ child(ren) living in the home.

4. This person ☐ works at *(place of work or business)* _____
    ☐ does not work outside the home.

5. This person ☐ earns *(give amount)* $ _____ per _____
    ☐ does not earn anything.

6. This person ☐ contributes about $ _____ per _____ towards the household expenses.
    ☐ contributes no money to the household expenses.

Form 13:   **Financial Statement (Support Claims)**   **(page 5)**   Court File Number

PART 7: PROPERTY

LAND

Kind of Property	Address of Property	Type of Ownership (Give your percentage of interest)	Estimated Market Value of Your Interest
matrimonial home	325 Traditional Lane London, Ontario, N6P 5L7	100%	$375,000.00
		83. TOTAL VALUE	$375,000.00

GENERAL ITEMS AND VEHICLES (including household goods and furniture, jewellery, cars, boats, tools, sports and hobby equipment)

Description (including where located, year and make)	Estimated Market Value (not replacement cost)
furniture and household goods, London, Ontario	10,000.00
2000 Dodge Caravan, London, Ontario	8,000.00
2002 Bombardier personal watercraft and trailer, London, Ontario	6,000.00
84. TOTAL VALUE	24,000.00

BANK ACCOUNTS, SAVINGS, SECURITIES AND PENSIONS (including R.R.S.P.'s other savings plans, cash, accounts in financial institutions, stocks, bonds, term deposits and controlling interest in an incorporated business)

Item/Type	Institution (include location)/ Description (including issuer and date)	Account Number	Date of Maturity	Amount/Estimated Market Value
Chequing account	TD Canada Trust, London, Ontario	4446609		1,426.91
Savings Account	CIBC, London, Ontario	78880995		568.00
			85. TOTAL VALUE	$1,994.91

LIFE AND DISABILITY INSURANCE (List all policies now in existence.)

Company, Type & Policy No.	Beneficiary	Face Amount	Today's Cash Surrender Value
		86. TOTAL VALUE	

BUSINESS INTERESTS (Show any interest in an unincorporated business owned today.)

Name of Firm or Company	Nature and Location of Business	Interest	Estimated Market Value of Your Interest
		87. TOTAL VALUE	

MONEY OWED TO YOU (including any court judgments in your favour, any estate money and any income tax refunds owed to you.)

Details (including name of debtors)	Amount Owed to You
88. TOTAL OF MONEY OWED TO YOU	

OTHER PROPERTY

Type of Property	Description and Location	Estimated Market Value
89. TOTAL VALUE OF OTHER PROPERTY		

90. TOTAL VALUE OF ALL PROPRETY Add items [83] to [89]	$400,994.91

Form 13: **Financial Statement (Support Claims)** **(page 6)**

Court File Number

PART 8: DEBTS AND OTHER LIABILITIES

Debts and other liabilities may include any money owed to the Canada Customs and Revenue Agency, contingent liabilities such as guarantees or warranties given by you (but indicated that they are contingent), any unpaid legal or professional bills as a result of this case, mortgages, charges, liens, notes, credit cards and accounts payable.

Type of Debt	Creditor	Details	Monthly Payments	Full Amount Now Owing
Bank, trust or finance company, or credit union loans	TD Canada Trust CIBC	mortgage car loan	1,146.72 367.00	105,376.84 7,463.00
Amounts owed to credit card companies	CIBC Mastercard			426.45
Other debts	City of London	property tax arrears		2,489.72
		91. TOTAL OF DEBTS AND OTHER LIABILITIES:		**$115,756.01**

PART 9: SUMMARY OF ASSETS AND LIABILITIES

	Amounts
TOTAL ASSETS *(from item [90] above)* $	$400,994.91
Subtract TOTAL DEBTS *(from item [91] above)* $	$115,756.01
92. NET WORTH $	285,238.90

☒ I do not expect changes in my financial situation.

☐ I do expect changes in my financial situation as follows:

☐ I attach a proposed budget in the format of Part 4 of this form.

NOTE: As soon as you find out that the information in this financial statement is incorrect or incomplete, or there is a material change in your circumstances that affects or will affect the information in this financial statement, you MUST serve on every other party to this case and file with the court:

- *a new financial statement with updated information, or*
- *if changes are minor, an affidavit in Form 14A setting out the details of these changes.*

Sworn/Affirmed before me at **CITY of LONDON**

municipality

in **the PROVINCE of ONTARIO**

province, state or country

on _____

date   Commissioner for taking affidavits
(Type or print name below if signature is illegible.)

_____
Signature
(This form is to be signed in front of a lawyer, justice of the peace, notary public or commissioner for taking affidavits.)

CHAPTER 9

DOMESTIC CONTRACTS UNDER THE *FAMILY LAW ACT*

The *Family Law Act*[1] allows parties to settle affairs between them without the necessity of having to resort to the courts. Different types of "domestic contracts" defined as marriage contracts, cohabitation agreements, separation agreements,[2] and paternity agreements can be entered into by the parties at different stages of the relationship. The requirements and enforceability of marriage contracts, cohabitation agreements, separation agreements, and paternity agreements will be discussed in this chapter.

MARRIAGE CONTRACTS

Marriage contracts can be entered into by two persons who are married to each other or intend to marry each other.[3] Therefore, a marriage contract can be entered into before marriage or at any time while the parties are married to each other. In a marriage contract, couples can agree on their rights and obligations during marriage and can also agree on what will happen if the parties should separate, divorce, annul their marriage, or if one party should die. Specifically, the parties can deal with:

- ownership in or division of property;

- support obligations;

- the right to direct the education and moral training of their children; and

- any other matter in the settlement of their affairs.

However, there are limits on what can be dealt with in a marriage contract. Clauses that deal with the custody of, or access to, the children and clauses that limit a spouse's right to possessing the matrimonial home under Part

---

[1] R.S.O. 1990, c. F.3, as amended [hereinafter "FLA"].

[2] FLA, s. 51. The definition of "domestic contract" has been amended to include paternity agreements and family arbitration agreements, but at the time of publication, this amendment has not been proclaimed in force.

[3] FLA, s. 52(1).

II of the Act are unenforceable.[4] Note that it is only the right of possession of the matrimonial home that is protected. Parties may specify who shall own the matrimonial home and that the value of the matrimonial home be excluded from a party's net family property. Such clauses would be enforceable in the event of separation, annulment, or death.

COHABITATION AGREEMENT

Two persons who are cohabiting, or intend to cohabit, can enter into a cohabitation agreement, which can deal with their rights during cohabitation, after their separation, or upon the death of one of them.[5] Like marriage contracts, cohabitation agreements can be entered into either before cohabitation begins or any time after cohabitation has begun. Parties to a cohabitation agreement can deal with the same matters as can be dealt with in a marriage contract, namely:

- ownership in or division of property;

- support obligations;

- the right to direct the education and moral training of their children; and

- any other matter in the settlement of their affairs.

Like marriage contracts, cohabitation agreements cannot deal with custody of or access to the children. However, since cohabiting couples do not have the same protection for possession of their homes as married couples do, clauses that deal with property possession after separation are enforceable.

If the parties to a cohabitation agreement marry, the cohabitation agreement automatically becomes a marriage contract.[6] If a clause deals with possession of property that then becomes a matrimonial home, when that cohabitation agreement becomes a marriage contract, such clause would no longer be enforceable.

SEPARATION AGREEMENTS

Two persons who were married to each other or cohabited with each other, and are living separate and apart, can enter into a separation agree-

---

[4] FLA, s. 52(2).
[5] FLA, s. 53(1).
[6] FLA, s. 53(2).

ment. Unlike marriage contracts or cohabitation agreements, there are no limits to what can be dealt with in a separation agreement.[7]

FORM AND CAPACITY

In order for a domestic contract to be enforceable, it must be in writing, signed by the parties, and witnessed. If the parties wish to amend or rescind a domestic contract, that agreement must also be in writing, signed by the parties, and witnessed.[8]

A minor (under 18 years of age) can enter into a domestic contract, but the court must approve the contract. Approval can be obtained either before or after the contract has been entered into.[9] With regard to mental incompetents, if the person has a guardian of property other than his or her spouse, the guardian may enter into a domestic contract of the person's behalf, but the contract must be approved in advance by the court.[10] Otherwise, it is the Public Guardian and trustee who would act for the mentally incompetent person.[11]

Application Questions

1. State whether each of the following is enforceable:

   (a) In a marriage contract, a clause stating that the mother of the children will raise the children in her faith.

   (b) In a cohabitation agreement between Cindy and Igor, a clause that states that in the event of a separation, Igor will immediately vacate the home. What would happen if, after signing the contract, Cindy and Igor marry?

   (c) In a marriage contract, a clause that the matrimonial home, will remain in Hanna's name only will not be included in Hanna's net family property.

   (d) In a separation agreement, a clause that the parents will have joint custody of the children and that their primary residence shall be with the mother, with specified times when the children will be with the father.

   (e) In a separation agreement, a clause that states that the husband has exclusive possession of the matrimonial home.

---

[7] FLA, s. 54.
[8] FLA, s. 55(1).
[9] FLA, s. 55(2).
[10] FLA, s. 55(3).
[11] FLA, s. 55(4).

2. Joshua, who is 17 years old, enters into a marriage contract a month before he is married. Does Joshua have to take any steps in order for that contract to be valid? When can he take those steps?

3. Betty and George have been married for five years. George is about to become a partner in his firm and wants Betty to sign a marriage contract that excludes the partnership from his net family property and releases any rights Betty has to any interest in the partnership. Would such a contract be valid?

4. Bill and Timothy have been living together for two years. They have decided to marry and want to enter in to a marriage contract. Can they? When can they?

5. Shortly after separation, Wayne and Peggy sit down together and draw up an agreement in which they divide their property between them and they both sign it. Does this agreement meet the requirements of a domestic contract?

ENFORCEABILITY OF DOMESTIC CONTRACTS

Custody, Access, and Child Support

The parties are free to enter into any domestic contract on any terms they wish, but the court will not necessarily be bound by the parties' agreement. The court can disregard any provision in a domestic contract having to do with the education, moral training, or custody of or access to a child, and may make an order in the best interest of the child.[12] With regard to child support, courts can override any clauses that are unreasonable or not in accordance with the *Guidelines*.[13]

As mentioned previously, the court can award an amount that is different from the *Guideline* amount where "special provisions" are made for the child,[14] or where the parties are consenting to an amount that is different from the *Guideline* amount, but the court is satisfies that "reasonable arrangements" have been made for the child's support, having regard to the *Guidelines*.[15]

---

[12] FLA, s. 56(1).
[13] FLA, s. 56(1.1).
[14] *Divorce Act*, s. 15.1(5), (6); FLA, s. 33(12), (13).
[15] *Divorce Act*, s. 15.1(7), (8); FLA, s. 33(14), (15).

> ### *Wright v. Zaver* (2002), 59 O.R. (3d) 26, [2002] O.J. No. 1098, 2002 CarswellOnt 887 (Ont. C.A.)
>
> The parties were the biological parents of child. The parties were never married to each other and their relationship broke up shortly after the child, Michael, was born on January 23, 1985. The mother began proceedings for custody and support and the parties signed Minutes of Settlement. In the Minutes of Settlement, the parties agreed that the father would make a lump-sum payment of $4,000 for child support without an admission of paternity. Access to the child was specifically "not granted." These Minutes of Settlement were embodied in a court order, on consent. In October 1990, Ms. Wright married Mr. Wright. They separated in July 1999. During their marriage they had one child, Amanda Wright, born October 31, 1992. Mr. Wright consented to an order that he pay child support for the two children. Mrs. Wright then also applied for child support from Mr. Zaver.
>
> Held:
>
> > . . .Mr. Zaver is Michael's biological father. The 1985 agreement did not relieve him of the continuing obligation to ensure that Michael's needs are properly met.. . . [At para. 105.] . . .[T]he "special provisions" exception does not apply to the circumstances of this case. While Mr. Wright's ongoing child support arguably does qualify as a special provision, that arrangement fails to meet the test in s. 37(2.3), since applying the child support guidelines would not be inequitable. [At para. 111.] . . .The *Ontario Guidelines* table amounts are designed to achieve that result based on the income of the payor(s). [At para. 105.] While it is true that neither Michael nor Mr. Zaver has had the opportunity of a personal relationship with the other, Mr. Zaver has had a holiday from support for many years. There is no indication that it will be an undue financial burden for him to pay support in accordance with the *Ontario Guidelines*. [At para. 106.] . . .I would dismiss the appeal and order Mr. Zaver to pay the *Ontario Guidelines* table amount of child support of $509.00 per month.. . . [At para. 126.]

Spousal Support

A clause in a contract that makes any right of a party dependent upon remaining chaste is unenforceable. However, a clause that causes rights to terminate when a party marries or cohabits with another is valid.[16] If the contract was entered into before March 1, 1986, a clause that ties a party's rights to that party remaining chaste is given effect as a clause that terminates the parties' rights upon remarriage or cohabiting with another.[17]

---

[16] FLA, s. 56(2).
[17] FLA, s. 56(3).

As mentioned previously, if the parties have entered into an agreement regarding spousal support, and an application is made under the *Divorce Act*, the court must take that agreement into account in deciding spousal support, but is not bound by it.[18] Under the *Family Law Act*, the court can set aside an agreement regarding spousal support, and decide spousal support, where any one of the following can be shown:

- the agreement for support or not to pay support results in circumstances that are unconscionable;

- the agreement results in a spouse qualifying to be supported out of public money; or

- the payor spouse has defaulted on the support payment.

The court can intervene in these circumstances, even if the contract says otherwise.[19]

Circumstances Surrounding Negotiation and Execution

The *Family Law Act* specifies that the court can set aside a domestic contract or a part of it if:

- a party failed to make full financial disclosure;

- a party did not understand the nature and consequences of a domestic contract; or

- otherwise in accordance with contract law.[20]

This section makes applicable all the defences that would be available in contract law, such as mental incapacity, duress, undue influence, mistake, and misrepresentation. It also imposes on the parties an obligation to disclose all significant assets, debts, and obligations.

---

[18] *Divorce Act*, s. 15.2(4).
[19] FLA, s. 33(4).
[20] FLA, s. 56(4).

Montreuil v. Montreuil (1999), [1999] O.J. No. 4450, 1999 CarswellOnt 3853 (Ont. S.C.J.), additional reasons at (2000), 2000 CarswellOnt 3566 (Ont. S.C.J.), affirmed by the Ontario Court of Appeal at (2002), [2002] O.J. No. 3891, 2001 CarswellOnt 3464 (Ont. C.A.)

The parties were married in 1978 and they separated in 1996. They had one son who was 12 years of age and who had been spending equal amounts of time with each parent following the separation. The parties owned a house worth $165,000. They also owned cars, a boat, and other recreational equipment. Since 1983, the husband operated a business called Mike's Marine. In 1984, the parties jointly purchased marina property on which they constructed premises that they rented to Mike's Marine. Both parties had RRSPs and other savings accounts. Following the wife's decision to separate, the husband's lawyer prepared a draft separation agreement. The wife brought the agreement to her lawyer. Her lawyer repeatedly advised her of the need for full financial disclosure before any resolution of issues could be finalized. Within two weeks, the parties arrived at a settlement that was incorporated into the agreement. Although the parties did not exchange financial statements before they signed the separation agreement, the wife asked the husband for financial information. He refused to complete a financial statement, but provided her with verbal information and showed her certain documentation relating to Mike's Marine and the bank accounts. Pursuant to the agreement, the parties had joint custody of their son and no spousal or child support was payable. The wife released any interest in Mike's Marine, the matrimonial home, and the marina property. One year after the agreement was signed, the husband disclosed a document to the wife that showed his net worth to be in excess of $1,000,000 and his net income to be $5,000 monthly. Pursuant to section 56(4) of the *Family Law Act*, the wife applied to set aside the agreement on the basis that the husband had grossly misrepresented his financial circumstances when they negotiated the agreement.

Held: Application allowed in part. The wife received independent legal advice prior to signing the agreement. Therefore, she knew the nature and the consequences of the agreement before she signed it. Although she was anxious and under stress as a result of the separation and the negotiations, she was not under duress or subjected to undue influence by the husband. Her bargaining position was not significantly weaker than that of the husband. However, the agreement was set aside pursuant to section 56(4)(a) of the Act and the common law doctrine of material misrepresentation. The husband made material misrepresentations regarding the value of his RRSP and the value of his interest in Mike's Marine. The wife relied on those representations in signing the agreement and was prejudiced as a result. Section 56(4)(a) of the Act placed a duty on each party to a domestic contract to divulge information without the other party having to take legal steps in order to compel disclosure. The wife did not have the onus to seek out the company's financial records to verify the husband's representations regarding the company's value. The husband was ordered to make an equalization payment of $272,000.

The *Family Law Act* also specifies that the court can set aside all or part of a contract if one party used the power to stop the other from being able to remarry with that party's faith to gain an advantage in the negotiations.[21] This applies to consent orders, releases, etc., as well as agreements, and even if the agreement specifies to the contrary.[22]

PATERNITY AGREEMENTS

A man and a woman who are not spouses can enter into a paternity agreement that deals with:

- paying a child's prenatal care and birth expenses;

- supporting a child;

- the funeral expenses of the child or mother.

A party to the agreement, or a Children's Aid Society, can apply to the Ontario Court of Justice or Family Court to incorporate the agreement into a court order.[23] The court must be satisfied that the agreement is reasonable, having regard to the *Guidelines*.[24]

If an application is made to incorporate an agreement into an order, the court can issue and order for a person's arrest if the court is satisfied that the person is about to leave Ontario and there are reasonable grounds for believing that the person intends to evade his or her responsibilities under the agreement.[25] The arrested person would have rights to bail under the *Provincial Offences Act*.

A minor can enter into a paternity agreement, but the agreement must be approved by the court. Approval can be obtained either before or after the agreement has been executed.[26]

---

[21] FLA, s. 56(5).
[22] FLA, s. 56(6), (7).
[23] FLA, s. 59(1).
[24] FLA, s. 59(1.1).
[25] FLA, s. 59(2).
[26] FLA, s. 59(4).

> **Application Questions**
>
> 1. Can a same-sex couple enter into a paternity agreement?
>
> 2. Can minors enter into paternity agreements?

REGISTERING A DOMESTIC CONTRACT WITH THE COURT

Domestic contracts and paternity agreements can be filed with the Ontario Court of Justice or Family Court. The person wishing to file the agreement must file an affidavit, stating that the agreement is in effect, and has not been set aside or varied.[27] Once the agreement has been filed, it can be enforced, varied, or, with respect to spousal support, indexed just like a court order.[28] The filed agreement can be set aside by the court in accordance with section 33(4).[29] An agreement can be filed and enforced despite a clause in the contract stating to the contrary.[30]

NEGOTIATING A DOMESTIC CONTRACT OR PATERNITY AGREEMENT

Traditional Negotiations

Negotiation of family law matters has customarily taken place through legal counsel. Lawyers, on the instructions of their clients, deal with each other to define what the issues between the parties are, get financial disclosure, and decide how assets will be valued. They deal with each other by telephone, in writing, or, more rarely, face to face. Each lawyer put forth his or her client's position, then attempts to negotiate with the other lawyer to obtain the best result possible for the client. This is called "positional bargaining". If negotiations are not producing the desired outcome, lawyers turn to the litigation process. Once litigation is commenced, lawyers can continue to negotiate to resolve some or all of the outstanding issues, but where resolution is not achieved, the court ultimately decides the unsettled issues.

There has been a great deal of dissatisfaction expressed for this process by clients, lawyers, and judges. Positional bargaining and litigation tend to intensify the conflict between the parties, which is undesirable, given that

---

[27] FLA, s. 35(1).
[28] FLA, s. 35(2).
[29] FLA, s. 35(3).
[30] FLA, s. 35(4).

the parties may still have to deal with each other on a regular basis, especially where children are involved. Alternative methods of resolving family law disputes have been developed and are gaining in popularity. Mediation, arbitration, and collaborative family law are the major alternatives to the traditional model.

Mediation

Instead of negotiating through lawyers, parties may choose to deal with each other directly with the help of a mediator to resolve their disputes. In family law in Ontario, mediation is a strictly voluntary process and both parties must agree to it before it can take place. The mediator is a neutral third party who is chosen by the parties and the parties usually split the mediator's fees. Negotiations are based on a different model, called "interest-based negotiations". Rather than putting forth their positions and making compromises, the role of the mediator is to help the parties explore the interests that lie beneath their positions, then to generate options for meeting the parties' interests. The goal is to arrive at "win-win" solutions rather than compromises. Generally, the parties negotiate in person and lawyers do not attend the mediation sessions. The mediator is not a decision maker and has no authority to impose an outcome on the parties. The mediator's role is to facilitate communication between the parties and help them to develop solutions and arrive at an agreement.

Mediation can take place at any stage in the proceedings. Usually, the parties simply agree to attend mediation, but mediation can also take place by court order. Section 3(1) of the *Family Law Act* allows a court to appoint a person whom the parties have selected to mediate any matters that the court specifies. Before the court can appoint a mediator, the mediator must have consented to act as mediator and have agreed to report to the court within a specified time.[31] The mediator must then confer with the parties, and may confer with the children if appropriate, and attempt to obtain an agreement between the parties.[32] The first step in this type of mediation is to get the parties to agree on whether is will be an "open" mediation or a "closed" mediation.[33] In an "open" mediation, the mediator will file a full report on the mediation, including anything he or she considers relevant; in a "closed" mediation, the mediator can only report on what agreement was reached by the parties or that the parties did not reach an agreement. The mediator must file the full or limited report with the clerk of the court and must give a copy of the report to the parties.[34] If

---

[31] FLA, s. 3(2).
[32] FLA, s. 3(3).
[33] FLA, s. 3(4).
[34] FLA, s. 3(5).

the parties have chosen closed mediation, then nothing that was said during the mediation can be used as evidence in the proceeding except with both parties' consent.[35] The court must require the parties to pay the mediator's fees and expenses, but may order one party to pay a larger proportion.[36] If paying the mediator's fees and expenses would cause serious financial hardship for one party, the court can order the other party to bear the entire cost of the mediation.[37]

Arbitration

Like meditation, arbitration is a voluntary process. Arbitrations in Ontario are governed by the *Arbitrations Act, 1991*.[38] In arbitration, the parties choose a mutually acceptable neutral third party to decide the issues in dispute between them. The parties are responsible for paying the arbitrator's fee. Arbitrations are more formal than mediations. Generally, the parties are represented by lawyers and evidence is called by the parties in a hearing. However, arbitrations are less formal than court proceedings; the rules of evidence are relaxed and the parties can choose which rules or laws will apply to the arbitration. At the end of the hearing, the arbitrator will make a decision that is binding on the parties. Under certain circumstances, the arbitrator's decision can be appealed to the court.[39]

There has been much debate over the proposed creation of a specialized arbitration tribunal that would apply Muslim religious law, called *sharia*, to family law disputes. Proponents of the tribunal argued that adults should be able to consent to family law disputes being settled in accordance with their religious and cultural beliefs. Opponents of the tribunal argued that vulnerable women may be coerced into agreeing to use the tribunals and that Muslim law is much less favourable to women than the laws of Canada and Ontario. Especially at risk are recent immigrants who do not know their rights under Canadian and Ontario law. The debate has expanded to include considering the question of whether arbitration based on religious or cultural principle should ever be allowed and whether arbitration and other alternative dispute resolution mechanisms are appropriate for family law matters at all. The Ontario government has passed legislation that amends the *Arbitration Act, 1991*, and the *Family Law Act* to disallow any arbitration based on religious principles and that all arbitrations must apply Canadian and Ontario law. At the time of publication, the amendments have not been proclaimed in force.

---

[35] FLA, s. 3(6).

[36] FLA, s. 3(7).

[37] FLA, s. 3(8).

[38] S.O. 1991, c. 17.

[39] *Arbitration Act*, s. 45.

Collaborative Family Law

Collaborative family law is a synthesis of the traditional negotiation model and the mediation model. The parties hire specially trained lawyers and sign into an agreement in which they commit themselves to settling the matter and agreeing that if a settlement is not reached, the lawyers must withdraw, and neither the lawyers nor their law firms can represent the clients in any subsequent litigation. Clients negotiate with each other, with their lawyers present more as advisors than lead negotiators. Negotiations are interest-based, cooperative, and collaborative, with all present attempting to generate options to resolve the dispute rather than taking a positional or adversarial approach. Although new, collaborative family law is expanding and has become very popular in some parts of Ontario.

APPENDIX 9A

THIS IS A SEPARATION AGREEMENT made this   day of November, 2006.

BETWEEN:

AIDAN CHRISTOPHER O'REILLY

(hereinafter referred to as the "husband")

-and-

FEROZA AHMED

(hereinafter referred to as the "wife")

I. DEFINITIONS

(1) In this agreement:

a) *"Canada Pension Plan Act"* means the *Canada Pension Plan Act*, R.S.C. 1985, c. C.8, and any successor:

b) *"Child Support Guidelines"* means the *Child Support Guidelines*, O. Reg. 391/97, and any successor;

c) *"Children's Law Reform Act"* means the *Children's Law Reform Act*, R.S.O. 1990, c. C.12, and any successor:

d) *"Divorce Act"* means the *Divorce Act*, R.S.C. 1985, c. C.3, and any successor:

e) *"Family Law Act"* means the *Family Law Act*, R.S.O. 1990, c. F.3, and any successor:

f) "matrimonial home" means the buildings and lot located at 15 Brockwood Crescent, in the City of Brampton, in the Regional Municipality of Peel;

g) "net family property" means net family property as defined in the *Family Law Act*;

h) *"Pension Benefits Act"* means the *Pension Benefits Act*, R.S.O. 1990, c. P.8, and any successor:

i) *"Succession Law Reform Act"* means the *Succession Law Reform Act*, R.S.O. 1990, c. S.26, and any successor:

j) *"Trustee Act"* means the *Trustee Act*, R.S.O. 1990, c. T.23, and any successor.

(2) An Act of the Legislature or of Parliament referred to by name will mean the Act in force at the material time, and includes any amendment or successor Act which replaces it.

2. BACKGROUND

(1) The parties were married on April 29, 1995, in Niagara-on-the-Lake, in the Province of Ontario;

(2) There are two children of the marriage, namely Randall Quentin O'Reilly, born March 23, 1998, and Kristen Yvette O'Reilly, born June 12, 2000.

(3) The parties have been living separate and apart from each other since April 1, 2006, and there is no reasonable prospect that they will resume co-habitation;

(4) The parties continue to live separate and apart and agree to settle all the rights and obligations which they may have or may otherwise acquire with respect to the custody, access and support of their children, the support of each other, possession, ownership and division of their property, and all other matters arising from the breakdown of their marriage.

3. DOMESTIC CONTRACT

(1) Each party acknowledges that this agreement is entered into under s. 54 of the *Family Law Act* and is a domestic contract that prevails over matters provided for in the *Family Law Act*.

(2) This agreement replaces and supersedes any prior agreements, whether oral or in writing, made between the parties.

4. LIVING SEPARATE AND APART

(1) The parties have lived separate and apart since April 1, 2006, and each shall be free from interference, authority and control, whether direct or indirect, by the other as if each were unmarried, except as may be necessary to implement the terms of this Separation Agreement or for the welfare of the children of the marriage.

5. PARENTING ARRANGEMENTS

(1) The wife will have sole custody of the children, and the primary residence of the children shall be with the wife.

(2) The husband shall have generous access to the children, which access will include, but not be limited to the following:

a) Tuesday evenings, from after school to 7:30 p.m.;

b) Every other weekend, from Friday after school to Sunday at 7:30 p.m.;

c) For a period of two weeks each summer vacation between July 1st and September 1st,

d) In even numbered years, from December 24th at 7:30 p.m. to December 25th at 7:30 p.m., and from December 31st at 12:00 noon to January 2nd at 12:00 noon, and the children shall be with the wife from December 23rd at 7:30 p.m. until December 24th at 7:30 p.m. In odd numbered years, the children shall be with the wife from December 24th at 7:30 p.m. to December 25th at 7:30 p.m., and from December 31st at 12:00 noon to January 2nd at 12:00 noon, and with the husband from December 23rd at 7:30 p.m. until December 24th at 7:30 p.m.

e) The children will spend Mother's Day weekend with the wife regardless of whether it falls on the husband's weekend, and Father's Day weekend with the husband regardless of whether it falls on the husband's weekend.

f) Other statutory and religious holidays will be enjoyed with the children on an alternating basis.

g) Such other times as arranged by the parties.

(3) The husband will notify the wife by May 15th of each year, which two weeks of the summer he wishes to exercise his access to his children.

(4) The parents will share information related to the health, welfare, education, activities, and significant events occurring in the children's lives. The parties will have full and equal access to all of the children's schools, doctors, dentists, therapists, coaches and other persons involved with the child, and may obtain all records and documentation regarding the children from such persons.

(5) The wife shall maintain her primary residence within a 15 kilometre radius of the City of Brampton. If the wife intends to move out of the radius, she shall give the husband at least three months notice of her intended move.

(6) Neither party will apply to change the names of the children without the express written consent of the other.

6. CHILD SUPPORT

(1) In accordance with the *Child Support Guidelines*, the husband will pay for the support of the children the table amount of $1,084.00 per month commencing December 1, 2006, based on his current income of $85,000.00 per annum. When one child

a) is no longer residing with the wife ("resides" includes living away from home for school, summer employment or vacation);

b) marries;

c) is at least 18 years of age and is no longer in full time attendance at an educational institution;

d) obtains at least one post secondary degree or diploma;

e) becomes self-supporting; or

f) dies;

support and maintenance shall terminate with respect to that child, and the monthly sum shall be reduced to the table amount for one child in accordance with the *Child Support Guidelines*, based on the income of the husband on the date the above-mention event occurred.

(2) The husband will pay 50% of the children's special and extraordinary expenses, within 7 days of the wife delivering to the husband proof of the expense. In the event that the parties disagree about a special and extraordinary expense, it will be resolved in accordance with the section of this agreement entitled "Dispute Resolution."

(3) If either party asks in writing for disclosure, the other party will provide in writing the following information, within 30 days of the request,

a) The documents required by s. 21(1) of the *Child Support Guidelines*;

b) Current information about the children's special or extraordinary expenses;

c) Any other information needed to review child support.

(4) The quantum of child support is subject to variation which includes rescission of any arrears of support based on a change of circumstances of either party or of the children. The parties will negotiate the change in child support, and if they cannot agree, child support will be resolved in accordance with the section of this agreement entitled "Dispute Resolution."

7. SPOUSAL SUPPORT

(1) The husband will pay spousal support of $1,000.00 a month starting December 1, 2006 and ending on December 1, 2014. The husband will make the payments on the first day of each month. On December 1, 2014, spousal support ends forever. This term cannot be changed.

(2) Spousal support ends when:

a) The wife dies,

b) The husband makes the final payment due on December 1, 2014, or

c) The husband dies, if the insurance required by this Agreement is in place. If it is not, the husband's estate will continue to pay the support. As the husband's estate will not be able to deduct the support payments for income tax purposes and the wife may not have to include the support in her taxable income, the monthly support payment will be reduced to the net after-tax monthly support the wife was entitled to receive immediately before the husband's death.

(3) On the first day of December in each year, starting on December 1, 2007, spousal support will increase by the percentage change in the All Items Consumer Price Index for Canada for April of that year.

(4) This Agreement has been negotiated in an unimpeachable fashion and fully represents the intentions and expectations of the parties. Both parties have had independent legal advice and all the disclosure they have asked for and need in order to understand the nature and consequences of this Agreement and to come to the conclusion, as they do, that the terms of this Agreement, including the release of all spousal support rights, constitutes an equitable sharing of both the economic consequences of their relationship and its breakdown.

(5) The terms of this Agreement substantially comply with the overall objectives of the *Divorce Act* now and in the future and the parties' need to exercise their autonomous rights to achieve certainty and finality.

8. DISPUTE RESOLUTION

(1) If the husband and the wife disagree about a reviewable aspect of this Agreement, they will try to resolve the dispute through negotiation.

(2) After exchanging any information required by this Agreement, the husband and the wife will meet personally, or through their personal representatives, to resolve the issues in dispute. If they come to an agreement, the parties will sign and date an amending agreement before witnesses.

(3) If the parties cannot agree within 30 days of the first negotiation meeting, they will try mediation first and then, if mediation does not result in an agreement, by court application.

(4) The parties wish Laura Masella to act as a mediator, but if she is unable or unwilling to act, they wish Marie Ferguson to act.

(5) The parties will share the costs of mediation equally.

9. MEDICAL AND DENTAL BENEFITS

(1) While required to pay child support under this Agreement, the husband will maintain the children as beneficiaries of medical, extended

health and dental coverage through his employment for as long as it is available to him

(2) The husband will:

a) promptly submit receipts given to him by the wife to the insurer, and

b) immediately endorse the reimbursement cheques from the insurer to the wife and deliver them to her.

10. LIFE INSURANCE

(1) The husband will keep a life insurance policy ("the policy") on his life in the amount of $200,000.00, naming the wife as the irrevocable beneficiary. The husband will not borrow against the policy while he is obligated to pay spousal or child or spousal support.

(2) When child and spousal support end, the husband's obligation to maintain the policy ends. When it does, the wife will provide the husband's insurer with a direction to withdraw the policy's irrevocable designation.

(3) Within 14 days of signing this Agreement, the husband will provide with a copy of the policy and the irrevocable beneficiary designation. The husband will sign the direction in the attached Schedule ("Authorization and Direction"), permitting the wife to confirm directly with the husband's insurer that the policy is unencumbered and in force.

(4) Within 14 days of the policy's anniversary date, the husband will give proof that he has paid the premium.

(5) When the husband dies, the husband's estate will pay support as if he were still alive adjusted to reflect that the wife may not have to pay tax on it and the estate cannot deduct it, until the wife receives the insurance proceeds.

(6) The husband authorizes a lien and first charge against his estate for the full amount of the policy proceeds if the policy is not in force on the husband's death.

(7) If the policy is not in force when the husband dies, in addition to any other remedy the wife may have against the husband's estate, she may apply under the *Succession Law Reform Act* for relief for herself or any child.

(8) If the husband's policy cannot be maintained for any reason, the husband will immediately obtain replacement coverage at a reasonable cost, ensuring no gap in coverage. If the husband learns that there may be a change in insurance coverage, he will advise the wife of the proposed change in coverage and the reason for the change.

11. PROPERTY

(1) The matrimonial home has been sold, and the closing is scheduled for December 1, 2006.

(2) The parties will direct the lawyer on the sale to pay these expenses from the matrimonial home sale proceeds:

a) real estate commission,

b) adjustments for taxes, utilities, municipal fees or levies,

c) amounts required to discharge registered encumbrances,

d) legal fees and disbursements relating to the sale, and

e) all other sale adjustments.

(3) After paying these amounts, the remaining proceeds will be divided equally between the parties. The lawyer will then deduct the amount of $34,334.00 from the husband's share, which the husband owes to the wife for equalization of their net family properties, and will add that amount to the wife's share, and pay to the parties the amount that each is owed.

(4) The husband and the wife acknowledge and agree that they have otherwise divided their property and their debts to their mutual satisfaction and that each of them has received all of the property to which he or she is entitled and that there is no other amount owing to one of them by the other by way of financial settlement or equalization payment under the Family Law Act or at common law or equity except as specified in this agreement.

12. RELEASES

(1) This Agreement is a full and final settlement of all issues between and the husband and the wife of all rights and obligations arising out of their relationship.

(2) Except as otherwise provided in this Agreement, and the husband and the wife release each other from all claims either may have against the other now or in the future under the terms of any statute or the common law, including all claims under the *Divorce Act*, the *Family Law Act*, and the *Succession Law Reform Act*, for:

a) possession of property,

b) ownership of property,

c) division of property,

d) compensation for contributions to property, and

e) an equalization payment.

except as otherwise provided in this Agreement, and each renounce any entitlement either may have in the other's will made before the date of this Agreement or to share in the estate of the other upon the other dying intestate.

(3) Except as otherwise provided in this Agreement, the husband and the wife release each other from all claims either may have against the other now or in the future under the terms of any statute or the common law, including claims for:

   a) a share in the other's estate,

   b) a payment as a dependant from the other's estate under the *Succession Law Reform Act*,

   c) an entitlement under the *Family Law Act*,

   d) an appointment as an attorney or guardian of the other's personal care or property under the *Substitute Decisions Act*, and

   e) participation in decisions about the other's medical care or treatment under the *Health Care Consent Act*.

13. SEPARATION AGREEMENT TO SURVIVE DIVORCE

(1) If a divorce judgment or order issues, all of the terms of this Agreement will continue.

14. GENERAL TERMS

(1) There are no representations, collateral agreements, warranties or conditions affecting this Agreement. There are no implied agreements arising from this agreement and this agreement between the parties constitutes the complete agreement between them.

(2) If the husband and the wife agree to try and reconcile their relationship but they cohabit for no longer than 90 days, this Agreement will not be affected. If they cohabit for more than 90 days, this Agreement will become void, except that any transfers or payments made to that time will not be affected or invalidated.

(3) Except as otherwise provided in this Agreement, the invalidity or unenforceability of any term of this Agreement does not affect the validity or enforceability of any other term. Any invalid term will be treated as severed from the remaining terms.

(4) The interpretation of this Agreement is governed by the laws of Ontario.

(5) This Agreement binds and the parties' heirs, executors, administrators and assigns.

(6) Any amendments to this Agreement must be in writing, signed by the parties, dated and witnessed.

(7) The husband and the wife will sign any documents necessary to give effect to this Agreement.

(8) The husband and the wife have disclosed their income, assets and other liabilities existing at the date of separation and the date of this Agreement.

(9) The husband and the wife have each investigated the other's financial circumstances to his or her satisfaction.

(10) The husband or the wife's failure to insist on the strict performance of any terms in this Agreement will not be a waiver of any term.

15. INDEPENDENT LEGAL ADVICE

(1) The husband and the wife and have both had independent legal advice, and each of them:

a) understands his or her rights and obligations under this Agreement and its nature and consequences,

b) acknowledges that this Agreement is fair and reasonable,

c) acknowledges that they are not under any undue influence or duress, and

d) acknowledges that both are signing this Agreement voluntarily.

e) Where consent is required under this Agreement, it will not be unreasonably withheld.

f) If the husband and the wife cannot agree whether consent is being reasonably withheld, they will use the section of this Agreement entitled "Dispute Resolution" to resolve the matter.

g) The effective date of this Agreement is the date on which the latter party signs it.

TO EVIDENCE THEIR AGREEMENT THE HUSBAND AND THE WIFE HAVE SIGNED THIS AGREEMENT BEFORE A WITNESS.

DATE: _____

_____   _____
Witness   AIDAN CHRISTOPHER O'REILLY

DATE: _____

_____   _____
Witness   FEROZA AHMED

CERTIFICATE OF INDEPENDENT LEGAL ADVICE

I, CHENIQUA DAVIS, of the City of Brampton in the Regional Municipality of Peel, Barrister and Solicitor, certify that I was consulted by AIDAN CHRISTOPHER O'REILLY, one of the parties to the attached Separation Agreement with respect to his rights and obligations under this Agreement.

I acted only for AIDAN CHRISTOPHER O'REILLY and fully explained to him the nature and effect of the Agreement. AIDAN CHRISTOPHER O'REILLY acknowledged that he completely understood the nature and effect of the Agreement. AIDAN CHRISTOPHER O'REILLY executed the Agreement in front of me and confirmed that he was entering into the Agreement of his own volition without any fear, threats, compulsion or influence by or any other person.

Dated at Brampton, Ontario, this   day of November, 2006:

_____

CHENIQUA DAVIS

CHAPTER 10

THE *CHILDREN'S LAW REFORM ACT*: EQUAL STATUS OF CHILDREN AND PARENTAGE

SCOPE OF ACT

The *Children's Law Reform Act*[1] governs a number of issues mainly relating to the legal status of Ontario children. The general topics covered by the CLRA include (a) the equal status of all children; (b) establishing parentage, including declarations of parentage; and (c) custody, access, and guardianship of children. The Act also addresses recognition and enforcement of custody and access orders, including those from other provinces and jurisdictions. Many of the actual rights of children flow from other legislation such as the *Family Law Act*,[2] which governs child support, and the *Succession Law Reform Act*,[3] which governs inheritance rights. This chapter will deal with the topics of equal status of children and declarations of parentage. The following chapter will deal with custody and access under the CLRA.

EQUAL STATUS OF CHILDREN

On March 31, 1978, the *Children's Law Reform Act* abolished the historical legal distinction between children born in wedlock and children born outside wedlock.[4] Prior to passing this legislation, a child born outside marriage was considered at common law to be "illegitimate" and was denied legal status for purposes such as support and inheritance rights. For all purposes of the law, a person is now considered to be the child of his or her biological parents, with the exception of legally adopted children,[5] whether or not the parents were married to each other at the time of the child's birth.[6] In addition, all other relationships flowing from the parent and child relationship must be determined in accordance with the CLRA.[7] A child's

---

[1] R.S.O. 1990, c. C.12, as amended [hereinafter the "CLRA"].
[2] R.S.O. 1990, c. F.3, as amended.
[3] R.S.O. 1990, c. S.26, as amended.
[4] CLRA, s. 1(4).
[5] CLRA, s. 1(2).
[6] CLRA, s. 1(1).
[7] CLRA, s. 1(3).

rights that could be affected include not only support and inheritance rights, but also many other statutory rights in such areas as insurance, immigration, and income tax.

Interpretation of Other Legislation and Documents

Unless there is a contrary intention expressed in the legislation, all statutes, regulations, orders, or by-laws passed after March 31, 1978, must be interpreted in a way that gives effect to the equal status of children, and kindred relationships flowing therefrom, as described in the CLRA.[8] Similarly, all documents, such as wills and trust documents made after March 31, 1978, which make reference to a person or class of persons described in terms of their blood or marriage relationships, must be construed to include children born inside and outside marriage.[9] Such terms in a will as "issue", "descendants" and "children" will be interpreted to include all biological children born inside and outside marriage, unless the testator clearly states a contrary intention.

ESTABLISHING PARENTAGE OF CHILDREN

Introduction

Prior to Part II of the CLRA, the issue of parentage of children born outside marriage was governed by the former *Child Welfare Act* in what were described as "affiliation" proceedings. There was no separate authority to make declarations of paternity or maternity but rather the issue was an ancillary one to child support. In addition to a mother's evidence of paternity, corroboration was required. There was also a two-year limitation period within which to commence a claim for child support for children born outside marriage. There is no longer any limitation period under the CLRA and there is no necessity for corroboration, although a person now has the right to secure blood tests.

---

[8] CLRA, s. 2.
[9] CLRA, s. 2.

Bagaric v. Juric (1984), 44 O.R. (2d) 638, 5 D.L.R. (4th) 78, 2 O.A.C. 35 (Ont. C.A.)

The fact that the Legislature severed from the declaration of parentage any issue as to expenses and maintenance, placing them in new and different statutes, is of significance. It is also of significance that the right was greatly widened involving all children and both mothers and fathers. The Legislature recognized by this legislation present social conditions and attitudes as well as recognizing that such declarations have significance beyond material ones.. . . [At para. 32.]

Who Can Apply For a Declaration of Parentage?

Part II of the CLRA deals with establishment of parentage. Any person having an interest may apply to a court for a declaration that a male person is recognized in law to be the father of a child or that a female person is the mother of a child. A mother can apply for a declaration that a male person is the father of her child; a child can apply for a declaration that a female person is his or her mother or a declaration of paternity. Similarly, a male person can apply to have a child declared to be his child and a female person can apply for a declaration that she is the mother of a child.

R. (J.) v. H. (L.) (2002), 2002 CarswellOnt 3445 (Ont. S.C.J.)

The applicants were common-law spouses who were unable to have children. They were accepted into an *in vitro* fertilization program at a Toronto hospital and signed the required consent form to participate. The applicants entered a gestational carriage agreement with the respondent and her husband. The respondent and her husband also signed the consent form. On February 9, 2002, the respondent, who was the carrier, gave birth to twins. The results of DNA testing on the applicants established that they were the biological mother and father of the twins. The respondent, who had carried the twins, swore an affidavit that she was not the mother of the children. The children lived with the applicant couple since birth pursuant to the agreement. The applicants applied for a declaration that they were the biological parents of the twins and a declaration that the respondent's husband was not the biological father of the children. In addition, they sought custody and an order directing the Registrar General to issue a Statement of Birth consistent with the declarations.

Held: All applications were granted.

The blood tests indicated that the probability that the applicants were the mother and father respectively was 99.99 per cent. The court therefore found that they were, on a balance of probabilities, the twins' genetic parents. Accordingly, pursuant to section 4(1) of the CLRA, J.K., the male applicant, was entitled to be "recognized in law" as the children's father and that J.R., the female applicant, was entitled to be "recognized in law" as the children's mother.

The respondent's husband did not contribute any genetic material and was not the biological father. He was only involved because he was the husband of the woman who was the gestational carrier of the twins. Pursuant to section 8(1) of the CLRA, he was presumed to be the father, but that presumption had been rebutted. The CLRA is quiet as to whether the court may make negative declarations. However, the *Courts of Justice Act* makes no distinction. The right to know whether or not one is a child's parent is of such significance that the issue may be the subject of a declaratory order pursuant to section 97 of the *Courts of Justice Act. (Raft v. Shortt* (1986), 2 R.F.L. (3d) 243 (Ont. H.C.).) The applicants had established that a declaration that the respondent's husband was not the father ought to be made in the circumstances.

Limitations upon Application

There is no time limitation upon an application for a declaration of parentage under the CLRA. However, where there is no person recognized in law to be a child's father under section 8 (presumptions of paternity), if a child applies for a declaration that a male person is his or her father or a male person applies to have a person declared to be his child, both people whose relationship is sought to be established must be living.[10] In such a situation, where no person is recognized under section 8 to be the father, a child's mother has no status to apply for a declaration of paternity. The application must be made by either the child or the potential father.[11]

Nature of Declaratory Order

A declaration of parentage made under the CLRA is a declaration *in rem* and is to be recognized for all purposes.[12] In other words, it is not just a declaration of a relationship that affects the two people involved. It affects the status of the parties with respect to the rest of the world in all circumstances.

---

[10] CLRA, s. 5(2).
[11] CLRA, s. 5(1).
[12] CLRA, s. 5(3).

Presumptions of Paternity

The CLRA establishes a set of circumstances, any one of which creates a rebuttable presumption that a male person is the father of a child. These presumptions can be rebutted if the contrary is proven on a balance of probabilities. The following are the circumstances that create a presumption of paternity:[13]

- the person is married to the mother at the time of the child's birth;

- the person was married to the child's mother and the marriage was terminated by death, nullity, or divorce within 300 days before the child's birth;

- the person marries the mother after the child's birth and acknowledges that he is the natural father;

- the person was cohabiting with the mother in a relationship of some permanence at the time of the child's birth or the child is born within 300 days after they ceased to cohabit;

- the person has certified the child's birth, as the child's father, under the *Vital Statistics Act* or a similar Act in another jurisdiction in Canada;

- the person has been recognized by a court of competent jurisdiction in Canada to be the child's father.

Conflicting Presumptions

Where circumstances exist that give rise to a presumption of paternity against more than one father, then no presumption will be made as to paternity and no one is recognized in law to be the father.[14] For example, a woman might be married to one man while cohabiting with another man at the time of her child's birth. Since there would be a presumption that both her husband and the man with whom she is cohabiting are the fathers of her child, neither would be recognized in law to be the father.

In a case where there is no person recognized in law under section 8 of the CLRA, either the child's father or the child can apply under section 5 of the Act for a declaration of paternity. This can only be done if both persons whose relationship is sought to be established are living. The child's mother has no status to bring an application for a declaration of paternity in such circumstances.

---

[13] CLRA, s. 8(1).
[14] CLRA, s. 8(3).

Application Questions

1. Which of the following persons can apply for a declaration of paternity?

   (a) a child born outside marriage whose father has recently died;

   (b) a mother who separated from her common-law partner six months prior to her child's birth;

   (c) a mother whose husband died two weeks prior to her child's birth;

   (d) a mother whose child was born while she was married to one man but living with another man;

   (e) a man who wants to obtain access to a child he claims is his child.

2. In each case, name the presumption that would apply, if any:

   (a) a married woman, who is separated from her husband, gives birth to a child;

   (b) a mother obtained an annulment from her husband two days prior to her child's birth;

   (c) a husband obtained a divorce one year before his ex-wife had a child;

   (d) a mother obtained a declaration of paternity by the British Columbia Supreme Court, but not in Ontario;

   (e) a mother is married to one man, but a different man has certified the child's birth under the *Vital Statistics Act*.

Proof of Parentage

Written Acknowledgement of Paternity

A written acknowledgment of parentage that is admitted in evidence in a civil proceeding against the person who made the acknowledgment is proof of parentage in the absence of any evidence to the contrary.[15]

Blood Tests

In a civil proceeding where there is an issue of parentage to be determined, the court may grant a party leave to obtain blood tests and to submit the results in evidence.[16] The court can name in the order the persons who must submit to the blood tests. An application for blood tests can be made

---

[15] CLRA, s. 9.

[16] CLRA, s. 10(1).

where the issue is a declaration of parentage, custody of a child, child support, or access to a child. There should be a genuine issue of parentage arising before the court will order blood tests.

G. (F.) v. G. (F.) (1991), 32 R.F.L. (3d) 252 (Ont. Gen. Div.)

The parties. . .separated [after 22 years of marriage]. The wife petitioned for divorce in 1989. The husband alleged that he had doubts about the youngest child's paternity based primarily on having seen other men in the home. The wife denied adultery and refused blood tests. The husband applied for leave to obtain blood tests. The Master denied the request because there were no reasonable grounds to contest paternity and the husband had not rebutted the presumption of paternity under s. 8 of the *Children's Law Reform Act* (Ont.).

The husband appealed.

Held: The appeal was dismissed.

The. . .Master was correct in deciding that the husband had to show, on the balance of probabilities, that someone else was the child's father. A real issue of paternity must arise before the court should order blood tests. The husband's failure to discharge the onus under s. 8(1) of the *Children's Law Reform Act* to rebut paternity meant that there was no issue for the Court to determine. [At 252-253.]

Other cases have held that a court should generally exercise its discretion to order blood tests unless the process of the blood test will harm the child's health or the request for leave is made in bad faith.[17]

Although advances in medical technology mean that blood tests can be used as compelling evidence that a man is a child's father, there is no test that proves it with one hundred per cent certainty. However, a blood test can exclude with certainty someone else as the father of a child. From a practical point of view, the blood test results will usually determine the issue of paternity one way or the other.

DNA Tests

DNA tests, although more expensive than blood tests, are a more sophisticated and accurate procedure. They are increasingly used where regular blood tests provide a less than 95 per cent probability of paternity. Some advantages of DNA testing over conventional blood testing are that DNA produces on average an accuracy of 99.99 per cent. This might be particularly critical where two potential fathers were closely related. Also,

---

[17] See *H. v. H.* (1979), 25 O.R. (2d) 219, 100 D.L.R. (3d) 364, 9 R.F.L. (2d) 216 (Ont. Fam. Ct.).

because DNA requires a very minimal blood sample, it can be performed on a newborn baby.

Inference from Refusal to Submit to Blood Tests

Once a person has been named in an order, if that person, male or female, refuses to submit to blood tests, the court is free to draw whatever inferences it thinks appropriate.[18] However, unless an order has been made, a person's refusal to submit to blood tests is not a relevant factor. It is within the judge's sole discretion whether or not to draw any inferences whatsoever, including no inference.[19] An appropriate inference in circumstances where an alleged father refuses to submit to court-ordered blood tests might be that he wished to avoid the risk that the results would indicate he was the father. On the other hand, if a person claiming to be the father refuses to attend for blood tests, an adverse inference may be drawn that he had something to hide, namely that he was not the child's father. If an alleged father applies for a declaration and the mother refuses to comply with a court order for blood tests, an appropriate inference might be that he is, in fact, the father of the child.

Charter *Issues and Blood Tests*

An order for blood tests under section 10(1) of the CLRA does not offend the right to life, liberty and security of the person under section 7 of the *Charter of Rights and Freedoms* since a party cannot be forced to submit to blood tests against his or her will.[20] The mere fact that an adverse inference can be drawn does not amount to compulsion.[21] Similarly, such an order does not violate section 8 of the *Charter*, the right to be free from unreasonable search and seizure.[22] Neither does an order pursuant to section 10(1) violate section 12 of the *Charter*, the right to be free from cruel and unusual punishment.[23]

Silber v. Fenske (1995), 11 R.F.L. (4th) 145 (Ont. Gen. Div.)

The parties were involved in an intimate relationship for a period of over two years until July 1993; the woman gave birth to a child in March 1994.

---

[18] CLRA, s. 10(3).

[19] See *T. (N.) v. C. (A.)* (2000), 2000 CarswellOnt 39 (Ont. S.C.J.).

[20] See *P. (K.) v. N. (P.)* (1988), 15 R.F.L. (3d) 110 (Ont. H.C.).

[21] See *Silber v. Fenske* (1995), 11 R.F.L. (4th) 145 (Ont. Gen. Div.).

[22] See *N. v. D.* (1985), 49 O.R. (2d) 490, 13 C.R.R. 26 (Ont. Fam. Ct.), judicial review dismissed as being premature: (1986), 54 O.R. (2d) 550, 16 O.A.C. 75 (Ont. Div. Ct.); *Silber v. Fenske, ibid.*

[23] See *Honsinger v. Kilmer* (1984), 12 C.R.R. 276 (Ont. Prov. Ct.).

The man certified under the *Vital Statistics Act* (Ontario) that he was the child's father. However, he subsequently denied paternity and refused to submit to a blood test voluntarily. The woman applied for leave to permit blood tests to determine the child's paternity as well as an order for interim interim child support and prenatal expenses. The man argued that an order for blood tests violated his rights under sections 7 and 8 of the *Charter*.

Held: Leave to obtain blood tests granted, interim interim support granted and issue of prenatal expenses was deferred.

> . . .In the case at bar, there was no evidence that a blood test would physically harm any of the parties, nor was there any question as to the bona fides of the application respecting blood testing. The man had voluntarily signed the *Vital Statistics Act* form regarding parentage. Accordingly, leave should be granted permitting such blood tests to be obtained.
>
> Given the wording of s. 10 of the *Children's Law Reform Act*, no one can take blood for purposes of a paternity test without that person's consent. No penalty of imprisonment is imposed for failing to take the test. The child's right to financial support from her father and her need to know who her father was, in order for the court to determine such support, should not be overlooked. It is in the interests of children in general that they be well taken care of and that they know their parentage. Therefore, there was no breach of the man's rights under s. 7 or s. 8 of the *Charter*. [At 146.]

JURISDICTION TO MAKE DECLARATION OF PARENTAGE

The court that has the jurisdiction to determine matters of parentage under the CLRA is either the Superior Court of Justice or the Family Court of the Superior Court of Justice.[24]

The Ontario Court of Justice has no jurisdiction to make a judgment *in rem*; i.e., for all purposes of the law. However, the CLRA does not deprive other courts in Ontario of jurisdiction to determine parentage as long as it is a material part of a dispute that is otherwise within that court's jurisdiction. Since the Ontario Court of Justice has jurisdiction under the *Family Law Act* to determine support of children born outside marriage, that court can decide paternity as a necessary incident of establishing the obligation for support.[25] The Ontario Court of Justice also has capacity to order blood tests under the CLRA where this is material to the issue of access to a child.[26] Even though the Ontario Court of Justice cannot make

---

[24] CLRA, s. 3.
[25] See *Sayer v. Rollin* (1980), 16 R.F.L. (2d) 289, [1980] O.J. No. 613, 1980 CarswellOnt 252 (Ont. C.A.).
[26] See *B. (R.) v. G. (L.)* (1992), 1992 CarswellOnt 3766 (Ont. Prov. Div.).

a declaration of parentage for all purposes, a finding that a person is a child's father in that court does create a rebuttable presumption under section 8 of the CLRA.

CHAPTER 11

CUSTODY UNDER THE
CHILDREN'S LAW REFORM ACT

INTRODUCTION

This chapter focuses upon custody and access of children under the *Children's Law Reform Act*. The meaning and rights associated with custody, joint custody, and access are the same under both the *Divorce Act* and the CLRA. The principles governing the award of custody under the CLRA also focus on the principle of the best interests of the child. The CLRA codifies in more detail the factors related to the child's best interests and in so doing provides a more in-depth perspective upon "best interests". The Act also creates its own unique jurisdictional requirements and applies to a broader group of potential custody claimants. Finally, the CLRA also addresses the recognition and enforcement of custody orders from other jurisdictions and the abduction of children from one jurisdiction to another.

EQUAL ENTITLEMENT OF PARENTS

Under the CLRA, the biological parents, whether or not they are married to each other, are equally entitled to custody of their child, unless there is a court order or agreement stating otherwise.[1] Where parents who have been living together separate and begin to live separate and apart, the child will usually continue to live with one of them. If a child lives with one parent, with the consent or approval of the other parent, the other parent's entitlement to custody is automatically suspended until a separation agreement or court order provides differently. However, the parent who loses custody does not lose the right to access to the child in those circumstances.[2] Once a separation agreement or court order is in place, the agreement or order will supersede any prior rights.[3]

---

[1] CLRA, s. 20(1).
[2] CLRA, s. 20(4).
[3] CLRA, s. 20(7).

WHO CAN APPLY FOR CUSTODY UNDER THE CLRA

Under the CLRA, not only the parents, but also any other person can apply for custody of a child.[4] Unless a married parent is seeking a divorce, he or she must apply for custody under the CLRA, rather than under the *Divorce Act*. All unmarried parents must apply for custody under the CLRA. In addition, any person, including grandparents, step-parents, adoptive parents, foster parents and extended family members can commence an application for custody under the CLRA.

JURISDICTION TO APPLY FOR CUSTODY

An application for custody under the CLRA may be brought in the Ontario Court of Justice, the Family Court, or the Superior Court of Justice.[5] The three bases upon which an Ontario court can assume jurisdiction are discussed below.

Habitual Residence in Ontario

The basic rule in the CLRA is that a court can only exercise jurisdiction where the child is habitually resident in Ontario at the commencement of the application.[6] Habitual residence is defined as the place where the child has resided (a) with both parents; (b) where the parents are living separate and apart, with one parent under a separation agreement, court order, or with the consent, express or implied, of the other; or (c) with a person other than a parent on a permanent basis for a significant period of time, whichever last occurred.[7]

There is no required length of time that a child must have resided in any of these situations in order for an Ontario court to have jurisdiction. A child could create his or her habitual residence within days of establishing a home with his or her parents.[8] However, where a child is living with a non-parent, it must be demonstrated that he or he has lived there "on a permanent basis for a significant period of time", which is unspecified. A child who is sent to Ontario to live with relatives while he attends school, but who returns home on school breaks would not be considered habitually resident in Ontario.

---

[4] CLRA, s. 21.
[5] CLRA, s. 18(1).
[6] CLRA, s. 22(1)(a).
[7] CLRA, s. 22(2).
[8] *Hartmann-Jorgensen v. Hartmann-Jorgensen* (1986), 50 R.F.L. (2d) 430, 1986 CarswellOnt 340 (Ont. U.F.C.).

One parent cannot unilaterally change the habitual residence of a child by abducting the child to another jurisdiction without the consent of the other parent having custody.[9] The only exception to this rule is where the parent having custody has acquiesced or has delayed in commencing proceedings to have the child returned.[10]

Child Physically Present in Ontario Coupled With Five Other Factors

If a child is not habitually resident in Ontario, an Ontario court may still assume jurisdiction if the child is physically present in Ontario at the commencement of the application and five other factors are *all* present. The five other factors that must be present include the following:

- substantial evidence concerning the best interests of the child is available in Ontario;

- no application for custody of, or access to, the child is pending before an extra-provincial tribunal in another place where the child is habitually resident;

- no extra-provincial order in respect of custody of, or access to, the child has been recognized by an Ontario court;

- the child has a real and substantial connection with Ontario; and

- on the balance of convenience, it is appropriate for jurisdiction to be exercised in Ontario.[11]

It is essential that all five of these criteria be satisfied before an Ontario court assumes jurisdiction, if the child is not habitually resident in Ontario.[12] Important witnesses who can testify about the child's best interests must be present in Ontario. Generally speaking, sporadic visits and vacationing in Ontario will not amount to having a "real and substantial connection" to Ontario.

---

[9] *Turner v. Viau* (2002), 2002 CarswellOnt 991, 26 R.F.L. (5th) 440 (Ont. C.A.); *Fulmer v. Kaleo-Fulmer* (2002), [2002] O.J. No. 3183, 2002 CarswellOnt 2718 (Ont. S.C.J.), additional reasons at (2002), 2002 CarswellOnt 2944 (Ont. S.C.J.). See also *Korutowska-Wooff v. Wooff* (2004), [2004] O.J. No. 3256, 2004 CarswellOnt 3203 (Ont. C.A.), leave to appeal refused (2005), 2005 CarswellOnt 3135 (S.C.C.); *Katsigiannis v. Kottick-Katsigiannis* (2001), 203 D.L.R. (4th) 386 (Ont. C.A.).

[10] CLRA, s. 22(3).

[11] CLRA, s. 22(1)(b).

[12] *Turner v. Viau, supra* note 9; *Brooks v. Brooks* (1998), 41 O.R. (3d) 191, 163 D.L.R. (4th) 715, 111 O.A.C. 177, 39 R.F.L. (4th) 187 (Ont. C.A.) (child must be physically present in jurisdiction to invoke this section).

Foucault v. Rouleau (2005), 2005 CarswellOnt 3583 (Ont. S.C.J.)

The mother and father lived in a common-law relationship in Quebec from 1990 to 2004 and two children, Jeffrey, aged 10, and Bianca, aged 7, were born of their relationship. When the parents separated in August 2004, the two children moved to Thunder Bay, Ontario, with their mother. The father continued to live in Quebec in the matrimonial home with his new partner. As soon as the mother moved to Thunder Bay, the father immediately followed her with the hope of having Bianca return with him to Quebec. When this failed to work out for him, he returned to Quebec and commenced an application for custody of both children. At that time, the mother opposed the application and the parties entered an agreement that the mother would have temporary custody until the end of June 2005 at which time the matter would return to the Quebec court. The agreement was filed with the court and was converted into a court order. The mother applied in Ontario to have the Ontario court accept jurisdiction over the custody hearing.

Held: The mother's application was dismissed. The Ontario court did not have jurisdiction to hear the custody matter.

The children had lived most of their lives in Quebec with the exception of the last ten months when they resided in Ontario. The actions of the father in following the mother to Thunder Bay, attempting to return with his daughter, and then commencing a custody action in Quebec clearly indicated that he did not consent to or acquiesce in the mother's move to Ontario. The children were therefore not habitually resident in Ontario. In addition, although the children had lived and attended school in Ontario for the past year, they had a far more lengthy and historical relationship with Quebec. Furthermore, by appearing in Quebec and signing the interim agreement, the mother had submitted to the jurisdiction of the Quebec court and by her actions agreed that the matter should be returned to the Quebec court.

Neither could the court assume jurisdiction under section 22(1)(b) of the CLRA because, although the children were physically present in Ontario, not all of the five criteria set out in that section were satisfied. In particular, there was already an application pending in another jurisdiction where the children were habitually resident.

Serious Harm to Child

Despite the jurisdictional requirements set out above, an Ontario court can assume jurisdiction, where it would not otherwise be permitted to do so, if the child is physically present in Ontario and the court is satisfied, on a balance of probabilities, that the child would suffer serious harm if he or she remains with or is returned to the person who is legally entitled to custody.[13]

Declining Jurisdiction

An Ontario court also has the power to refuse jurisdiction if it is of the opinion that it is more appropriate for jurisdiction to be exercised elsewhere.[14] In deciding whether to decline jurisdiction under section 25 of the CLRA, the court will look to the purposes of Part III of the Act, one of which is to avoid the concurrent exercise of custody jurisdiction over the same child by different jurisdictions.[15] This section is most likely to play a role where Ontario has jurisdiction because the child is habitually resident in Ontario, but the child has a real and substantial connection to another jurisdiction.[16]

CLRA and the *Divorce Act*

If there is a prior order under the *Divorce Act*, a court cannot decide custody under provincial legislation such as the CLRA, based on the doctrine of paramountcy.[17] The CLRA specifically provides that where an application for divorce is commenced under the *Divorce Act*, any custody or access application under the CLRA that has not been determined is stayed, unless there is leave of the court to continue such application.[18] However, once an order has been made under the CLRA, it will remain in force and binding unless or until a new order is made in a divorce proceeding.

Application Questions

1. Tamara and Seiji were married for 11 years and had three children. During their marriage, the family had lived in Japan, France, and the United States, but the children had spent most of their lives in Japan. Tamara had some immediate family members living in Ontario and the family had visited Ontario frequently on holidays, but had never carried on their daily life in Ontario. Most of the witnesses who could testify about the children's best interests lived in Japan. When the parties separated, Tamara relocated to Ontario with the children.

---

[13] CLRA, s. 23.
[14] CLRA, s. 25.
[15] CLRA, s. 19(b); *Wickham v. Wickham* (1983), 35 R.F.L. (2d) 448 (Ont. C.A.).
[16] See *Starr v. Adam* (2003), 2003 CarswellSask 170 (Sask. Q.B.).
[17] See *French v. Mackenzie* (2003), 2003 CarswellOnt 1748, 38 R.F.L. (5th) 81 (Ont. S.C.J.).
[18] CLRA, s. 27.

(a) In which country are the children habitually resident under the CLRA?

(b) Could Tamara change the children's habitual residence by moving to Ontario without Seiji's consent?

(c) Would the Ontario court have jurisdiction to hear and determine the issue of custody of the children under the CLRA? Why or why not?

(d) If the Ontario court did not have jurisdiction, what other court would have jurisdiction? On what basis?

2. Francine and Michel had lived in New Brunswick for ten years with their two children, now aged 8 and 6, until Francine decided to move to Ontario with the children without Michel's consent. After the children moved to Ontario, Francine enrolled them in school and arranged for them to attend a local church. Francine then started a custody action in Ontario and served the father in New Brunswick with her application. Michel had already commenced an action for custody in New Brunswick.

(a) In which province are the children habitually resident under the CLRA?

(b) Does the Ontario court have jurisdiction to make a custody order with respect to the children? Why or why not?

(c) Does the New Brunswick court have jurisdiction to hear the custody matter? If so, on what basis?

3. Lisa and David were married for 14 years and during that time they lived in Manitoba with their two children. After the separation, Lisa took the children to live in Ontario. David immediately applied for divorce in Manitoba and obtained an order for interim custody of the children under the *Divorce Act*. Lisa applied for custody in Ontario under the CLRA. The children had lived in Ontario for six months at the time of the application.

(a) In what province are the children habitually resident?

(b) Does the Ontario court have jurisdiction under the CLRA to hear Lisa's custody application? Why or why not?

(c) Could Lisa commence a variation application in Ontario of David's interim order under the *Divorce Act?* Why or why not?

PRINCIPLES DETERMINING THE MERITS OF CUSTODY

Best Interests of the Child

Just as under the *Divorce Act*, custody and access applications are to be determined according to the best interests of the child.[19] The CLRA provides a detailed set of child-centred criteria that must be considered by the court in determining the child's best interests. Other factors related to the needs and circumstances of the child can also be considered. The factors related to the child's best interests are often interrelated and the court is required to make an integrated assessment of all the relevant factors and circumstances. The legal principles must be applied to the particular facts of each case.[20] A court is not authorized to give more weight to one factor in section 24 of the CLRA than to another.[21] The factors in the CLRA are discussed separately below.

Love, Affection and Emotional Ties

The emotional bonds between the child and the parties involved in a custody dispute are an important factor. The legislation requires the court to consider the child's ties to three different classes of people, namely: (a) each person claiming custody or access; (b) other members of the child's family who live with the child; and (c) people involved in the child's care and upbringing.[22]

The courts have come to accept the central role played by the child's 'psychological parent' in determining the child's best interests. In the Supreme Court of Canada case of *Gordon v. Goertz*,[23] Madame Justice L'Heureux-Dubé stated:

> The assessment of the child's best interests also involves a consideration of the particular role and emotional bonding the child enjoys with his or her primary caregiver. The importance of preserving the child's relationship with his or her psychological parent has long been recognized by this Court on a number of occasions. . ... There is a growing body of evidence that this relationship may well be the most determinative factor on the child's long-term welfare. As I mentioned in *Young, supra*, at p. 66, the vital link between

---

[19] CLRA, s. 24(1).

[20] See *Poole v. Poole* (1999), 45 R.F.L. (4th) 56, 1999 CarswellBC 649 (B.C. C.A.).

[21] *Cox v. Stephen*, 2002 CarswellOnt 2321, 30 R.F.L. (5th) 54, [2002] O.T.C. 499 (Ont. S.C.J.), affirmed (2003), 2003 CarswellOnt 4554 (Ont. C.A.).

[22] CLRA, s. 24(2)(a).

[23] 19 R.F.L. (4th) 177, 141 Sask. R. 241, [1996] 2 S.C.R. 27 (S.C.C.).

continuity in the emotional bonding of the child with his or her psychological parent and the best interest of the child finds ample support in the literature:[24]

The child's psychological bond to his or her caregiver has even taken precedence over racial, biological, and cultural ties.[25]

> ### N. (M.) v. B. (M.) (2000), 2000 CarswellOnt 2108 (Ont. S.C.J.), additional reasons at (2000), 2000 CarswellOnt 2433 (Ont. S.C.J.)
>
> A mother and father and their two very young children fled the political oppression in Iran and took refuge in a camp in Iraq. When war broke out between Iraq and Kuwait, followed by the Gulf war, their lives were again endangered. At that time, the parents made the difficult decision to allow an organization to take their children, then aged 6 and 3, along with one thousand other children, out of the war zone to a place of safety. In 1990, the two children left Iraq, and after several stops, ended up with a couple who lived in Ottawa, Ontario. The children were registered in school, learned English and adjusted extremely well to their lives in Canada. By all accounts they were intelligent, happy, outgoing and well-liked children. They loved their new family as parents and the couple loved them as their own children.
>
> For several years, the biological parents had no knowledge of where their children were but they eventually tracked them down and made contact. They unsuccessfully attempted to enter Canada as refugees and ended up in Denmark as refugees instead. The biological mother eventually gained entrance to Canada, went immediately to Ottawa where she brought an unsuccessful motion for custody of the children, with a view to returning to Denmark with them. During the time she was in Canada, the biological mother exercised some access, but some of her actions proved to be disruptive to the children's lives. The children took the position that they wanted to remain in Ottawa with their new family. They regarded this as their home and family and did not wish to be parted from the life they now knew. Although the biological parents wished to live as a family in Canada, this was highly unlikely in view of the father's false representations to Canadian immigration authorities initially and his alleged association with an organization viewed as terrorist by Canadian authorities. The biological parents commenced an application for custody under the CLRA, which was opposed by the "psychological parents" who themselves sought custody of the children.

---

[24] *Gordon v. Goertz, ibid.* at para. 121.

[25] See *R. (A.N.) v. W. (L.J.)* (1983), 36 R.F.L. (2d) 1, 24 Man. R. (2d) 314, [1983] 2 S.C.R. 173 (S.C.C.) (as important as child's Indian heritage was, duration and strength of child's relationship with non-Indian adoptive parents took precedence); *Catholic Children's Aid Society of Metropolitan Toronto v. M. (C.)* [1994] 2 S.C.R. 165 (S.C.C.) (child's psychological bond to foster parents given precedence over rights of birth parents).

Held: The application of the biological parents was dismissed. The application of the "psychological parents" was granted and custody was awarded to them.

The decision as to the children's custody had to be made in accordance with the children's best interests and after considering the criteria in section 24 of the CLRA. In the circumstances of this case, serious harm may be occasioned by removing the children from their present surroundings and placing them in the custody and care of someone who will likely be quite a stranger to them. In addition, if the biological parents were to gain custody, the children would most likely be relocated to Denmark where they would have to learn another new language and culture. Considering that the children were thriving in Ottawa in all aspects of their lives, it was not in their best interests to uproot them.

The courts have generally found it important to keep siblings together so that brothers and sisters can share their childhood together, show their affection to one another, support one another, and experience a sense of solidarity. Relationships with extended family, such as grandparents, aunts, uncles, and cousins have increasingly become an important factor in awarding custody. Also relationships with daycare providers are relevant in awarding custody because these are persons directly involved in the child's care and upbringing.[26]

Views and Preferences of the Child

In determining custody and access under the CLRA, the child's views and preferences are one important factor to be considered.[27] However, it is important that the court examines the dynamics behind a child's express wishes to be sure they are arrived at independently.[28] Sometimes a young child will merely express a parent's wishes or will tell adults around them what the child thinks they want to hear. In other cases, a child may choose to live with one parent out of concern for that parent's health or well-being.[29] Also, the child's wishes must not be confused with the child's welfare or best interests, as his or her wishes may not always correspond with his or her best interests. For example, a child may choose to live with his father because his mother is more influential in establishing rules about school work.[30]

---

[26] See *O'Hara v. O'Hara* (September 26, 2002), Doc. Brockville 01-0300 (Ont. S.C.J.).

[27] CLRA, s. 24(2)(b).

[28] See *Boukema v. Boukema* (1997), 31 R.F.L. (4th) 329, 33 O.T.C. 190 (Ont. Gen. Div.), additional reasons at (1997), 1997 CarswellOnt 5151 (Ont. Gen. Div.) (Court refused to make order based on an 11 year old's wishes where they were not arrived at on child's own).

[29] See *Medeiros v. Medeiros* (2003), 2003 CarswellOnt 712 (Ont. S.C.J.).

[30] See *Jespersen v. Jespersen* (1985), 1985 CarswellBC 564, 48 R.F.L. (2d) 193 (B.C. C.A.).

A child's age is important in deciding what weight to attribute to the child's wishes.[31] The court will usually give greater weight to the views of teenaged children because they are assumed to be more capable of responsible thought, and also for practical reasons. With teenaged children, the court is less concerned with how the child's views were arrived at, because a strong-willed child will not usually comply with an order that violates his or her wishes.

Length of Time in a Stable Home Environment

The length of time that a child has lived in a stable home environment is another factor to be considered under the CLRA.[32] This is sometimes referred to as the *status quo* factor. In awarding custody, a court generally seeks to maintain a reasonable stability in a child's residence and continuity in a child's care. *Status quo* implies the relationships and way of life of the child in a particular location and not merely a geographic or physical locale.[33] The home, neighbourhood, school, church, friends, lifestyle, and recreational amenities need to be taken into account when considering the child's *status quo*.

Ability and Willingness to Provide Guidance, Education, Necessaries and Special Needs

The court must consider the ability and willingness of each person seeking custody to provide the child with guidance and education, necessaries of life, and any special needs of the child.[34] The focus is upon the child as a whole person and the respective capacities and motivation of the parents to nurture the child and look after the child's long-term development. Both willingness and ability on the part of the parent or custody claimant must be demonstrated. Willingness is insufficient if a parent cannot demonstrate that he or she has the corresponding ability to meet the child's needs.[35]

One important aspect of this factor is a parent's ability and willingness to place the child's needs ahead of his or her own. This could range from a parent organizing their work time to maximize his or her availability to the children,[36] to facilitating the child's contact with the other parent.[37]

---

[31] *Kosokowsky v. Kosokowsky* (1992), 95 D.L.R. (4th) 309 (Ont. Gen. Div.).

[32] CLRA, s. 24(2)(c).

[33] See *Poole v. Poole*, *supra* note 20.

[34] CLRA, s. 24(2)(d).

[35] *Blackwell v. Burden* (1996), 1996 CarswellOnt 362 (Ont. Gen. Div.).

[36] *Bosch v. Bosch* (1985), 49 R.F.L. (2d) 157 (Sask. Q.B.); see also *Peterson v. Scalisi* (2001), 2001 CarswellOnt 2404 (Ont. S.C.J.), additional reasons at (2001), 2001 CarswellOnt 3198 (Ont. S.C.J. [In Chambers]).

[37] *C. (S.W.) v. C. (T.L.)* (1996), 20 O.T.C. 63, 1996 CarswellOnt 5025 (Ont. Gen. Div.).

Another aspect includes the ability and motivation of a parent to take a long-term view of the child's educational needs and to take time to nurture the child's religious and cultural roots. In a bi-racial situation, the parent who would most likely promote respect for the child's other racial background will be more favourably regarded.[38]

Where a child has a special emotional or physical need, the parent who can demonstrate the fine-tuned parenting skill to address that need might tip the scale in his or her favour.

Van de Perre v. Edwards, 19 R.F.L. (5th) 396, [2001] 11 W.W.R. 1, [2001] 2 S.C.R. 1014 (S.C.C.)

Kimberly, a young, single Caucasian woman living in Vancouver, and a married African-American professional basketball player carried on an 18-month sexual affair. A son was born of the relationship. The father already had twin daughters from his marriage and he and his family were based in North Carolina. When the child was 3 months old, the mother brought an action for custody and child support under the British Columbia legislation and the father, who remained married, also sought sole custody. The mother was granted sole custody of the child and the father was granted access. The trial judge found that the father had a weak and unstable marriage that would impact the parenting support he would receive. On the other hand, the mother would likely have her own parents' support until their death and she was found to be a good mother. The trial judge also found that the father spent extremely long periods away from home, was very active in the professional basketball social scene when at home, and had had several extra-marital affairs. His two daughters were very upset about his relationship with the mother of the present child. These factors, combined with the fact that he always left the day-to-day childcare activities to his wife, cast the father's parenting ability into doubt.

The father appealed the decision, his wife applied for admission as a party, and on appeal, the father and his wife were awarded joint custody with generous access to the mother. The mother then appealed the decision to the Supreme Court of Canada.

Held: The appeal was allowed and the trial decision awarding sole custody to the mother was restored.

There was no indication that the trial judge made an error in considering the factors that he did, or that he ignored relevant factors. The narrow power of appellate review did not allow the appeal court to delve into a custody case in the name of the best interests of the child where there was no material error.

---

[38] *Ho v. Gallinger* (2002), 2002 CarswellOnt 5308 (Ont. S.C.J.).

There was no credence to the finding of the Court of Appeal that the trial judge failed to give consideration to the issues of race and to the interracial problems that the child might face. The question to be determined in a bi-racial situation is which parent will best be able to contribute to a healthy racial socialization and overall healthy development of the child. In the present situation, the child would have exposure to both sides of his racial and cultural heritage since one biological parent would have custody and the other would have access. No evidence was introduced to suggest that greater exposure to cultural background through custody as opposed to access was in the child's better interests in every case. The limited findings of the trial judge on the race issue reflected the minimal weight that the parties themselves placed on the issue at trial. The trial judge clearly viewed the possible benefits provided by the father with regard to fostering a positive racial identity as not outweighing the negative findings relating to the father.

Plans for the Care and Upbringing of the Child

Any plans for the care and upbringing of the children that are proposed by the parents must be considered under the CLRA.[39] Each parent's plan will be assessed in terms of how it meets the needs of the children involved. Such plans may include parents' work schedules and childcare plans as well as the neighbourhood in which they intend to raise the child.

Permanence and Stability of Proposed Family Unit

The permanence and stability of the family unit where the child will live is an important factor under the CLRA.[40] This factor focuses on the stability of the individual family units of each party seeking custody of the children. Considerations relevant to this inquiry are such things as the living arrangements of each parent, their hours and type of employment, their personal relationships, and their economic circumstances. Particular factors examined by the court include the length of time the parties have lived in their current accommodation, the length and quality of the relationships in the family unit, and the amount of conflict in the family unit.

In assessing the stability and permanence of a family unit, support from extended family members in the household or close by in the neighbourhood seems to be an important factor in creating stability for the children.[41]

---

[39] CLRA, s. 24(2)(e).
[40] CLRA, s. 24(2)(f).
[41] *T. (K.A.) v. T. (J.)* (1989), 23 R.F.L. (3d) 214 (Ont. U.F.C.); see also *Riley v. Parsons* (2002), 2002 CarswellOnt 1847 (Ont. C.J.); *Rosien v. McCulloch* (2000), 2000 CarswellOnt 1738 (Ont. S.C.J.), additional reasons at (2000), 2000 CarswellOnt 2284 (Ont. S.C.J.), affirmed (2001), 2001

Same-sex family units are considered equally as capable of providing stability for children as heterosexual couples.[42]

Relationship to the Parties by Blood or Adoption

The child's relationship by blood or adoption to each person who applies for custody is a factor to be taken into consideration under the CLRA.[43] However, the blood or adoption connection between a child and the persons competing for custody is only one factor to be considered in determining the child's best interests.[44] The law is clear that the best interests of the child is the only consideration even where the contest is between a natural parent and a stranger.[45] The fact that a person is a biological parent of a child does not, in and of itself, guarantee any right to custody or access.

Past Conduct as a Factor

Past conduct of a person who applies for custody is only considered if the conduct is relevant to the person's ability to act as a parent to the child.[46] Therefore, a father's infidelity towards his spouse or a mother's occupation as an exotic dancer is not necessarily relevant to his or her ability to be a good parent. However, a parent who has shown an unsupportive attitude toward the other parent or who has systematically alienated the children from the other parent will have his or her own parenting abilities questioned. This kind of conduct is not in the children's best interests. Similarly, the exposure of children to drunkenness or violence on the part of either parent would be considered conduct detrimental to the children's well being.[47] Sexual or physical abuse of children is conduct that will usually result in custody being awarded to the other non-offending parent.[48] Although there is no presumption that a person who is an abusive spouse is disentitled to custody, domestic violence that includes the children is definitely related to parenting ability. A proposed new provision in the

---

CarswellOnt 1562 (Ont. C.A.); *Parent v. Parent* (2001), 2001 CarswellOnt 4962 (Ont. S.C.J.); *Murphy v. Laurence* (2002), 2002 CarswellOnt 1281 (Ont. S.C.J.).

[42] See *Boots v. Sharrow* (2004), 2004 CarswellOnt 25 (Ont. S.C.J.) (mother, who was in lesbian relationship, awarded custody of four children where she had always been primary caregiver).

[43] CLRA, s. 24(2)(g).

[44] *K. (K.) v. L. (G.)*, 1985 CarswellNWT 54, [1985] 1 S.C.R. 87, 16 D.L.R. (4th) 576, 44 R.F.L. (2d) 113 (S.C.C.); see also *D. (S.) v. B. (T.C.)* (2000), 2000 CarswellOnt 3378 (Ont. S.C.J.).

[45] *H. (M.E.) v. F. (R.M.)* (1994), 1994 CarswellSask 32, 10 R.F.L. (4th) 77 (Sask. C.A.).

[46] CLRA, s. 24(3).

[47] *Mooney v. Coutts* (1996), 1996 CarswellOnt 3927 (Ont. Gen. Div.); *Nairn v. Lukowski* (2002), 2002 CarswellOnt 1119 (Ont. S.C.J.), additional reasons at (2002), 2002 CarswellOnt 2319, 29 R.F.L. (5th) 117 (Ont. S.C.J.).

[48] *A. (S.J.) v. A. (S.C.)* (1994), 1994 CarswellOnt 4337 (Ont. Gen. Div.).

CLRA would make domestic violence a consideration in assessing a person's parenting ability, whether or not it involves the children directly.

Application Questions

1. During a six-month relationship, Dean, aged 18, and Vanessa, aged 16, conceived a child, but they separated before the child was born. Vanessa wanted to complete her schooling and become a court and tribunal agent, so when the child was born, she gave the little girl to her dear friends Grant and Crystal to raise. Dean disappeared, and when Vanessa told him about the child, he denied that he was the father and told her to "prove it!" Grant and Crystal treated the child as their own; the child viewed them as her parents and she became part of their family, blending in with the couple's other two children. Vanessa visited occasionally and the child had never met Dean, her biological father. When the child was almost 3 years old, Dean decided, since he was the biological father, that he had a right to custody over Grant and Crystal who were not even related to the child at all.

   (a) Does Dean have the status to apply for custody in Ontario? If so, under what statute can he apply?
   (b) Does Dean have an automatic right to custody because he is the biological father of the child?
   (c) What are the important factors that the court will consider in this case to determine the child's best interests?

2. Ed and Linda were married for 15 years and have four children. Throughout the marriage, Linda was always the primary caregiver of the children. The couple separated when Linda confessed that she was lesbian. She is now living in a same-sex relationship with another woman. Ed is very hurt and claims that Linda is unfit to be a mother to his children. Also Ed is black and Linda is white and he wants his children to grow up knowing their black roots. Linda respects the children's black heritage and promises to make sure the children are raised with an appreciation of this. On the other hand, Ed calls Linda "white trash". The oldest girl, who is 14 years old, insists upon living with her father, Ed. She wants nothing to do with her mother, as she is very embarrassed by the relationship. The 9 year old also wants to live with her father. The other two children have expressed no preference.

   (a) Will Linda's lesbian relationship disentitle her to custody? How will it be regarded by the courts?

> (b) Will the court follow the wishes of the 14-year-old girl? What about the wishes of the 9 year old? Why or why not in each case?
>
> (c) How is the court likely to view the racial factor in the circumstances?
>
> (d) What factors will be most important in determining the children's best interests?

TYPES OF CUSTODY ORDERS

The court has the power to make custody or access orders similar to those under the *Divorce Act*. Sole or joint custody orders are possible under the CLRA[49] and joint custody may be shared between parents and non-parents; e.g., between a parent and a grandparent. However, there is no presumption in favour of joint custody. The principles of joint custody under the *Divorce* Act are equally applicable under the CLRA. The court may also decide any aspect or incident of custody or access.[50] Thus, any one incident of custody, such as making medical decisions, can be awarded exclusively to one parent, while making educational decisions may be the exclusive domain of the other parent.

VARIATION OF CUSTODY OR ACCESS ORDERS

A custody or access order, by its very nature, is never final. A custody order reflects what is in the best interests of a child at the time the order was made. If the order no longer reflects the child's best interests, the legislation authorizes a judge to change the order. The CLRA gives a court the power to vary an original custody order only where there has been a material change in circumstances that affects the child's best interests.[51] A variation application is different from an appeal as it treats the original judgment or order as correct at the time it was made. The onus is on the person who is seeking the variation to show that circumstances have changed since the first order was made to the extent that the existing childcare arrangements are no longer in the child's best interests.[52]

---

[49] CLRA, s. 28(a).
[50] CLRA, s. 28(b).
[51] CLRA, s. 29.
[52] *Gordon v. Goertz*, [1996] 2 S.C.R. 27, 19 R.F.L. (4th) 177 (S.C.C.).

Material Change in Circumstances

A material change in circumstances is a substantial continuing change, not merely a temporary change such as a temporary leave from work.[53] The change should usually include the occurrence of some unanticipated event or the failure of an expected event to take place. Variation involves a two-step process: first, the applicant must show a material change that gives the court the power to review the original order; second, the person applying must prove that as a result of the changed circumstances, the prior order is no longer in the child's best interests.[54]

There are several common changes that a party can raise as a material change in circumstances. Since parental contact is considered an important factor under both the *Divorce Act* and the CLRA, a parent's subsequent conduct restricting or impeding contact with the other parent is conduct warranting a change in the custodial arrangement.[55] If one or both parents remarry or form new relationships, this is generally regarded as a material change in circumstances. Remarriage introduces new financial and emotional responsibilities as well as new caregivers, and sometimes new conflicts, into the family unit. A change in a parent's employment circumstances can amount to a material change if new job commitments affect the ability to meet the child's needs, either in terms of availability or financial means. As children grow older, their wishes are subject to change and the court is reluctant to ignore the express wishes of a teenaged child to change a custody or access arrangement. In today's mobile society, a variation application is often based upon a custodial parent's desire to move with the child to another province or country. This type of change will certainly affect the child's best interests because it not only affects the child's relationship with the other parent and extended family but may also disrupt the child's *status quo* in terms of school, friends, community and extra-curricular activities.

COURT ASSISTANCE IN CUSTODY MATTERS

Custody Assessments

In a custody or access dispute, an assessment can be ordered by a judge where the court finds that it requires a professional to assess and report

---

[53] See *McLeod v. Impey* (2003), 2003 CarswellSask 289 (Sask. Q.B.).
[54] See *Talbot v. Henry* (1990), 25 R.F.L. (3d) 415 (Sask. C.A.).
[55] *Boukema v. Boukema* (1997), 31 R.F.L. (4th) 329 (Ont. Gen. Div.), additional reasons at (1997), 1997 CarswellOnt 5151 (Ont. Gen. Div.).

on the child's needs and the parties' ability to meet those needs.[56] It is not necessary that one of the parties request an assessment in order for a judge to make such an order.[57] The court will try to appoint a person that the parties can agree upon, but if they cannot agree, the court can choose the assessor,[58] as long as the person consents to act.[59] Usually an assessor is a qualified social worker, psychologist, or psychiatrist. The assessment normally involves meeting with each parent and the children, assessing the interaction of the children with each party seeking custody, and sometimes interviewing other important people in the children's lives, such as doctors and teachers.

The court will not routinely order an assessment merely to obtain another opinion.[60] Only in cases where there are "clinical issues" that require the special knowledge of an expert, or to obtain insight or information that would not be discoverable otherwise, should an assessment be ordered.[61] Routine changes that result from the parents' separation do not automatically give rise to clinical issues.[62] The CLRA does not authorize the court to delegate the final decision as to what arrangement is in the child's best interests to the assessor.[63] The role of the assessor is limited to assisting the court by providing helpful evidence.

The court can require the parties, the child, and any person to attend an assessment.[64] If a person refuses to participate in the assessment when he or she has been ordered to do so, the court may draw an inference about that person's ability and willingness to meet the needs of the child that it thinks appropriate.[65] The assessor will file a report with the court and copies are given to each party and counsel for the child, if any.[66] In addition to the report being admitted at trial,[67] any party can call the assessor as a witness.[68] The parties must pay the assessor's fees in whatever proportion the court directs.[69]

---

[56] CLRA, s. 30(1).

[57] CLRA, s. 30(2).

[58] CLRA, s. 30(3).

[59] CLRA, s. 30(4).

[60] *Linton v. Clarke* (1994), 10 R.F.L. (4th) 92, 21 O.R. (3d) 568, 76 O.A.C. 363 (Ont. Div. Ct.).

[61] *Linton v. Clarke, ibid.; Mantesso v. Mantesso* (1991), 4 F.L.R.R. 128 (Ont. Gen. Div.).

[62] *Hodgson v. Hanson* (2000), 2000 CarswellOnt 3769 (Ont. C.J.).

[63] *Van Delft v. Colosimo* (1996), (sub nom. *J. V-D. v. E.C.*) 14 O.T.C. 159, 1996 CarswellOnt 3595 (Ont. Gen. Div.) (Court considering both assessor's report and report of parental alienation syndrome expert; although both reports of great value, final decision of what was in child's best interests had to be made by Court).

[64] CLRA, s. 30(5).

[65] CLRA, s. 30(6).

[66] CLRA, s. 30(7), (8).

[67] CLRA, s. 30(9).

[68] CLRA, s. 30(10).

[69] CLRA, s. 30(12), (13).

Mediation

At the request of the parties in a custody or access application, the court may make an order appointing a person to mediate specific issues between the parties.[70] In mediation, a neutral third party helps the parties to reach an agreement without going to court. However, if the parties cannot come to an agreement, then the mediator has no authority to impose a solution. In that case, the parties must return to court to have the judge make a final decision, after hearing all the evidence. The parties must choose the mediator,[71] who must consent to act and agree to file a report within a time specified by the court.[72] The parties must decide before the mediation whether the mediator is to make a full report or merely a report setting out the final agreement or the fact that no agreement was reached.[73] If the parties choose the second form of report, then if the matter is not settled, no admissions made in the mediation are admissible as evidence at the trial.[74] The parties themselves are required to pay the mediator's fees in whatever proportion the court orders.[75]

PROCEDURE

Application

A custody or access application under the CLRA must be commenced in the municipality where the child ordinarily resides, unless the case meets one of the exceptions in section 22 of the CLRA.[76] If there is an immediate danger that the child might be abducted from Ontario or immediate danger to the child's or a party's safety, then the case may be started in any municipality.[77] After a motion is heard, the case will usually be transferred by the court back to the appropriate municipality.[78]

A person who is making a custody application must complete and file with the court an Application (Form 8) under the Rules.[79] Usually a claim for custody is combined with a claim for child support, which is made by

---

[70] CLRA, s. 31(1).
[71] CLRA, s. 31(1).
[72] CLRA, s. 31(2).
[73] CLRA, s. 31(4).
[74] CLRA, s. 31(7).
[75] CLRA, s. 31(8), (9).
[76] *Family Law Rules*, O. Reg. 114/99 as amended, Rule 5(1)(b); see also s. 22(1)(b) of CLRA where the court may assume jurisdiction even though the child is not habitually resident in Ontario if certain factors are present.
[77] Rule 5(2).
[78] Rule 5(2).
[79] Rule 8(1).

checking the appropriate boxes on the same Application. The form provides space to set out the specific claims the party is making and a space to set out the facts that support each claim. In a claim for custody, the applicant would set out those facts that favour the child's best interests, based on section 24(2) of the CLRA. Other claims for spousal support and property division under the FLA can also be made in the same application, if necessary. Financial statements are not normally required where only custody and access are claimed, but a court may order the parties to file one if it deems it appropriate.[80] When the application is filed, the court clerk seals the application and sets a court date.[81] The application is then immediately served on all other parties by special service (usually be leaving a copy with the person to be served), unless the party is an agency or government department.[82] A person who starts an application must also prepare and file a continuing record and serve it on all other parties in the application. The continuing record must be filed with the court along with an affidavit of service.[83] The formal requirements for a continuing record are discussed in the chapter dealing with the *Family Law Rules*.

Answer

A person who is responding to an application for custody or access under the CLRA must serve and file an answer in Form 10 within 30 days after being served with the application.[84] If the application is served outside Canada or the United States, then the person has 60 days in which to serve and file an answer.[85]

The answer may also include a claim by the person who is responding.[86] For example, the respondent may wish to claim custody him- or herself or make a claim for access.

Variation

If a party is seeking a variation of an order or agreement with respect to custody under the CLRA, this must be done by motion under Rule 15.[87] The notice of motion to change the order or agreement must be served by special service at least 30 days prior to the motion date. If the person

---

[80] Rule 13(3).
[81] Rule 8(4).
[82] Rule 8(5), (6).
[83] Rule 9(1).
[84] Rule 10(1).
[85] Rule 10(2).
[86] Rule 10(3).
[87] Rule 8(2).

being served lives outside Canada or the United States, then it must be served at least 60 days before the motion is heard.[88] An affidavit must accompany the notice of motion, setting out the particulars of the children involved, the current custodial arrangement, the specific changes sought, and the circumstances upon which the change is based.[89]

INTERNATIONAL CHILD ABDUCTION – *THE HAGUE CONVENTION*

What is the *Hague Convention?*

The *Hague Convention* is an agreement between international states to enforce custody orders and agreements made in those states. It addresses the situation where a child is abducted from his or her lawful custodian and taken to another country, often by another parent who does not have the right to do so. Only certain countries and states in the United States have signed the agreement and only those countries have the authority to enforce custody orders in another state or country. Each contracting country must proclaim its own legislation in force for this purpose. Ontario brought its legislation into force in 1982 as a Schedule to the CLRA.

Purpose

The purpose of the *Convention* is to protect children from the harmful effects of being wrongfully removed from the parent who has legal custody. It establishes similar procedures in each country to make sure that children are returned promptly to their place of habitual residence. The *Convention* does not have any authority to decide custody issues on the merits. Once a child is back in his or her place of habitual residence, if custody is an issue, it must be decided under the appropriate legislation (such as the CLRA in Ontario).[90]

How it Works

The *Convention* applies where a child has been "wrongfully removed or retained" in violation of existing custody rights under the law of the child's habitual residence. A person might have custody rights by operation of

---

[88] Rule 15(1).
[89] Rule 15(7).
[90] See *Thomson v. Thomson*, [1994] 3 S.C.R. 551 (S.C.C.) for a complete discussion of the scope of the *Hague Convention*.

law (common law or statute), by court order, or by an agreement such as a separation agreement. Most commonly, the *Convention* is used to return children who have been abducted by the non-custodial parent after separation or divorce. The person whose custody rights have been violated can apply, either in Ontario or in the place where the child was taken, seeking the child's immediate return. Sometimes a parent will have lawful access to his or her child when he or she initially takes the child to another country. However, if the access parent refuses to return the child at the end of the access period, this will amount to unlawful retention and the custodial parent can then start procedure to have the child returned to him or her under the *Convention*. Similarly, if a child is wrongfully brought to Ontario from another country that has signed the *Convention*, the person who has lawful custody in the other country can apply in the Ontario courts for the child's return.

Application Questions

Jane was awarded custody of her three children pursuant to an Ontario court order under the *Divorce Act*. Howard was entitled to summer access for two weeks and was permitted to take the children out of the country during that period of time. Howard took the children to London, England, during his two-week access period, but at the end of the access period, he refused to return the children to Ontario. England is one of the countries that has signed the *Hague Convention*.

(a) Did Howard wrongfully take or retain the children in this case? If so, explain which actions were wrongful.

(b) If Jane wants to apply to have the children returned, does she have to do it in England or Ontario?

(c) Does Jane have to show that it would be in the children's best interests to be with her in order to have them returned?

(d) What would happen if the custody order were made in England instead of Ontario and Howard brought them to Ontario, contrary to the British order? Would the Ontario courts return the children to England?

APPENDIX 11A

ONTARIO

ONTARIO COURT OF JUSTICE	Court File Number
(Name of court)	*Family Law Rules, O. Reg. 114/99*
at **311 Jarvis Street, Toronto, Ontario, M2N 1G8**	**Form 8: Application**
Court office address	**(General)**

(SEAL)

Applicant(s)

Full legal name & address for service – street & number, municipality, postal code, telephone & fax numbers and e-mail address (if any).	*Lawyer's name & address – street & number, municipality, postal code, telephone & fax numbers and e-mail address (if any).*
Angelina May Sampagnaro **265 Balliol St., Apt. 205** **Toronto, Ontario** **M2N 1P6**	**Shannon Fitzpatrick** **Barrister & Solicitor** **320 St. Clair Ave. East, Unit 107** **Toronto, Ontario** **M2N 1G5** **Tel: (416) 299-7777** **Fax: (416) 299-7778**

Respondent(s)

Full legal name & address for service – street & number, municipality, postal code, telephone & fax numbers and e-mail address (if any).	*Lawyer's name & address – street & number, municipality, postal code, telephone & fax numbers and e-mail address (if any).*
Bradley James Quarry **242 Merton Street** **Toronto, Ontario** **M2N 1P6**	

TO THE RESPONDENT(S):

A COURT CASE HAS BEEN STARTED AGAINST YOU IN THIS COURT. THE DETAILS ARE SET OUT ON THE ATTACHED PAGES.

☒ **THE FIRST COURT DATE IS** *(date)* **Mon. April 10, 2006** **AT 10:00** ☒ a.m. ☐ p.m. or as soon as possible after that time, at: *(address)*

311 Jarvis Street, Toronto, Ontario, M2N 1G8

NOTE: If this is a divorce case, no date will be set unless an Answer is filed. If you have also been served with a notice of motion, there may be an earlier court date and you or your lawyer should come to court for the motion.

☐ **THIS CASE IS ON THE FAST TRACK OF THE CASE MANAGEMENT SYSTEM.** A case management judge will be assigned by the time this case first comes before a judge.

☐ **THIS CASE IS ON THE STANDARD TRACK OF THE CASE MANAGEMENT SYSTEM. No court date has been set for this case** but, if you have been served with a notice of motion, it has a court date and you or your lawyer should come to court for the motion. A case management judge will not be assigned until one of the parties asks the clerk of the court to schedule a case conference or until a notice of motion under subrule 14(5) is served before a case conference has been held. If, after 200 days, the case has not been scheduled for trial, the clerk of the court will send out a warning that the case will be dismissed in 30 days unless the parties file proof that the case has been settled or one of the parties asks for a case conference or a settlement conference.

IF YOU WANT TO OPPOSE ANY CLAIM IN THIS CASE, you or your lawyer must prepare an Answer (Form 10 – a blank copy should be attached), serve a copy on the applicant(s) and file a copy in the court office with an Affidavit of Service (Form 6B). **YOU HAVE ONLY 30 DAYS AFTER THIS APPLICATION IS SERVED ON YOU (60 DAYS IF THIS APPLICATION IS SERVED ON YOU OUTSIDE CANADA OR THE UNITED STATES) TO SERVE AND FILE AN ANSWER. IF YOU DO NOT, THE CASE WILL GO AHEAD WITHOUT YOU AND THE COURT MAY MAKE AN ORDER AND ENFORCE IT AGAINST YOU.**

Form 8: Application (General)   **(page 2)** | Court File Number |

Check the box of the paragraph that applies to your case

☒ This case includes a claim for support. It does not include a claim for property or exclusive possession of the matrimonial home and its contents. You **MUST** fill out a Financial Statement (Form 13 – a blank copy attached), serve a copy on the applicant(s) and file a copy in the court office with an Affidavit of Service even if you do not answer this case.

☐ This case includes a claim for property or exclusive possession of the matrimonial home and its contents. You **MUST** fill out a Financial Statement (Form 13.1 – a blank copy attached), serve a copy on the applicant(s) and file a copy in the court office with an Affidavit of Service even if you do not answer this case.

IF YOU WANT TO MAKE A CLAIM OF YOUR OWN, you or your lawyer must fill out the claim portion in the Answer, serve a copy on the applicant(s) and file a copy in the court office with an Affidavit of Service.

- If you want to make a claim for support but do not want to make a claim for property or exclusive possession of the matrimonial home and its contents, you **MUST** fill out a Financial Statement (Form 13), serve a copy on the applicant(s) and file a copy in the court office.

- However, if your only claim for support is for child support in the table amount specified under the Child Support Guidelines, you do not need to fill out, serve or file a Financial Statement.

- If you want to make a claim for property or exclusive possession of the matrimonial home and its contents, whether or not it includes a claim for support, you **MUST** fill out a Financial Statement (Form 13.1, not Form 13), serve a copy on the applicant(s), and file a copy in the court office.

YOU SHOULD GET LEGAL ADVICE ABOUT THIS CASE RIGHT AWAY. If you cannot afford a lawyer, you may be able to get help from your local Legal Aid Ontario office. *(See your telephone directory under LEGAL AID.)*

_____   _____
        Date of issue   *Clerk of the court*

Form 8: Application (General)	(page 3)	Court file number

FAMILY HISTORY

APPLICANT: Age: **25**   Birthdate: *(d,m,y)* **9 July 1980**

Resident in *(municipality & province)*   **Toronto, Ontario**

since *(date)* **9 July 1980**

Surname at birth: **Sampagnaro**   Surname just before marriage:

Divorced before?   ☒ No   ☐ Yes *(Place and date of previous divorce)*

RESPONDENT: Age: **33**   Birthdate: *(d,m,y)* **16 October 1972**

Resident in *(municipality & province)*   **Toronto, Ontario**

since *(date)* **19 January 1990**

Surname at birth: **Quarry**   Surname just before marriage:

Divorced before?   ☒ No   ☐ Yes *(Place and date of previous divorce)*

RELATIONSHIP DATES:

☐ Married on *(date)*   ☒ Started living together on *(date)* 29 August 2003

☒ Separated on *(date)* 10 March 2006   ☐ Never lived together   ☐ Still living together

THE CHILD(REN)

List all children involved in this case, even if no claim is made for these children.

Full legal name	Age	Birthdate (d,m,y)	Resident in (municipality & province)	Now Living With (name of person and relationship to child)
Mary Lou Sampagnaro-Quarry	2	3 February 2004	Toronto, Ontario	Angelina May Sampagnaro, mother
Sherry Lyn Sampagnaro-Quarry	2	3 February 2004	Toronto, Ontario	Angelina May Sampagnaro, mother

PREVIOUS CASES OR AGREEMENTS

Have the parties or the children been in a court case before?

☒ No   ☐ Yes *(Attach a Summary of Court Cases – Form 8E.)*

Have the parties made a written agreement dealing with any matter involved in this case?

☒ No   ☐ Yes *(Give date of agreement. Indicate which of its terms are in dispute. Attach an additional page if you need more space.)*

Form 8:	Application (General)	(page 4)	Court file number

CLAIM BY APPLICANT

I ASK THE COURT FOR THE FOLLOWING:
(Claims below include claims for temporary orders.)

Claims under the *Divorce Act* *(Check boxes in this column only if you are asking for a divorce and your case is in the Family Court of the Superior Court of Justice.)*	**Claims under the *Family Law Act* or *Children's Law Reform Act***	**Claims relating to property** *(Check boxes in this column only if your case is in the Family Court of the Superior Court of Justice.)*
00 ☐ a divorce 01 ☐ support for me 02 ☐ support for child(ren) – table amount 03 ☐ support for child(ren) - other than table amount 04 ☐ custody of child(ren) 05 ☐ access to child(ren)	10 ☐ support for me 11 ☒ support for child(ren) – table amount 12 ☐ support for child(ren) - other than table amount 13 ☒ custody of child(ren) 14 ☐ access to child(ren) 15 ☐ restraining/non-harassment order 16 ☐ indexing spousal support 17 ☐ indexing same-sex partner support 18 ☐ declaration of parentage 19 ☐ guardianship over child's property	20 ☐ equalization of net family properties 21 ☐ exclusive possession of matrimonial home 22 ☐ exclusive possession of contents of matrimonial home 23 ☐ freezing assets 24 ☐ sale of family property
Other claims 30 ☒ costs 31 ☐ annulment of marriage 32 ☐ prejudgment interest	50 ☐ Other *(Specify.)*	

Give details of the order that you want the court to make. *(Include any amounts of support (if known) and the names of the children for whom support, custody or access is claimed.)*

1. Custody of the twins, Mary Lou Sampagnaro-Quarry and Sherry Lyn Sampagnaro-Quarry, born 3 February, 2004;.

2. Support for the said children in the table amount in the Child Support Guidelines;

3. Costs.

Form 8:	**Application (General)**	**(page 5)**	Court File Number

IMPORTANT FACTS SUPPORTING MY CLAIM FOR DIVORCE

☐ **Separation:** The spouses have lived separate and apart since *(date)* _____ and

    ☐ have not lived together again since that date in an unsuccessful attempt to reconcile.

    ☐ have lived together again during the following period(s) in an unsuccessful attempt to reconcile: *(Give dates.)*

☐ **Adultery:** The respondent has committed adultery. *(Give details. It is not necessary to name any other person involved but, if you do name the other person, then you must serve this application on the other person.)*

☐ **Cruelty:** The respondent has treated the applicant with physical or mental cruelty of such a kind as to make continued cohabitation intolerable. *(Give details.)*

IMPORTANT FACTS SUPPORTING MY OTHER CLAIM(S)

(Set out below the facts that form the legal basis for your other claim(s). Attach an additional page if you need more space.)

1. The children have lived with the applicant since separation and the applicant has been their primary caregiver since birth. It would be in the children's best interests to remain in the custody of the applicant.

2. The respondent is employed as an auto technician at Honest Auto Services and he earns $45,000 per year.

Put a line through any space left on this page. If additional space is needed, extra pages may be attached.

_____	_____
Date of signature	*Signature of applicant*

LAWYER'S CERTIFICATE

For divorce cases only

My name is: _____
and I am the applicant's lawyer in this divorce case. I certify that I have complied with the requirements of section 9 of the *Divorce Act*.

_____	_____
Date	*Signature of Lawyer*

CHAPTER 12

THE *FAMILY LAW RULES*

It used to be that the *Family Law Rules*[1] only applied to the Family Court, and the Ontario Court of Justice and the Superior Court each had their own rules of procedure. Eventually, *Family Law Rules* were extended to the Ontario Court of Justice, and as of July 1, 2004, to the Superior Court of Justice. This means that every court in Ontario that handles family law matters is now governed by the same rules.[2]

The Rules apply to all family law matters.[3] In this chapter, we will focus on the rules that would be used most often in cases where support, custody and/or property issues are in question.

THE PRIMARY OBJECTIVE

The primary objective of the Rules is to enable the court to deal with all matters justly,[4] which includes:

- ensuring that the procedure is fair to all parties;
- saving expense and time;
- dealing with the case in ways that are appropriate to its importance and complexity; and
- giving appropriate court resources to the case while taking account of the need to give resources to other cases.[5]

The court is required to apply the rules so as to promote the primary objective, and the parties and their lawyers must help the court to promote the primary objective.[6]

---

[1] Made under the *Courts of Justice Act*, O. Reg. 114/99, as amended [hereinafter the "Rules"].

[2] Rule 1(2).

[3] Rule 1(2).

[4] Rule 2(2).

[5] Rule 2(3).

[6] Rule 2(4).

DUTY TO MANAGE CASES

One of the ways that the court promotes the primary objective is by actively managing cases. Case management means that judges and judicial officers are more actively involved in cases, with an emphasis on full disclosure, expediency, settlement, and control of costs for the litigants and for the judicial system. Case management includes:

- at an early stage, identifying the issues and separating and disposing of those that do not need full investigation and trial;
- encouraging and facilitating the use of alternatives to the court process;
- helping the parties to settle all or part of the case;
- setting timetables or otherwise controlling the progress of the case;
- considering whether the likely benefits of taking a step justify the cost;
- dealing with as many aspects of the case as possible on the same occasion; and
- if appropriate, dealing with the case without parties and their lawyers needing to come to court, on the basis of written documents or by holding a telephone or video conference.[7]

The rules relating to case management in the various courts will be discussed later in this chapter.

TIME

Where the Rules or an order specify the number of days between two events, the following rules apply to counting days:

- do not count the first day;
- do count the last day;
- if the period specified is less than seven days, then do not count Saturdays, Sundays, or other days when all court offices are closed (holidays). Conversely, if the period specified is seven days or more, then every day is counted, regardless of whether it is a weekend or holiday; and
- if the last day is a weekend or holiday, then the period ends on the next day that the courts are open.

---

[7] Rule 2(5).

Application Questions

Using the calendars provided, state which is the last day to do the following within the time limit:

SEPTEMBER

Sunday	Monday	Tuesday	Wednesday	Thursday	Friday	Saturday
			1	2	3	4
5	6	7	8	9	10	11
12	13	14	15	16	17	18
19	20	21	22	23	24	25
26	27	28	29	30		

OCTOBER

Sunday	Monday	Tuesday	Wednesday	Thursday	Friday	Saturday
					1	2
3	4	5	6	7	8	9
10	11	12	13	14	15	16
17	18	19	20	21	22	23
24	25	26	27	28	29	30
31						

1. The court orders on September 8 that the respondent has five days to file an updated financial statement.

2. The respondent is served with an application on September 14 and has 30 days to serve and file an answer. Note that October 11 is Thanksgiving and the courts are closed.

3. The respondent is served with an application on September 10, and has 30 days to serve and file an answer. Note that October 11 is Thanksgiving, and the courts are closed.

4. The applicant must file an updated financial statement at least seven days before the case conference, which is scheduled for September 23.

The court can, by order, lengthen or shorten any time set out in the rules or in an order (except a timetable for child protection cases) and in most cases, the parties can consent to lengthen or shorten time periods.[8] The court staff must refuse to accept documents that are out of time unless the time has been extended by a court order or on consent.[9]

---

[8] Rule 3(5), (6).
[9] Rule 3(7).

STARTING A CASE

Application

The general rule is that a case is to be started in the municipality where a party resides, but if the case deals with custody or access to a child, it must be started where the child ordinarily resides.[10] To start a case, the applicant files an application. The applicant must select the proper application form. If the applicant is seeking only a divorce, then Form 8A is used (see Chapter 3 for procedure for an uncontested divorce), but if the applicant is also seeking corollary relief under the *Divorce Act*, or anything under the *Family Law Act* or the *Children's Law Reform Act*, etc., then Form 8 is used. If the parties or the children have been in a court case before, then a Summary of Court Cases (Form 8E) must be prepared as well.[11]

Financial Statement

If the application contains a claim for support, a property claim, or a claim for exclusive possession of the matrimonial home, then the applicant must also serve and file a financial statement with the application.[12] If the claim is for support, but no property claim or claim for exclusive possession is made, then the applicant prepares a Financial Statement in Form 13.[13] If the applicant is making a property claim or a claim for exclusive possession of the matrimonial home, then a Financial Statement in Form 13.1 is required.[14] However, if the application is only for child support in the *Guideline* table amount, a financial statement is not required.[15] A financial statement is also not required where only custody and access are being sought, unless the court orders it.[16] If the only claim is for spousal support in a divorce, then a financial statement is not required if the parties either agree not to serve and file financial statements, or agree to a specified amount of support or to no support.[17]

Each party is required to make full and frank disclosure in his or her financial statement and to attach proof of his or her current income (a pay cheque stub, an employment insurance stub, etc.). Each party must also attach copies of income tax returns and notices of assessment or a direction to

---

[10] Rule 5(1).
[11] Rule 8(1).
[12] Rule 13(1).
[13] Rule 13(1.1).
[14] Rule 13(1.2).
[15] Rule 13(1.3).
[16] Rule 13(3).
[17] Rule 13(9).

the taxation branch to disclose that person's income tax returns and notices of assessment.[18] If the required documents are not attached, the clerks must not accept the financial statement for filing.[19]

Continuing Record

The applicant is also required to prepare a continuing record.[20] However, a continuing record is not required in the following circumstances:

- a joint application for divorce case;
- an uncontested divorce case, except that if the respondent files an answer, the respondent shall start the continuing record on filing the answer;
- the applicant files a Change Information Form (Form 15), except that if the respondent files an affidavit that sets out any disagreement, the respondent shall start the continuing record on filing the affidavit;
- the case is started in the Superior Court of Justice, other than the Family Court of the Superior Court of Justice, before July 1, 2004 and a party files a Notice of Change in Representation (Form 4) or a party's lawyer files a notice of motion to be removed as lawyer on or after July 1, 2004; or
- the parties file a consent motion for a final order.[21]

A continuing record must meet the requirements set out in a document entitled "Formal Requirements of a Continuing Record Under The Family Law Rules", which is included as Appendix 12A to this chapter. It is also available online at www.ontariocourtforms.on.ca.

Service of Documents

The application and the accompanying documents must be served by special service.[22] Special service of a document is carried out by:

- leaving a copy with the person to be served,
- leaving a copy with the person's lawyer of record in the case, or with a lawyer who accepts service in writing on a copy of the document;
- mailing a copy to the person, together with an acknowledgment of service in the form of a prepaid return postcard (Form 6), all in an envelope that is addressed to the person and has the sender's return

---

[18] Rule 13(6).
[19] Rule 13(7).
[20] Rule 9(1).
[21] Rule 9(2).
[22] Rule 8(5).

address (but service under this clause is not valid unless the return postcard, signed by the person, is filed in the continuing record); or

- leaving a copy at the person's place of residence, in an envelope addressed to the person, with anyone who appears to be an adult person resident at the same address and, on the same day or on the next, mailing another copy to the person at that address.[23]

There are particular rules for special service if the person being serves is mentally incompetent, a child, a corporation, or a Children's Aid Society.

Documents served after 4 p.m. or on a day when the courts are not open (weekends and holidays) count as having been served the next day that the courts are open.[24]

If a party cannot locate the person to be served, or if there is difficulty in serving a party, the court may, on motion, order substituted service,[25] or can even dispense with service.[26]

Service of a document by special service is proved by:

- an acceptance or admission of service, written by the person to be served or the person's lawyer;

- an Affidavit of Service (Form 6B);

- the return postcard mentioned in clause (3)(c); or

- the date stamp on a copy of the document served by deposit at a document exchange.[27]

ANSWERING A CASE

Answer

The person served with the application has 30 days to serve and file an Answer (Form 10) if he or she wishes to defend the application.[28] If the person is served outside of Canada or the U.S.A., then he or she has 60 days to serve and file the answer.[29] The answer can include a claim against the respondent or any other person (who then becomes a respondent in the case).[30]

---

[23] Rule 6(3).
[24] Rule 6(7).
[25] Rule 6(15).
[26] Rule 6(7).
[27] Rule 6(19).
[28] Rule 10(1).
[29] Rule 10(2).
[30] Rule 10(3).

Financial Statement

If the application contains a claim for support, a property claim, or a claim for exclusive possession of the matrimonial home, or if the answer contains any such claims, then the respondent must also serve and file a financial statement.[31] If the claim or answer is for support, but no property claim or claim for exclusive possession is made, then the respondent prepares a Financial Statement in Form 13.[32] If the applicant or the respondent is making a property claim or a claim for exclusive possession of the matrimonial home, then a Financial Statement in Form 13.1 is required.[33] However, if the application and/or the answer is only for child support in the *Guideline* table amount, a financial statement is not required.[34] A financial statement is also not required where only custody and access are being sought, unless the court orders it.[35] If the only claim is for spousal support in a divorce, then a financial statement is not required if the parties either agree not to serve and file financial statements, or agree to a specified amount of support or to no support.[36]

Each party is required to make full and frank disclosure in his or her financial statement and to attach proof of his or her current income (a pay cheque stub, an employment insurance stub, etc.). Each party must also attach copies of income tax returns and notices of assessment or a direction to the taxation branch to disclose that person's income tax returns and notices of assessment.[37] If the required documents are not attached, the clerks must not accept the financial statement for filing.[38]

Continuing Record

All parties have an obligation to maintain the continuing record.[39] If the continuing record has not been separated, then the respondent must serve and file any documents that are not already in the continuing record and serve with the documents an updated cumulative table of contents listing the documents being filed. If the continuing record has been separated, then the respondent must serve and file any documents that are not already in the party's separate record and serve with the documents an updated

---

[31] Rule 13(1)(b).
[32] Rule 13(1.1).
[33] Rule 13(1.2).
[34] Rule 13(1.3).
[35] Rule 13(3).
[36] Rule 13(9).
[37] Rule 13(6).
[38] Rule 13(7).
[39] Rule 9(11).

cumulative table of contents listing the documents being filed in the party's separate record.[40]

Service of Documents

The answer and the accompanying documents may be served by regular service. Regular service of a document on a person is carried out by:

- mailing a copy to the person's lawyer or, if none, to the person;

- sending a copy by courier to the person's lawyer or, if none, to the person;

- depositing a copy at a document exchange to which the person's lawyer belongs;

- faxing a copy to the person's lawyer or, if none, to the person; or

- carrying out special service.[41]

If the documents are being served by mail, then service is effective on the fifth day after it was mailed.[42] If they are being couriered, then service is effective on the day after the courier picks it up.[43] Service by deposit at a document exchange is effective only if the copy deposited and an additional copy of the document are date-stamped by the document exchange in the presence of the person depositing the copy and then service is effective on the day after the stamp's date.[44]

If the documents are being served by fax, they can only be served before 4 p.m. on a day the court offices are open, unless the parties consent or the court order otherwise.[45] Documents served by fax must include a fax cover page, containing the following information:

- the sender's name, address, telephone number, and fax number;

- the name of the person or lawyer to be served;

- the date and time of the fax;

- the total number of pages faxed; and

- the name and telephone number of a person to contact in case of transmission difficulties.[46]

---

[40] Rule 9(12).
[41] Rule 6(2).
[42] Rule 6(9).
[43] Rule 6(10).
[44] Rule 6(11).
[45] Rule 6(8).
[46] Rule 6(12).

Document cannot be served by fax if there are more than 16 pages (including the cover page) unless the parties consent in advance or the court orders.[47] Also, a trial record, appeal record, factum, or book of authorities may not be served by fax at any time unless the person to be served consents in advance.[48]

REPLY

The applicant can, if he or she wishes, serve and file a Reply (Form 10A) within ten days of being served with the Answer.[49] The Reply is served by regular service.

MANDATORY INFORMATION PROGRAM

The Mandatory Information Program only applies to cases that are started in the Superior Court of Justice in Toronto after July 1, 1998. It does not apply to cases that are uncontested, such as cases where the parties are only asking for costs and for the incorporation of terms of an agreement or prior court order. It also does not apply to motions to change a final order.[50]

The purpose of the program is to provide the parties with information about separation and the legal process, and may include the following information:

- the options available for resolving differences, including alternatives to going to court;

- the impact on children when parents separate; and

- resources available to deal with problems arising from separation.[51]

When the application is filed, the applicant must arrange an appointment to attend the program. At the program, the applicant obtains an appointment for the respondent to attend the program and must serve the appointment with the application.[52] Attendance is compulsory and the parties must attend within 45 days of the case being started.[53]

---

[47] Rule 6(13).
[48] Rule 6(14).
[49] Rule 10(6).
[50] Rule 8.1(1).
[51] Rule 8.1(3).
[52] Rule 8.1(5).
[53] Rule 8.1(4).

The parties are given a certificate of attendance, which the parties must file as soon as possible, but not later than 2:00 p.m. two days before the case conference.[54] A party cannot take any steps in the case until the certificate of attendance is filed, unless the party can show urgency or hardship, or some other reason in the interest of justice.[55]

MOTIONS FOR TEMPORARY ORDERS

A party in the case can make a motion for:

- a temporary order for a claim made in the application;

- directions on how to carry on the case; or

- a change in a temporary order.[56]

A motion may be made by a party in the case or by a person with an interest in the case.[57] The party making a motion on notice must serve, on all other parties at least four days before the motion, the following: a Form 14 Notice of Motion, a Form 14A Affidavit (General), and any other evidence he or she will be relying on in the motion.[58] Motion documents are served by regular service. These materials should be filed as soon as possible, but must be filed by 2:00 p.m. at least two days before the motion date.[59] However, if the motion is limited to procedural, uncomplicated, or unopposed matters, the party making the motion may use a Motion Form (Form 14B) instead of a notice of motion and affidavit.[60] A Form 14C Confirmation must also be filed by 2:00 p.m. two days before the motion date.[61]

However, no motion material may be served, and no motion may be heard, until a case conference has taken place,[62] unless it is a situation of urgency or hardship.[63] Certain types of motions are exempted from this rule.[64]

In addition to attendance at the courthouse, motions can also be made by telephone or video conference.[65]

---

[54] Rule 8.1(6).
[55] Rule 8.1(7), (8).
[56] Rule 14(1).
[57] Rule 14(2).
[58] Rule 14(11)(a).
[59] Rule 14(11)(b), (11.1).
[60] Rule 14(10).
[61] Rule 14(11)(c).
[62] Rule 14(4).
[63] Rule 14(4.2).
[64] Rule 14(6).
[65] Rule 14(8).

Motions without Notice

A motion may be made without notice if:

- the nature or circumstances of the motion make notice unnecessary or not reasonably possible;

- there is an immediate danger of a child's removal from Ontario, and the delay involved in serving a notice of motion would probably have serious consequences;

- there is an immediate danger to the health or safety of a child or of the party making the motion, and the delay involved in serving a notice of motion would probably have serious consequences; or

- service of a notice of motion would probably have serious consequences.[66]

Unless the court orders otherwise, documents for a motion without notice must be filed by the day before the motion date.[67] The order made on a motion without notice, and all of the materials used on the motion, must be served immediately on all parties affected by the motion.[68] The order made on motion without notice (Form 14D) must require the matter to come back to the court and, if possible, to the same judge, within 14 days or on a date chosen by the court.[69]

Browne v. McLaughlin (1988), [1988] O.J. No. 1066, 1988 CarswellOnt 2563 (Ont. Dist. Ct.)

Ex parte custody orders in family law cases undoubtedly give the successful applicant a leg up in the proceedings. That party's de facto custody is then supported by an order of the Court or, the order has changed custody. There then follows the usual exchange of affidavits, in many cases cross-examinations on the affidavits and before long, months have past providing a so-called "status quo" which is by intent without blemish.

The other party has this state of affairs cast upon them as if by ambush in which the Court exercising what can only be described as an extraordinary remedy has participated.

The Rule requires "full and fair disclosure of all material facts". The meaning of that Rule is clear that nothing short of that should give rise to an order. [At paras. 5-7.]

---

[66] Rule 14(12).
[67] Rule 14(13).
[68] Rule 14(15).
[69] Rule 14(14).

CONFERENCES

The rules provide for three kinds of conferences: case conferences, settlement conferences, and trial management conferences. In each contested case, a judge must hold at least one case conference and may conduct settlement conferences and case management conferences.[70] A judge can order that conferences be combined.[71]

Case Conferences

The purposes of a case conference include:

- exploring the chances of settling the case;

- identifying the issues that are in dispute and those that are not in dispute;

- exploring ways to resolve the issues that are in dispute;

- ensuring disclosure of the relevant evidence;

- noting admissions that may simplify the case;

- setting the date for the next step in the case;

- if possible, having the parties agree to a specific timetable for the steps to be taken in the case before it comes to trial;

- organizing a settlement conference, or holding one if appropriate; and

- giving directions with respect to any intended motion, including preparing a specific timetable for the exchange of material for the motion and ordering the filing of summaries of argument, if appropriate.[72]

A case conference generally must be held before a motion can be brought.[73] The party who asks for the case conference must serve and file a Case Conference Notice (Form 17)[74] and must also serve and file a Case Conference Brief—General (Form 17A) not later than seven days before the case conference. The other party must serve and file a Case Conference Brief not later than four days before the case conference.[75] Each party must confirm his or her attendance by filing a Confirmation (Form 14C) by 2:00 p.m. on the day before the conference.[76] The lawyers and the

---

[70] Rule 17(1).
[71] Rule 17(7).
[72] Rule 17(4).
[73] Rule 15(4).
[74] Rule 17(4.1).
[75] Rule 17(13.1).
[76] Rule 17(14).

clients attend the conference,[77] which may be held by telephone or video, if the judge gives permission in advance.[78] Case conference briefs do not form part of the continuing record, unless the court orders otherwise.[79]

Settlement Conferences

The purposes of a settlement conference include:

- exploring the chances of settling the case;

- settling or narrowing the issues in dispute;

- ensuring disclosure of the relevant evidence;

- noting admissions that may simplify the case;

- if possible, obtaining a view of how the court might decide the case;

- considering any other matter that may help in a quick and just conclusion of the case;

- if the case is not settled, identifying the witnesses and other evidence to be presented at trial, estimating the time needed for trial, and scheduling the case for trial; and

- organizing a trial management conference or holding one if appropriate.[80]

A settlement conference must be held before a matter is scheduled for trial, unless a court orders otherwise.[81] The party who asks for the settlement conference must serve and file a Settlement Conference Brief—General (Form 17C) not later than seven days before the settlement conference. The other party must serve and file a Settlement Conference Brief not later than four days before the settlement conference.[82] Each party must confirm his or her attendance by filing a Confirmation (Form 14C) by 2:00 p.m. on the day before the conference.[83] The lawyers and the clients attend the conference,[84] which may be held by telephone or video, if the judge gives permission in advance.[85] Settlement Conference Briefs and anything that is prepared for or discussed at a settlement conference are confidential, unless an agreement is reached or the court orders

---

[77] Rule 17(15).
[78] Rule 17(16).
[79] Rule 17(22).
[80] Rule 17(5).
[81] Rule 17(10).
[82] Rule 17(13.1).
[83] Rule 17(14).
[84] Rule 17(15).
[85] Rule 17(16).

otherwise.[86] Also, the judge who hears an issue at the settlement conference cannot hear that same issue at trial.[87]

Trial Management Conferences

The purposes of a trial management conference include:

- exploring the chances of settling the case;

- arranging to receive evidence by a written report, an agreed statement of facts, an affidavit or another method, if appropriate;

- deciding how the trial will proceed;

- ensuring that the parties know what witnesses will testify and what other evidence will be presented at trial;

- estimating the time needed for trial; and

- setting the trial date, if this has not already been done.[88]

Trial management conferences are not mandatory. The party who asks for the trial management conference must serve and file a Trial Management Conference Brief (Form 17E) not later than seven days before the trial management conference. The other party must serve and file a Trial Management Conference Brief not later than four days before the trial management conference.[89] Each party must confirm his or her attendance by filing a Confirmation (Form 14C) by 2:00 p.m. on the day before the conference.[90] The lawyers and the clients attend the conference,[91] which may be held by telephone or video, if the judge gives permission in advance.[92] Trial Management Conference Briefs *do* form part of the continuing record.[93]

CASE MANAGEMENT

Case management is one of the methods by which the primary objective of the Rules is fulfilled. Case management varies slightly in the Family Court, the Ontario Court of Justice, and the Superior Court of Justice.

---

[86] Rule 17(23).
[87] Rule 17(24).
[88] Rule 17(6).
[89] Rule 17(13.1).
[90] Rule 17(14).
[91] Rule 17(15).
[92] Rule 17(16).
[93] Rule 17(21).

Family Court

In Family Court, cases are placed on either the fast track or a standard track. Applications for a divorce or a property claims and motions to change a final order are standard track cases; all others are fast track cases.[94] In fast track cases, the first court date is set when the application is filed.[95] In a standard track case, the clerk does not set a court date when the application is filed, but will schedule a case conference at the request of either party.[96] Before the first date, the clerk's duties are to:

- confirm that all necessary documents have been served and filed;
- refer the parties to sources of information about the court process, alternatives to court (including mediation), the effects of separation and divorce on children, and community resources that may help the parties and their children;
- if an answer has been filed in response to an application, or if an affidavit has been filed in response to a motion to change a final order or agreement, confirm that the case is ready for a hearing, case conference, or settlement conference and schedule it accordingly;
- if no answer has been filed in response to an application, send the case to a judge for a decision on the basis of affidavit evidence or, on request of the applicant, schedule a case conference; and
- if no affidavit has been filed in response to a motion to change a final order or agreement, send the case to a judge for a decision on the basis of affidavit evidence or, on request of a party who made the motion, schedule a case conference.[97]

In a fast track case, a case management judge is assigned the first time the case comes before a judge.[98] In a standard track case, the case management judge is assigned when a case conference or a motion is scheduled, whichever comes first.[99] A case management judge assigned to a case:

- shall generally supervise its progress;
- shall conduct the case conference and the settlement conference;
- may schedule a case conference or settlement conference at any time, on the judge's own initiative;
- shall hear motions in the case, when available to hear motions; and

---

[94] Rule 39(4), (7).
[95] Rule 8(4).
[96] Rule 39(8).
[97] Rule 39(5).
[98] Rule 39(6).
[99] Rule 39(8).

- may, on motion, set aside an order of the clerk under subrule (12).[100]

If, for any reason, a case management judge cannot continue, another case management judge can be assigned for all or part of the case.[101]

In both fast track and standard track cases, the case must be scheduled for trial within two hundred days after it is started, or the clerk will serve a notice on the parties that the case will be dismissed unless one of the parties:

- files an agreement signed by all parties and their lawyers, if any, for a final order disposing of all issues in the case, and a notice of motion for an order carrying out the agreement; or

- arranges a case conference or settlement conference for the first available date.[102]

If neither of these is done by any party, after 30 days the clerk sends out a notice to all the parties that the case has been dismissed, without costs.[103]

Ontario Court of Justice

In the Ontario Court of Justice, a court date is set when the Application is filed.[104] The clerk has duties to perform before the first court date, which are exactly the same as the clerk performs in Family Court before the first court date.[105] As in Family Court, the case must be scheduled for trial within two hundred days after it is started, or the clerk will serve a notice on the parties that the case will be dismissed unless one of the parties:

- files an agreement signed by all parties and their lawyers, if any, for a final order disposing of all issues in the case, and a notice of motion for an order carrying out the agreement; or

- arranges a case conference or settlement conference for the first available date.[106]

If neither of these is done by any party, after 30 days the clerk sends out a notice to all the parties that the case has been dismissed, without costs.[107]

---

[100] Rule 39(9).
[101] Rule 39(10).
[102] Rule 39(11).
[103] Rule 39(12), (13).
[104] Rule 8(4).
[105] Rule 40(4).
[106] Rule 40(5).
[107] Rule 40(6), (7).

Superior Court of Justice

In the Superior Court of Justice, the clerk does not set a court date when the application is filed, and the case comes before the court when a case conference or a motion is scheduled, whichever comes first. The clerk schedules a case conference on any party's request.[108] As in the other courts, the case must be scheduled for trial within two hundred days after it is started. If neither party files an agreement settling or disposing of the case, or schedules a case conference or settlement conference, then after 30 days of sending out the notice that the case will be dismissed, the clerk sends out a notice to all the parties that the case has been dismissed, without costs.

MOTIONS TO CHANGE A FINAL ORDER OR AGREEMENT

If a person wishes to change a final order, whether the order was made under the *Divorce Act* or the *Family Law Act*, or an agreement for support filed under section 35 of the *Family Law Act*, the procedure under Rule 15 must be followed. The person wishing to change the order must serve the Notice of Motion by special service, at least 30 days before the motion is to be heard (or 60 days, if the Notice is served outside of the U.S. or Canada).[109] However, the motion cannot be heard until a case conference has been held.[110] Rule 15(7) sets out the information that must be included in the affidavit in support of the motion. A copy of the existing order or agreement must be attached as an exhibit to the affidavit.[111] Alternatively, a party asking for a change to a child support order can serve and file a Change Information Form (Form 15), with all the required attachments, instead of an affidavit.[112] The responding party may serve and file an affidavit if he or she disagrees with any of the evidence.[113] If either party is claiming that the amount of child support should not be the table amount, then the parties must serve and file affidavits containing information on why the order should be an exception to the presumptive rule (e.g., split custody, income over $150,000) and financial statements.[114]

If the parties are in agreement as to what the child support order should be, then, instead of proceeding by way of a motion, they can simply file the following materials:

---

[108] Rule 41(4).
[109] Rule 15(1).
[110] Rule 15(2.1).
[111] Rule 15(8).
[112] Rule 15(12)(a).
[113] Rule 15(12)(b).
[114] Rule 15(12)(c).

- a Change Information Form (Form 15);
- a Consent (Form 15A);
- five copies of a draft order;
- a stamped envelope addressed to each of the parties;
- a support deduction order information form; and
- a draft support deduction order.[115]

The clerk then presents this material to a judge. If everything is in order, the judge will sign the order and copies will be sent to the parties in the envelopes provided.[116] This avoids the necessity of anyone having to appear in court.

---

[115] Rule 15(10).
[116] Rule 15(11).

APPENDIX 12A[117]

Formal Requirements of the Continuing Record
under the *Family Law Rules*

Published by: The Family Rules Committee
Dated: November 1, 2005
Available at: www.ontariocourtforms.on.ca

TABLE OF CONTENTS

I. Introduction
II. Formal Requirements

    1. Contents of the record

    2. Preparation of the Record

       (a) Record Cover

       (b) Filing Documents

       (c) Contents of sections

          (i) Table of Contents

          (ii) Endorsements

          (iii) Pleadings

          (iv) Financial Statements

          (v) Other Documents

       (d) Affidavits of Service

       (e) Further volumes

       (f) Separate or combined records

    3. Additional requirements for distinct records

       (a) Support enforcement continuing record

       (b) New record where motion to change made

       (c) Children's Lawyer record

APPENDIX A – SUMMARY OF CONTENTS

APPENDIX B – SAMPLE COVER

APPENDIX C – SAMPLE TABLE OF CONTENTS

---

[117] From: http://www.ontariocourtforms.on.ca/english/forms/family/continuing_record/index.jsp.

I. Introduction

The "Formal Requirements of the Continuing Record under the *Family Law Rules*" is published by the Family Rules Committee and available at the following website: www.ontariocourtforms.on.ca. These requirements must be followed in all cases, except child protection cases, governed by the *Family Law Rules*. The Family Rules Committee has the authority to make court rules for the practice and procedure in family cases, subject to the approval of the Lieutenant Governor in Council.

The formal requirements of the continuing record for child protection cases are set out in the "Formal Requirements of the Child Protection Continuing Record under the *Family Law Rules*", published by the Family Rules Committee and available at www.ontariocourtforms.on.ca.

The *Family Law Rules* provide for a continuing record to be established and maintained by both parties in every case. The Family Rules Committee has approved the following variations to the continuing record to broaden its format and to permit it to be tailored to the case type:

Separate records – The record may be separated into an Applicant's Record and Respondent's Record. Any party in a standard track case under Rule 41 can elect, on filing their first document in the case, to have separate records. In all cases, a party may request that the continuing record be separated, and the court may order that the continuing record by separated or that a separated record be combined.

Distinct records – There are distinct records for cases involving support enforcement and a motion to change a final order. A party may request or the court may order at any time that a record in these cases be separated.

The substantive requirements of the continuing record are set out in Rule 9. There are provisions in Rules 13 and 17 that set out the types of documents that may be excluded from the record. The formal requirements for the preparation and maintenance of the continuing record, including separate and distinct records, are set out in this document, and in the following appendices:

Appendix A – Summary of Contents
Appendix B – Sample Cover
Appendix C – Sample Table of Contents

II. Formal Requirements

1. Contents of the record

Unless otherwise indicated, the continuing record consists of four sections, which comprise Part I of the record: table of contents, endorsements, pleadings (documents starting or answering a case), and financial statements.

Documents other than pleadings and financial statements must be filed in a second, separately bound part of the record (Part II). If a continuing record has been separated into an applicant's record and a respondent's record, the endorsements section must appear in the applicant's record only.

The formal requirements of a continuing record also apply to a new record made where there is a motion to change a final order.

If the Children's Lawyer prepares a separate record, the record will consist of a table of contents and documents section only.

A support enforcement continuing record includes a table of contents, an endorsements section and a documents section only. There is no option to create a Part II.

A summary of the contents of each record is set out in a chart at Appendix A.

2. Preparation of the Record

(a) Record Cover

A sample record cover is attached at Appendix B. All elements of the sample cover must appear on a party's record cover. The title of the record (e.g. "Continuing Record") must appear in bold, font size 20, or an equivalent size, below the names of the parties to the case. The cover must identify the Part of the record and volume number, if applicable. Please see section (e), below, for additional information about further volumes.

(b) Filing Documents

Documents must be filed in chronological order, with the most recently filed document at the back. All documents filed in the record must be punched in standard three-hole format.

Other than in a support enforcement continuing record, each document filed must be identified by a numbered tab. Tabs within sections must be in sequential order. A new section must start with a new tab sequence starting with tab 1. For example, if there are three documents in the pleadings section and three documents in the financial statements section, the tabs in the pleadings section must be labelled 1 to 3, and the tabs in the financial statements section must be labelled 1 to 3. If there is a Part II to the continuing record, it must start with a new tab sequence. For example, the first tab in Part II must be labelled 1.

Pages between numbered tabs shall be numbered consecutively. Page numbers are not required to appear in the table of contents.

(c) Contents of sections

It is not necessary to create any of the sections referred to in Appendix A unless there is a document to be filed in it.

Each section, other than the table of contents, must be identified by a tab showing the name of the section.

(i) Table of Contents

A sample table of contents is attached at Appendix C. The table of contents must list documents in the order in which they are filed, indicate the tab that locates the document, the kind of document, which party filed it, and the date it was filed. For an affidavit or transcript of evidence, the name of the person who gave the affidavit or the evidence must also be shown.

The table of contents must be updated every time a document is filed.

(ii) Endorsements

The endorsements section must contain three (3) blank sheets (or more if necessary), on which the judge dealing with any step in the case will note the disposition of that step and the date. The court's file copy of each order made in the case must be put into the endorsement section after the endorsement pages.

(iii) Pleadings

The pleadings section must contain all documents which start or answer the case.

(iv) Financial Statements

The financial statements section must include all financial statements and documents that are required by the *Family Law Rules* to be attached to it (three years of notices of assessment and Form 13A: Directions to Canada Revenue Agency, if applicable).

(v) Other Documents

If there are other documents filed in the case, they must be filed in Part II. This part will contain documents such as reports ordered by the court, motions documents (including motions to enforce orders other than a support order), documents to enforce a payment order other than a support order, and trial management conference briefs.

If there is an applicant's record and a respondent's record, a report ordered by the court must be filed in Part II of the applicant's record. A report requested by a party must be filed in the record of the party who requested it.

(d) Affidavits of Service

Affidavits of service must be filed in a separate section of the court file labelled "affidavits of service".

In a support enforcement continuing record, affidavits of service are filed in the documents section.

(e) Further volumes

If the clerk determines that a part of a continuing record needs to be continued in another volume, then the party filing the next document must create a new volume. A new volume of Part I consists of a table of contents, pleadings section and a financial statements section.

(f) Separate or combined records

Where the court orders that the continuing record be separated, or that separate court records be combined,

- court staff must supervise the separation or the combination of separate records;
- the clerk must destroy the table of contents that existed just before the record is separated or combined;
- if the record is separated, each party must prepare and update a table of contents reflecting the contents of their record; and
- if separated records are combined, the party directed to combine the record shall prepare and update a table of contents that reflects the contents of the combined record.

3. Additional requirements for distinct records

(a) Support enforcement continuing record

The documents section must be separated from the endorsements section by a labelled tab. The documents section must contain each document filed in the case, numbered consecutively and arranged in order, with the most recently filed document at the back. All affidavits of service must be filed in this section.

(b) New record where motion to change made

The cover must identify the order that is the subject of the motion. Below the title of the record state: "Motion to Change Final Order of Mr./Madam Justice . . . ., dated . . . ., with respect to . . . ."

A motion for an order to refrain under s. 35(1) of the *Family Responsibility and Support Arrears Enforcement Act, 1996* must be filed in Part II of a motion to change final order record.

(c) Children's Lawyer record

Documents filed in the documents section of a Children's Lawyer record will include any pleadings and documents filed by the children's lawyer.

APPENDIX A – SUMMARY OF CONTENTS

CONTINUING RECORD			
SINGLE RECORD	SEPARATE RECORDS		
Continuing Record	Applicant's Record	Respondent's Record	Children's Lawyer Record
- red cover	- red cover	- blue cover	- red cover
Part I - Table of contents - Endorsements (only in 1st volume) - Pleadings - Financial statements	Part I - Table of contents - Endorsements (only in 1st volume) - Pleadings - Financial statements	Part I - Table of contents - Pleadings - Financial statements	Part I - Table of contents - Documents
Part II - All other documents	Part II - Applicant's other documents	Part II - Respondent's other documents	

SUPPORT ENFORCEMENT CONTINUING RECORD			
SINGLE RECORD	SEPARATE RECORDS		
Support Enforcement Record	Director's Enforcement Record	Payor's Enforcement Record	
- green cover	- green cover	- green cover	
- Table of contents - Endorsements (only in 1st volume) - Documents (incl. affidavits of service)	- Table of contents - Endorsements (only in 1st volume) - Documents (incl. affidavits of service)	- Table of contents - Documents (incl. affidavits of service)	

NEW RECORD: MOTION TO CHANGE			
SINGLE RECORD	SEPARATE RECORDS		
Continuing Record	Applicant's Record	Respondent's Record	Children's Lawyer Record
- red cover	- red cover	- blue cover	- red cover
Part I - Table of contents - Endorsements (only in 1st volume) - Pleadings - Financial statements	Part I - Table of contents - Endorsements (only in 1st volume) - Pleadings - Financial statements	Part I - Table of contents - Pleadings - Financial statements	Part I - Table of contents - Documents
Part II - All other documents	Part II - Applicant's other documents	Part II - Respondent's other documents	

APPENDIX B – SAMPLE COVER

ONTARIO

Court File Number / *Numéro de dossier du greffe*

_____

(Name of court / Nom du tribunal)

at / *situé(e) au* _____

Court office address / *Adresse du greffe*

Part and Volume / *Partie et volume* : _____

Applicant(s) / *Requérant(e)(s)*

Full legal name & address for service — street & number, municipality, postal code, telephone & fax numbers and e-mail address (if any). *Nom et prénom officiels et adresse aux fins de signification — numéro et rue, municipalité, code postal, numéros de téléphone et de télécopieur et adresse électronique (le cas échéant).*	Lawyer's name & address — street & number, municipality, postal code, telephone & fax numbers and e-mail address (if any). *Nom et adresse de l'avocat(e) — numéro et rue, municipalité, code postal, numéros de téléphone et de télécopieur et adresse électronique (le cas échéant).*

Respondent(s) / *Intimé(e)(s)*

Full legal name & address for service — street & number, municipality, postal code, telephone & fax numbers and e-mail address (if any). *Nom et prénom officiels et adresse aux fins de signification — numéro et rue, municipalité, code postal, numéros de téléphone et de télécopieur et adresse électronique (le cas échéant).*	Lawyer's name & address — street & number, municipality, postal code, telephone & fax numbers and e-mail address (if any). *Nom et adresse de l'avocat(e) — numéro et rue, municipalité, code postal, numéros de téléphone et de télécopieur et adresse électronique (le cas échéant).*

(Title of record in bold, font size 20 or equivalent / Intitulé du dossier en caractères gras; police de taille 20 ou l'équivalent)

Read these notes if this is an **Applicant's Record** or a **Respondent's Record**. / Veuillez prendre connaissance des remarques suivantes s'il s'agit d'un **Dossier du(de la) requérant(e)** ou d'un **Dossier de l'intimé(e).**

Note to the Respondent: If you are served with an **Applicant's Record**, you must serve and file a separate Respondent's Record.

À l'intimé(e) : *Si vous recevez signification d'un **Dossier du(de la) requérant(e)**, vous devez signifier et déposer un **Dossier de l'intimé(e)** distinct.*

Note to the Applicant: If you are a served with a **Respondent's Record** after you have prepared the Continuing Record, the Continuing Record will be renamed **Applicant's Record.**

Au(à la) requérant(e) : *Si vous recevez signification d'un **Dossier de l'intimé(e)** après avoir préparé le dossier continu, le dossier continu sera par la suite intitulé **Dossier du(de la) requérant(e).***

APPENDIX C – SAMPLE TABLE OF CONTENTS

ONTARIO

Court File Number

_____
(Name of court)

at _____

Court office address

**Cumulative Table of Contents
(Continuing Record)**

Applicant(s)

Full legal name & address for service — street & number, municipality, postal code, telephone & fax numbers and e-mail address (if any).	Lawyer's name & address — street & number, municipality, postal code, telephone & fax numbers and e-mail address (if any).

Respondent(s)

Full legal name & address for service — street & number, municipality, postal code, telephone & fax numbers and e-mail address (if any).	Lawyer's name & address — street & number, municipality, postal code, telephone & fax numbers and e-mail address (if any).

Document (For an affidavit or transcript of evidence, include the name of the person who gave the affidavit or the evidence.)	Filed by (A = applicant or R = respondent)	Date of Document (d, m, y)	Date of Filing (d, m, y)	Part/Section/Tab
Application	A	11/10/00	20/10/00	Part I, P – 1
Summary of Court Cases	A	11/10/00	20/10/00	Part I, P – 2
Financial Statement	A	11/10/00	20/10/00	Part I, F – 1
Answer	R	6/12/00	6/12/00	Part I, P – 3
Financial Statement	R	6/12/00	6/12/00	Part I, F – 2
Notice of Contempt Motion	R	5/6/02	5/6/02	Part II – 1
Affidavit (name of person)	R	5/6/02	5/6/02	Part II – 2
Affidavit in Response (name of person)	A	4/7/02	4/7/02	Part II – 3

☐ *Continued on next sheet*

(Français au verso)

CHAPTER 13

ENFORCING SUPPORT ORDERS
AND AGREEMENTS

After a support order was obtained, if the support payor was not complying with the order, the support recipient still had the problem of enforcing the order. This could be an expensive, time-consuming and frustrating endeavour. Non-compliance with support orders became such a problem that, in 1985, the Ontario government passed the *Support and Custody Orders Enforcement Act, 1985*, which created an office to enforce support orders on behalf of support recipients. This office was immediately overwhelmed with work. Since then, there have been several changes to the legislation and currently the governing legislation is the *Family Responsibility and Support Arrears Enforcement Act, 1996.*[1] Despite the changes, problems with this office continue.

According to the Standing Committee on Public Accounts Report of July 2004,[2] during the 2002/2003 fiscal year, the Family Responsibility Office (FRO) administered approximately 180,600 family support cases, with 1,200-1,400 new cases coming in each month. The FRO had collected approximately $561 million from support payors, but payment arrears at the end of the fiscal year totalled $1.3 billion, an increase of 8 per cent since the 1999 audit. At the time of the audit, approximately one-third of payors were in full compliance, one-third were in partial compliance (at least 85 per cent of current monthly obligations), and one-third were non-compliant.

The Ontario government has recently announced changes to the legislation, and operational changes that hopefully will improve the service this office is able to provide.

THE DIRECTOR'S ROLE

The Act creates the position of the Director of the Family Responsibility Office.[3] The Director may appoint employees as enforcement officers for

---

[1] S.O. 1996, c. 31, as amended.

[2] Available at www.ontla.on.ca/committees/Family%20Resp%20Office%20Report.pdf.

[3] *Family Responsibility and Support Arrears Enforcement Act, 1996*, s. 2 [hereinafter "FRSAEA"].

the purposes of the Act.[4] It is the Director's duty to enforce support orders (and the related support deduction orders) that are filed with the office and to pay the amounts collected to the persons to whom they are owed.[5] The definition of a "support order" is very broad and includes retroactive support, payment of legal fees, and the provisions in a domestic contract or paternity agreement that have been filed with the court.[6] The Director can decide how to enforce the order and can use any mechanism in this or any other Act.[7] In fact, the Director can enforce orders by more than one means at a time.[8] However, once an order is filed with the Director's office, only the Director can enforce it.[9] The Director can also refuse to enforce a support order under certain circumstances.[10] If the support order contains a cost of living clause, the director can enforce the cost of living clause, so long as the clause requires the cost of living increase to be calculated in accordance with the *Family Law Act*.[11]

SUPPORT ORDERS AND SUPPORT DEDUCTION ORDERS

Every support order made in Ontario should contain the following clause:[12]

> . . .[U]nless the order is withdrawn from the Director's office, it shall be enforced by the Director and that amounts owing under the order shall be paid to the Director, who shall pay them to the person to whom they are owed.

However, if the court considers it appropriate to do so, it can order that the support order cannot be withdrawn from the Director's office.[13]

Unless it states otherwise, a support order and a support deduction order can be withdrawn at any time from the Director's office.[14] In order to withdraw a support order, a written notice must be signed by both the payor and recipient if the payor is in compliance with the order. If the payor is not in compliance, the order can be withdrawn by a written notice

---

[4] FRSAEA, s. 3(1).
[5] FRSAEA, s. 5(1).
[6] FRSAEA, s. 1(1).
[7] FRSAEA, s. 6(1).
[8] FRSAEA, s. 6(6).
[9] FRSAEA, s. 6(6).
[10] FRSAEA, s. 7(1).
[11] FRSAEA, s. 7(4).
[12] FRSAEA, s. 9(1).
[13] FRSAEA, s. 9(2).
[14] FRSAEA, s. 16(1).

signed only by the recipient. However, the order can be re-filed at any time by either the payor or the recipient.[15]

The court that makes the support order is required to make a support deduction order at the same time.[16] A support deduction order is, in essence, a garnishment order. Before making the support deduction order, the court must make inquires of the parties to determine the names and addresses of each income source of the payor, and the amounts paid by each income source.[17] The clerk or registrar of the court that made the orders files the support order and the support deduction order with the Director promptly after they are made.[18]

Income Source

The Director gives notice to each income source, setting out the amount of support owed and any arrears and the amount required to be paid by the income source to the Director. The payor is also sent a copy of these notices.[19] The income source is required to deduct the amount in the notice and pay it to the Director.[20] However, the income source cannot deduct more than 50 per cent of the net amount owed to the payor.[21] But, one hundred per cent of a tax refund or other lump sum payments can be paid to the Director.[22]

A person or company that is served with a notice has ten days to notify the Director in writing, disputing being an income source. Either the Director or the alleged income source can then make a motion to have the court determine the matter. Also, either the Director or the income source can make a motion to have the court determine whether the income source has failed to comply with the order or the amount that should be deducted.[23]

If an income source does not make the required payments to the Director, then income source is liable to pay any amount it failed to deduct and pay to the Director.[24]

---

[15] FRSAEA, s. 16(4).
[16] FRSAEA, s. 10(1).
[17] FRSAEA, s. 11(2).
[18] FRSAEA, s. 12.
[19] FRSAEA, s. 20.
[20] FRSAEA, s. 22(1).
[21] FRSAEA, s. 23(1).
[22] FRSAEA, s. 23(3).
[23] FRSAEA, s. 26(1)-(3).
[24] FRSAEA, s. 26(7).

Dispute by Payor

The support payor can also bring a motion if the payor believes that the wrong amount is being deducted or to seek relief for an amount that is being deducted for arrears.[25] However, the payor cannot dispute that the recipient is entitled to support.[26] The payor is presumed to have the ability to pay the amount being deducted, and the court can only vary the amount being deducted if the payor satisfies the court that he or she cannot pay that amount for valid reasons.[27]

Application Questions

1. Chelsea has just recently obtained a child support order against Kirk. Kirk is in compliance with the order. Kirk would rather make support payments directly to Chelsea, rather than to the Director of the FRO. Can he?

2. Brigit has a support order against Aaron filed with the FRO. Aaron is in arrears. Brigit has heard that Aaron is about to receive a large inheritance. She wishes to issue a garnishment order against the estate trustee so that she can get payment of her arrears directly from the estate. Can she?

3. A notice regarding a support deduction order was sent to Corey's employer. Corey's employer is now deducting 50 per cent of Corey's net wages and forwarding them to the Director of the FRO. Corey wishes to dispute the amount being deducted on the basis that his financial situation has changed and that the amount of support awarded is too high. Is this a valid ground to dispute the support deduction order? What should Corey do?

4. Chris's employer has just received a support deduction order regarding Chris. Chris asks her employer not to deduct anything from her wages and promises to make the payments directly to the Director of the FRO herself. If the employer agrees to this, what risk is Chris's employer taking?

SUSPENSION OF DRIVERS' LICENCES

Where a support order is in default, the Director can serve a notice on the payor that his or her driver's licence may be suspended within 30 days.

---

[25] FRSAEA, s. 27(1).
[26] FRSAEA, s. 27(3).
[27] FRSAEA, s. 27(6).

The payor has three choices if he or she wants to stop his or her licence from being suspended: 1) the payor makes arrangements with the Director to comply with the order and to pay the arrears; 2) the payor can pay off all the arrears; or 3) the payor can obtain an order to refrain.[28] The payor must do one of these within the 30-day period.

Motion to Refrain

In order to get an order to refrain, the support payor must commence a proceeding to vary the support order in the court that originally made the support order,[29] or must undertake to commence such proceeding, or must appeal the support order.[30] The motion for an order to refrain must also be made in the court that made the original support order.[31] The order to refrain must be obtained within 30 days.[32]

Final Notice

If the payor makes an arrangement with the Director, or obtains a motion to refrain, or if support is changed, and if the payor does not fulfill the terms of the agreement or order, the Director may send a Second and Final Notice to the payor.[33] Unless the payor complies within 15 days, his or her licence will be suspended.[34]

Direction to Reinstate

After a licence has been suspended, the Director can have the payor's licence re-instated if the payor pays off all the arrears; comes into compliance with an arrangement, order to refrain, or support order; makes new arrangements satisfactory to the Director; or the support order is withdrawn.[35]

---

[28] FRSAEA, s. 34.
[29] FRSAEA, s. 35(1).
[30] FRSAEA, s. 35(4).
[31] FRSAEA, s. 35(5).
[32] FRSAEA, s. 35(10)-(13).
[33] FRSAEA, s. 36(1).
[34] FRSAEA, s. 37(2).
[35] FRSAEA, s. 38(1).

DEFAULT HEARING

The Director may request a financial statement and proof of income from a payor in default.[36] The payor has 15 days to deliver the financial statement. The Director may serve a statement of arrears on the payor in default and require the payor to appear before the court to explain the default.[37] The court may require a person who is financially connected to the payor to file a financial statement and may add that person as a party to the default hearing.[38] The payor is presumed to have the ability to pay and it is up to the payor to prove that he or she cannot.[39] Unless the payor shows that he or she cannot pay the arrears for valid reasons, the court can make an order that the payor pays the arrears, or pays a certain amount per month, or can order imprisonment for up to 180 days.[40] The court can make orders also against a person financially connected to the payor.[41] Even if the payor is imprisoned, imprisonment does not discharge arrears and the payor would still owe those amounts.[42]

OTHER ENFORCEMENT MECHANISMS

Registration against Land

A support order may be registered against the payor's land and the obligation under the order becomes a charge on the property.[43] This charge can be enforced by a sale of property.[44]

Registration under the *Personal Property Security Act*

The Director can register arrears against all the personal property that the payor owns in Ontario, or acquires afterward, under the *Personal Property Security Act*.[45] Arrears owing or accruing have priority over any subsequent registration.[46]

---

[36] FRSAEA, s. 40(1).
[37] FRSAEA, s. 41(1).
[38] FRSAEA, s. 41(4), (5).
[39] FRSAEA, s. 41(9).
[40] FRSAEA, s. 41(10).
[41] FRSAEA, s. 41(12).
[42] FRSAEA, s. 41(17).
[43] FRSAEA, s. 42(1).
[44] FRSAEA, s. 42(2).
[45] FRSAEA, s. 43(1).
[46] FRSAEA, s. 43(2).

Garnishment of Joint Accounts

A Notice of Garnishment issued by the Director and served on a financial institution attaches 50 per cent of a joint account.[47] The financial institution must pay 50 per cent of the money in the account to the Director within ten days and must notify the co-holders of the account.[48] The co-holder may file a dispute with the Director within 30 days, claiming ownership of all or part of the money.[49]

Deduction from Lottery Prize

If the payor wins a lottery prize of $1,000 or more, the Ontario Lottery Corporation must deduct the amount of arrears from the prize and send it to the Director.[50] If the payor wins a non-monetary prize, the Ontario Lottery Corporation must promptly disclose information about the prize and the payor to the Director.[51]

Report to Consumer Reporting Agency

The Director may report a payor in default to a consumer reporting agency.[52]

Arrest of Absconding Debtor

The Ontario Court of Justice or Family Court can issue warrant for the payor's arrest where it is satisfied that the payor is about to leave Ontario and intends to evade his or her support obligations.[53]

Director's Access to Information

The Director can demand from any person or public body any information indicating the payor's address, employment, wages, income, liabilities, and other enforcement-related information.[54]

---

[47] FRSAEA, s. 45(1).
[48] FRSAEA, s. 45(2).
[49] FRSAEA, s. 45(3).
[50] FRSAEA, s. 46(2).
[51] FRSAEA, s. 46(3).
[52] FRSAEA, s. 47.
[53] FRSAEA, s. 49(1).
[54] FRSAEA, s. 54(2).

Application Questions

1. Jack has received a first notice that his driver's licence will be suspended for non-payment of support. What can Jack do? How much time does he have? What will happen if Jack does nothing?

2. Bruce is objecting to his joint bank account being garnished because support is already being deducted by his employer pursuant to a support deduction order. Is this a valid ground for objecting to the garnishment? Who can object to the garnishment?

3. Frank is upset because the arrears of child support he owed were deducted from his winnings by the Ontario Lottery Corporation. Frank objects because he won the lottery long after he had separated from his ex-wife and feels that she is therefore not allowed to touch the lottery winnings. Is he correct?

APPENDIX 13A

ONTARIO

SEAL	**Superior Court of Justice Family Court Branch**	Court File Number **123456**

(Name of court)

at **470 Water Street, Peterborough, Ontario, K9H 3M3**

Court office address

Family Law Rules, O. Reg. 114/99

Form 25: Order (general)

☐ **Temporary**
☒ **Final**

Applicant(s)

Full legal name & address for service — street & number, municipality, postal code, telephone & fax numbers and e-mail address (if any).	*Lawyer's name & address — street & number, municipality, postal code, telephone & fax numbers and e-mail address (if any).*
Sarah Diane Johnston **334 Landsdowne St.** **Peterborough, Ontario** **K9H 2T1**	**Jasmin Manning** **Barrister & Solicitor** **123 George St., Suite 303** **Peterborough, Ontario** **K9H 3M3**

Donovan

Judge (print or type name)

Respondent(s)

March 3, 2006

Date of order

Full legal name & address for service — street & number, municipality, postal code, telephone & fax numbers and e-mail address (if any).	*Lawyer's name & address — street & number, municipality, postal code, telephone & fax numbers and e-mail address (if any).*
David Allan Johnston **123 Peter St.** **Peterborough, Ontario** **K9H 2T2**	

The court heard an application/motion made by *(name of person or persons)*

Sarah Diane Johnston

The following persons were in court *(names of parties and lawyers in court)*
Jasmin Manning, Sarah Diane Johnston, David Allan Johnston

The court received evidence and heard submissions on behalf of *(name or names)*
Sarah Diane Johnston and David Allan Johnston

THIS COURT ORDERS THAT:

1. The applicant, Sarah Diane Johnston, shall have custody of the children, Julie Ann Johnston, born on October 2, 1996 and Michael Allan Johnston, born on May 26, 1999.

2. The respondent, David Allan Johnston, shall have reasonable access to the said children.

3. The respondent shall pay child support in accordance with the Child Support Guidelines in the amount of $927 per month for the two children.

4. The respondent shall pay spousal support in the amount of $500 per month.

5. Unless the support order is withdrawn from the office of the Director of Family Responsibility, it shall be enforced by the Director and amounts owing under the support order shall be paid to the Director, who shall pay them to the person to whom they are owed.

Form 25:   **Order (general)**   **(page 2)**

Court File Number
123456

Put a line through any blank space left on this page. If additional space is needed, extra sheets may be attached.

_____   _____
            Date of signature   *Signature of judge or clerk of the court*

APPENDIX 13B

SUPPORT DEDUCTION ORDER
ORDONNANCE DE RETENUE DES ALIMENTS

Family Responsibility and Support Arrears Enforcement Act, 1996
Loi de 1996 sur les obligations familiales et l'exécution des arriérés d'aliments

Court File No. / *N° de dossier du tribunal*

Name of Court / *Nom du tribunal*

Location / *Lieu*

Judge / *Juge*

Date

Between / *Entre*

Applicant / Petitioner / Plaintiff
Requérant / Demandeur

and / *et*

Respondent / Defendant
Intimé / Défendeur

SUPPORT DEDUCTION ORDER / *ORDONNANCE DE RETENUE DES ALIMENTS*

Upon making an order this day which provides for the payment of support and on making the necessary inquiries required by section 11 of the *Family Responsibility and Support Arrears Enforcement Act, 1996*:

Après avoir rendu ce jour une ordonnance qui prévoit le versement d'aliments et après avoir fait les recherches nécessaires exigées par l'article 11 de la Loi de 1996 sur les obligations familiales et l'exécution des arriérés d'aliments :

1. **THIS COURT ORDERS THAT**
   LE TRIBUNAL ORDONNE QUE

   (Name of Payor / *nom du payeur*)

   pay support as set out in the attached information form.
   verse des aliments comme le prévoit la formule de renseignements ci-jointe.

2. **THIS COURT ORDERS THAT** any income source that receives notice of this support deduction order make payments to the Director of the Family Responsibility Office in respect of the payor out of money owed to or paid by the income source to the payor.

   LE TRIBUNAL ORDONNE *que toute source de revenu qui reçoit avis de la présente ordonnance fasse à l'égard du payeur des versements au directeur du Bureau des obligations familiales à même les sommes qu'elle doit au payeur ou qu'elle lui verse.*

   Signature of Judge, Registrar or Clerk of the Court
   Signature du juge ou du greffier du tribunal

FRO-019 (June 15, 2005 / 15 juin 2005)

CHAPTER 14

THE *CHANGE OF NAME ACT*

The *Change of Name Act*[1] provides the mechanism to formally change an adult or a child's first name, last name, or both. It is not necessary to go through this procedure if a person wants to change his or her last name as a result of getting married. You can simply start using your spouse's last name, or a hyphenated combination of your last name and your spouse's last name. Most organizations, communities, and government offices accept this practice, with proof of marriage. Going through the change of name procedure set out in the Act results in a legal change of name, and a change of name certificate or a new birth certificate will be issued.

When a new name is chosen under the Act, the person must have both a first name and a last name.[2]

ELECTION BY SPOUSE

Married Spouses

At any time after marriage, a spouse can change his or her surname to the surname of the other spouse, or a combination of his or her surname and that of the other spouse, with or without a hyphen. Also at any time during the marriage, a person can change back to the surname he or she was using before marriage.[3] Within 90 days of divorce, annulment, or death, a spouse can elect to change his or her name back to the name he or she was using immediately before marriage. In order to do any of these, the spouse must file an Election to Change Surname (Form 1), all birth certificates and change of name certificates in his or her possession, a police records check (if required), and pay the prescribed fee.[4] It is not necessary to notify the spouse of an application for a change of name.[5] The Registrar General will then register the change of name and issue a change of name certificate, and, if the person was born in Ontario, a new birth certificate.[6]

---

[1] R.S.O. 1990, c. C.7, as amended.
[2] *Change of Name Act*, s. 2(3).
[3] *Change of Name Act*, s. 3(1).
[4] *Change of Name Act*, s. 3(3), (3.1).
[5] *Change of Name Act*, s. 3(8).
[6] *Change of Name Act*, s. 3(4).

Common-Law Spouses

A common-law spouse can also choose to change his or her surname to his or her spouse's surname, or to a combination of his or her surname and that of the other spouse, with or without a hyphen. The procedure and documentation is the same for married spouses, except that common-law spouses must also file a Joint Declaration of Conjugal Relationship (Form 3).[7] If the person wishes to resume his or her former name after the conjugal relationship ends, the person may do so by filing a Declaration that Conjugal Relationship has Ended (Form 4) along with the other required documents.[8]

Application Questions

1. Chris Rodgers and Katie Holmes were married last month. Katie wishes to legally change her last name to Holmes-Rodgers. Can she do this? Does she need to notify Chris? Can Chris change his surname to Holmes-Rodgers as well? Can he change his last name to Holmes?

2. Vern Cooper and Charlotte Scott have been living together for a number of years. Charlotte wishes to legally change her surname to Cooper. Can she do so? Does she need to notify Vern?

CHANGE OF CHILD'S NAME

A person who has lawful custody of a child may apply to change a child's forename or surname or both. The child must be either born in Ontario and be ordinarily resident there, or must have been ordinarily resident in Ontario for at least one year before the application is commenced.[9] The written consent of any person who also has lawful custody of the child, and of any person whose consent is necessary because of a court order or separation agreement, is required. If the child is 12 years of age or older, the child's consent is also required,[10] unless a medical practitioner states in writing that the child does not have the capacity to consent.[11] If consent cannot be obtained or is refused, the applicant may apply to the court to dispense with the consent.[12] The court determines the application in accordance with the best interest of the child.[13]

---

[7] *Change of Name Act*, s. 3(6).
[8] *Change of Name Act*, s. 3(7).
[9] *Change of Name Act*, s. 5(1).
[10] *Change of Name Act*, s. 5(2).
[11] *Change of Name Act*, s. 5(3).
[12] *Change of Name Act*, s. 5(4).
[13] *Change of Name Act*, s. 5(6).

The consent of a person who has access to the child is not required; however, the applicant must give notice to every person who is lawfully entitled to access.[14] If such person objects to the name change, he or she must bring an application to the court for an order prohibiting the change of name.

Belisle v. Poole (1994), [1994] O.J. No. 364, 1994 CarswellOnt 372 (Ont. Gen. Div.)

Wesley was born on March 8, 1988, and is therefore almost six years old. He is enrolled in kindergarten under the surname "Poole," being the name of his mother since her marriage to Bruce Poole on April 27, 1991. This application was commenced on January 14, 1993. [At para. 2.]

In November 1992, Mr. Belisle received notice that Mrs. Poole was intending to change Wesley's surname from "Belisle" to "Poole." Mr. Belisle refused to consent and requested the Registrar General to stay the application until this matter is disposed of. [At para. 8.]

Mrs. Poole, as indicated, has taken the surname of her new husband. There is a child of that marriage, born May 28, 1992, and the respondent is presently expecting another child.. . . [At para. 9.]

. . .Mr. Belisle believes that his former wife is attempting to replace him as the father in Wesley's life and to reinforce this by changing Wesley's surname to that of her present husband. [At para. 12.]

The "best interest of the child" has consistently been the threshold test to determine what should be done in matters of a change of name application, both before and after the Act was proclaimed. [At para. 41.]

The factors which I perceive to be applicable are:

(a) the age of the child;
(b) the length of time that the custodial parent has had sole custody of the child;
(c) whether there is a continuing close relationship between the child and the noncustodial parent; and
(d) whether there are any siblings of the child and, if there are, the surname used by the siblings. [At para. 50.]

. . .[T]he onus of proof that the change of name should not proceed lies with Mr. Belisle. Having regard to the factors that I have enunciated, I am satisfied that on the balance of probabilities he has established that the proposed change would not be in the best interests of Wesley at this time. [At para. 55.]

---

[14] *Change of Name Act*, s. 5(6).

If an applicant proposes to change the child's name to the name of his or her new spouse or common-law partner, then the applicant must give notice to the new spouse or common-law partner.[15]

A child who is 16 years of age or older, and who has been ordinarily resident in Ontario for at least one year, may apply to change his or her own first name or surname or both.[16] The child must obtain the written consent of every person who has lawful custody of the child.[17] If consent cannot be obtained or is refused, the child can apply to the court to dispense with the consent,[18] and such applications are determined on the basis of the best interest of the child.[19]

Application Questions

David Abrahams and Irene Phillips were married in 1985 and divorced in 2000. They have one child, Ian Abrahams, born on July 20, 2003. Irene married Alex Starsky in May of 2005. She is now pregnant with Alex's child. Irene changed her name to Starsky when she got married and now wishes to legally change Ian's last name to Starsky as well.

1. If the divorce granted joint custody of Ian to Irene and David, would Irene need David's consent, or to give notice to David, to change Ian's name?

2. If the divorce gave custody to Irene and access to David, would Irene need David's consent, or to give notice to David, to change Ian's name? If David objected to the change of name, what could he do?

3. If the divorce gave custody to Irene and access to David, but a separation agreement stipulated that neither party could change the child's name without the consent of the other, and David refused consent to change Ian's name, is there any thing Irene can do?

4. Would Irene need Alex's consent, or to give notice to Alex, to change Ian's name?

5. Would Irene need Ian's consent, or to give notice to Ian, to change Ian's name?

---

[15] *Change of Name Act*, s. 5(7).
[16] *Change of Name Act*, s. 4(1).
[17] *Change of Name Act*, s. 4(3).
[18] *Change of Name Act*, s. 4(4).
[19] *Change of Name Act*, s. 4(5).

PROCEDURE

A person who wishes to change his or her name or the name of his or her child must fill out an Application for Change of Name (Form 5).[20] This form requires the applicant to give information about the applicant's marital status, names of his or her parent, details of criminal convictions and law enforcement orders outstanding, judgments, executions, bankruptcy, etc., as well as the reason why the applicant wishes to change his or her name. Required consents must be included with the application,[21] as well as a statement that everyone who is entitled to notice has been given notice. If notice is required, then the applicant must give notice at least 30 days before filing the application, by registered or certified mail, or must obtain an Acknowledgment of Notice (Form 6).[22]

A Statement of Guarantor (Form 8) must accompany the Application.[23] The Guarantor can be a member of the prescribed class (such as a doctor, lawyer, school principle, etc.) who knows the applicant and knows that the applicant has resided in Ontario for at least one year,[24] or can be someone else, who has known the applicant for at least five years, and knows that the applicant has resided in Ontario for at least one year.[25]

The application must also be accompanied by all birth certificates and change of name certificates in the applicant's possession.[26] If the applicant has disclosed any criminal offences or law enforcement orders, a Police Records check must also be included.[27]

DUTY OF THE REGISTRAR GENERAL

If the application complies with the Act, the Registrar General must issue a change of name certificate. If the person was born in Ontario, the Registrar General must note the change of name on the birth registration and issue a new birth certificate. If the person was not born in Ontario, the Registrar General simply notes the change of name and issues the certificate.[28] However, if the Registrar General has reasonable grounds to believe the change of name is for an improper purpose, he or she must refuse the application and notify the applicant that the application has been refused

---

[20] *Change of Name Act*, s. 6(2).
[21] *Change of Name Act*, s. 6(6).
[22] *Change of Name Act*, s. 6(7).
[23] *Change of Name Act*, s. 6(3).
[24] *Change of Name Act*, s. 6(4).
[25] *Change of Name Act*, s. 6(5).
[26] *Change of Name Act*, s. 6(8).
[27] *Change of Name Act*, s. 6(9)-(11).
[28] *Change of Name Act*, s. 7(1).

and that the applicant may apply to the court.[29] Such application must be made within 30 days after being notified of the refusal.[30]

Before granting the change of name, the Registrar General must check with the Ministry of the Solicitor General to find out if the Ministry has any information on the applicant that would be included in a police record check.[31]

After registering the change of name, the Registrar General must publish a notice in *The Ontario Gazette* and must enter the change of name under the *Vital Statistics Act*. If there was any information disclosed regarding criminal offences, judgments, etc., then the Registrar General must also give notice to the Ministry of the Solicitor General, the sheriff, the Registrar in Bankruptcy, etc.[32]

If the Attorney General certifies that the change of name is intended to prevent significant harm to the person, as for example someone going into a witness protection program, then all the records related to the change of name are sealed and no notice is published.[33]

OFFENCES

A person who obtains a change of name by fraud or misrepresentation is guilty of an offence and is liable to a fine of up to $2,000.[34] Using a name obtained by fraud or misrepresentation is also an offence, for which the fine is up to $2,000.[35] It is also an offence to use a name that was applied for, but refused. The fine for this offence is also up to $2,000.[36] If the change of name is granted, it is an offence to use a birth certificate or change of name certificate showing the old name. Again, the fine for this offence is up to $2,000.

---

[29] *Change of Name Act*, s. 7(2) .
[30] *Family Law Rules*, O. Reg.114/99, s. 35(1).
[31] *Change of Name Act*, s. 7.1(1).
[32] *Change of Name Act*, s. 8(1).
[33] *Change of Name Act*, s. 8(2).
[34] *Change of Name Act*, s. 12(1).
[35] *Change of Name Act*, s. 12(2).
[36] *Change of Name Act*, s. 12(3).

CHAPTER 15

CHILD AND FAMILY SERVICES ACT

INTRODUCTION

Scope of Legislation

The *Child and Family Services Act*[1] governs a number of more peripheral family-related topics that are not covered by other family law statutes. The topics covered by the Act include situations where state intervention is required to assist families and preserve the welfare of children. In particular, the legislation deals with:

1. the creation, function, and powers of Children's Aid Societies (C.A.S.), which deal with the welfare of children in Ontario;
2. agreements with parents who have a temporary need for assistance or who have children with special needs;
3. the protection of children whose parents are unable or unwilling to care adequately for them;
4. the creation and maintenance of a child abuse register;
5. programs for young offenders in Ontario;
6. the rights of children who are removed from their parents and are in the care of the state; and
7. the adoption of Ontario children and access to adoption records.

This chapter will focus mainly upon agreements with parents and state intervention where children are in need of protection.

Purpose of Legislation

The paramount purpose of the CFSA is to promote the best interests of children, their well-being and protection.[2] The Act also recognizes the integrity of the family unit and the need to help parents to cope with

---

[1] R.S.O. 1990, c. C.11 as amended [hereinafter the "CFSA"].
[2] CFSA, s. 1(1).

problems encountered in raising their children. Because the Act gives the state the power to intervene in the life of the family, the Act recognizes that the least restrictive course of action should be followed with respect to each child. In providing services to further the interests of children, the goal is to ensure stable family relationships and take into account the individual, cultural, religious and regional differences between children, as much as possible. Finally, wherever possible, native people should be permitted to provide their own services, and any services provided to them should recognize their unique cultural heritage and traditions.[3]

CHILDREN'S AID SOCIETIES

Children's Aid Societies are designated and approved by the Minister of Community and Social Services to operate with specified territorial jurisdictions.[4] The functions of a C.A.S. include:

- investigating whether children under 16 are in need of protection;
- protecting children who are in the C.A.S.'s care;
- providing guidance and counselling to families for the protection of children;
- providing care to children who are committed to supervision;
- placing children for adoption; and
- performing other duties related to protecting children.[5]

Every Children's Aid Society must have a local Director who must advise, supervise, and exercise the powers or functions of the C.A.S. and designate a place of safety for the protection of children in his or her area.[6]

AGREEMENTS FOR CHILDREN'S CARE

Temporary Care Agreements

A temporary care agreement is a contract between a Children's Aid Society and the child's parents, wherein the C.A.S. agrees to have custody and care of a child or children for a specified period of time, with a view to returning the child to the parents upon the expiry of the agreement. This type of agreement is usually entered in a situation where a parent is unable to care for a child due to a temporary circumstance and there is no family

---

[3] CFSA, s. 1(2).
[4] CFSA, s. 15(2).
[5] CFSA, s. 15(3).
[6] CFSA, s. 17.

member available to assist the parent. For example, the parent might need to go into drug rehabilitation and voluntarily surrenders his or her child for a limited period of time. The key to this type of arrangement is that it is completely voluntary on the parent's part. There is no court order requiring the parent to give up care of his or her child. The Act provides authority for this kind of agreement to be made.[7]

A temporary care agreement cannot be entered into with respect to a child who is over 16 years of age. Neither can such an agreement involve a child over 12, unless the child is a party to the agreement.[8] The length of the agreement cannot be more than six months, but the parties can extend it to a maximum of 12 months, on consent.[9] A child cannot be in the care of a Society for more than 12 months, if the child is under 6 years of age. If the child is over 6, the maximum length of time is 24 months.[10]

Each agreement must contain certain mandatory terms or statements. The child's care and custody are legally transferred to the C.A.S. The parent must acknowledge that the placement is voluntary and that he or she is temporarily unable to care for the child. Since the goal is to return the child to his or her parent, the parent must agree to maintain contact with the child or designate another person to do so, if this is not possible. The name of the primary contact person with the C.A.S. must be stated along with any other relevant provisions.[11]

Special Needs Agreements

A special needs agreement is an agreement between a Children's Aid Society and a child's parent(s) to provide special services to a child who has special needs that the parents are unable to meet on their own. The Act states that a special needs agreement may provide for the special needs to be met by the C.A.S. or it may provide that the C.A.S. supervise or have custody of the child.[12]

The term of the agreement must be stated in the contract but it can be extended for a further specified period of time.[13] A child who is over age 16 and is no longer in the care of his or her parents also has the capacity to enter a special needs agreement to meet his or her own special needs.[14]

---

[7] CFSA, s. 29(1).
[8] CFSA, s. 29(2).
[9] CFSA, s. 29(5).
[10] CFSA, s. 29(6).
[11] CFSA, s. 29(8).
[12] CFSA, s. 30(1).
[13] CFSA, s. 30(3).
[14] CFSA, s. 31.

Larcade v. Ontario (Minister of Community & Social Services) (2005), 197 O.A.C. 287, 16 R.F.L. (6th) 156, 18 C.P.C. (6th) 21 (Ont. Div. Ct.)

. . .[The CFSA empowers Children's Aid Societies and/or the Minister] to enter into Special Needs Agreements to provide services for profoundly disabled children whose parents were unable to provide the services required because of the children's special needs. In 1997, notwithstanding the legislative provision for these agreements, the Ministry unilaterally directed that no new Special Needs Agreements would be entered into. The plaintiffs allege that this directive was part of a budget reduction strategy. The plaintiffs further allege that in the absence of the Special Needs Agreement program, parents unable to meet the needs of their disabled children could only obtain assistance for their children by giving up custody to the Children's Aid Society. This, they alleged, was a breach of statutory duty, breach of a common law duty of care, breach of *parens patriae* obligations and negligent. [At para. 2.]

The plaintiffs' motion for certification of their action as a class proceeding was dismissed on the basis that the statement of claim failed to disclose a cause of action. The plaintiffs appealed.

Held: The appeal was allowed and an order was issued certifying the action as a Class Proceeding.

The motions judge misapprehended the theory of the plaintiffs' case.

. . .[T]he plaintiffs' case is not really about the level of budget commitments or the allocation of scarce resources as a question of government policy and priority. Rather, the plaintiffs argue this was an operational decision as to the *manner* in which services would be provided, with the government deciding to ignore the statutorily mandated route and with the result that children's needs were not met at all or parents lost custody of their children so that the needs were met through the Children's Aid Society. [At para. 9.]

It is not correct to say that the plaintiffs' argument in this regard has no chance of success.

The statement of claim also raises an arguable cause of action in respect of misfeasance in public office. Although a breach of statute cannot create a cause of action in and of itself, it can be one of the elements of the tort of misfeasance in a public office. Therefore, it is possible that this breach of statutory duty could support a damage claim for misfeasance in public office.

. . .[A] class action is the preferable procedure to deal with the common issues in this proceeding.. . .The families affected by the government's actions number at least in the hundreds. They are, by definition, parents who have been unable to provide for their own children's special needs. What then can be inferred about their financial ability to carry on this sophisticated litigation against the government? Furthermore, individual claims might not be large in quantum, making individual actions too expensive to justify for the damages available. Requiring separate actions for all claimants would likely prove to be an obstacle to justice for the hundreds of potential plaintiffs. Finally, it is not desirable to have hundreds of individual cases all raising common issues of law and fact. If there was a multiplicity of such proceedings, no doubt all parties would be seeking some sort of consolidation. There would also be a risk of inconsistent verdicts.. . . [At para. 20.]

Termination of Agreements

All temporary care and special needs agreements automatically terminate on the child's 18th birthday.[15] Also, an agreement can be terminated by either party at any time by the party giving written notice, which becomes effective five days after, unless the agreement itself states otherwise. Once the agreement is terminated, the child must be returned by the Children's Aid Society to the parent(s) or person who made the agreement. If the C.A.S. believes that the child would not be properly cared for if he or she were returned to the parent(s), then the C.A.S. must bring the child before the court so that the court can determine whether the child is in need of protection.[16]

Application Questions

1. Jimmy, who is 13 years old, has lived with his mother since his father died tragically in a car accident a few months ago. Jimmy's mother suffered an emotional breakdown as a result of her husband's death and she requires psychiatric hospitalization for several months. There is no one else in Jimmy's family who is able to care for Jimmy.

(a) What kind of agreement could Jimmy's mother enter with the Children's Aid Society so that Jimmy will be cared for while she is recuperating?

(b) Is there anyone else besides Jimmy's mom and the C.A.S. who needs to sign the contract? If so, who and why?

(c) How long can the agreement last?

(d) In case Jimmy's mother is unable to visit him while she is in the hospital, what does she need to include in the contract?

(e) If Jimmy's mother returns home from the hospital and wants Jimmy back home before the agreement expires, what must she do?

(f) If, when it is time to return Jimmy to his mother, the C.A.S. believes that his mother is not able to care properly for him, what action must the C.A.S. take?

---

[15] CFSA, s. 32.
[16] CFSA, s. 33.

CHILD PROTECTION

Overview of Child Protection Law

Child protection law is a legal system that provides for intervention by the government into the family's life where the child's caretakers are either unable or unwilling to provide a minimum standard of care that is tolerable to our society. The original legislation only provided for a minimum standard with respect to the child's physical well-being. The CFSA now provides protection for the child's emotional and developmental well-being also. In addition, the minimum standard now includes a *risk* of harm to a child by reason of a "pattern of neglect" by a parent and does not always require actual proof of harm that has already occurred.

Child Protection Distinguished from Custody

As we have seen in an earlier chapter, custody is a private dispute between a child's two caretakers, usually the parents, as to who can best meet the child's needs and interests. Child protection, on the other hand, is a dispute between the child's caretakers, or parents, and the state, which arises only where the parents fail to meet the minimum standard required of parents in our society. A protection proceeding represents the community's responsibility towards children who are inherently powerless and who sometimes require state protection.

Conflict between Community and Family Privacy Interests

The CFSA recognizes both the community's interest in protecting children and the parents' right to privacy in raising their children, free from state intervention. The legislation attempts to establish a balance between the two conflicting interests. One example of this conflict occurs when a parent attempts to deny a life-saving medical procedure to a child on the ground of religious beliefs. Frequently, the state will intervene in this kind of situation, giving priority to the child's life over family privacy and freedom of religion. However, the intervention is usually only for as long as it takes to complete the medical procedure and then the child is returned to its caretakers.

B. (R.) v. *Children's Aid Society of Metropolitan Toronto*, 9 R.F.L. (4th) 157, 21 O.R. (3d) 479 (note), [1995] 1 S.C.R. 315 (S.C.C.)

The child, born prematurely, exhibited many physical ailments. Her parents consented to her receiving medical treatment but, for religious reasons, objected to her receiving blood transfusions. When the child was one month old, the doctors believed that her life was in danger and that, as a result, she might need a blood transfusion. Protection proceedings were instituted and a Provincial Court judge granted wardship of the child to the Children's Aid Society for 72 hours. The wardship was extended for an additional 21 days on a status review application. During that period the child received a blood transfusion. The wardship was later terminated and the child was returned to her parents. The parents appealed the wardship orders. A District Court judge dismissed the appeal and awarded costs against the Attorney General for Ontario, who had intervened in the proceedings. The Court of Appeal dismissed the parents' appeal and the Attorney General's cross-appeal on costs.

The parents appealed to the Supreme Court of Canada on the [basis that the provisions of the child welfare legislation] offends the *Canadian Charter of Rights and Freedoms*. [At 158 (R.F.L.).]

Held: The appeal was dismissed.

. . .Liberty [under section 7 of the *Charter*] means more than freedom from physical restraint and includes the right to make decisions of fundamental personal importance. The rights to nurture a child and to make decisions that ensure his or her welfare in such matters as medical care are part of a parent's liberty interest. Child protection legislation recognizes the right of parents to raise and care for their children by promoting a policy of minimal intervention.

Parents should be able to make decisions for their children. Although the state may intervene to protect a child's interests, that intervention must be justified. The state may properly interfere in situations in which parental conduct falls below a standard that is considered socially acceptable. In doing so, it is limiting the constitutional rights of parents, not vindicating the constitutional rights of children.

In the case at bar, the application of the *Child Welfare Act* deprived the parents of their right to decide which medical treatment their child should receive. As a result, their parental "liberty," protected by s. 7 of the *Charter*, was infringed. That fundamental right was, however, limited in accordance with the principles of fundamental justice. The state has the power to intervene to protect children whose lives are in jeopardy and to promote their well-being. [The child welfare legislation] is compatible with a modern conception of life that includes the notion of quality of life, and the general procedure under the Act accords with the principles of fundamental justice. Accordingly, the parents' *Charter* rights under s. 7 had not been violated. [At 158-159 (R.F.L.).]

Who is a "Child in Need of Protection"?

The CFSA is very specific about what kind of action, inaction, or circumstances on the part of a parent or caretaker render a child in need of protection. The definitions set out in the Act do not apply to children who are 16 years of age or older, unless the child is already the subject of a child protection order.

Physical Harm or Risk of Physical Harm

A child is in need of protection if the child suffers physical harm caused by the person in charge of the child, or harm resulting from that person's failure to protect the child, or a pattern of neglect.[17] A child can suffer physical harm through intentional abuse or through neglect or lack of supervision. This section focuses upon *actual* harm that must be demonstrated by proof such as broken bones, scald burns, or cigarette burns on the child's body. However, equally serious injuries can befall a child if he or she tumbles from an apartment balcony or almost drowns in a bathtub because the person in charge has neglected to supervise the child's activities.

The Act also finds a child who is at *risk* of suffering the same physical harm to be a child in need of protection.[18] Some children live in an environment that is an accident waiting to happen. If a toddler is permitted to run barefoot on a floor with broken glass or stick a metal fork into an electrical outlet, the child is likely to suffer physical harm sooner or later. The legislation no longer waits until the child has suffered harm, if the likelihood is present.

Molestation or Risk of Molestation

A child is in need of protection if that child has been sexually molested or exploited by the person having charge of the child or with the knowledge of the person in charge, if that person fails to protect the child.[19] A mother who turns a blind eye to her husband or partner's sexual exploitation of her child renders her child in need of protection. A parent who would knowingly fail to protect his or her child places his or her own needs ahead of the physical and emotional welfare of the child. Similarly, even a risk that a child will suffer sexual molestation or exploitation is sufficient

---

[17] CFSA, s. 37(2)(a).
[18] CFSA, s. 37(2)(b).
[19] CFSA, s. 37(2)(c).

to make the child in need of protection.[20] If a child is living with someone who has a criminal record for sexual abuse of children and that person has received no treatment since his or her conviction, there is a risk that the child might be molested by that person.

Denial of Medical Treatment

If a child is in need of medical treatment and the person in charge either fails or refuses to provide the necessary treatment, the child is in need of protection.[21] A parent might deny medical treatment to a child through neglect or because they refuse to recognize the child's problem or for some religious or other reason of conscience. If a court determines that a child requires life-saving treatment that a parent refuses or neglects to provide, the child will be found in need of protection and the court will have the authority to intervene for the purpose of providing the treatment.

Emotional Harm or Risk of Emotional Harm

If a child has suffered emotional harm and there are reasonable grounds to believe that the harm resulted from the actions or failure to act or pattern of neglect of the person in charge of the child, the child is in need of protection.[22] The child's emotional harm must be demonstrated by anxiety, depression, withdrawal, self-destructive or aggressive behaviour, or delayed development. Whether or not the emotional harm was caused by the person in charge of the child, if that person fails to provide the services to meet the child's need, the child is in need of protection.[23] Similarly, a risk that the child is likely to suffer such emotional harm resulting from the caretaker's actions or inactions[24] or the caretaker's failure to provide treatment or prevention[25] is sufficient to place the child in need of protection. A child who lives in an environment of chronic verbal abuse and humiliation might come within the risk category.

Mental, Emotional, or Developmental Condition

A child who suffers from a mental, emotional, or developmental condition that requires attention and the caretaker or parent fails to provide the

---

[20] CFSA, s. 37(2)(d).
[21] CFSA, s. 37(2)(e).
[22] CFSA, s, 37(2)(f).
[23] CFSA, s. 37(2)(f.1).
[24] CFSA, s. 37(2)(g).
[25] CFSA, s. 37(2)(g.1).

child with the necessary services is a child in need of protection.[26] This differs from emotional harm as it is more akin to a condition that is either congenital or at least not caused by the actions or inactions of the caregiver. The child is only in need of protection if the parent or caregiver refuses or fails to provide treatment or services that would help the child.

Other Situations

A child whose parents have abandoned the child or whose parents have died without making adequate provision for the child places the child in need of protection. [27] A child under 12 who has killed or seriously injured someone is in need of protection.[28] It should be noted that only a child over 12 can be dealt with as a young offender under the *Youth Criminal Justice Act*. Similarly, a child is in need of protection if he or she is under 12 and has, on more than one occasion, injured another and caused damage to property with the encouragement of the parent or because of the parent's failure to supervise.[29] Finally, a child can be brought before the court, as a child in need of protection, with the consent of the parent, or the consent of the child if he or she is 12 years or older, if the parent is unable to care for the child.[30]

Application Questions

Which category, if any, does "child in need of protection" fall under in each of the following situations? Explain.

1. A 7-year-old girl is confined to her bedroom, not permitted to socialize with friends, and fed only bread and water for several months.

2. A mother frequently leaves her 9-month-old infant alone, asleep in his crib, while she goes to a bar with her boyfriend for the evening.

3. A mother is aware that her husband is sexually abusing her 5-year-old child, but does nothing about it.

4. Paula's parents refuse to admit that their daughter needs help, even though the school psychologist and family doctor insist she has a serious learning disability that requires attention. Paula is becoming discouraged because she is doing poorly in school.

5. Sammy's parents are drug addicts and Sammy is constantly living in an atmosphere of domestic violence, although Sammy himself has never suffered any physical harm.

---

[26] CFSA, s, 37(2)(h).
[27] CFSA, s. 37(2)(i).
[28] CFSA, s. 37(2)(j).
[29] CFSA, s. 37(2)(k).
[30] CFSA, s. 37(2)(l).

Parties to the Proceeding

Children's Aid Society

The applicant in a child protection proceeding is almost always the Children's Aid Society. The C.A.S. acts as the state's delegate in the investigation and prosecution of alleged child protection concerns. Occasionally, the applicant is a private citizen. If the C.A.S. is not the applicant, then it is always a party to the proceedings.

Parents

The respondent is usually the child's mother. The child's father will only be respondent if he meets the definition of parent in section 37(1) of the Act. A father must come within the definition in section 8(1) of the *Children's Law Reform Act*, which was discussed in Chapter 11. A parent also includes a person other than a biological parent if that person has shown a settled intention to treat the child as a member of their family. Similarly, a parent can include a person who by court order or written agreement has a right to custody, access, or a support obligation with respect to the child.

Representative of Native Band

In addition, if the child is a native person, a representative of the child's band or native community is also made a party.[31]

Director

A Director appointed by the Minister may be made a party at any stage in the proceedings upon his or her application.[32] This may occur, for example, if the position of the Minister is adverse to that of the Children's Aid Society or there is an issue of public significance before the court.

Possessory Parents

Possessory parents include foster parents who have had possession of the child within six months prior to the hearing. Possessory parents are given

---

[31] CFSA, s. 39(1).
[32] CFSA, s. 39(2).

qualified party status. They are entitled to be advised of the hearing, to be present at the hearing, to have legal representation, and to make submissions.[33]

Child

A child who is 12 years of age or over and is subject of the application is a party to the proceeding unless the court is satisfied that the child's presence at the hearing would cause emotional harm to the child.[34] On the other hand, a child who is under the age of 12 is not entitled to notice of the proceedings and cannot be present as a party unless the court decides that the child will understand the proceedings and will not suffer emotional harm if present. If the court determines in favour of the child on these matters, then the child, even though under 12, is given all the rights of a party.[35]

Jurisdiction of Courts

The courts that have exclusive jurisdiction over child protection proceedings are the Ontario Court of Justice or the Family Court Branch of the Superior Court of Justice. A child protection proceeding takes priority over any other family law proceeding affecting the child. Any prior custody order will be superseded by a child protection order, if the prior custody order is inconsistent with the child protection order.

Commencement of Child Protection Application

The child who is subject of the application comes before the court either by a process of apprehension or an application.

Apprehension

Apprehension refers to the process of physically removing a child from his or her environment and taking them to a place of safety until the hearing of the application.

---

[33] CFSA, s. 39(3).
[34] CFSA, s. 39(4).
[35] CFSA, s. 39(5).

With a Warrant

A child protection worker or a peace officer can carry out an apprehension of a child under the authority of a warrant issued by a justice of the peace. In order to obtain a warrant, a person must satisfy a justice of the peace on reasonable grounds that the child is in need of protection and that a less restrictive course of action would not be sufficient to protect the child.[36]

Without a Warrant

In addition, a child protection worker can carry out an apprehension without a warrant if the worker has reasonable grounds to believe the child is in need of protection and there is urgency involved.[37] There must be evidence that waiting to obtain a warrant or complete an application would create a substantial risk to the health and safety of the child. A child protection worker can seek the assistance of a peace officer in carrying out an apprehension.[38] If a child protection worker or peace officer believes a child is in need of protection at certain premises, the CFSA gives them the power of entry and search of the premises where the child is believed to be. The worker or peace officer can use force, if necessary, as long as the power of entry is exercised in accordance with the CFSA regulations.[39]

Within five days of a child's apprehension and being taken to a place of safety, the child must be brought before the court for the hearing. If this does not happen, the child must be returned to the person who last had charge of the child or the person with custody. Otherwise, a temporary care agreement must be made.[40]

Application

A Children's Aid Society is entitled to apply to court to determine whether a child is in need of protection.[41] A private citizen can bring an application to court, where the C.A.S. has made no application on its own. If the court believes the child is in need of protection, the court may order the person in charge of the child to produce the child in court at a set time and date to determine if the child is in need of protection.[42]

---

[36] CFSA, s. 40(2).
[37] CFSA, s. 40(7).
[38] CFSA, s. 40(8).
[39] CFSA, s. 40(11)-(13).
[40] CFSA, s. 46.
[41] CFSA, s. 40(1).
[42] CFSA, s. 40(4).

Application Questions

1. A neighbour calls the local Children's Aid Society because she believes that there are three young children, under the age of 7, who have been left alone next door. When the C.A.S. worker arrives, he finds the three children alone. The 5 year old is playing with a cigarette lighter while the 6 year old is trying to give the 3 year old a bath in the tub, which is overflowing with scalding water. What kind of action can the C.A.S. worker take in this situation?

2. The three children in the above situation live with their mother and her common-law partner whom they view as their dad and who treats them as his own children. The mother also receives child support from the children's biological father. If the C.A.S. commences a child protection proceeding, who must be made parties to the application? Do the children themselves have a right to be in court?

3. If the C.A.S. worker decides to remove the children from the home immediately, how soon must the C.A.S. bring the matter before the court?

4. If the matter is adjourned, where must the children be placed until the hearing? What are the factors the court must consider?

Who May be Subject of a Child Protection Proceeding?

In order for the court to have jurisdiction, the child must be under the age of 16 at the time the protection proceeding is commenced. It does not matter whether the child is over 16 at the time of the hearing as long as he or she was under 16 when the proceeding began.[43] However, the consent of a child over 16 is required before any services can be provided, unless the court orders the treatment over the child's consent.[44] The courts have established that the CFSA does not give a fetus any status or right to protection under the Act.

> ### Winnipeg Child & Family Services (Northwest Area) v. G. (D.F.), [1997] 3 S.C.R. 925, 31 R.F.L. (4th) 165 (S.C.C.).
>
> A pregnant mother was heavily addicted to glue-sniffing which had a strong potential to cause permanent damage to the foetus. She had previously given birth to three children, of whom two had sustained permanent injuries as a result of the mother's glue-sniffing addiction. All of these children had been made Crown wards. A local child welfare agency applied for and was granted

---

[43] CFSA, s. 47(3).
[44] CFSA, s. 27(1).

> an order that the mother be placed in the custody of the provincial director of child and family services and detained at a hospital to follow a course of treatment respecting her addiction. The order was stayed two days later and the decision to grant the order was subsequently reversed on appeal. . ..
> [At 167 (R.F.L.).]

The child welfare agency appealed further to the Supreme Court of Canada.

Held: The appeal was dismissed.

Per McLachlin J. (for the majority):

> . . .[T]he law does not recognize the unborn child as a legal or juridical person. This principle applies generally, whether the case falls under family law, tort law or succession law.
>
> The extension of the court's parens patriae power to permit the protection of unborn children should be rejected for the same reasons as those enunciated in connection with the argument that tort law should be extended to the unborn. The ramifications of such a change would be complex and significant. The law is clear that the courts do not have parens patriae over unborn children. To allow it to extend to unborn children would not be an incremental change but a change of major impact. It would seriously intrude on the rights of women. The legislature was in a much better position to weigh the competing interests and arrive at a solution which was principled and minimally intrusive to pregnant women. [At 167-168 (R.F.L.).]

Child Protection Hearing

Adjournment

Considering that the matter must be brought before the court within five days of a child's apprehension,[45] the hearing will not likely proceed on that date and the matter is almost always adjourned. However, the CFSA does not permit an adjournment for more than 30 days unless all of the parties consent.[46] If the hearing is adjourned, the court must make some order for temporary custody of the child. The child must remain in the custody of the person who had charge of the child immediately prior to the intervention of the C.A.S. unless the court is satisfied that there are reasonable grounds to believe there is a risk the child is likely to suffer harm if returned to that person. The risk must also be one that cannot be adequately met by imposing terms or conditions of supervision upon the person having custody.[47]

---

[45] CFSA, s. s. 46.

[46] CFSA, s. 51(1).

[47] CFSA, s. 51(3).

Hearing in Private

As a general rule, all hearings are held in the absence of the public. The press, radio, and television media may attend at the court's discretion. Publishing a report of the hearing may be prohibited by the court. In any event, there can be no publication of a child's name or information that may identify the child. In the absence of the court's permission, only a party to the proceedings or solicitor may have a copy of a transcript of the court's proceedings.[48]

Preliminary Findings

Before the court determines that a child is in need of protection, the judge must make certain preliminary findings with respect to the child. In particular, the court must determine the child's age and name; the child's religious faith, if any; whether the child is a native or Indian person, and if so the child's community and band; and the place from which the child was removed.[49]

Finding of Child in Need of Protection

Before a child is found to be in need of protection, there must be a significant departure from the average standard of care for a child of a given age. The child must also fall within at least one of the definitions set out in section 37(2) of the CFSA. Although there is an initial standard below which no child must fall, the case law has indicated that here is a secondary standard based upon the parent's age and the cultural or socio-economic community in which the family lives. For example, different standards would apply to parents of native ancestry living in a small rural community in northern Ontario than to white, middle-class parents living in a large city in southern Ontario.[50] At this stage of the hearing, the "best interests" test is not relevant.

Orders the Court May Make

If a child is found to be in need of protection under section 37(2) of the CFSA, the court has four potential options with respect to the disposition

---

[48] CFSA, s. 45.

[49] CFSA, s. 47.

[50] See *M. (E.C.D.), Re,* (sub nom. *E., Re*) [1980] 4 W.W.R. 296, (sub nom. *E., Re*) 17 R.F.L. 274 (Sask. Prov. Ct.); *Mooswa v. Saskatchewan (Minister of Social Services)* (1976), 30 R.F.L. 101 (Sask. Q.B.).

and these options are governed solely by the child's best interests.[51] In addition to the four potential orders, the court may order that the child simply be returned to the person who had charge of the child immediately before the state's intervention. Sometimes the court can determine that, although a child is found in need of protection, no actual protective order is warranted.[52]

Supervision Order

The court may order that the child be returned to the parent or another person, subject to the supervision of the C.A.S. The supervision order must last for at least three months but no longer than 12 months. The court may also impose reasonable terms and conditions relating to the child's care and supervision upon the person with whom the child is placed, the supervising society, the child, or any other person participating in the hearing.[53]

Society Wardship

The court may order that the child be made a ward of the Children's Aid Society for a specified period not exceeding 12 months. This means that the child is placed in the care and custody of the C.A.S., who will usually place the child in a foster home during this temporary period of time. The focus is still upon the parents' rehabilitation so that the child can eventually be returned.

Crown Wardship

The court may order that the child be made a ward of the Crown until the wardship is terminated or expires. In such a case, the child is also placed in the care of the C.A.S. However, the focus has shifted from the parents' rehabilitation to permanent placement of the child in a substitute home where the child might ultimately be adopted. Once an order for Crown wardship has been made, there is a presumption against access between the child and his or her parent.[54] Then, if no access is ordered, the child may be placed in a home with a view to adoption. Once the child has been placed in a potential adoptive home, no further application

---

[51] CFSA, s. 57(1).
[52] CFSA, s. 57(9).
[53] CFSA, s. 57(8).
[54] CFSA, s. 59(2).

for access can be made. Neither can a status review application be made with respect to a child who is so placed.[55]

Consecutive Orders of Society Wardship and Supervision

The court may order that a child be made a ward of the Children's Aid Society for a specified period of time and then the child be returned to the parent or other person for a period or periods not exceeding a total of 12 months.

Considerations in Making Order

Before a court makes a final order, there must be evidence that such an order is necessary to protect the child in the future.[56] The court must also inquire into the efforts made to make use of community resources prior to the order.[57] The court must not make an order that removes the child from the care of the person who had charge immediately prior to the intervention unless the court is satisfied that this is the least disruptive alternative for the child.[58] The court must always consider placing the child, if possible, with a relative, neighbour, or member of the child's community, before making an order.[59] All orders made must be governed by the best interests of the child.[60]

Status Review

Application

Where a child is the subject of a supervision order, or C.A.S. wardship or Crown wardship order under section 57(1) of the Act, the C.A.S. may, at any time, apply to the court to review the child's status. In any event the C.A.S. must apply for a status review before the existing order expires.[61] An application to review the child's status can also be made by: (a) the child, if he or she is over 12 years of age; (b) a parent; (c) a person with whom the child has been placed; or (d) a representative of the child's band or native community.[62] However, where a child is a Crown ward and has

---

[55] CFSA, s. 58(7).
[56] CFSA, s. 57(1).
[57] CFSA, s. 57(2).
[58] CFSA, s. 57(3).
[59] CFSA, s. 57(4).
[60] CFSA, s. 58.
[61] CFSA, s. 64(2).
[62] CFSA, s. 64(4).

lived with the same foster parent continuously for two years immediately preceding the application, an application for review cannot be made by a child's parent unless the court grants permission.[63]

Orders on Status Review

On a status review, the court has the power to vary or terminate the original order, order the original order to terminate on a specified future date, or make a further order under section 57 of the CFSA, on the basis of the child's best interests.[64]

> ### *Catholic Children's Aid Society of Metropolitan Toronto v. M. (C.),* 2 R.F.L. (4th) 313, 18 O.R. (3d) 160 (note), 71 O.A.C. 81, [1994] 2 S.C.R. 165 (S.C.C.)
>
> The child in question was born in 1986. During the first three years of her life she was taken into protection by the Catholic Children's Aid Society on several occasions. Each time she was returned to her mother subject to a supervision order. Throughout this period the Society worked with the mother to improve her parenting skills. In 1989 the child was again taken into care and was, with the mother's consent, made a ward of the Society for four months. Even though the Society continued to assist the mother and facilitated regular visits between the mother and the child, the two were not able to bond. In December 1989, after a second four-month wardship, the Society brought a status review application to have the child made a Crown ward, without access by the mother, for adoption purposes. The mother opposed the motion and in February 1992 the Ontario Court of Justice (Provincial Division) directed that the child be returned to her. The Ontario Court of Justice (Provincial Division) judge found that the child was no longer in need of protection; he did not consider the child's best interests. The Society had the order stayed. It appealed to the Ontario Court of Justice (General Division), but without success. On a further appeal, the Ontario Court of Appeal admitted fresh evidence of the child's relationships with her mother and with her foster family; it then allowed the appeal, set aside the order for the return of the child, and made the child a Crown ward, without access, so that she could be placed for adoption.
>
> The mother appealed the order to the Supreme Court of Canada. The Society again sought to adduce fresh evidence, this time of the child's assertions that she considered her foster family, her real family and that she did not want to see her mother, and also of the unsuccessful attempts to implement access. [At 314 (R.F.L.).]
>
> Held: The appeal was dismissed. Fresh evidence was allowed.

---

[63] CFSA, s. 64(5).
[64] CFSA, s. 65(1).

. . .The fresh evidence submitted to the Supreme Court of Canada was essential. It had not been available earlier in the proceedings, it provided an accurate picture of the current state of the child's relationships with her mother and her foster family, it had the potential to help the court to make a decision on the child's best interests, and it was credible.. . .

The court should not consider, on a status review hearing, whether the original protection order should have been made, but whether the child is still in need of protection. Children's needs change constantly and any changes in circumstances must be taken into account.. . .

. . .The court must first decide whether the child continues to be in need of protection and then consider the best interests of the child. The Act directs that a flexible approach be taken in making that decision so that the best interests of the child will be balanced with the need to prevent indefinite State intervention.. . .

The most important factors in this case were the psychological bonding of the child to her foster parents and the adverse effects she would suffer if she were taken from them. Maintaining a family unit is important only if to do so is in the best interests of the child. Different solutions are needed to meet these interests as the child grows older, but, in any event, the child's interests should be given precedence over the parent's interests. Whether a child needs continued protection does not depend solely on the parent's ability to care for him or her. It also involves whether the child, in light of the intervening events, continues to require State protection. Based on the facts of the case, the child needed continued protection. [At 314-315 (R.F.L.).]

Appeals

An appeal can be made to the Superior Court of Justice by: (a) the child, if he or she is able to participate in the hearing; (b) the parent; (c) the person who has charge of the child; (d) the Director; or (e) the band, if the child is native.[65]

---

[65] CFSA, s. 69.

APPENDIX 15A

ONTARIO

(SEAL)	**ONTARIO COURT OF JUSTICE** *(Name of Court)* at 1911 Eglinton Avenue East, Toronto, Ontario, M4S 1G1 *Court office address*	Court File Number *Family Law Rules, O. Reg. 114/99* **Form 8B: Application (Child Protection and Status Review)**

Applicant(s) *(In most cases, the applicant will be a children's aid society.)*

Full legal name & address for service — street & number, municipality, postal code, telephone & fax numbers and e-mail address (if any).	*Lawyer's name & address — street & number, municipality, postal code, telephone & fax numbers and e-mail address (if any).*
Catholic Children's Aid Society of Toronto **1530 Markham Road** **Toronto, Ontario** **M4S 1G2**	**Daniel Jefferson Stone** **Barrister & Solicitor** **1530 Markham Road** **Toronto, Ontario** **M4S 1G2** **Tel: (416) 284-2222** **Fax: (416) 284 2223**

Respondent(s) *(In most cases, a respondent will be a "parent" within the meaning of section 37 of the Child and Family Services Act.)*

Full legal name & address for service — street & number, municipality, postal code, telephone & fax numbers and e-mail address (if any).	*Lawyer's name & address — street & number, municipality, postal code, telephone & fax numbers and e-mail address (if any).*
Shandra Miriam Ahmed **Amir Mohammed Aguar** **2988 Kennedy Road** **Toronto, Ontario** **M4S 1L7**	**Nazira Jamal** **1777 Kennedy Road, Suite 707** **Toronto, Ontario** **M4S 1L8** **Tel: (416) 298-4444** **Fax: (416) 298-4445**

Children's Lawyer

Name & address of Children's Lawyer's agent for service (street & number, municipality, postal code, telephone & fax numbers and e-mail address (if any)) and name of person represented.

TO THE RESPONDENT(S):

A COURT CASE HAS BEEN STARTED AGAINST YOU IN THIS COURT. THE DETAILS ARE SET OUT ON THE ATTACHED PAGES.

THE FIRST COURT DATE IS *(date)* **Friday April 7, 2006**   **AT**   **10:00**   a.m./p.m.
or as soon as possible after that time, at: *(address)*

1911 Eglinton Ave. East, Toronto, Ontario, M4S 1G1

If you have also been served with a notice of motion, there may be an earlier court date and you or your lawyer should come to court for the motion.

IF YOU WANT TO OPPOSE ANY CLAIM IN THIS CASE, you or your lawyer must prepare an *Answer* (Form 10 – a blank copy should be attached), serve a copy on the children's aid society and all other parties and file a copy in the court office with an *Affidavit of Service* (Form 6B).

YOU HAVE ONLY 30 DAYS AFTER THIS APPLICATION IS SERVED ON YOU (60 DAYS IF THIS APPLICATION IS SERVED ON YOU OUTSIDE CANADA OR THE UNITED STATES) TO SERVE AND FILE AN ANSWER. IF YOU DO NOT, THE CASE WILL GO AHEAD WITHOUT YOU AND THE COURT MAY MAKE AN ORDER AND ENFORCE IT AGAINST YOU.

Check this box if this paragraph applies   ☐   The children's aid society is also making a claim for child support. You **MUST** fill out a *Financial Statement* (Form 13 – a blank copy attached), serve a copy on the society and file a copy in the court office with an *Affidavit of Service* even if you do not answer this case.

Form 8B:	**Application (Child Protection and Status Review)**	**(page 2)**	Court File Number

WARNING: This case is subject to case management, which means that the case runs on a timetable. That timetable says that the following steps have to be finished by the following number of days from the start of this case:

Service and filing of answers and plans of care	*30 days*	*Settlement conference*	*80 days*
Temporary care & custody hearing	*35 days*	*Hearing*	*120 days*

You should consider getting legal advice about this case right away. If you cannot afford a lawyer, you may be able to get help from your local legal aid office. *(See your telephone directory under LEGAL AID).*

_____
Date of issue

_____
Clerk of the court

Form 8B:	Application (Child Protection and Status Review)	(page 3)	Court File Number

THE CHILD(REN): *(List all children involved in this case.)*

Child's Full Legal Name	Birthdate	Age	Sex	Full Legal Name of Mother	Full Legal Name of Father	Child's Religion	Child's Native Status
Shema Akari Ahmed	15 Nov. 1998	7	F	Shandra Miriam Ahmed	Sukeer Anka Ahmed	Catholic	
Anastur Kami Ahmed	3 Jan. 2001	5	M	Shandra Miriam Ahmed	Sukeer Anka Ahmed	Catholic	
Natasha Sundeep Aguar	21 Mar. 2003	3	F	Shandra Miriam Ahmed	Amir Mohammed Aguar	Catholic	

CLAIM BY APPLICANT

NOTE: If this case is an application for a status review or for access only, strike out paragraph 1 and go immediately to paragraph 2.

1. The applicant children's aid society asks the court to make a finding under Part III of the *Child and Family Services Act* that the child(ren) named in this application is/are in need of protection because:

(Check the applicable box(es). In each checked paragraph, delete those portions of the text that are not relevant.)

☐ the child(ren) has/have suffered physical harm, inflicted by the person having charge of the child(ren) or caused by that person's

  ☐ failure to care for, provide for, supervise or protect the child(ren) adequately [subclause 37(2)*(a)(i)*].

  ☐ pattern of neglect in caring for, providing for, supervising or protecting the child(ren) [subclause 37(2)*(a)(ii)*].

☐ there is a risk that the child(ren) is/are likely to suffer physical harm inflicted by the person having charge of the child(ren) or caused by that person's

  ☐ failure to care for, provide for, supervise or protect the child(ren) adequately [subclause 37(2)*(b)(i)*].

  ☐ pattern of neglect in caring for, providing for, supervising or protecting the child(ren) [subclause 37(2)*(b)(ii)*].

☐ the child(ren) has/have been sexually molested or sexually exploited, by the person having charge of the child(ren) or by another person where the person having charge knows or should know of the possibility of sexual molestation or sexual exploitation and fails to protect the child(ren) [clause 37(2)*(c)*].

☐ there is a risk that the child(ren) is/are likely to be sexually molested or sexually exploited, by the person having charge of the child(ren) or by another person where the person having charge knows of should know of the possibility of sexual molestation or sexual exploitation and fails to protect the child(ren) [clause 37(2)*(d)*].

☐ the child(ren) require(s) medical treatment to cure, prevent or alleviate physical harm or suffering and the child(ren)'s parent or the person having charge of the child(ren) does not provide, or refuses or is unavailable or unable to consent to, the treatment [clause 37(2)*(e)*].

☒ the child(ren) has/have suffered emotional harm, demonstrated by serious anxiety, depression, withdrawal, self-destructive or aggressive behaviour, or delayed development and there are reasonable grounds to believe that the emotional harm suffered by the child(ren) results from the actions, failure to act or pattern of neglect on the part of the child(ren)'s parent or the person having charge of the child(ren) [clause 37(2)*(f)*].

☐ the child(ren) has/have suffered emotional harm, demonstrated by serious anxiety, depression, withdrawal, self-destructive or aggressive behaviour, or delayed development and the child(ren)'s parent or the person having charge of the child(ren) does not provide, or refuses or is unavailable or unable to consent to, services or treatment to remedy or alleviate the harm [clause 37(2)*(f.1)*].

☒ there is a risk that the child(ren) is/are likely to suffer emotional harm, demonstrated by serious anxiety, depression, withdrawal, self-destructive or aggressive behaviour, or delayed development resulting from the actions, failure to act or pattern of neglect on the part of the child(ren)'s parent or the person having charge of the child(ren) [clause 37(2)*(g)*].

☐ there is a risk that the child(ren) is/are likely to suffer emotional harm, demonstrated by serious anxiety, depression, withdrawal, self-destructive or aggressive behaviour, or delayed development and that the child(ren)'s parent or the person having charge of the child(ren) does not provide, or refuses or is unavailable or unable to consent to services or treatment to prevent the harm [clause 37(2)*(g.1)*].

Form 8B: **Application (Child Protection and**   **(page 4)**   Court File Number
            Status Review)

☐ the child(ren) suffer(s) from a mental, emotional or developmental condition that, if not remedied, could seriously impair the child(ren)'s development and the child(ren)'s parent or the parent having charge of the child(ren) does not provide, or refuses or is unavailable or unable to consent to, treatment to remedy or alleviate the condition [clause 37(2)*(h)*].

☐ the child(ren) has/have been abandoned [clause 37(2)*(i)*].

☐ the child(ren)'s parent has died or is unavailable to exercise his or her custodial rights over the child(ren) and has not made adequate provision for the child(ren)'s care and custody [clause 37(2)*(i)*].

☐ the child(ren) is/are in a residential placement and the child(ren)'s parent refuses or is unable or unwilling to resume the care and custody of the child(ren) [clause 37(2)*(i)*].

☐ the child(ren) is/are less than twelve years old and has/have killed or seriously injured another person or caused serious damage to another person's property; services or treatment are necessary to prevent a recurrence; and the child(ren)'s parent or the person having charge of the child(ren) does not provide, or refuses or is unavailable or unable to consent to, those services or treatment [clause 37(2)*(j)*].

☐ the child(ren) is/are less than twelve years old and has/have, on more than one occasion, injured another person or caused loss or damage to another person's property, with the encouragement of the person having charge of the child(ren) or because of that person's failure or inability to supervise the child(ren) adequately [clause 37(2)*(k)*].

☐ the child(ren)'s parent is unable to care for the child(ren) and the child(ren) is/are brought before the court with the person's consent and, where the child(ren) is/are twelve years of age or older, with the child(ren)'s consent, to be dealt with under Part III of the *Child and Family Services Act* [clause 37(2)*(l)*].

2.   The applicant asks for an order,

☐ that the child(ren) be placed with *(name of custodian)* _____

subject to the supervision of *(full legal name of supervising society)*

for a period of _____ months, on the terms and conditions set out in the Appendix on page 6 of this Application form.

☐ that the child(ren) be made (a) ward(s) of *(full legal name of society)*

for a period of _____ months

☒ that the child(ren) be made (a) ward(s) of *(full legal name of society)*
The Catholic Children's Aid Society of Toronto

for a period of   **six (6)** _____ months and then returned to *(name of custodian)*
Ankara Shimoda Ahmed

subject to the supervision of *(full legal name of supervising society)*
The Catholic Children's Aid Society of Toronto

for a period of   **six (6)** _____ months, on the terms and conditions set out in the Appendix on page 6 of this Application form.

☐ that the child(ren) be made (a) ward(s) of the Crown and placed in the care of *(full legal name of caretaker society)*

☐ that *(name of homemaker)* _____
be authorized to remain on the premises at *(address of premises where homemaker is placed)*

until *(date)* _____ or until the person who is entitled to custody of the child(ren) returns to care for the child(ren), whichever is sooner.

☐ relating to access, the details of which are as follows: *(Specify details of order to be sought, including any claim for a restraining order under section 80 of the Child and Family Services Act.)*

☐ relating to payment of support while the child(ren) is/are in care, the details of which are as follows:

☒ court costs.

☐ *(Other; specify.)* _____

Form 8B: **Application (Child Protection and Status** **(page 5)**
 Review)

Court File Number

3. To the applicant's best knowledge, the child(ren)

   ☒ has/have never before been in the care of a society under an out-of-court agreement.

   ☐ has/have been in the care of a society under an out-of-court agreement. The details are as follows: *(Set out the number of times each child was in society care, when the care began and how long it lasted.)*

4. To the applicant's best knowledge, the parties or the child(ren)   ☐ have   ☒ have not
been in a court case before relating to the supervision, wardship (guardianship) or custody of or access to the child(ren). *(If you checked the first box, attach a summary of court cases – Form 8E.)*

5. The parties   ☐ have   ☒ have not
made a written agreement dealing with any matter involved in this case. *(If you checked the first box, give date of agreement and indicate which of its terms are in dispute. Attach an additional page if you need more space.)*

6. The following is a brief statement of the facts upon which the applicant is relying in this application.
(Set out the facts in the numbered paragraphs. If you need more space, you may use the other side or attach a page, but you must date and sign each additional page.)

1. The respondents have cohabited as a family with the three children since 31 December 2004.

2. The relationship between the respondents frequently invovles incidents of drinking alcohol, conflict, domestic violence and abusive behaviour. These incidents involve the respondents yelling, swearing, demeaning each other and threatening each other with acts of violence in the presence of the children.

3. The respondent, Amir Mohammed Aguar admits that he is addicted to alcohol.

4. As a result of the parents' pattern of behaviour, the two oldest children have exhibited symptoms of chronic anxiety and depression as reported by teachers and social workers.

5. The pattern of domestic violence engaged in by the respondents has been emotionally harmful to the children and places the children at risk of further emotional harm if they are not removed from their present environment.

Put a line through any blank space left on this page.

_____
Date of signature

_____
If applicant is a children's aid society, give office or position of person signing.

_____
Signature

_____
Print or type name.

INDEX

ACCESS
defined, 88
factors relevant to, 89
reasonable access, 88
rights of access parent, 88
specified access, 88-89
supervised access, 89

ADULTERY, see **DIVORCE**

ANNULMENT
affidavit in support of
application, sample, 34-35
application, sample, 29-33
defined, 21
marriages of convenience not
eligible for, 26
procedure, 28
void *ab initio* marriages, grounds
age, 22
consanguinity and affinity,
22-23
duress, 23
mental incapacity, 23
mistake, 24
prior subsisting marriage, 22
voidable marriages, grounds
age, 24
inability to consummate, 24-
26

**APPREHENSION OF
CHILDREN,** 290-291

ARBITRATION, 187

ASSESSMENTS
custody cases, 224-225

BARS TO DIVORCE, 45

**BEST INTERESTS OF THE
CHILD**
Children's Law Reform Act, 215-
221
Divorce Act, 81

BLOOD TESTS
parentage, to determine, 204-
206

CASE MANAGEMENT
conferences, 246-247
Family Court, 249-250
generally, 236
Ontario Court of Justice, 250
Superior Court of Justice, 251

CHANGE OF NAME
certificate, issuance, 277
Change of Name Act, 274-278
children
aged 16 or older, 276
consents required, 274-276
factors applicable, 275
notice required, 276
election of spouse
common-law spouses, 274
married spouses, 273
offences, 278
procedure, 277
Registrar General, duties, 277-
278
Statement of Guarantor, 277
Vital Statistics Act, 278

***CHANGE OF NAME ACT,* 274-
278**

CHILDREN, see also **ACCESS;
CHANGE OF NAME; CHILD
PROTECTION; CHILD
SUPPORT; CUSTODY;
PARENTAGE**
apprehension of child in need of
protection, 290-291
equal status under *Children's Law
Reform Act,* 199-200

***CHILD AND FAMILY SERVICES
ACT,* 279-303,** see also **CHILD
PROTECTION**
purpose of legislation, 279-280
scope of legislation, 279

CHILD PROTECTION
application
commencement, 291
hearing
adjournment, 293

findings required, 294
  private, 294
  sample application, 299-303
apprehension of children
  defined, 290
  with warrant, 291
  without warrant, 291
child in need of protection
  abandonment by parents,
    288
  child under 12 committing
    serious offence, 288
  defined generally, 286
  emotional harm or risk
    thereof, 287
  mental, emotional,
    developmental condition,
    287-288
  molestation or risk thereof,
    286-287
  physical harm or risk
    thereof, 286
children's aid societies, 280
community and privacy interests,
  conflict between, 284-285
courts having exclusive
  jurisdiction, 290
custody, distinguished from, 284
orders, 294-296
  consecutive orders, 296
  considerations in making,
    296
  Crown wardship, 295-296
  society wardship, 295
  supervision order, 295
parties to proceeding
  child over 12, 290
  Children's Aid Society, 289
  Director, 289
  native band representative,
    289
  parents, 289
  possessory parents, 289-290
special needs agreements, 281-
  283
state intervention, when
  appropriate, 284
status review

application, 296-297
  potential orders, 297-298
temporary care agreements,
  280-281, 283
who is subject of legislation,
  292-293

CHILDREN'S AID SOCIETIES,
280-283, *see also* **CHILD
PROTECTION**

CHILDREN'S LAW REFORM ACT,
see also **CUSTODY**
equal status of children, 199-200
parentage, *see* PARENTAGE
scope of Act, 199

CHILD SUPPORT, *see also* **CHILD
SUPPORT GUIDELINES**
Divorce Act,
  amount, determination of,
    see CHILD SUPPORT
    GUIDELINES
  "child of the marriage"
    defined, 63-64
  person standing in place of
    parent, 64-65
  variations, 90
enforcement, *see*
  ENFORCEMENT OF
  SUPPORT
Family Law Act
  application for child support
    and custody under CLRA,
    sample, 230-234
  application for spousal
    support, sample, 166-176
    application, 166-170
    financial statement, 171-
      176
  "child" defined, 160-161
    settled intention to treat
      child as member of
      family, 160-161
  comparison with *Divorce Act*
    provisions, 161
  divorce proceedings, effect
    of, 162
  procedure

application and financial
statements, 163-164
motion for temporary
order, 164
motion to change final
order or agreement,
164-165
variations, 162-163
income tax implications, 63
motion to change child support,
93-100
change information form,
95-100
notice of motion, 93-94
support order, sample, 269-279

CHILD SUPPORT GUIDELINES
application to *Family Law Act*,
161-162
children over age of majority, 68
commencement of, 63
how they work generally, 66-67
incomes over $150,000, 68-69
objectives, 66
presumptive rule, 67
shared custody, 70-71
special and extraordinary
expenses, 67
split custody, 69
spouse in place of parent,
application to, 69
undue hardship, 71

CIVIL MARRIAGE ACT, 15, 73

**COHABITATION
AGREEMENTS,** 178

COLLABORATIVE FAMILY LAW,
188

COLLUSION
as bar to divorce, 45

COMMON-LAW SPOUSES
custody and child support
application, sample, 230-234
custody, status to apply, 210
election to change name, 274
exclusion from equalization
regime, 102-103

exclusion from matrimonial
home provisions, 142
spousal support, entitlement to,
153-154

CONDONATION
as bar to divorce, 45

CONFERENCES
case conference, 246-247
settlement conference, 247-248
trial management conference,
248

CONNIVANCE
as bar to divorce, 45

**CONSUMMATION OF
MARRIAGE,** see
ANNULMENT, voidable
marriages

CONTINUING RECORD
answer, 241-242
application, 239
formal requirements, 253-257
sample cover, 259
sample table of contents, 260
summary of contents, 258

**COURT OF APPEAL FOR
ONTARIO,** 9, 11

COURT SYSTEM
chart, 11
Court of Appeal for Ontario, 9
Ontario Court of Justice, 7
Superior Court of Justice, 7-9
Divisional Court, 8
Family Court, 8-9
Small Claims Court, 8
Supreme Court of Canada, 10

CRUELTY, see **DIVORCE**

CUSTODY, see *also* **ACCESS**
annulment, on, 28
Children's Law Reform Act
application for custody and
support, sample, 230-234
assessments, 224-225
"best interests of the child"
principle

ability and willingness to
meet child's needs,
218-219
blood relationships, 221
child's views, 217-218
cultural and racial
factors, 219-220
love, affection, emotional
ties, 215-217
past conduct, 221-222
permanence, stability of
family unit, 220-221
plans for care and
upbringing, 220
stable home
environment, 218
compared to *Divorce Act*,
209
divorce proceedings, effect
upon, 213
equal entitlement of parents,
209
international child abduction,
see *HAGUE CONVENTION*
jurisdictional requirements
child physically present
in Ontario with other
factors, 211-212
court declining
jurisdiction, 213
habitual residence, 210-
211
serious harm to child,
212-213
mediation, 226
procedure, 226-228
status to apply, 210
types of orders, 223
variations, 223-224
material change in
circumstances, 224
defined, 79
Divorce Act
"best interests of the child"
principle, 81
conduct of parent as factor,
82

maximum contact principle,
82-84
status to apply, 80
"child of the marriage"
defined, 80
non-spouses, 80
spouses, 80
variations, 92
joint custody
defined, 84-85
when awarded, 85-87
parallel parenting, 87
shared custody, child support
guidelines, 70-71
split custody, child support
guidelines, 69

**CUSTODY ASSESSMENTS, 224-
225**

DEATH OF SPOUSE, see
**FAMILY PROPERTY;
MATRIMONIAL HOME,**
possession

**DECLARATION OF
PARENTAGE,** see
PARENTAGE

DEDUCTIONS, see **FAMILY
PROPERTY,** net family
property

DIVORCE
affidavit for divorce, sample, 56-
59
application for uncontested,
sample, 51-55
bars
collusion, 45
condonation, 45
connivance, 45
reasonable arrangements for
child support, 45
certificate, 47
corollary relief, see CHILD
SUPPORT; SPOUSAL
SUPPORT; CUSTODY;
ACCESS
court, duty of, 44

foreign divorces, recognizing, 47-48

grounds

adultery, 41-43

defined, 41

evidence of, 43

same-sex adultery, 41-42

cruelty, 43-44

cohabitation rendered impossible, 43

"grave and weighty", 43

living separate and apart, 40-41

reconciliation attempts, effect of, 41

under same roof, 40-41

history, 2-3

jurisdiction

courts, 37

geographical jurisdiction, 37-39

legislation governing, 37

legal advisor, duty of, 44

order, sample, 60-61

procedure

defended divorce, 48-49

generally, 48

uncontested divorce, 49-50

DIVORCE ACT

bars to divorce, 45

child support, 63-65

custody, 80-85

foreign divorces, recognition, 47

grounds, 40-44

jurisdiction, 37-39

spousal support, 72-77

DNA TESTS

parentage, to determine, 205-206

DOCTRINE OF "SEPARATE PROPERTY", 2

DOMESTIC CONTRACTS

arbitration, 187

capacity to enter, 179

cohabitation agreements, 178

collaborative family law, 188

enforceability

custody, access, child support, 180-181

spousal support, 181-182

formal requirements, 179

marriage contracts, 177-178

mediation of, 186-187

negotiating, 185-186

paternity agreements, 184

registering with court, 185

separation agreements, 178-179

sample agreement, 189-198

setting aside by court

grounds for, 182-184

DRIVERS' LICENCE SUSPENSION, see **ENFORCEMENT OF SUPPORT**

ENFORCEMENT OF SUPPORT

absconding debtor, arrest, 267

compliance, statistical analysis, 261

consumer reporting agency, reporting to, 267

default hearing, 266

Director of Family Responsibility

access to information, 267

role, 261-262

dispute of amount by payor, 264

Family Responsibility and Support Arrears Enforcement Act, 1996, 261-267

garnishment of joint accounts, 267

income source, obligations, 263

land, registration of order against, 266

lottery winnings, deduction from, 267

Personal Property Security Act, registration under, 266

Support and Custody Orders Enforcement Act, 1985, 261

support deduction order

defined, 263

sample order, 271

withdrawal, 262

support order

defined, 262

sample order, 269-270
suspension of drivers' licences,
    264-265
    final notice to payor, 265
    motion to refrain, 265
    reinstatement, 265

EQUALIZATION PAYMENT, *see*
FAMILY PROPERTY

EXCLUSIONS, *see* **FAMILY**
PROPERTY, net family
property

FAMILY COURT
    as part of Ontario court system,
        8-9, 11
    case management, 249-250

FAMILY LAW ACT
    child support, 160-176
    domestic contracts, 177-198
    family property, 101-140
    matrimonial home, 141-152
    spousal support, 153-160

FAMILY LAW LEGISLATION, *see*
    also specific statutes by name
    division of powers, 6
    federal, 6
    provincial, 6

FAMILY LAW RULES, 235-260
    answering case
        answer, 240
        continuing record, 241-242
            formal requirements,
                253-257
            sample cover, 259
            sample table of contents,
                260
            summary of contents,
                258
        financial statement, 241
        service of documents, 242-
            243
    case management, 236, *see also*
        CASE MANAGEMENT
    commencement of case
        application, 238
        continuing record, 239

formal requirements,
    253-257
    sample cover, 259
    sample table of contents,
        260
    summary of contents,
        258
financial statement, 238-239
service of documents, 239-
    240
conferences
    case conference, 246-247
    settlement conference, 247-
        248
    trial management
        conference, 248
Mandatory Information Program,
    243-244
motion to change final order or
    agreement, 251-252
objective, 235
reply, 243
temporary orders, motions
    on notice, 244
    without notice, 245
time
    counting, 236
    lengthening or shortening,
        237

FAMILY PROPERTY, *see also*
MATRIMONIAL HOME
application for equalization,
    sample, 124-140
    application, 124-128
    financial statement, 129-137
    net family property
        statement, 138-140
death of spouse
    election of surviving spouse
        priority of spouse's
            entitlement, 118
        spouse dying intestate,
            117
        spouse leaving will, 116-
            117
equalization payment,
    calculation, 115
limitation periods, 105

"net family property"
   deductions
      debts and liabilities, 109
      matrimonial home
         excepted, 110
      property owned on date
         of marriage, 109-110
   defined, 108-109
   exclusions
      damages for personal
         injuries, 112
      gift or inheritance, 111
      income from gift or
         inheritance, 111-112
      life insurance proceeds,
         112
      property excluded by
         domestic contract,
         114-115
      tracing, 112-113
   sample calculation of, 121-
      123
   steps in calculating, 115-116
philosophy behind legislation,
   101-102
procedure, 119-120
"property" defined, 105-107
status to apply for equalization
   exclusion of common-law
      spouses, 102-103
   married spouses, 102
   surviving spouse on death of
      spouse, 102
unequal division, 118-119
valuation date
   death of spouse, 105
   improvident depletion, 104
   separation date, 104

**FAMILY RESPONSIBILITY AND
SUPPORT ARREARS
ENFORCEMENT ACT, 1996,
261-267**

FINANCIAL STATEMENT
answering case under *Family Law
   Rules*, 241
child support application, 163-
   164

commencing case under *Family
   Law Rules*, 238-239
equalization of net family
   property, sample, 129-137
spousal support, sample, 171-
   176

FORMS AND PRECEDENTS
annulment, affidavit, 34-35
annulment application, 29-33
child protection application, 299-
   303
continuing record
   sample cover, 259
   sample table of contents,
      260
   summary of contents, 258
custody and child support
   application, 230-234
divorce, affidavit, 56-59
divorce application, 51-55
divorce order, 60-61
equalization of net family
   property
      application, 124-128
      financial statement, 129-137
      net family property
         statement, 138-140
motion to change child support,
   93-100
separation agreement, 189-197
   certificate of independent
      legal advice, 198
spousal support application
   application, 166-170
   financial statement, 171-176
support deduction order, 271
support order, 269-270

**GARNISHMENT OF JOINT
ACCOUNTS**
support enforcement, 267

HAGUE CONVENTION
defined, 228
operation of, 228-229
purpose, 228

HISTORY
adoption of English law, 1
divorce, 2-3

family law generally, 1-5
marriage as partnership, 4, 101-102
married women, legal status, 1-2
property division, 4-5
support orders, 3

JOINT CUSTODY, 84-87

LOTTERY WINNINGS
support enforcement, use in, 267

MANDATORY INFORMATION PROGRAM, 243-244

MARRIAGE
Civil Marriage Act, 15
defined, 13
formalities
defined, 16
failure to comply, consequences, 19-20
licence, 17
parental consent if minor, 16-17
publication of banns, 17
solemnization
form of ceremony, 18-19
officials who can perform ceremony, 17-18
legal capacity
age, 16
marital status requirement, 15-16
parties who can marry, 15
marriage of convenience, 26
same-sex marriage, 13-15

MARRIAGE ACT, 16-21

MARRIAGE CONTRACTS, 177-178

MARRIAGE OF CONVENIENCE, 26
MARRIED WOMEN'S PROPERTY ACT, 2

MATRIMONIAL HOME
defined, 141-142

designation, 144-145
joint tenancy and right of survivorship, 151-152
more than one home, 143
partition and sale, 147-148
part used for other purposes, 143-144
possession
death of spouse, on, 145
equal right of spouses, 145
exclusive possession, 145-147
factors governing, 146
occupation rent, 146
payments to cover maintenance, 146-147
shares in corporation holding title to home, 143
special place in family law, 141
spousal consent to sale or mortgage, 149-151
status to claim special rights to, 141

MAXIMUM CONTACT PRINCIPLE, 82-84

MEDIATION,
custody disputes, 226
domestic contracts, 186-187

NEGOTIATION, 185-186

NET FAMILY PROPERTY, see **FAMILY PROPERTY**
Net Family Property Statement, sample, 138-140

ONTARIO COURT OF JUSTICE
as part of Ontario court system, 7, 11
case management, 250
child protection proceedings, 290

PARALLEL PARENTING, 87

PARENTAGE
declaration of parentage
jurisdiction to make, 207-208

limitations upon application, 202

nature of order, 202

separate from maintenance, 201

who can apply, 201-202

former "affiliation" proceedings, 200

presumptions of paternity, 203

conflicting presumptions, 203

proof of

blood tests, 204-205

Charter issues, 206-207

inference from refusal to submit to, 206

DNA tests, 205-206

written acknowledgement, 204

PARENTAL SUPPORT

obligation of child, 161

PATERNITY AGREEMENTS, 184

PERSONAL PROPERTY SECURITY ACT, **266**

PRESUMPTIONS OF PATERNITY, 205

PROCEDURE, see *FAMILY LAW RULES*

PROPERTY

defined for purposes of equalization, 105-107

PUBLICATION OF BANNS, see **MARRIAGE**

RULES, see *FAMILY LAW RULES*

SAME-SEX MARRIAGE, 13-15

"SEPARATE AND APART", see **DIVORCE**

SEPARATION AGREEMENTS, 178-179

SPECIAL AND EXTRAORDINARY EXPENSES, see **CHILD SUPPORT GUIDELINES**

SPECIAL NEEDS AGREEMENTS, 281-283

SPOUSAL SUPPORT

Divorce Act

factors to be considered, 73-75

pre-existing agreement, effect upon, 74-75

objectives, 75-77

status to apply, 72-73

former spouses, 73

same-sex couples, 73

types of orders, 73

variations, 90-91

Family Law Act

divorce proceedings, effect, 159

domestic contracts, effect upon, 156-157

factors to be considered, 157

indexing, 158-159

purposes of order, 157

status to apply, 153-155

"cohabit" defined, 154

common-law partners, 153-154

polygamous marriages, 153

same-sex couples, 154

void or voidable marriages, 153

types of orders, 158

variations, 159-160

income tax implications 72

Spousal Support Advisory Guidelines, proposed, 77-78

SPOUSAL SUPPORT ADVISORY GUIDELINES, 77-78

STATUS REVIEW APPLICATIONS, 296-298

SUPERIOR COURT OF JUSTICE

as part of Ontario court system, 7-9

case management, 251

chart indicating, 11

Divisional Court, 8

Family Court, 8-9
Small Claims Court, 8

SUPPORT AND CUSTODY ORDERS ENFORCEMENT ACT, 1985, 261.

SUPPORT DEDUCTION ORDER, 262-263, 271

SUPREME COURT OF CANADA, 10, 11

TEMPORARY CARE AGREEMENTS, 280-281, 283

TIME
counting under *Family Law Rules*, 236-237

UNCONTESTED DIVORCE PROCEDURE, 49-50

VALUATION DATE, 104-105

VARIATIONS
Children's Law Reform Act
custody, 223-224
Divorce Act,
child support, 90
custody, 92
spousal support, 90-91
Family Law Act
spousal support, 159-160
motion to change child support, sample, 93-100
motion to change final order or agreement, 251-252

VITAL STATISTICS ACT, 278

VOID AB INITIO MARRIAGES, see **ANNULMENT**

VOIDABLE MARRIAGES, see **ANNULMENT**